CULINARY AMERICANA

Woodcut from The Bettmann Archive

Preparations for a Family Dinner, 1869

CULINARY AMERICANA

Cookbooks published in the cities and towns of the United States of America during the years from 1860~~~~~~through~~~~~~1960

BY ELEANOR AND BOB BROWN

FOREWORD BY CLIFTON FADIMAN

Limited Edition Facsimile

Of the

Original Edition

ISBN 1-888262-21-4

MARTINO PUBLISHING
P.O. BOX 373
MANSFIELD CENTRE, CT 06250

Foreword

I feel pleased to be asked to say a word about Bob and Eleanor Brown's *Culinary Americana*. And, if I may, a word about Bob. Bob Brown belonged to a bohemian culture far more wholesome and fruitful than the one we are now developing. His non-conformism took a pleasing rather than a dismal shape. He had an extraordinary zest for life, for people, for happy memories. And for food and wine, and the talk that goes with them when they are good. I miss him.

This book is a genuine contribution to Americana, as is indicated by Eleanor Brown's all-too-modest Introduction. The history of what we Americans have eaten over the last hundred years or so, and why we have eaten it, and how we have eaten it—this can tell us more about ourselves than a carload of commercial and industrial statistics. *Culinary Americana*, though it seems basically a mere bibliography, if carefully read and thoughtfully interpreted, can throw a significant and diverting light on us as a people. It makes clear, for example, in the most unpretentious way, how stubborn, how resistant to change, are those outgrowths of pioneer institutions, the Ladies' Aid Society, the church group, the women's clubs. The charming little cookbooks they issued (and continue to issue) are an index of the sturdiness of village culture. It has not all gone neon-light.

Amateurs of food and amateurs of Americana will find *Culinary Americana* a delightful addition to their shelves. Good fortune to it!

CLIFTON FADIMAN.
NEW CANAAN, CONN.

Introduction

Man is a voracious eater. At the dawn of human time, his daylight hours were spent in obtaining food, preparing it, eating and tossing the bones over his shoulder. We can therefore say that most of his life was given to solving the food problem.

Modern man has a more complicated and individual approach to food. But he too spends the principal part of his life catering to his appetite. People eat for various reasons. Some people just eat; others desire better health, hope for the restoration of manhood, or seek miraculous cures in a new, exotic diet. But there are some men and women who eat because they like it—every blessed mouthful. They, with their never ending search for finer taste sensations, have left us with a rich heritage of recipes to make life more delightful. Happily, for whatever reason people were interested in food, someone wrote a book about it.

Now we have written a book about the books. Our study is concerned mainly with "the regionals," the personal, local cookbooks compiled by women's clubs and church groups in the towns throughout the United States. These little books are peculiarly American in concept, just as the groups that compiled them were typical American institutions. The ladies' aid societies, the women's clubs were a development of the pioneer community where women organized quilting parties, husking bees, sewing circles as social gatherings where time would not be "a-wasting." To raise money, these women gave church suppers. To raise more money, they donated favorite recipes to make little cookbooks for sale. Title pages of the books show the range of community responsibility: for "the benefit" of the church, for missions, for "The Home for the Friendless," for a new roof for the school building.

It is said that the earliest of these regional cookbooks were brought out to provide funds for the Sanitary Commissions during the Civil War. Certainly it was after the War that we find them printed in many states of the Union. A survey of 200 cookbooks of our own collection, published at various times during this last century in Massachusetts showed that they came from seventy-four different cities and villages. In the case of many of the smaller places, these titles constitute the only books ever printed in these localities, which makes them important landmarks in the history of bookmaking in the state.

The regional cookbooks are a treasure trove of original recipes, as well as a record of old "receipts," reflecting the nationality background of the settlers of the community. Thus you will expect, and find, German foods in the old books of Lancaster County, Pennsylvania, Scandinavian receipts in the pamphlets of the midwest, and Spanish dishes in the booklets published in the southwest. Some books were illustrated: kitchen-dining room scenes of the period, pictures of many an old church, adorn cover or frontispiece, wonderful drawings of equipment and house furnishings told our ancestors what to buy. These are the home and hearth records of a people. It is interesting to think that you and I are the product of them—there isn't one of us that doesn't have some of the recipes in us. The little books, some in the handwriting of the contributor, often with signed recipes, give us a glimpse of the gallant women who proudly cooked these meals and generously gave up their secrets "for the benefit of . . ." others.

We have included a sampling of cook books brought out by established publishers in the urban centers throughout the century. We offer these as a background against which to place the regionals. The authors include the cooking-school teachers: Parloa, Lincoln, Farmer and Rorer. Then there are the books of fad and fancy: Mr. Graham of cracker fame, Horace Fletcher advocating the long chew in the face of all custom to the contrary, Dr. Drews' "Unfired Food" and "Tropho-Therapy." There are books about eating to grow slim or fat, or even perhaps, medium. There are recipes from all around the world. You can trace the development of nutrition, note the increase in such books during periods of economic reversal; learn about substitute foods to meet scarcity. Indeed when war shrank the pocketbook, muskrat became king, horsemeat was not scorned and whale-steaks were considered a delicacy. War gave impetus to the scientific study of foods as regarded growing, cooking and nutritive content.

Other types of books which printed cooking articles, menus and recipes are the almanacs, and the advertising booklets. These, too, mirror customs of the century. Oh, the medical recipes, the Kickapoo Indian Balm, and how Mrs. X, Mrs. Y and Mrs. Z were helped by Lydia Pinkham! Yes, she brought out a cookbook, too. The advertisements in the almanacs and the regionals are a study in themselves. One thing we've never found is a receipt for funeral meats, even though there is a booklet sponsored by the Jeffersonville Cemetery Association. But we have heard of the Swedish custom of frosting little funeral cakes in white with black edgings, or in black with white decorations.

Bob Brown first got together a cookbook collection for reference when he began to write about cooking. He had 1500 volumes which were purchased promptly by a grocery chain store as nucleus for their research library. It was then necessary for him to start a new collection. This was the origin of an interest in cookery books which lasted, and grew, to the end of his life. Bob saw cook books as social and cultural history in America; particularly those regional books which were so close to the heart of the country. His plan for a bibliography of regionals was "the delight of my slippered years."

After Bob's sudden death I've continued work on this bibliography. *Culinary Americana* includes listings of all the regional cookbooks we could either locate or obtain information about. It runs the gamut from "Fifteen Cent Dinners for Families of Six" to the extravagant and elaborate collations of Oscar of the Waldorf. In the bibliography there will be books with recipes to enchant everybody, from the glutton to the most fastidious feeder.

In a sense, everybody helped in the preparation of this book. Like all collectors, we have traded books and information with other collectors, dealers, libraries. Our heart-felt thanks go to so many friends who have sent encouraging letters, information, book lists of their own libraries: Mr. and Mrs. Philip Brown, Mrs. Thomas Scruggs, Mrs. Julia Hindley, Mrs. Edward Hansen, Mrs. C. F. Fordyce, Mr. Paul Fritzsche, Mr. J. George Frederick, President of the Gourmet Society, and to Mr. James Gourley who has supplied titles which did not appear in his bibliography, *Regional American Cookery*. Other bibliographies were studied and consulted, primarily those focused on cookbooks printed in America: the Lincoln-Lowenstein *American Cookery Books*, 1742-1860; *Gastronomic Bibliography* by K. G. Bitting, and the *California in the Kitchen* of Liselotte and William Glozer.

Every time we thought we were finished with this bibliography, we found more books we just had to put in. We expect you to find many we have never heard of, and to write and tell us about them. Maybe there will have to be a supplement some day. In any case, as Bob once said, "Eating is still a delightful necessity."

ELEANOR PARKER BROWN
NEW YORK, 1961

Table of Contents

Arrangement of the Book

A word about how to use this book. The body of the book is arranged alphabetically by state and in chronological order within each state. There are indexes by author, title of book, and place of publication. There is also a partial list of book prices which can be used in assessing the value of a collection. We hope it will be both useful and interesting.

CULINARY AMERICANA

Alabama

1 GULF CITY COOK BOOK. Compiled by the Ladies of the St. Francis Street Methodist Episcopal Church, South Mobile, 1878. 252p.

2 GULF CITY COOK BOOK. Compiled by the Ladies of St. Francis Street Methodist Episcopal Church, 1878. Revised by the Aid Society. South Mobile, 1911. 252p. and ads.

3 BASHINSKY, MRS. ELIZABETH BURFORD (Compiler). Tried and True Recipes, 2nd book. Illus. Alabama Division, United Daughters of the Confederacy. Troy, 1926. 384p. and ads.

4 MAGUIRE, CLYDE MERRILL. The Cokesbury Dinner and Banquet Book. Holiday ideas from Alabama, told in personal, chatty style. Decorative end papers. Nashville, Tenn.: Abingdon — Cokesbury (1953). 1st ed. 153p.

5 KITCHEN NOTES. Compiled by the Knox Music Club. An offset collection of signed recipes of much interest and value. Circular plastic bdg. An original, hand-written & illus. Anniston, nd. (recent). 350p. and ads.

6 PASTRY & SWEETS. Wraps. Illus. 140 recipes. Birmingham.

Alaska

7 LADIES' AID SOCIETY COOK BOOK. Autographed recipes. Valdez, Alaska: no pub., 1916. 115p. and ads. Wraps.

8 A COLLECTION OF CHOICE RECIPES. Compiled by the Anchorage Womans Club. Anchorage: 1921. Photo Mt. McKinley, map of the government railroad in Alaska. Some autographed recipes, many interesting ads. 80p.

9 OUT OF ALASKA'S KITCHENS. By members of Alaska Crippled Children's Ass'n. "All Alaska has contributed recipes for this book. Exceptionally beautifully colored illus. Pictorial bds. Recipes for Julie Kaka (Christmas bread), Roast Reindeer Saddle, etc. Printed by The Ketchikan Alaska Chronicle, Anchorage, 1947.

10 CLEVELAND, BESS A. Frontier Formulas. An Alaskan Cookbook. Sourdough, Berries, Favorite Salmon Derby Recipes. Looseleaf, Spiral bdg. June, 1952. Juneau, 212p.

11 ESKIMO COOK BOOK. By the Students of Shishmaref Day School. Signed by the children. Wraps. For the Alaska Crippled Children's Ass'n. Anchorage. n.d. 36 pages.

Arizona

12 THE ARIZONA COOK BOOK. Press of the Morning Journal, Albuquerque, N.M., 1911. 418p.

13 ARIZONA FISH AND GAME LAWS AND COOK BOOK. Compiled and pub-

lished by C. E. Golding, State game warden. Illus. Phoenix (1923). 63 (1)p. and ads.

14 TREASURER'S CACTUS BARREL FULL OF ARIZONA RECIPES. Apache Co. Elk Dinner, Coconino Co. Roast Duck, Gila Co. Quail Dinner, etc. Autographed recipes, by Eleanor Roosevelt, Mrs. V-P Garner, and others. Col. pictorial wraps. Compliments of William (Bill) Petersen to Greek War Relief Ass'n., Phoenix (c. 1940). 55p.

15 ARIZONA MEXICAN COOK BOOK. (see Foreign sec.)

16 ARIZONA RECIPES FOR YOU. Compliments of William "Bill" Petersen, Large format, col. wraps. Flagstaff. n.d. 72p.

17 THE WOMAN'S CLUB COOK BOOK. Autographed recipes. Compiled by the Household Economics Department from submitted recipes. Ads. Wraps. Flagstaff. n.d. 95p.

Arkansas

18 COURSE OF LESSONS IN DOMESTIC SCIENCE. Little Rock P.S., dept. of household arts. Little Rock: no pub. (1913). 128p.

19 MCKNIGHT, LILLIE. Tested and Tried Recipes. Blytheville: Acton Printing Co. (1926). 248p. and ads. Wraps.

19a DAVIS, J. B. Ham Gravy, and other Essays on Victuals. Siloam Springs: Bar D Press, 1939. 30p. (some of them upside down).

20 PINKLEY-CALL, CORA. From My Ozark Cupboard. A Basic Ozark Cook Book. Wraps. 1950. 98p.

21 MAGNOLIA SELECTED RECIPES. Autographed recipes, ads. Pictorial wraps. Spiral plastic binding. Illus. St. James Auxiliary, Magnolia. 73p.

California

22 CALIFORNIA RECIPE BOOK. By Ladies of California. San Francisco: Bruce's Printing House, 1872. 45p. Wraps.

23 HOW TO KEEP A HUSBAND, OR CULINARY TACTICS. San Francisco, Cubery & Co., 1872. 76p. Wraps.

24 ALMANAC AND FAMILY RECEIPT BOOK FOR 1874. San Francisco: Coffin and Mayhew. Pamphlet, 24p. and drug store ads. Wraps.

25 CALIFORNIA RECIPE BOOK by Ladies of California. San Francisco: Cubery, 1875. 80p. and ads. Wraps.

26 FITCH, FANNIE C. (Anon.) The Gem Cook Book by a New England Lady. San Francisco: Cubery & Co., 1875. 309p. (Gems of New England recipes, culinary couplets, and household remedies).

27 POND, HELEN W. Helps for Young Housekeepers. Prepared for the Fair given by "The Bethany Band of Merry Workers," Monday and Tuesday Evening, Dec. 20 and 21, 1875. Revised for the benefit of the church building fund. San Francisco: Bacon & Co., 1879. 82p. Wraps.

28 BOHEMIAN CLUB OF SAN FRANCISCO. History, records, menus from 1872-1880. Text & pictures by talented members. 2 vols. Ltd. ed. (600), San Francisco, 1881. 243 & 246p.

29 Fisher, Mrs. Abby. What Mrs. Fisher knows about Old Southern Cooking. Awarded 2 medals at the San Francisco Mechanics' Institute Fair, diploma at Sacramento State Fair. (Book dictated by an author who could neither read nor write.) But she knew her subject! San Francisco: Women's Co-operative Printing Office, 1881. 72p.

30 The California Practical Cook Book. Oakland: Pacific Press, 1882. 56p. Wraps.

31 Plymouth Church Cook Book. Edited by the ladies and their friends of the church. San Francisco: Jos. Winterburn, 1882. 122p.

32 Clayton, H. J. Clayton's Quaker Cook-Book. The result of life-long experience in catering to a host of highly cultivated tastes. San Francisco: Women's Co-operative Printing Office, 1883. 80p. Frontis. port. of author.

33 Harland, Marion. Cookery for Beginners. Familiar lessons for young housekeepers. San Francisco: Golden Age Bazaar, n.d. (c. 1884). 157p.

34 Cronkite, Mrs. H. Mrs. Cronkite's Cook Book. Over 700 useful recipes for cooking all kinds of soups, fish, etc. Sacramento: G. W. Herr, 1885. 279p.

35 Harder, Jules Arthur. The Physiology of Taste. Practical American Cookery (6 vols.) Vol. I. American Vegetables: the plants, cultivation, art of cooking. By Chef de Cuisine, Palace Hotel, San Francisco: 1885. 432p. Frontis. port. of author. (Remaining vol. not published).

36 Elphick, Levy Simpson. Eat and Drink to Live, and not Live to Eat and Drink. How to keep young till eighty. Obey Nature's laws and live. San Francisco: the Author, 1886. 22p. Wraps.

37 Smith, Mrs. Mary G. Temperance Cook Book. Written for the benefit of all housekeepers. 2nd ed. San Jose: Mercury Book and Job Printing House, 1887. 261p. and ads.

38 "Still Another" Cook Book. Ladies' Aid Society, Congregational Church, Oakland. Pacific Press Pub. Co., 1888. 3rd ed. 120p.

39 Cookery For Working-Men's Wives. The Helping Hand Club, Issue No. 1. From Reports from the Consuls of the U.S., No. 107. Published by a quick-silver company to aid in preventing an industry disease among employees in mining and handling its products. New Almaden, 1890. 50p. Wraps.

40 1001 Useful Recipes. San Francisco: A. J. Leary, 1890. 256p. 1st ed. Mar. 1. (See No. 228).

41 A Practical Cook Book. Compiled from the choicest recipes of many good housewives. For The Froebel Society. Sacramento: Good & Carrington, 1890. 47p. Paper.

42 Lizzie's Cook Book edited by "The Bachelette." San Jose: Smith & Wilcox, 1891. 114p.

43 O'Connell, Daniel. The Inner Man by one of the founders of the Bohemian Club. Good things to eat and drink and where to get them. San Francisco: The Bancroft Company, 1891. 160p.

44 Tilton, E. Stevens. Home Dissertations . . . San Francisco: Goldberg Bowen & Co., 1891. (See 401).

45 Golden Rule Bazaar Encyclopedia of Cookery and Reliable Recipes. Recipes written and pasted in. Oilcloth cover. Patrons of Golden Rule Bazaar. San Francisco (1892). Portland, Oregon. 309 plus 103p.

46 Hinckley, Mrs. E. M. Progressive Cookery compiled from a series of lessons given at the School of Cookery. San Francisco; San Francisco Printing Co., 1892. 150p. Wraps.

47 How We Cook in Los Angeles. A Practical Cook-Book containing 600 or more Recipes Selected and Tested by over 200 well known Hostesses, including a French, German and Spanish Department. Autographed recipes. Boards. Ladies' Social Circle, Simpson M. E. Church, Los Angeles, 1894. 382p. and interesting ads.

48 Choice Recipes collected by the Ladies of the Guild of the Church of St. Matthew, San Mateo, 1897. 117p. Wraps.

49 Tracy, Suzy. Twelve Lessons in Scientific Cookery. San Francisco; H. S. Crocker Company, 1897. 62p.

50 Wachtmeister, Constance and Davis, Kate Buffington. (editors). Practical Vegetarian Cookery. San Francisco: Mercury Pub. Co. (1897). 179p. (Pub. simultaneously in Chicago, New York, Minneapolis, London).

51 San Rafael Cook Book. Compiled by the ladies of San Rafael. San Rafael, 1898. 136p. and ads.

52 What We Eat and How We Cook It. Autographed recipes. Wraps. Woman's Auxiliary of the First Unitarian Church, Oakland, 1898. 19p.

53 Colcord, Mrs. Anna L. A Friend In The Kitchen. What to Cook and How to Cook It. About 400 Choice Recipes Carefully Tested. Illus. Pictorial boards. Pacific Press Publishing Co., Oakland (1899). 126p.

54 Forbes, Ernest. The Other Way. Respectfully dedicated to all good housewives. Illus. of various stoves, general essays, and chapters of recipes. San Francisco: Ernest Forbes (1899). 186p.

55 Choice Recipes, compiled by practical housekeepers of Sonoma County . . . San Francisco: The Whitaker & Ray Co. (1900). 57p.

56 New Century Belgian Hare Manual and Cook Book. For breeders. A treatise on breeding, feeding, management, diseases, cooking, etc. Los Angeles: Corbett & Langley (1900). 31p. Wraps.

57 The Berkeley Cook Book. 400 Practical receipts used by Berkeley

women. Compiled by the Women's Association of the First Congregational Church. Berkeley: 1903. 169p. and ads. Wraps.

58 THE GOLDEN BANQUET and other functions during reception of President Roosevelt. San Francisco: no pub., May, 1903. 100p.

59 LUMMIS, CHARLES F. LANDMARKS CLUB COOK BOOK. A California Collection of Choicest Recipes from Everywhere. Including chapter of Most Famous Old Californian and Mexican Dishes. Autographed recipes. Illus. 16 full page photos of Calif. landmarks. Out West Company, Los Angeles, 1903. 261p.

60 THE RAISIN CENTER COOK BOOK. Fowler Improvement Association . . . Fowler: Fowler Ensign Press (1903). 390p.

61 FULTON, E. G. Vegetarian Cook Book. You can find out what 'Frizzled Protose' is. Mountain View: Pacific Press Pubg. Co. (1904). 268p. and ads.

62 MCLAREN, L. L. (compiled by) High Living. Recipes from Southern Climes. Preface by Edward H. Hamilton. Decorations by W. S. Wright. Benefit Telegraph Hill Neighborhood Assn. Paul Elder; San Francsco (1904). 62p.

63 SOUTHWORTH, MAY E. (compiled by) 101 CHAFING DISH RECIPES. Wraps. Paul Elder & Co., San Francisco (1904). 93p.

64 SOUTHWORTH, MAY E. Book of 101 Entrees. San Francisco: Paul Elder and Company, 1904. 83p.

65 SOUTHWORTH, MAY E. Book of 101 Sandwiches. San Francisco: Paul Elder and Co., 1904. 81p. Wraps.

66 THE BRIDE'S COOK BOOK. Wraps. E. Bryant Ashman: 20th Century Press, San Diego (c. 1905). Ads.

67 ECHOES FROM THE SOUTHERN KITCHEN. Compiled and published by the Robert E. Lee Chapter, United Daughters of the Confederacy, No. 278. Los Angeles: 1905. 147p. and ads. Paper boards.

68 COSMOPOLITAN RECIPES contributed by the Woman's Improvement Club and its friends. Most recipes autographed. St. Helena: 1905. 99p. and ads. Paper.

69 HAINES. Ye Gardeyne Boke. Illus. San Francisco, 1906. 72p.

70 SOUTHWORTH, MAY E. (compiled by) 101 Beverages. Wraps. Paul Elder & Co., San Francisco (1906). 87p.

71 SOUTHWORTH, MAY E. 101 Sauces. San Francisco: Paul Elder & Company, 1906. 77p. Wraps.

72 COLE, LIZZIE. City of Roses Best Recipes. Chico: 1907. 72p. Wraps.

73 COOKERY. Recipes compiled by St. Mary's Guild. Mill Valley: 1907. 128p. 2nd ed.

74 EAT CALIFORNIA FRUIT by one of the eaters. San Francisco: Passenger Dept., Southern Pacific Co., 1907. 32p. Wraps.

75 JONES, MRS. NETTIE M. (WARE), San Rafael Cook Book. "Mrs. W. F. Jones," editor. (San Rafael), 1907. 222p. and ads.

76 McLaren, Linie Loyall. High Living. Recipes from Southern climes. 2nd ed. San Francisco and New York: P. Elder and Co. (1907). 62p.

77 Porter, Arina L. and Ball, Eva B. Crumbs from Everybody's Table. A cook book. 3rd ed. Compiled for the Ladies of St. Paul's guild, Salinas. Salinas: Monterey County Democrat Print, 1907. 362p. Wraps. Ads.

78 Southworth, May E. 101 Desserts. Wraps. Paul Elder & Co., San Francisco, 1907. 73p.

79 Southworth, May E. 101 Layer Cakes. San Francisco: Paul Elder and Company (1907). 103p. Wraps.

80 Temple Workers Recipes. Cloth book. Temple Workers of Plymouth Church, San Francisco, 1907. 143p.

81 Tilden, Major Joseph. Joe Tilden's Recipes for Epicures. San Francisco: A. M. Robertson, 1907. 135p.

82 Hirschler, Mrs. David. Council Cook Book published by the San Francisco section of the Council of Jewish Women. San Francisco: 1908-1909. 192p. and Ads.

83 The Reappear. A book of choice recipes, compiled by the Ladies' Aid Society of the Fulton Presbyterian Church . . . Sonoma County, Calif. (Santa Rosa: Press of C. A. Wright & Co.), 1908. 147p.

84 San Anselmo Cook Book. By the Ladies of St. Anselm's Church. San Anselmo: 1908. 168p. and ads.

85 San Antonio Cook Book. Published by the Ladies of St. Anthony's Parish. Oakland: 1908. 189p. and ads. Paper.

86 Tracy, Suzy. Practical Cook Book . . San Francisco: Payot, Stratford & Kerr Print, 1908. 75, 4p.

87 Good Things From Good Cooks. Autographed recipes. Compiled and sold for the benefit of The Cottage Hospital, Santa Barbara. Illus. with photographs of places near Santa Barbara. Pacific Coast Publishing Co. for The Managers; Santa Barbara, 1909. 256p.

88 Ladies Aid Cook Book. Autographed recipes. Oilcloth covers. Ladies of the Presbyterian Church, Dinuba, 1909. 97p. and ads.

89 Middleton, May. Recipes from Old Mexico. (see For. sec.)

90 Miyagawa, Y. Entree and Salad Cookery. (see Foreign section)

91 Thomas, May Robinson. Recipes of the Woman's Club of San Mateo. San Mateo: (Woman's Club of San Mateo), 1909. 103p. Wraps. Ads.

92 Aunt Flo's Cook Book. Wraps. San Diego (?), 1910. 41p.

93 Corona Club Cook Book. Autographed recipes. Oilcloth covers. Rincon Publishing Co., San Francisco (1910). 248p. and ads.

94 Gilbreth and Bossue. Chinese and English Cook Book. (see Foreign sec.)

95 Hirtzler, Victor. Hotel St. Francis Book of Recipes and Model

Menus—L'Art Culinaire. By the hotel's famous chef. Putney Haight, Telegraph Press, San Francisco, 307p. and ads.

96 Los Angeles Times Cook Book Number Three. Cooking and Other Recipes by Skilled Housewives. Autographed recipes with address of each contributor. The Times-Mirror Co., Los Angeles (before 1911). 224p.

97 Goodhue, Isabel. Good Things, Ethical Recipes for Feast Days and Other Days, with Graces for all the Days. Decorations by Walter Francis. San Francisco: Paul Elder & Co., 1911. 50p.

98 Home Tried Recipes. Autographed recipes. Many interesting local ads. Wraps. Ladies of the First Universalist Church, Los Angeles (c. 1911). 176p.

99 James, George Wharton. The 1910 Trip of the H.M.M.B.A. to California and the Pacific Coast. Illus. with photos of the trip. Descriptions of hotels of Calif. Bolte and Braden Co., San Francisco, 1911. 377p.

100 300 Favorite Recipes. Published by the Floral League of the First Congregational Church of San Francisco. Church Fair, Nov. 23, 1911. San Francisco: Thos. J. Davis, 1911. 167p. illus. Autographed recipes.

101 The Bride's Cook Book. San Francisco: Original Bride's Cook Book Pub., 1912. 127p. and ads.

102 Briggs, Edgar William (Compiler). The Bride's Cook Book . . . San Francisco: The California Bride's Cook Book Pub. Co. (1912). 110p.

103 Evans, Edna. Home Bakings. Drawings by Harold Evans. San Francisco: H. S. Crocker Co. (1912). 96p. Wraps.

104 Ohata, Susumu Ichitaro. Cook's Cook Book. (see Foreign sec.)

105 Vail, Mary Beals. Home Economics. Recipes. Berkeley; Univ. of California Press, 1912. 44p. Wraps.

106 Chinese and English Cook Book. (see Foreign sec.)

107 Hoff, A. C. Specialties of the World Famous Chefs—United States, Canada, Europe, from the International Cooking Library. Los Angeles: International Pub. Co., Wraps. Illus. of World famous hotels and portraits of the contributing chefs. N.D. (c. 1913).

108 Tried and True Cook Book. Autographed recipes. Soft leather cover. Women of Christ Church, Los Angeles, 1913. 168p.

109 Bride's Cook Book; Helpful recipes and useful information. Los Angeles: Los Angeles Bride's Cook Book Co. (1914). 123p. and ads. Wraps.

110 Edwords, Clarence E. Bohemian San Francisco. Its Restaurants and Their Most Famous Recipes —The Elegant Art of Dining.

Paul Elder & Co., San Francisco (1914). 136p.

111 HONBERGER, MAUD MITCHELL (compiler). Tried Receipts of Pasadena. Pasadena: Pasadena Stationery and Print. Co., 1914. 112p. and ads.

112 ROASTS AND ENTREES. Wraps, in case. International Cooking Library, Los Angeles, 1914. 64p.

113 ROBERTS, W. K. Health from Natural Foods. Self Culture Series. An Argument for the Fruitarian Diet. Sunnyvale: (c. 1914). 90p. Paper.

114 ROPER, DORA C.C.L. Scientific Feeding. Oakland: R. S. Kitchener, Printer, 1914. 260p.

115 SOUPS AND CONSOMMES. Wraps, in case. International Cooking Library. Los Angeles, 1914. 64p.

116 SOUTHWORTH, MAY E. (compiler). 101 Mexican Dishes. San Francisco: Paul Elder and Co., 1914. 86p.

117 SOUTHWORTH, MAY E. Midnight Feasts. 202 salads and chafing dish recipes. San Francisco: Paul Elder and Company, 1914. 135p.

118 STEAKS, CHOPS, EGGS. Wraps, in case. International Cooking Library. Los Angeles, 1914. 64p.

119 TRIED RECEIPTS OF PASADENA. Autographed recipes. Ads. Compiled for the benefit of The William A. Scripps Home for Aged People, The Pasadena Charitable League, The Pasadena Children's Training Society, The Pasadena Day Nursery. California (1914). 112p.

120 BROOKS, WILLIAM H. Modern Practical Cake Baking. Palo Alto: Times Pub. Co., 1915. 87p. Frontis. port. of the author. Illus.

121 IMMANUEL AID SOCIETY COOK BOOK. Autographed recipes. Ads. Picture of Church on front cover. Wraps. Crescent Printing Co., O. E. Goodale, Los Angeles, 1915. 96p.

122 LEHNER, JOSEPH CHARLES. World's Fair Menu and Recipe Book. A collection of the most famous menus exhibited at the Panama-Pacific International Exposition. San Francisco: The Lehner and Sefert Publishing Company, 1915. 144p.

123 MCLAREN, LINIE LOYALL. The Pan-Pacific Cook Book. Savory bits from the world's fare. San Francisco: Blair, Murdock Co., 1915. 170p.

124 ST. FRANCIS COOK BOOK. Wraps. Friends of the Sisters of St. Francis Technical School: San Francisco, 1915. 115p. and ads.

125 BARTLETT, JOSEPHINE. The Bulletin Cook Book. Prize recipes. San Francisco; The Bulletin, 1916. 116p. Wraps.

126 WILLIAMSON, SARAH MINNIE (complier). A California Cook Book . . . San Francisco: Town Talk Press, 1916. 47p.

127 ANDERSON, H. S. Food and Cookery. By the nutritionist at Loma Linda Sanitarium, Calif. No meat recipes . . . Mountain View:

Pacific Press Publishing Association, 1917. 163p.

128 THE BRIDE'S COOK BOOK. San Francisco: Pacific Coast Pub., 1917. 130p. and ads.

129 CUSIMANO, JACK. Economical Italian Cook Book. (see Foreign sec.)

130 LIBERTY COOK BOOK. State Council of Defense: Woman's Committee. Los Angeles City Teachers Club, Los Angeles (1917). 27p.

131 CONSERVATION RECIPES. Compiled by The Mobilized Women's Organizations. Emphasize economy in cooking. Rev. ed. Pict. wraps. Berkeley, 1918. 176p.

132 CUPID'S BOOK OF GOOD COUNSEL. The Cupid books were published for various Coast States and given to Brides and Grooms. Pictorial boards. E. F. Kiessling & Son: Oakland, 1918. 109p. and ads.

133 SAN DIEGO COOK BOOK . . . Compiled by the Ladies of the Methodist Episcopal Church, San Diego. Garrett & Smith, printers (191-?). 100p. and ads.

134 DELICIOUS RECIPES. For peaches. Colored illustrations. Booklet, wraps. California Peach Growers: Fresno, 1920. 32p.

135 ANDERSON, H. S. SCIENCE OF FOOD & COOKERY. Diet, menus and recipes. Pacific Press: Mountain View, 1921: Illus. 282p.

136 CASTELAR CRECHE COOK BOOK. Los Angeles, 1922. 296p.

137 DE GRAF, BELLE. Mrs. De Graf's Cook Book; by the editor of the San Francisco Chronicle's cooking page. San Francisco: H. S. Crocker Co., 1922. 372p. Frontis. port. of author.

138 WELLS, HELEN M. Everywoman's Cook Book. Recipes and food combinations for the household. The author, dietitian National League for Woman's Service. San Francisco: National League for Woman's Service (1922). 47p. Pict. wraps.

139 VANDEGEER, DIRK. The Chef de Cuisine. Proven Recipes for the Cook, Baker, Pastryman and Confectioner. Illus. by the author. No place, no pub. (1923). 319p. Copyright dated 1923 at Oceanside.

140 WYMAN, A. L. (Edited by). LOS ANGELES TIMES PRIZE COOK BOOK. Recipes for A Mystery Dish, Bungalow Soup etc. The editor, chef in famous cooking establishments of Europe, Egypt, India and the Orient. Boards. Los Angeles, 1923. 340p. and ads.

141 BURBERRY, RUTH. HINDU DIETETICS FOR BODY BUILDERS. About herbs and seeds and spices and their effects. Wraps. Sonoma, 1924. 69p.

142 GAY, AUGUSTE AND PAGE, ANNE. NEW PRESENTATION OF COOKING WITH TIMED RECIPES. Ringsmith and Wellman, San Francisco (1924). 1st ed. 500p. and adv. of Occidental Stovetop Gas Ranges.

143 BELLE, FRANCES P. (compiler). California Cook Book. An unusual

collection of Spanish dishes and typical California foods for luncheons and dinners. Chicago: Regan Pub. Corp., 1925. 154p.

144 CORONA CLUB COOK BOOK. Corona Club, San Francisco. San Francisco: Press of John Kitchen Jr. Co. (1925.) Front. 235p.

145 PERRY, EVADNA KRAUS AND PHIPPS, O. W. Vegetable Salads for Health. From Garden to Table —no cooking. Needles: no publisher (1925). 35p. Wraps.

146 RICHTER, VERA M. Mrs. Richter's Cook-less Book with Scientific Food Chart. 10th ed. Los Angeles: Los Angeles Service and Supply Co., 1925. 61p. Wraps.

147 THE BRIDE'S BOOK. Household Economy, helpful cooking recipes. With some of one bride's private shopping lists in July, 1926. Arts & Crafts Press, San Diego. 96p. and ad.

148 CARQUÉ, OTTO. Natural Foods. The Safe way to Health. 2nd ed. Pub. by Carqué Pure Food Co., Inc. Los Angeles, 1926. 356p. and ads.

149 DE GRAF, BELLE. Spark Cook Book for Spark lid-top gas stoves. Edited and approved by Mrs. De Graf. Oakland: Hammer-Bray Co. (1926). 123p. and ads.

150 MCCOY, FRANK. The Fast Way to Health. An exposition of the fasting cure and its application to prevalent disorders. Diets for the well. 11th ed. Los Angeles: McCoy Publications, Inc., 1926. 333p. Frontis. portrait of author.

151 PIRKEY, M. UVA. The U.V.A. Cook Book. Los Angeles: Gem Publishing Company (1926). 104p.

152 VASEY, ANN. Favorite English, Dutch, German, French Recipes. Los Angeles: Gem Publishing Company (1926). 22p. Wraps.

153 WATT, WALTER. CORRECT EATING THRU BALANCED MEALS. A simple, non-technical treatise. Correct Eating Society, Los Angeles (1926) 176p.

154 BELL, KATHARIN. Mammy's Cook Book. Trade Printing Co.: Los Angeles, 1927. 160p.

155 FIVE HUNDRED WAYS TO COOK CALIFORNIA SEA FOOD. Compiled by State Fish Exchange, Calif. Dept. of Agriculture. Sacramento: California State Printing Office, 1927. 119p.

156 GRETHER, ERNEST. The Bride's Book . . . by a chef known in Europe, etc. Los Angeles (1927). 200p. illus. Wraps.

157 LOVELL, PHILIP M. AND PRESS-LOVELL, LEAH. Diet for Health by Natural Methods. Menus and recipes. Cure without the use of drugs. Los Angeles: The Times-Mirror Press, 1927. 428p.

158 THE OLD VANITY FAIR tea room recipes gathered from far and near. (Los Angeles: C. A. Bundy Quill & Press, 1927). 160p.

159 THOMPSON, MRS. J. DOUGLAS. The Health Recipe Book. 1st ed. Oakland: Thompson Publications (1927). 59p. Wraps.

160 WYMAN, ARTHUR LESLIE, M. C.A. DAILY HEALTH MENUS. With special articles by Dr. W. D. Sansum of the Potter Metabolic Clinic. Wyman Food Service, Los Angeles (1927). 502p.

161 BARTON, MRS. FLORENCE GIBSON. The California Orange Cook Book. Complete and explicit directions for the making of candied and glace fruits, jellies, marmalades, orange and grapefruit rinds. Also recipes for desserts and salads and Spanish dishes. San Bernardino: 1928. Illus. 88p.

162 CORLEY, BUREN L. The Food Way to Health. By the author of "Health and Beauty." San Francisco: Public Health Institute (1929). 159p. Frontis. port. of author.

163 FASHIONS IN FOODS. Beverly Hills Woman's Club. Los Angeles, 1929. 189p.

164 LADIES' AID COOK BOOK. Compiled by The Ladies' Aid Society of First Methodist Episcopal Church. Cloth. San Pedro, 1929. 144p. and local ads.

165 VAUGHN, KATE BREW. "My Best Recipes." A Selection from 20 Years' Experience. Los Angeles: 1929. 138p. and ads.

166 BRAGG, PAUL CHAPPIUS. Live Food Cook Book and Menus. Hollywood: Live Food Products, 1930. 170p. Wraps.

167 THE JUNIOR LEAGUE RECIPE BOOK. Los Angeles: 1930. 206p.

168 WEISKIRCH, LAUREL ELIZABETH. The Clew Cook Book. Privately published. Los Angeles: American Lithograph Company (1930). 333p. It's the "Clew to 1500 American and Foreign Recipes."

169 FASHIONS IN FOODS IN BEVERLY HILLS. Autographed recipes. Foreword by Will Rogers. Compiled by The Book Section of the Woman's Club. Cover design and titles by Vivian V. Robeson, Beverly Hills Woman's Club, Beverly Hills, 1931. 239p.

170 DRAKE, NELLIE M. Dee-Licious Recipes. Compiled by the Women's City Club of Oakland and the East Bay. Oakland: the club, 1932. 198p. and ads. Autographed recipes.

171 FOOD TABLES AND RECIPES FOR LOW SALT DIETS. Special Diet Laboratory, Stanford Univ. Hospital. San Francisco: 1932. 44p.

172 KNIGHT, MRS. MIDGIE. Hollywood's Famous Recipes of the Movie Stars. 100 culinary secrets with 100 exclusive portraits. Clark Gable, John Gilbert, Marlene Dietrich as they were. Wraps. Illus. Los Angeles: Goodan-Jenkins Furniture Co. (1932). 96p.

173 LOYALTY COOK BOOK. Native Daughters of the Golden West, Santa Rosa Parlor No. 217. Santa Rosa, 1932. 192p.

174 SOUP TO NUTS. Cook book for Epicures. 3rd ed. rev. Choice recipes collected to create work for girls at Sisterhood House. San Francisco: Emanu-El Sisterhood, 1932. 184p. loose-leaf.

175 THOMPSON, J. DOUGLAS. Eating Your Way to Health. The natural way to health by the Oakland diet specialist. 7th ed. Oakland: Thompson Health Publications (1932). 197p.

176 ASSISTANCE LEAGUE OF SOUTHERN CALIFORNIA. The Palatists Book of Cookery . . . Hollywood, 1933. 230p.

177 CALIFORNIA SEA FOODS. Recipes compiled by State Fish Exchange. Issued by Div. of Fish and Game Dept. of Natural Resources, San Francisco. Sacramento: California State Printing Office, 1933. 97p. Paper.

178 KWONG, GEORGE I. AND MAGPIONG, PACIFICO. Oriental Culinary Art. (See Foreign section)

179 THE PALATISTS BOOK OF COOKERY. Foreword by Mrs. Anita M. Baldwin. Compiled and published by the Assistance League of Southern California. Hollywood: 1933. 230p.

180 STEWART, MARION. One Hundred Favorite Foreign Recipes. 12 full-page illus. and end papers by Margaret Schoch. Los Angeles: Saturday Night Publishing Co., 1933. 152p.

181 PRETORIUS, MARTIN W. with the collaboration of Miss Lillian Bournman and Mrs. Agnes White Gillanders. Scientific Cooking. Health recipes arranged according to their respective classes. 2nd ed. Hollywood: The Food Chemistry Educational Institute (1934). 112p.

182 P.T.A. COOK BOOK. National Congress of Parents & Teachers, 1897. 12th District of Calif., 1934. Ventura: Free Press. Signed recipes. 112p. Wraps.

183 SCHULMAN, B. DONALD. Favorite Recipes of the Famous Movie Stars . . . (B. Donald Schulman.) (Milwaukee), 1934. 80p. illus.

184 MEADE, MARTHA. Modern Meal Maker. The cook book that does everything: makes 1115 menus for every meal in the year, gives 744 "perfected" receipts, 2000 "recipettes" and other valuable information. San Francisco: Sperry Flour Co., 1935. 428p.

185 CERWIN, HERBERT. Famous Recipes by Famous People. Tested and sampled by a group of the American Ass'n. of Gourmets. Illus. by Paul Whitman. Del Monte: Hotel Del Monte, 1936. Frontis. autographs, recipe donors' names and occupations. 43p. Wraps.

186 MCNEILL, BLANCHE AND EDNA V. First Foods of America. Los Angeles: Suttonhouse, Ltd. (1936). 150p. and sketches.

187 PACKMAN, ANA BIGUE DE. Early California Hospitality. The Cookery Customs of Spanish California, with authentic recipes and menus of the period. Glendale: Arthur H. Clark Co., 1938. 182p. Frontis.

188 SUNSET'S BARBECUE BOOK. Construction section by George A. Sanderson. Cookery section edited by Virginia Rich. Illustrations by Norman Gordon. Spiral binding;

wood covers. Sunset Magazine, San Francisco (1938). 1st ed. 64p.

189 Sunset's New Kitchen Cabinet Cook Book. All the recipes published over a period of nearly 10 years. Illus. Spiral binding. Sunset Magazine, San Francisco, 1938. 223p.

190 Yeates, Lilian Lyford. "I'd Like the Recipe." Recipes wangled from friends, relatives, chefs. Pasadena: Pub. by the Compiler, Oct. 1938. (Bickley Printing Co.). 145p.

191 Lease, Rex & Harlan, Kenneth. "What Actors Eat—When They Eat." Photos of actors with their favorite recipes, autographed. Los Angeles, Lymanhouse, 1939. 241p.

192 Sunsweet. Fruit recipes. Booklet, wraps, illustrated. California Prune & Apricot Growers: San Jose, 1939. 40p.

193 Cerwin, Herbert: Famous Recipes by Famous People. From Gertrude Stein to Walt Disney. Large format. Illus. by Paul Whitman. San Francisco, Hotel Del Monte, 1940. 62p.

194 Hollywood Glamour Cook Book. "For Health and Beauty. A Thousand Ways to Make Yourself Beautiful." Photograph of Mariposa, boards, pictorial cover. Pub. by Glamour Publications, Mariposa, 1940. 427p.

195 Sunset's Host and Hostess Book. Ideas for menus, recipes, and entertainment. From the Magazine. Compiled by Helen Kroeger Muhs. Illus. by Phyllis Gregg. Lane Publishing Co. San Francisco, 1940. 180p.

196 Walker. Diet & Salad Suggestions. Wraps. Los Angeles, 1940. 103p.

197 Sunset's Barbecue Book. Construction section edited by George A. Sanderson. Cookery section edited by Virginia Rich. Illus. by Norman Gordon. Sunset Magazine, San Francisco (1941). 71p.

198 Auerbach, Maurice H. "Old Smoky" and Auerbach, Herbert R. "Smoky." Handbook for Rumpus Room Chefs and Barbecuers. Unusual cookery and writing about it. Decorations. Wraps. Maurice H. "Smoky" Auerbach, San Francisco, 1942. 48p.

199 Gregg, Marion (edited by) The American Women's Voluntary Services Cook Book. A book for wartime living. Spiral binding. A.W.V.S., San Francisco: 1942. 191p.

200 Sunset Barbecue Book. How to build them, how to use them. Illus. Decorative end papers. Lane Publishing Co., San Francisco, 1945. 96p.

201 Callahan, Genevieve. The California Cook Book. Decorations by Philip Little, drawings and end papers. M. Barrows, New York, 1946. 1st ed. 381p.

202 Sunset Kitchen Cabinet Recipes. Vol. 2 . . From the magazine. Illus. Lane Publishing Co., San Francisco (1946). 128p.

203 Dunham, Wayland A. It's a Date. Illus. San Marino, 1948. 156p. & bibliog.

204 Loyality Cook Book. Favorite recipes of members of Native Daughters of the Golden West and friends. Compiled and published by Willow Borba, Sebastopol, 1948. Wraps over spiral binding. 288p.

205 The California Way. Brighter Dinners, More Glamorous Parties, Planned for easy entertaining. Illus. in color. Wraps. Wine Advisory Board, San Francisco, 1950. 31p.

206 Beck, Neill and Fred. The Farmers Market Cook Book. Stall-by-stall with recipes to match. California cookery. Drawings by Ernest Maxwell. Henry Holt: New York, 1951. 1st ed. 246p.

207 Blake, Mary. The Cook's Handbook. Autographed by Gracie Allen. Illus., many in color. Spiral binding; wraps. Carnation Co., Los Angeles (1951). 96p.

208 Sunset Barbecue Cook Book. 251 tested recipes, 37 sauces, 26 barbecue menus and recipes, index. Colorful pages, illus. Lane Publishing Co., Menlo Park (1951). 96p.

209 Barbour, Fanny. One Man's Family. The 20th Anniversary Souvenir. Mother Barbour's Favorite Recipes. Family photos; Wraps. Miles Laboratories, Elkhart, Ind. 1952. 48p.

210 Sunset Barbecue Book. The complete barbecue book; how to build, and use. Illus. Lane Publishing Co., Menlo Park (1952). 96p.

211 San Pascual. The Cook Key. Herbs, spices, recipes & information. Chatty notes from the Calif. coast. Carmel; the author, 1954. Mimeo. 9p.

212 San Pascual. The How About Herbs. Vol. IV, a cook-booklet by an expert with recipes from his friends: Zabaione to serve with candlelight, and Curry-Ben (who is an artist). Illus. by Edmond Ronaky. Carmel: the author, 1954. 14p. mimeo.

213 Medic Menu Magic. Favorite recipes of the Univ. of Calif. Doctors' Wives Assn. Signed recipes. Spiral. San Francisco, 1957. 91p.

214 The Times Cook Book, No. 3 . . . Los Angeles: Times-Mirror Co. (19-?) 240p. and ads.

215 Califene Cook Book. Recipes specially selected from numerous recipes submitted by California's best cooks. *Do not confuse this with previous issues.* San Francisco: Western Meat Co., n.d. 76p. Wraps.

216 California Street M. E. Church Cook Book. Compiled and published for the benefit of The Ladies' Aid Society. San Francisco, Brunt Press, n.d. 104p. and ads. Wraps.

216a Elegant but Easy Recipes with California Ripe Olives. Prepared by California Foods Research Institute. Illus. Wraps. Olive Advisory Board, San Francisco (n. d.). 14p.

217 Choice Receipts Edited and Compiled by Members of the Eastern Star of Sacramento. Sacramento: Eastern Star Hall Ass'n., ~~n.d. 157~~p. illus. Ads.
w-2 copies, 160 p. [1935?] and [1938]

218 Chuck's On. Selected and Prize Beef Recipes. Compiled by the Kern County Cow Bells. Photos of beef cattle and brands of the cattlemen of several counties. Bakersfield: n.d. 181p. Spiral, wraps.

219 Glendale Sanitarium Vegetarian Cook Book. Wraps. Pub. by Glendale Sanitarium, Glendale, 64p.

220 Haffner - Ginger, Bertha. California Mexican-Spanish Cook Book. (see For. sec.)

221 Hazeldine, Norton F. W. Therapeutic Dietetics or the Science of Health Foods and their Medical Values. By the principal of the Venice Health School, Venice-on-Sea, Cal. Los Angeles: the author, n.d. 147p. Frontis. port. of author.

222 Hints to the Hostess. San Francisco: Nathan-Dormann Co., n.d. (1900). 62p. Wraps. Illus.

223 Home Tested Recipes. Compiled by Los Angeles Tenth District California Congress of Parents and Teachers, Mrs. W. R. Goddard, Pres. Signed recipes. Los Angeles: n.d. no pub. 8, 48, 19, 116, 17, 8p. Spiral bdg. [1940?]

224 Kiessling, E. F. and Son. Cupid's Book of Good Counsel. Oakland; E. F. Kiessling & Son, n.d. (1918 see p. 93). 104p. Ads.

225 Milliers, G. W. Servants and Stars; conditions under which we labor. Also favorite dishes of the movie stars. Hollywood: G. W. Milliers, n.d. 144p. Wraps.

226 The Mission Cook Book. Immanuel Baptist Church. San Francisco, n.d. 180p. and ads for a sewing machine.

227 Modern Meatless Cook Book. 500 Recipes for Preparing Foods, with Special Reference to Cooking Without Meat. San Jose: House of Rest, n.d. 135p. Wraps.

228 1001 Useful Recipes and valuable hints about cooking and housekeeping. San Francisco: Dutton H. Partridge, n.d. 192p. and many ads. Wraps. (See No. 40)

229 P.E.O.'S in the Kitchen. Whittier, n.d. (recent). 368p. 1947

230 Raw Food Menu & Recipe Book. Booklet. Illus. Los Angeles, n.d. 58p.

231 Warren, Jane. San Francisco Economical Cook Book. A practical guide to every-day cookery with minute directions how to buy, dress, cook, serve and carve. 300 standard recipes, and a chapter on pickling & candying. San Francisco: Sullivan, Burtis & Dewey, n.d. 96p. Wraps.

232 Wise Ways with a Gas Range. Prepared by Home Service Dept., Southern Counties Gas Co. Wooden binder, loose leaf, hinged. Los Angeles. 92p. 1941.

Colorado

233 Colorado Cook Book. Young Ladies' Mission Band. Central Presbyterian Church. Collier & Cleaveland, printers: Denver (1883). 40p.

234 Nash, Mrs. William H. Cloud City Cookbook. Herald Democrat Print. House: Leadville, 1889. 48p.

235 Mitchell, Clara G. Choice Recipes. Denver: W. H. Kistler Stationery Co. (1897). 161p.

236 The Highland Cook Book, containing practical receipts. Pub. by St. Paul's Church, Highlands, Colo . . . Denver; Zalinger Print. Co. (189-?). 65p. and ads.

237 Colorado Cook Book, published by the Young Ladies' Mission Band of the Central Presbyterian Church. Denver: Collier & Cleaveland (1901). 608p. illus. Frontis.

238 Norton, Caroline Trask. The Rocky Mountain Cook Book . . W. F. Robinson Print. Co., 1903. Denver, 327p.

239 How We Cook in Colorado. Pub. by the M. E. Church, Grand Junction, 1908.

240 Borst, Mrs. Ella Henry (compiler). The Court of Honor Cook Book . . . Denver: J. D. Dillenback (1915). 126p.

241 Mitchell, Clara G. The "Original Book" of Choice Recipes. 3rd ed. Denver: Smith-Brooks Printing Co. (1915). 240p.

242 Norton, Caroline T. The Rocky Mountain Cook Book. 3rd ed. Denver: C. T. Trask (1918). 286p.

243 Brighton Blade Cook Book, adapted to use in high altitudes. Brighton Printing Co., Brighton, 1921. 2nd ed. rev. 96p.

244 Tilden, J. H., M.D. Food. Its combination, etc. Appendix on Cooking. J. H. Tilden, M.D., Denver (1923). 306p.

245 The Bride's Book. Colorado Springs: Bride's Book. Pub. (c. 1925). 270p. and ads. Wraps.

246 Seamster, Albert Silas. The Housewives' Handy Baking Recipes. Denver: The Franklin Press, (1925). 64p. Wraps. Portrait.

247 Tilden, J. H. Practical Cook Book Including Suggestions Regarding Proper Food Combinations with Illustrative Menus Compiled and Approved by Dr. Tilden. Denver: the author (1926-1927). 217p. Frontis. port. of author.

248 Baking Quick Breads and Cakes at High Altitudes, a guide to housewives. Bulletin 366 of the Colorado Agricultural Experiment Station, Fort Collins. Fort Collins: Colorado Agricultural College, 1930. 48p.

249 Peterson, Mrs. Marjorie W. Baking Flour Mixtures at High Altitude. Bulletin 366 of Colo. Agric. Experiment Station, Colo. Agric. College, Fort Collins, 1930. 180p.

250 ALLEN, MRS. IDA BAILEY. THE SERVICE COOK BOOK. A book by "the home maker." Spiral binding. F. W. Woolworth: Colorado Springs, 1933. 192p.

251 KANDY, LILIAN S. SELECTED HIGH ALTITUDE RECIPES. Tested in the Solitaire Kitchen. Revised and enlarged. Lavishly illus. in color. Ring binder, pict. wraps. Pub. by the Morey Mercantile Co., Denver, 1947. 212p.

252 THE DENVER QUAKER COOK BOOK. Compiled by the Ladies' Aid Society of Friends' Church, North Denver. . . Denver: Alexander & Meyer, printers (190-?). 127p.

Connecticut

253 LYMAN, JOSEPH B. AND LAURA E. THE PHILOSOPHY OF HOUSE-KEEPING. A Scientific and Practical Manual; including the preparation of food. Goodwin and Betts, Hartford: 1867. 1st ed. 560p.

254 ORR, MRS. N. DE WITT'S CONNECTICUT COOK BOOK AND HOUSE-KEEPER'S ASSISTANT. Plain styles of cooking, and preserving. Robert M. De Witt, New York, 1871. 192p. and book ads.

255 CHOICE RECEIPTS SELECTED FROM THE BEST MANUSCRIPT AUTHORITIES. Published for the benefit of Christ Church Fair. Worthington, Dustin & Co., Hartford, 1872. 66p.

256 ELLET, (ELIZABETH FRIES). The New Cyclopaedia of Domestic Economy and Practical Housekeeper. All the household interests and arts included. Over 200 engravings. Frontis and one col. plate. Norwich: Henry Bill Pub. Co., 1872. 603p.

257 CHOICE RECEIPTS. Pub.'d toward the erection of a girls' school at Walla Walla. Hartford, 1873. 68p.

258 ELLET, MRS. E. F. The New Cyclopedia of Domestic Economy. Norwich: 1873. (See No. 256).

259 HOW TO MAKE CANDY. A Manual of Plain Directions for the Manufacture of the more popular forms of Confectionery. Wraps. N. P. Fletcher & Co., Hartford (1875). 168p.

260 THE HANDY COOK BOOK. Published by the Ladies of Grace Church. 2nd ed. Wraps. John Kirschner, New Haven, 1882. 44p. and ads.

261 METHODIST COOK BOOK. Pub. by the Ladies' Aid Society of the Methodist Episcopal Church, Bristol, Conn. M. W. Dowd & Co., Winsted, 1882. 69p. and ads.

262 G.A.R. RECIPE BOOK. With such recipes as stewed pigeons, roast partridges. Sedgwick Post, No. 1, Norwich, 1885. 45p.

263 MERIDEN COOK BOOK. Autographed recipes. Poem by Ella Wheeler Wilcox. Pub. by Ladies of the Hospital Fund, Republican Book Department, Meriden, 1885. 144p. and ads.

264 THE UNITED WORKERS' COOK BOOK. Autographed recipes. Wraps. Tuttle, Morehouse & Taylor, 1885. New Haven. 40p.

265 Household Companion and Family Directory. . . . suggestions relating to business, health, law, and cookery. Just about 9/10 advertising. See the celebrated sponge cake beater. New Haven: Phineas E. Austin, 1886. 274p.

266 250 Tried and Tested Recipes. Autographed recipes of the Ladies of the Methodist Episcopal Church, Waterbury, Conn. 1886. Malone & Cooley, Printers. 88p. and ads.

267 Choice Recipes, The Elm City Cook Book. A Collection of Recipes Tried and Approved by Ladies of Dwight Place Church. Wraps. Stafford Printing Co., New Haven, 1889. 58p. and ads.

268 Healy & Bigelow's New Cook Book. Wraps. New Haven, 1890. 64p. and ads.

269 The Mansfield Cook Book. Published by W. H. Mansfield & Co., Putnam, 1890. 108p.

270 New Cook Book. Valuable cooking receipts. Wraps. Healy & Bigelow, New Haven, 1890. 64p. & Illus. ads. of Kickapoo Indian Remedies.

271 Cook Book. Published by the Ladies' Benevolent Society of the Congregational Church, Terryville, Conn. Press of Dowd Printing Co., Winsted, 1891. 66p. and ads.

272 Family Cook Book. Distributed with advertising of Kickapoo Indian remedies, including *Indian Worm Killer*. Wraps. Healy & Bigelow, New Haven, 1891. 48p.

273 Ladies' Hand Book of Reliable Receipts. Autographed recipes. Wraps. Pub. by the Ladies of St. James' Episcopal Guild, Winsted, 1891. 19p. and ads.

274 The New Britain Cook Book. Autographed recipes. Pub. by the Ladies of the Trinity Methodist Episcopal Church. New Britain Record Printers, New Britain, 1891. 64p.

275 The Lucile Cook Book. Conn. 1892. 279p. and ads.

276 Parish Cook Book containing useful Household Receipts. By the Ladies of the Grand Avenue Congregational Church. Wraps. J. T. Hathaway: 297 Crown St., New Haven, 1893. 52p. and ads.

277 Whatsoever Circle, King's Daughters, Cook Book. Wraps. New Haven (c. 1895). 48p. and many ads.

278 The Cook Book of the Meriden Young Women's Christian Association. Republican-Record Print, Meriden, 1896. 48p. and ads.

279 Litchfield Cookery. Choice Recipes, tested by the Ladies of Methodist Episcopal Church and Others. Oilcloth wraps. Graham & Gerrard: Torrington, 1897. 89p. and ads.

280 Molasses Cook Book. 100 Family Recipes for the use of Porto Rico Molasses. Leaflet. J. D. Dewell & Co., New Haven, October 1897. 28p.

281 The Handy Cook Book. A Collection of Tested Recipes, con-

tributed by Ladies of the Methodist Episcopal Church. Wraps. Press of A. C. Northrop & Co., Waterbury, 1898. 140p. and ads.

282 McMurphy, Harriet S. (edited by). The Ideal Receipt Book. Illus. Wraps. Peck, Stow & Wilcox Co., Southington (1898). 64p.

283 Meriden Cook Book. Pub. by the Woman's Executive Committee of the Meriden Hospital. Autographed recipes. Meriden Journal Printers, Meriden, 1898. 166p. and Ads.

284 The Universal Cook Book. The Universal Food Chopper advertising leaflet. Wraps. Pictorial cover. Landers, Frary & Clark, New Britain (c. 1898). 44p.

285 A Book for the Cook. Old Fashioned Receipts for New Fashioned Kitchens. Autographed recipes. Many interesting ads. Pub. under Auspices of The Village Improvement Society of Greenfield Hill, Conn. Bridgeport, 1899. 100p. and ads.

286 The Priscilla Cook Book of Tried and Proved Recipes. Autographed recipes. Wraps. Pub. by the Ladies' Aid Society of the Main Street Baptist Church, Meriden. n. d. (1890'c). 68p. and ads.

287 A Book for the Cook; Old fashioned receipts for New-fashioned Kitchens. Pub. by Village Improvement Society, Greenfield Hill, Conn. Bridgeport: Hurd & Taylor Co., 1900. 100p.

288 Drinking Terms. Illustrated amusing. Small booklet, wraps. Heublein: Hartford, 1901. 30p.

289 The Norwich Cook Book. Autograph recipes of the Ladies of Trinity Methodist Episcopal Church. Picture of Church on cover. Boards. Norwich, 1901. 62p. and ads.

290 Middlebrook's New-England Almanac. Wraps. Standard Association, Bridgeport, 1903. 64p. and ads.

291 A New Cook Book—The Reliable. Contains a collection of valuable and reliable recipes, thoroughly tested by many of the skilful housekeepers of the Ladies' Benevolent Society of the Congregational Church. Wraps. Rocky Hill, 1903. 28p. and ads.

292 The New England Almanac for 1903. Some paragraphs on food. New London, 1903. 98p.

293 The Reliable Cook Book. Recipes compiled by Ladies Benevolent Society of the Congregational Church. Signed. Wraps. Rocky Hill, 1903. 28p. & ads.

294 Book of Recipes. Wraps. Ladies Social and Benevolent Society, 1st Baptist Church, Meriden (c. 1904). 40p. and ads.

295 Hartford Branch Cook Book. More than 500 Recipes from our best Housekeepers. Pub. by Hartford Branch of the Connecticut Children's Aid Society. Hartford, 1904. 179p. and ads.

296 Leap Year Cook Book. West Hartford Bazaar. Wraps. Press of D. S. Moseley, Hartford, 1904. 64p.

297 Middlebrook's New-England Almanac. Wraps. Standard Association. Bridgeport, 1904. 62p. and ads.

298 Proved Receipts. Autograph recipes. Illus. with photographs of public buildings. Wraps. The Ladies of the W.C.T.U. of Clinton, Madison, Guilford, 1904. 52p. and ads.

299 Terryville Cook Book. Signed recipes. Wraps. Ladies Benevolent Society. Terryville, 1904. 125p.

300 Receipt Book. Arranged by the Ladies' Aid Society of the 1st Baptist Church of Middletown, Conn. Wraps. 1905. 48p. and ads.

301 Middlebrook's New-England Almanac for 1906. Wraps. Standard Assoc., Bridgeport, Conn. 64p. and ads.

302 Receipts. Collected by the Ladies of Christ Church. Autographed recipes. Wraps. West Haven, 1906. 48p.

303 Middlebrook's New-England Almanac for 1907. Wraps. Standard Association, Bridgeport, Conn. 64p. and ads.

304 The New England Almanac and Farmers' Friend for 1907. Wraps. L. E. Daboll, New London. 98p. and ads.

305 Receipts. Arranged by the Flower Committee of the Benevolent Society of the Center Congregational Church. Autographed recipes. Wraps. Torrington, 1907. 52p.

306 Y.M.C.A. Womens' Auxiliary Cook Book. Choice Receipts compiled by the Ladies of the Society. Autographed recipes. Wraps. New Haven, 1907. 64p. and ads.

307 Middlebrook's New-England Almanac for 1908. Wraps. Standard Association, Bridgeport, 64p. and ads.

308 The Elm City Free Kindergarten Receipt Book. Compiled by Mrs. Mary Twining Gridley with the Assistance of the Board of Officers and Friends. Autographed recipes. Boards. Conn., 1909. 102p. and ads.

309 Middlebrook's New-England Almanac for 1909. Wraps. Standard Assoc., Bridgeport, 64p. Ads.

310 Middlebrook's New-England Almanac for 1910. Wraps. Standard Assoc., Bridgeport, 62p. Ads.

311 Tested Receipts from Mount Carmel. Autographed recipes. Compiled by the Mount Carmel Library Association. Wraps. Mount Carmel (c. 1910). 90p. and ads.

312 Underhill, Jennie E. Sunshine Cook Book. A collection of valuable recipes and menus. New London: the Author. 1910. 173, 13p.

313 Trinity Parish Cook Book. Autographed recipes. Revised and Enlarged. Wraps. Torrington, 1911. 101p. and ads.

314 THE COVENTRY BI-CENTENNIAL COOK BOOK. Tried and Approved Receipts. Compiled by Ladies Association of the 1st Congregational Church. Autographed recipes, photos. Wraps. South Coventry, 1912. 91p.

315 FREDERICK, CHRISTINE. Meals That Cook Themselves and Cut the Costs . . . featuring the Sentinel Automatic Cook Stove. New Haven: The Sentinel Manufacturing Co. (1915). 69p.

316 RUSSWIN COOK BOOK. Recipes for dishes prepared with the Russwin Food Cutter. Illus. wraps. Russell & Erwin Mfg. Co., New Britain (c. 1915). 32p.

317 WEBBER, CAROLYN PUTNAM. The Sentinel Book of Automatic Cooking. New Haven: The Sentinel Mfg. Co. (1915). 176p.

318 RECIPES. Collected by the Thursday Thimble Club. Autographed recipes. Wraps. December, 1917. 29p.

319 MIDDLEBROOK'S NEW-ENGLAND ALMANAC FOR 1918. Wraps. Standard Assoc., Bridgeport, 48p. & ads.

320 COMMUNITY COOK BOOK. Autographed recipes. Wraps. Civic Union, Home Economics Committee and Girls' Club. Watertown (c. 1920). 63p. and ads.

321 HAYES, MAUD E. Uses of Connecticut Grown Foods. Bulletin No. 24 of the Extension Service, Connecticut Agricultural College. Storrs: August, 1920. 12p.

322 NEW FAIRFIELD CONGREGATIONAL CHURCH COOK BOOK. Autographed recipes. Wraps. Mimeographed pages, unnumbered. Dedicated to the Building Fund of the New Church, New Fairfield, 1921.

323 CONNECTICUT COLLEGE COOK BOOK. Principally cakes, cookies & puddings originated by Mrs. Sarah Colfax (Aunt Colie). Small handbook. Connecticut College Endowment Fund, Connecticut College, New London, 1922. 106p.

324 COOK BOOK FROM LADIES' AID SOCIETY. Wraps. 1st Baptist Church, Southington, 1922. 32p. and ads.

325 FALES, WINIFRED AND NORTHEND, MARY H. The Wallace Hostess Book. Col. frontis. illus. Wallingford: R. Wallace & Sons Mfg. Co. (1922). 36p.

326 THE HARTFORD WOMAN'S CLUB COOK BOOK. Wraps. Hartford, 1922. 147p. and ads.

327 COOK BOOK. Compiled by the Members of Ethel Chapter No. 28, Order of the Eastern Star. Autographed recipes. Wraps. Pub. by Procter & Way, New Haven (c. 1923). 40p. and ads.

328 55TH ANNIVERSARY SOUVENIR. Tested Recipes and Household Hints. The 1st Methodist Episcopal Church. Wraps. The Ladies' Aid Society and Ladies' Guild. West Haven, 1923. 144p. and ads.

329 FARMERS' ALMANAC FOR 1924. Wraps. The Stratford Trust Co., Stratford, Ads.

330 ALMANAC and Manual of Useful Information. Wraps. The New Milford Times, New Milford, 1925. 44p. and ads.

331 PLYMOUTH CHURCH COOK BOOK. A Book of Tested Recipes. Autographed. Wraps. New Haven (c. 1925). 84p.

332 TERRYVILLE COOK BOOK. Autographed recipes. Wraps. Press of the Thomaston Printing Co., Thomaston, 1925. 96p.

333 FARMERS' ALMANAC FOR 1926. Wraps. 1st National Bank, Litchfield. Ads.

334 THE HARTFORD WOMAN'S CLUB COOK BOOK. Wraps. Hartford, 1926-1927. 147p. and ads.

335 HOUSEHOLD REFERENCE BOOK. Autographed recipes. Wraps. Parent Teacher Association, Bunker Hill School, Waterbury, 1928. 32p. and ads.

336 GUILFORD COOK BOOK. Autographed recipes. Compiled by a Committee of the Improvement Society of the 1st Congregational Church. Wraps. Guilford, 1929. 72p.

337 MAGIC MAID KITCHEN MIXER AND JUICE EXTRACTOR. Col. illus. 12p. advertising leaflet. (c. 1930).

338 THE POST-TELEGRAM. Leaflet. Presenting Foods of the Nation. Cooking School at the Pyramid Mosque, Bridgeport, 1930. 8p.

339 SIMPLIFIED HOSPITALITY WITH SERVEL HERMETIC. Col. illus. Advertising booklet. 1932. n.p. 48p.

340 FARMERS' ALMANAC FOR 1933. Wraps. Community Service, Inc. n.p. Ads.

341 SMITH, MARGARET (Compiled by). SALAD PARADE-ICE BOX DESSERTS. Oilcloth wraps. Sandpiper Shop (Madison). 1933. 40p.

342 EASTON, ALICE. Dictionary of Sea Food. One of the little gold books. Stamford: J. O. Dahl, 1935. 40p.

343 DAHL, J. O. Dictionary of 1001 Menu terms—foods, wines, spirits, cocktails. A little gold book. Stamford: J. O. Dahl, 1936. 47p.

344 FINK, B. ROBERT JR. (Colonel) —Cooking with Rum. Old recipes, well revived with Ronrico Rum. Stamford: J. O. Dahl (1937). 54p.

345 DEGOUY, L. P. Cooking with Apple Brandy. Over a hundred specialties compiled for Hildick Apple Brandy. Stamford: J. O. Dahl, 1939. 63p.

346 WATERBURY WOMEN'S CLUB COOK BOOK 1889-1939. Autographed recipes written in hand of contributor. Spiral binding. Pictorial boards. Illus. Waterbury, November 1939. 1st ed. 320p.

347 THE COUNTRY HOUSE-WIVES GARDEN. Containing Rules for Herbs & Seeds . . also Divers new Knots for Gardens. Facsimile of London, 1637 ed. 1940. 30p.

348 EASTON, ALICE. Recipes and Menus for Restaurant Profits. Stamford: The Dahls, 1940. 212p.

349 500 FAVORITE RECIPES. Autographed recipes. Wraps. Compiled by Dorcas Society. Emanuel Lutheran Church, Manchester, 1940. 150p. and ads.

350 ROBINSON, K. C. (autographed) Types of Persons with Diets to Match. Not for cure of disease, but to be well fed. Private printing, Greenwich, 1940. 1st ed. 167p.

351 ELLSWORTH AND WINTER, PATRICIA. ABC of Herb Cooking. Canaan, 1941. 48p.

352 SWEDISH SMORGASBORD AND 500 OTHER FAMOUS RECIPES. (see Foreign sec.)

353 TRIED AND TRUE RECIPES. Autographed recipes. Oilcloth wraps. Mimeographed. Immanuel Woman's Club, Meriden, 1941. 46p.

354 DAKIN, MARION EVANS. THE UNIVERSITY OF CONNECTICUT EXTENSION SERVICE—HOME CANNING. Leaflet. April 1942. 18p.

355 THE CONNECTICUT COOK BOOK. Compiled by The Woman's Club of Westport. Illustrated by Connecticut's famous artists, including Karl Anderson, Kerr Eby, Helen Hokinson and Rollin Kirby. Harper, New York, 1943, 1st ed. 261p.

356 DAHL, J. O. (Compiled by) 200 WAYS TO CONTROL FOOD COSTS IN QUANITY COOKERY. Hotel management's cookery. The Dahls, Stamford: 1944.

357 WINTER, PAT. RECIPE MAGIC. 20th Ed. Wraps. House of Herbs, Inc., Salisbury, 1944. 48p.

358 WINTER, PATRICIA (ed.) SEASONING TRICKS. Scores of simple easy ways to give a chef-like touch to everyday dishes with herbs and herb-flavored condiments. Pictorial wraps. House of Herbs, Salisbury, 1945. 16p.

359 SPEED COOKING with your new 1947 General Electric Automatic Electric Range. Pictorial wraps. Bridgeport, 1947. 54p.

360 THE STAMFORD COOK BOOK. 2nd. Edition, revised. Autographed recipes, handwritten by contributors. Spiral binding. Illus. Pictorial wraps. Pub. by the Stamford Hospital Aid Society, Stamford, 1947. 370p. and ads.

361 DIETZ, F. MEREDITH. Let's Talk Turkey. Adventures and Recipes of the White Turkey Inn, (Danbury) Old American recipes. Color photographs & illus. Dietz Press, Richmond, Va. (1948). 340p.

362 RIELLO, MARY CARMEN. Italian Cook Book. (see Foreign sec.)

363 GAYLORD. Cooking with an Accent. The Herb Grower's Cookbook. Spiral. Falls Village, 1949. 116p.

364 THE ABC'S OF HERB COOKERY. Lists of herbs, a few recipes. Attractive folder by the House of Herbs, Inc., Salisbury, 1950.

365 COOK BOOK OF FAVORITE RECIPES. Autographed recipes handwritten by contributors. Spiral binding. Illus. Pictorial board covers. Ads. Compiled by Members of Group A and their Friends, Center Con-

gregational Church, Manchester, 1951. 176p.

366 THE NORFIELD COOK BOOK. Autographed recipes. Pictorial wraps. Compiled by the Norfield Junior Guild of the Norfield Congregational Church, Weston, 1951. 1st Edition. 76p.

367 WOODBURY'S TREASURE OF PERSONAL RECIPES. Autographed recipes. Illus. Spiral binding. Pictorial wraps. Compiled by the St. Teresa's Guild of the Catholic Church, Woodbury (1952). 44p.

368 AT HOME ON THE RANGE. By the Calendar Staff. Autographed recipes. Spiral. Wraps. Illus. Ladies' Benevolent Society, Congregational Church, Ellington, 1953. 116p. & Index.

369 DE GROS, J. H. TODAY'S WOMAN CANDY COOK BOOK. History and art of candy making; how to do it. Illustrated profusely. Wraps. Fawcett Publication, Greenwich, 1953. 144p.

370 ANN PILLSBURY'S NEW COOK BOOK. 100 Prize Winners from the 5th Grand National Recipe Contest. Illustrated. Drawings by June Kirkpatrick. Wraps. Fawcett, Greenwich, 1954. 144p.

371 COLEBROOK, CONN., PERSONAL RECIPES. Autographed recipes. Spiral binding. Pictorial cover. Ads. By Women's Church Union, Colebrook Congregational Church, 1956.

372 AUXILIARY COOK BOOK. Picture of the Y.M.C.A. as frontispiece. Wraps. Ads. Pub. by the Woman's Auxiliary to the Y.M.C.A., Winsted. n.d. 74p.

373 BOWERING, MISS FLORRIE BISHOP. THE MIXING BOWL. WTIC. A series of cooking lessons. Wraps. Hartford. n.d.

374 BRANFORD COOK BOOK. Revised Edition. Selected recipes pub. by the Comfortable Society of the 1st Congregational Church. Pictorial wraps. Branford. n.d. 96p.

375 THE CHAFING DISH. MANNING-BOWMAN TESTED RECIPES. Advertising booklet. Illus. Pictorial wraps. n.d. n.p. 32p.

376 CLOTHO CANDY BOOK. A little booklet of candy recipes. Wraps. Few ads. New Haven. n.d. 20p.

377 COOK BOOK. Autographed recipes. Wraps. Ways and Means Committee, Meriden Woman's Club. Meriden. n.d. 72p.

378 COOK BOOK. Autographed recipes. Compiled by the Ladies of Washington. n.d. Wraps. 39p. Ads.

379 HARVEST COOK BOOK THOMASTON, CONN. Pictorial wraps. Linotype Printing Co., Waterbury. n.d. 108p.

380 HOUSEKEEPERS' FRIEND—TRIED RECIPES. Wraps. Pub. by Stanley Relief Corps, No. 12, Auxiliary to the G.A.R., New Britain. n.d. 44p.

381 IMMANUEL WOMAN'S CLUB. Autographed recipes. Oilcloth wraps. Mimeographed. Meriden. n. d. 48p.

382 THE JUNIOR LEAGUE OF WATERBURY, INC., COOK BOOK. Compiled and illustrated by its members. Spiral. n.d. 217p.

383 MILK. EMERGENCY FOOD SERIES, No. 8. By Millicent Sears. Pub. by the Conn. Agricultural College Extension Service—Conn. Committee of Food Supply. Leaflet. n.d. 10p.

384 THE MIXING BOWL. Based on Mixing Bowl Radio program. Pictorial Wraps. WTIC, Hartford. n.d. 41p.

385 OUR FAVORITE RECIPES. Autographed recipes. Ads. Pictorial wraps. Plastic binding. Service League of St. John's Church. n.p. n.d. 140p.

386 PRESBYTERIAN COOK BOOK. Illus. with photo of church. Oiled paper wraps. Ads. The Woman's Guild, the Noroton Presbyterian Church, Noroton. n.d. 77p.

387 THE REVISED TRIED AND TRUE COOK BOOK, 3rd Edition. Compiled by Members of Auxiliary to St. Joseph's Hospital and Their Friends. Autographed recipes. Wraps. Chronicle Print, Willimantic. n.d. 91p.

388 SWEETS AND MEATS AND OTHER THINGS TO EAT. Wraps. Ads. The Philathea Circle of South Methodist Episcopal Church, Waterbury. n.d. 43p.

389 TILL WE EAT AGAIN. Recipes collected by the Cause Girls of the South Congregational Church. Signed by the persons who submitted them. Spiral. Pictorial wraps. Hartford. n.d. 68p.

390 TRIED AND TRUE RECIPES. Autographed recipes. Ads. Wraps. Canaan. n.d. 48p.

391 TRINITY PARISH COOK BOOK. Wraps. Torrington. n.d. 90p. and ads.

392 UNIVERSAL COOK BOOK. Economical recipes. Booklet, wraps. Adv. for cutlery and kitchen equipment. Landers, Frary & Clark, New Britain. n.d. 56p.

393 THE WATERBURY JUNIOR LEAGUE COOK BOOK. Autographed recipes. Wraps. Waterbury. n.d. 38p.

394 WHAT'S COOKIN'? BRIDGEWATER. Compiled by the P.T.A. Augraphed recipes. Spiral binding. Pictorial wraps. Bridgewater, 44p. and ads.

395 WHAT TO COOK AND HOW TO COOK IT—TRUE AND TRIED COOKING RECIPES. Autographed recipes. Wraps. Ads. From the Ladies' Aid Society of the 1st Baptist Church, Waterford. n.d. 16p.

395a THE HOUSEHOLD DIGEST AND DIRECTORY. Cold pack canning chart. Signed recipes. Wraps. Mothers' Guild, St. John's Episcopal Church, Waterbury. 56p. and ads.

Delaware

396 TRINITY PARISH COOK BOOK. Compiled by the Ladies Parish Aid Society of Holy Trinity Church. Wilmington: J. M. Rogers' Press, 1892. 200p. illus.

397 Bush, Rebecca Gibbons Tatnall. What and How: a practical cook book for every-day living. Pub. by Miss Edna N. Taylor. Wilmington: New Amstel Magazine Co., 1910. 336p.

398 Taylor, Edna N. What to Have and How to Cook It. A practical cook book for every-day living. Wilmington: the author, 1910. 336p.

399 Blue Hen's Chickens' Cook Book . . . Recipes gathered by the ladies of the Milford New Century Club. Milford: Milford Pub. Co., 1921. 112p. (2nd ed.)

400 Peninsula Cook Book. Compiled by Senior Bykota Class of Peninsula Methodist Church. Wraps. Wilmington. n.d. 150p.

District of Columbia

401 Tilton, E. Stevens. Home Dissertations: an Offering to the Household for economical and practical skill in cookery . . and nicety in the appointments of home. Excerpts from favorite authors . . Washington; John H. Magruder (1885). 174p. (See No. 44).

402 Brown, Margaret. Margaret Brown's French Cookery Book. (See Foreign sec.)

403 Gillette, Mrs. Fanny Lemira. White House Cook Book. A selection of choice recipes original and selected during 40 years' practical housekeeping. Frontis. Vanderbilt dining room and 4 full-page plate portraits of wives of the presidents. Chicago: R. S. Peale & Co., 1887. 521p.

404 Harrison, Mrs. Benjamin, and Others. Statesmen's Dishes and How to Cook Them. Washington: The National Tribune, 1890. 222p.

406 Fitts, Emma Frances. The Universal Cook-Book, compiled from tested recipes of practical cooks. Washington, D.C., Age Printing Co. (1894). 179p. and ads. Wraps.

407 Ralston Model Meals. Wraps. Ralston Health Club, Washington, 1895. 46p.

408 Presidential Cook Book. Adapted from the White House Cook Book. Photos of Mrs. McKinley and Mrs. Cleveland. Pictorial wraps. Illus. 1896. 440p.

409 Panelli, Dodrigo (compiled by) The White House Kitchen Companion. 1000 recipes. Frontis. portraits of Mrs. McKinley, Mrs. Harrison, Mrs. Cleveland. Small book. Wraps. Geo. M. Hill: Chicago (1898). 274p.

410 Stewart, Bessie. Two Hundred Recipes. Washington: The Neale Publishing Company, 1901. 109p.

411 The Nordhoff Guild Cook Book . . . Washington: Press of McGill & Wallace (1902). 69p.

412 Kauffmann, Alphonse, et al. The new White House dishes. . . A complete cook book and household economist. The authors; David Chidlow, Mrs. Myra Russell Gar-

rett, Mary B. Vail, Ella Shuart, Eben E. Texford, R. W. Webster. Chicago, Ill.: G. W. Ogilvie & Co., 1903. 508p. Frontis. Illus.

413 The Ralston Health Club Book of New Ralstonism. "The Ralston Clan for Health, Home, Happiness and Long Life." Pictorial wraps. Washington, 1903. 206p.

414 Woods, C. D. Meats: Composition and Cooking. U. S. Dept. of Agriculture, Washington, 1904.

415 The Presidential Cook Book. Adapted from The White House Cook Book. Photos of Mrs. Theodore Roosevelt and Mrs. Wm. McKinley. Chicago, Ill.: Saalfield Pub. Co., 1905. 440p. illus. Book ads.

416 Ralston Meals for every day in the year and how to prepare them. The luxury of eating for health without dieting. Washington: Ralston Co. (1905). 63p. Wraps.

417 Teaching the Rudiments of Cooking. Primary methods for use of teachers in the Indian Schools. Dept. of the Interior, Office of Indian affairs. Washington: Gov't Printing Office, 1906. 62p. Wraps.

418 Langworthy, C. F. Fish as Food. U. S. Dept. of Agriculture, Washington, 1907.

419 Colcord, Mrs. Anna L. A Friend in the Kitchen. 400 choice recipes. Illus. Photograph of author. Wraps. 16th ed. Review & Herald Pub. Co., Washington, 1908. 112p.

420 Atwater, Helen W. Bread and Bread Making. Farmer's Bull. 389, U. S. Dept. Agriculture, Washington, 1910. Wraps. 47p.

421 Bush, Mrs. What and How. A Practical Cook Book for Everyday Living. Miss Edna N. Taylor, Washington, 1910.

422 Langworthy, C. F. Hunt, Caroline L. Economical Use of Meat in the Home. Farmers' Bulletin 391. Pamphlet. U. S. Dept. of Agriculture, Washington, 1910. 30p.

423 Uncle Sam's Cook Book. U. S. Dept. of Agri. Bulletins on Meat, Fish, Sugar, Vegetables, Fruit, Charts and illustrations. Colored end papers and page edges. Govt. Printing Office, Washington, 1903 to 1910. 761p. plus Bulletin lists.

424 Lord, Clara Sophia. Recipes. Washington: Press of the Hayworth Pub. House, 1911. 100p. Ads.

425 Cheese and its Economical Uses in Diet. U. S. Farmer's Bulletin. U. S. Dept. Agri., 1912.

426 Fryer, Jane Eayre. The Mary Frances Cook Book. Adventures Among the Kitchen People. For little girls who like to help mother. Illustrations by Margaret G. Hays and Jane Allen Boyer. Copyright by the author, 1912. 1st ed. 175p.

427 Recipes of Quality. Pictorial boards. Chr. Heurich Brewing Co., Washington (1912). 224p.

428 Robertson, Georgia. Efficiency in Home-making and First-aid to Good Cooking. Washington: Robertson (1915). 157p.

429 STEVENSON, MATILDA COXE. The ethnobotany of the Zũni Indians. From the 30th annual report of the Bureau of American Ethnology. Washington: Government Printing Office, 1915. 102p. Frontis.

430 ABEL, MARY HINMAN. BEANS, PEAS AND OTHER LEGUMES AS FOOD. Wraps. U. S. Department of Agriculture, Washington, 1916. 36p.

431 BITTING, A. W. (M.D.) AND BITTING, K. G. (M.S.). CANNING. How to Use Canned Foods. Illus. National Canners Ass'n., Washington (1916). 191p.

432 MANUAL FOR ARMY COOKS. Storage, handling and preparation of food. Prepared under Commissary General of Subsistence. Washington, 1916. 306p.

433 NORCROSS, MR. AND MRS. T. W. (Compiled by) FOREST SERVICE RECIPES. A bound notebook of mimeographed pages of recipes, December, 1916. 58p.

434 VAN VOAST, ELLEN. Eating for Life, Health and Happiness. Washington: "Wednesday Club," (1916). 49p. Wraps.

435 LANGWORTHY, C. F. & HUNT, CAROLINE, L. CHEESE AND ITS ECONOMICAL USES IN THE DIET. Wraps. U. S. Department of Agriculture, Washington, 1917. 40p.

436 MANUAL FOR ARMY BAKERS. Prepared under direction of the Quartermaster General. By order of the Secretary of War. A Small hard cover pocket book. Washington. Government Printing Office, 1917.

437 PARLOA, MARIA. CANNED FRUIT, PRESERVES & JELLIES. Household methods of preparation. U. S. Dept. of Agriculture, Washington, 1917. 101p.

438 ROUND AND LANG. PRESERVATION OF VEGETABLES BY FERMENTATION AND SALTING. Wraps. U. S. Department of Agriculture, Washington, 1917. 16p.

439 ASHBROOK AND ANTHONY. KILLING HOGS AND CURING PORK. Pictorial wraps. U. S. Department of Agriculture, Washington, 1918. 40p.

440 HOME CANNING AND DRYING OF VEGETABLES AND FRUITS with Directions for making Jellies and Fruit Butters . . National War Garden Commission. Wraps. Washington, 1918. 32p.

441 HUNT AND WARD. SCHOOL LUNCHES. Pictorial wraps. U. S. Department of Agriculture, Washington, 1918. 32p.

442 INSPECTION MANUAL FOR DEPOT QUARTERMASTER, CAMP QUARTERMASTERS, SUBSISTENCE OFFICERS AND INSPECTORS OF THE SUBSISTENCE DIVISION (1918). Bulletins in looseleaf binder. Data contributed by experts. Washington.

443 MCCANN, ALFRED W. THE SCIENCE OF EATING. How to insure stamina, endurance, vigor, strength and health in infancy, youth and age. Evans Brothers, London. Printed in the U.S.A. (1919). 408p.

444 CORNFORTH, GEORGE E. Good Food, How to Prepare It. Nearly 500 Carefully Selected Recipes. Washington, D. C., Review and Herald Pub. Assoc. (1920). 224p. illus. Frontis. of author.

445 GILLETTE, MRS. F. L. AND ZIEMANN, HUGO. The White House Cook Book. A comprehensive cyclopedia of information for the home. Chicago, N. Y.: Saalfield Pub. Co., 1920. Portr. of Mrs. Wilson. Illus. (over 600p.)

446 WESSLING, HANNAH. BAKING IN THE HOME. Wraps. Illus. Farmers' Bulletin 1136, U. S. Dept. Agriculture. (1921). 40p.

447 WOOD-COMSTOCK, BELLE. The Home Dietitian or Food and Health. Tacoma Park, Washington: Review and Herald Pub., 1922. 352p. Frontis. of author.

448 KUHLMANN, MARY L. PERRIE. The White Ribbon Recipe Book. Washington (1923). 209p.

449 MANN, MRS. I. T. (Compiled by) SUPERIOR RECIPES. Oilcloth binding. Washington, 1923. 226p.

450 NAIDEN, MARY S. Luncheon and Dinner Menus. With recipes for every day in the year. No place: the author (1923). 175p.

451 BOOK OF RECIPES, published by the Calvary Baptist Church Sunday-school. Washington: Press of Judd & Detweiler, 1924. 149p.

452 LEWIS HOTEL TRAINING COURSE. Lessons 36 through 50; three on food. Illus. Bound booklets. Lewis Hotel Training Schools, Washington, 1924. Booklets paged separately—from 16 to 32p. ea.

453 DINNER TO THE AMBASSADOR OF FRANCE AND MRS. JULES JEAN JUSSERAND BY THE PEOPLE OF THE CITY OF WASHINGTON. Illus. With menu, program and list of guests. Wraps. Washington, January 10, 1925. 28p.

454 GILLETTE, MRS. F. L. AND ZIEMANN, HUGO. DAGUE, MRS. E. (Revised by) THE WHITE HOUSE COOK BOOK. A comprehensive cyclopedia of information for the home. Frontispiece, Mrs. Coolidge. Illustrated. Saalfield Publishing: Akron, Ohio, 1925. 609p.

455 AUNT SAMMY'S RADIO RECIPES. 70 menus and 300 recipes. Wraps. Bureau of Home Economics, U. S. Dept. Agri. Washington, 1926. 85p.

456 GRAY, GETA. CONVENIENT KITCHENS. Pictorial Wraps. U. S. Department of Agriculture, Washington, 1926. 30p.

457 MCNALLY, CLARA LOUISE, et al. Chevy Chase Cook Book, compiled and published by Mrs. William J. McNally, Mrs. Thomas F. Keane . . Washington: C. H. Potter & Co., Inc. (c. 1926). 119p.

458 THE CONGRESSIONAL CLUB COOK BOOK, favorite national and international recipes . . . Compiled and published by the Congressional Club. Washington, 1927. 799p. illus.

459 The Cook Book of the United States Navy, 1927. Washington. U. S. Government Printing Office, 1927. 144p.

460 Gavin, Molly. Molly Gavin's Own Cook Book. Oilcloth boards. The Grimes Co., Washington, 1928. 160p.

461 Gillette, Mrs. F. L. and ziemann; Hugo. Rev. by Mrs. Mary E. Dague. The White House Cook Book. Frontis portrait, Mrs. Hoover. Ohio, 1928. (See No. 454).

462 Potter, Adele G. Practical Instructions and Recipes for Cooking and Canning in the Pressure Cooker. Washington: C. H. Potter & Co., Inc. (c. 1929). 49p.

463 Marshall, Ann Parks. Martha Washington's Rules for Cooking Used Every Day at Mt. Vernon; those of her neighbors, Mrs. Jefferson, Mrs. Madison, Mrs. Monroe. George Washington bicentennial edition, 1732-1932. Washington: Ramsdell Inc. (1931). 160p. illus. Ads.

464 The Cook Book of the United States Navy, 1932. Washington: Government Printing Office, 1932. 196p.

465 Theiss, Helen E. A Cook Book for a Bride. Washington, 1932. 100p. Loose-leaf book.

466 Williams, Mrs. John R. Thrift Shop Cook Book. Ring binder, illus. Much material from foreign embassies. Thrift Shop Cook Book Club, Washington, 1932.

467 The Congressional Club Cook Book. Rev. ed. Washington, 1933. 834p. illus. (See No. 458).

468 Everybody's Cook Book. A collection of Tested Recipes. Pictorial wraps. Frederick J. Haskin; Washington (1934). 64p.

469 Romer, Frank. The History of Harvey's. As related by Harvey Host, Julius Lulley. A pageant of personalities since 1858. Illus. Wraps. Private printing, Washington, 1934. 32p.

470 Gillette, Mrs. F. L. and Ziemann, Hugo. Rev. by Mrs. E. Dague. The White House Cook Book. 1935. Frontis portrait of Mrs. Roosevelt. (See No. 454).

471 Honey and Some of its Uses. Prepared in the Bureau of Home Economics by Elizabeth Whiteman and Fanny Yeatman. Ways of using cooked and uncooked honey. Pamphlet No. 113. U. S. Dept. of Agriculture, Washington (1936). 8p.

472 Fletcher, W. F. The Native Persimmon. Pictorial wraps. U. S. Department of Agriculture. Revised. Washington, 1942. 22p.

473 Harvey's Famous Restaurant. 84th Anniversary Booklet about the far famed epicurean resort of the Nation's Capital. History, photographs, famous people, Nast Cartoons, and a few recipes (marginal). Washington. Harvey's, Inc. (1942). 32p. and ads.

474 KING, FLORENCE B. HOMEMADE BREAD, CAKE AND PASTRY. Wraps. U. S. Dept. of Agriculture, Washington, 1942. 30p.

475 THE COOK BOOK OF THE U. S. NAVY. U. S. Gov't. Ptg. Office: Washington, 1945. 465p.

476 CONGRESSIONAL CLUB RECIPES. Autographed recipes reproduced in handwriting of contributor. Illus. Pictorial wraps. Plastic spiral binding. Whitman Publishing Co. for the Congressional Club, Washington (c. 1946). 401p.

477 ROBERTS, LYDIA J. The Road to Good Nutrition. Diets for children, in collaboration with members of Children's Bureau Staff. Wraps. Federal Security Agency, Children's Bureau, Washington, 1948. 52p.

478 EMERGENCY COOK BOOK. Favorite Recipes, many from Old Virginia Families. Good autograph recipes. Benefit of Emergency Hospital. Washington, 1949. 79p.

479 FOODS AND COOKING. Home Economics. Price list II—42nd ed. Supt. of Documents, Washington, 1949. Wraps. 14p.

480 THE GEORGETOWN COOK BOOK. Compiled by St. Stephen's Guild. Autographed recipes reproduced in handwriting of contributor. Pictorial wraps. Plastic spiral binding. Illus. Christ Church Parish, Georgetown, 1949. 1st ed. 273p.

481 FAMILY FARE. Food Management and Recipes. Pictorial wraps. U. S. Dept. of Agriculture, Washington (1950). 96p.

482 THE FAMILY CIRCLE DESSERT AND FRUIT COOK BOOK. Illustrated; color photos. Decorative cover and end papers. Family Circle; USA, 1954. 144p.

483 WHO SAYS WE CAN'T COOK. By the Members of the Women's National Press Club. Autographed recipes. Illus. Pictorial wraps. Plastic spiral binding. Washington, 1955. 176p.

484 ATECO SIMPLIFIED CAKE DECORATING. Explicit directions. Profusely illustrated. August Thomsen & Co., U.S.A., n.d. 81p.

Florida

485 HARCOURT, HELEN. Florida Fruits and How To Raise Them. Rev. and enlarged ed. Elaborate Index of Subjects. Many recipes using fruits & nuts. Louisville, Ky., 1886. 347p.

486 THE FLORIDA TROPICAL COOK BOOK. Published by the Aid Society, First Presbyterian Church, Miami, Fla. (Chicago: Printed by E. F. Harmen & Co., 1912). 224p. incl. front. 1st ed. Ads.

487 HARRIS, FRANCES BARBER. FLORIDA SALADS. Wholesome, well balanced recipes. H. & W. B. Drew Co., Jacksonville, 1918. 87p.

488 FLORIDA SALADS. A Collection of Wholesome, Well Balanced, Easily Prepared Salad Recipes. Revised & enlarged edition, Boston, Mass., 1926. 85p.

489 ANDREA, A. LOUISE. The Modern Home-Maker; cookery, canning and preserving. Menus for gaining or reducing weight. Food charts and food combinations from E. Christian; health and hygiene chapters by Rebekah S. Hufcut. St. Petersburg: Gift Publishing (1929). 239p. Illus.

490 STENNIS, MARY A. Florida Fruits and Vegetables in the Family Menu. Bul. No. 46, New Series. Tallahassee, Florida: Department of Agriculture, 1931. 100p. illus.

491 DENISON, GRACE E. Burdine's Cookbook. Col. & other plates. Miami (1932). 537p.

492 COACHMAN, JESSE CANDLER. MRS. COACHMAN'S FLORIDA RECIPES. Kumquat Sweet Shop, Coachman Station, Clearwater (1938). 144p.

493 HORTON, WALDO, M.D. AND THURSBY, ISABELLE S. FLORIDA HONEY AND ITS HUNDRED USES. Illustrated with good plant photographs. Department of Agriculture, Tallahassee (1938). 79p.

494 RAWLINGS, MARJORIE KINNAN. Cross Creek Cookery. Charming conversational discussion, with recipes & menus. Drawings by Robert Camp. New York: Charles Scribner's Sons, 1942. 230p. 1st ed.

495 RATION BY-PASS. War-Time Recipes Collected by members of the Garden Club of the Halifax country. Autographed recipes. Wraps. Daytona Beach, 1944. 36p.

496 KATCH'S KITCHEN. Signed and illus. recipes. Spiral, pictorial cover. Letter from "Katch" Goodue. Dept. of Applied Education of The Women's Club, West Palm Beach, 3rd ed., 1945. 355p. and ads.

497 THE KEY WEST COOK BOOK. Many signed recipes. Illus., mimeo, spiral pictorial cover. Key West Woman's Club, Key West, 1948. 298p. and ads.

498 PUTCAMP, LOUISE AND GOULET, VIRGINIA Z. CONCH COOKING. Key West Recipes. Spiral binding. Central Press: Miami, 1948. 93p.

498a BECKER, HELEN E. (compiler). Food Favorites of Olde St. Augustine. Regional Recipes. Humbly dedicated to Clara Lopez Mier. Handsome photos of the oldest town in America. Recipes from Fat Hen Pilau to Peach Leather. St. Augustine, 1959. p.

499 THE DAYTONA BEACH COOK BOOK. The Pennsylvania Club, Daytona Beach, n.d. 73p.

500 JACKSON, JOSEPHINE. THE POCO COOK BOOK. Jacksonville, n.d. 254p. and ads.

500a SERVED IN PALM BEACH. Signed recipes. Contributions from winter residents of Palm Beach. Oblong, wraps, small book. Guild of The Church of Bethesda-by-the-Sea.

Georgia

501 WILCOX, MRS. ESTELLE WOODS (complied by). The New Dixie Cook-Book and Practical Housekeeper. Rev. ed. L. A. Clarkson: Atlanta, 1883. Frontis. Illus. 688p.

502 Hints from Southern Epicures. Compiled by the Flower Committee of the Independent Presbyterian Church, Savannah, Ga. Pub. by A. H. Pugh Print. Co., Cincinnati, Ohio, 1892. 42p.

503 Bailey, Ida D. The Atlanta Exposition Souvenir Cook Book. Compiled under direction of Woman's Domestic Science Comm. Washington, D.C.: R. L. Pendleton, 1895. 60p.

504 Wilson, Mrs. Henry Lumpkin (compiled by). Tested Recipe Cook Book. Illus. Foote & Davies Co.: Atlanta, 1895. 148p.

505 Souvenir Cook Book of Free Kindergarten Association of Columbus . . . Columbus: T. Gilbert, printer, 1902. 80p.

506 Dennis, Annie E. New Annie Dennis Cook Book. Compendium of Popular Household Recipes. Original edition came out in the early '90's. Very successful, revised many times, continued to sell even after 1920. Frontispiece portrait of the author. Quaint ads. Wraps. Atlanta (1905). Mutual Pub. Co. 359p.

507 The Baptist Cook Book. Compiled by a Committee of the Building Fund Association of the First Baptist Church of Albany, Ga., May, 1907. Columbus: Gilbert Print. Co., 1907. 158p. and ads.

508 Macon Cook Book; a collection of recipes tested principally by members of Benson-Cobb Chapter, Wesleyan College Alumnae. Macon: The J. W. Burke Co., 1909. 284p.

509 Favorite Southern Recipes. Southern Ruralist: Atlanta, 1912. 222p.

510 The Gate City Cook Book. Pub. by the Ladies' Aid Society of the Ponce de Leon Baptist Church. 1st ed. compiled by Committee two . . . 1905; 2nd ed. by Committee five . . . 1907; 3rd ed. compiled by Committee one . . . 1915. Atlanta, 1915. 90p. and ads.

511 The New, Reliable Cook Book. Pub. by the J. D. Franklin Chapter, United Daughters of the Confederacy, Tennille (Tennille,) 1918. 40p.

512 Wing, Mrs. Newton C. Atlanta's Woman's Club Cook Book. Decorations by Miss Marie Haines, censored by Miss Mary Pinckney Means. (Atlanta: Johnson Dallis Co., 1921). 250p. illus. Ads.

513 Dahle, C. D. A Manual for Ice Cream Makers. The Manufacturing Process. Formulas. Layless, Atlanta (1927). 1st ed. 158p.

514 Dull, Henrietta Stanley. Southern Cooking. By the editor of the Home Economics page of the Atlanta Journal. Atlanta; The Ruralist Press, 1928. 350p.

515 Miller, Mrs. J. D. P.T.A. Interpretations of Food; Nutrition, Efficiency, Happiness. Contributions by members, arranged & supplemented by the author. Atlanta: Walter S. Brown Pub. Co. (1928). 782p. illus. Bibliographies.

516 KUGEL, DAISY ALICE. Spillman College Bulletin, Recipes for foods classes. Atlanta: The Atlanta University Press, 1930. 209p.

517 ALLEN, IDA BAILEY. When You Entertain, What to Do and How. Illus. Atlanta, 1932.

518 CALVERT, MAUDE RICHMAN. RICHARDSON, ANNA E. The New First Course in Home Making. Lessons for the Junior Home Maker. Primarily for use in schools. Illustrated by Mary Clemmitt. Turner E. Smith; Atlanta (1932). 507p.

519 COLQUITT, HARRIET ROSS (Collected & Edited by) THE SAVANNAH COOK BOOK. Very old receipts, and some from Mrs. Habersham's cooking school. Introduction by Ogden Nash. Decorations by Florence Olmstead. Farrar & Rinehart: New York, 1933. 1st ed. 186p.

520 COASTAL COOKERY. Recipes of the coastal section of Georgia. Illustrations hand drawn to carry out coastal atmosphere. Spiral binding. Cassina Garden Club of St. Simon's Island, 1937. 264p.

521 COASTAL COOKERY. St. Simon's Island: 1940. (See No. 520).

522 MCREE, PATSIE (autographed) The Kitchen and the Cotton Patch. Dalton: 1948. 94p.

523 MCCLAIN, CHARLEEN (Editor) HOLLAND'S SOUTHERN COOK BOOK. Cooking with a Southern Accent. Decorative end papers with measurements and equivalents. Decorations by Jerry Turney. Tupper & Love: Atlanta, 1952. 1st ed. 312p.

Hawaii

524 THE HAWAIIAN COOK-BOOK. Autographed recipes. Wraps. Illus. ads. Pub. by The Ladies of Fort Street Church. Honolulu, 1879. 49p.

525 ALEXANDER, AGNES B. Hawaiian Fruit. How to use fruit products. Honolulu, 1912. 73p.

526 HAWAIIAN FISH and How to Cook Them. Published by The Women's Committee of the Territorial Food Commission and Federal Food Administration, June, 1918. 19p. Wraps.

527 HAWAIIAN COOK BOOK compiled by the Woman's Society of Central Union Church. 6th ed. Honolulu, Honolulu Star-Bulletin, 1920. 134p.

528 99 TEMPTING PINEAPPLE TREATS. Made with crushed or grated Hawaiian pineapple. Wraps. Col. illus. on covers. Assoc. of Hawaiian Pineapple Canners; San Francisco (1922). 32p.

529 EPICURE IN HAWAII. The Tsukiyaki, Lawalu Fish, Sai Men, Kanaka Stew. San Francisco, 1938. 56p.

530 BAZORE, KATHERINE. Hawaiian and Pacific Foods. Exotic dishes, with menus, decorations, garnishes. New York: M. Barrows, 1953. 288p.

531 LING, NEWI-MEI. CHOP SUEY. Simplified Recipes for American Homes. Booklet, illus. Honolulu, 1953. 34p.

532 LUCK, LUCKY. LUCKY LUCK'S FAVORITE ISLAND RECIPES. More than 300 exotic dishes recommended by one of Hawaii's most famous personalities. Spiral binding. Tongg: 1953. Honolulu. 108p.

533 KAY, TUTU. Wiki Wiki Kau Kau. Quick Cooking Recipes from Hawaii. Chinese and Japanese and Hawaiian dishes; a special Gourmet section. Honolulu: Watkins Printery, Ltd., 1954. 77p. illus. and Index. Wraps.

534 YOUR BLUE FLAME NOTEBOOK. 1904-1954 GOLDEN ANNIVERSARY. Beginning with a recipe from "The Hawaiian Cook Book" of 1896, thru recipes contributed by the first citizens and finest restaurants. Small, gay booklet. Honolulu Gas Co., Hawaii, 1954. 14p. of recipes.

535 KAU-KAU KEEPSAKE KOOK BOOK. 1st Methodist. Illus. Honolulu. 124p.

536 MORI, MAX I. Kona Inn Famous Recipes, by its Chef. From a Poi Cocktail to Macadamia Nut Sauce. With a coconut Beef Stroganoff besides. With the compliments of the Kona Inn, Hawaii. n.d. Unnumbered pages—28.

537 SUKIYAKI. The Art of Japanese Cooking & Hospitality by Fumiko. Pleasantly illus. Decor. wraps. Honolulu. n.d.

Idaho

538 COOK BOOK of the Ladies Aid Society of the First Methodist Episcopal Church. Boise: Journal Printing Co., 1904. 137p.

539 SWEETS AND MEATS AND OTHER GOOD THINGS TO EAT. Pub. by Ladies Aid Society, Methodist Episcopal Church, Montpelier . . . Laramie, Wyo.: The Laramie Republican Co., 1917. 80p. and ads.

540 JOHNSON, INGRID N. War Economy Cook Book: containing 200 receipts for making delicious and economical dishes from potatoes, vegetables, fish, fowls and game. Coeur d'Alene, Idaho, Journal Publishing Co., 1918. 40p.

541 GOOD EATS BY THE REBEKAHS OF IDAHO. Pub. by Odd-Fellows, Independent Order of . . . Caldwell: Caxton Printers (1929). 169p.

542 SQUIRE, MARIAN. THE STAG AT EASE, A COOK BOOK. Being the Culinary Preferences of a Number of Male Citizens of the World. 100 Famous feeders from George Ade to Paul Whiteman. Caldwell: Caxton Printers, 1938. 1st ed. 164p.

543 KITCHEN TREASURES. Typical Idaho menus, autographed recipes, local ads. An attractive book with pleasantly humorous drawings by Pat Miller. Spiral binding. The Women's Society of Christian Service, First Methodist Church, Lewiston, 1959. 162p.

Illinois

544 OWEN, MRS. T. J. V. Mrs. Owen's Illinois Cook Book. Springfield: J. H. Johnson, 1871. 360p.

545 HAMILTON, ALEXANDER V. The Household Cyclopaedia of Practical Receipts and Daily Wants. Includes Receipts for Domestic

Cookery, with over 100 illus. Springfield: W. J. Holland & Co., 1873. 423p.

546 TRIED AND TRUE RECIPES. The Home Cook Book of Chicago. Recipes contributed by ladies of Chicago and other cities and towns; for the benefit of the Home for the Friendless. Chicago: J. Fred. Waggoner, 1874. 288p.

547 THE HOME COOK BOOK. Tried and True Recipes, compiled from recipes contributed by the ladies of Chicago. Published for the Home for the Friendless. Autographed recipes. F. Fred Waggoner, Chicago, 1875. 336p. (See No. 546).

548 TRIED, TESTED, PROVED. The Home Cook Book. 3rd ed. 10th thousand. Originally published for the benefit of the Home for the Friendless. Chicago: J. Fred. Waggoner, 1876. 394p. (See No. 546).

549 THE HOME COOK BOOK. Tried and True Recipes, compiled from recipes contributed by the ladies of Chicago. Pub. for the Home for the Friendless. Autographed recipes. Waggoner, Chicago, 1877. (See No. 546).

550 THE HOME GUIDE. A book by 500 ladies embracing 1000 recipes & hints. From the Home Dept. of the Chicago Daily Tribune. Colored end papers. Taylor, Elgin: 1877. 160p.

551 BROWN, MRS. W. W. (compiler). The Illinois Cook Book. Recipes contributed by the ladies of Paris, pub. for the benefit of Grace Episcopal Church. Claremont, N. H.: Claremont Mfg. Co., printer, 1881. 164p.

552 THE HOME COOK BOOK. Recipes contributed and autographed by the ladies of Chicago and other cities and towns. Benefit Home for the Friendless. Waggoner: Chicago, 1882. 400p. (See No. 546).

553 ENSWORTH, H. B. The St. Andrews Cook Book. Published for the benefit of the young ladies' society of St. Andrews Church, Chicago: St. Andrews Church Society, 1883. 146p. Autographed recipes.

554 OUR DAILY BREAD; OR, COMMON SENSE COOK BOOK. Compiled and published by the Ladies' Aid Society of the Second Universalist Church. Boards. Printers, Jameson & Morse, Chicago, 1883. 99p.

555 CHICAGO WOMAN'S CLUB COOK BOOK. 175 choice recipes mainly furnished by members of the Club. Pub. for the benefit of the Club Kindergarten. Chicago: C. H. Kerr & Co., 1887. 77p.

556 MCCLURE, MRS. J. C. (Anon.). Gathered Crumbs. A Peoria Cook Book . . . Peoria: Transcript Publishing Co., 1888. 320p. illus. Ads. Frontis.

557 PAR EXCELLENCE, a Manual of Cookery. St. Agnes Guild of the Church of Epiphany, Chicago, 1888, 162p.

558 A Book of Tried Recipes. Cover-title: Choice Recipes from our Friends and Neighbors. (Chicago: 1890?). 51p.

559 The Housekeeper's Friend. Published by The Young Ladies Missionary Society of Grace Methodist Episcopal Church. Imitation alligator cover. Chicago, 1891. 96p.

560 The Universal Cook Book, pub. by the Ladies' Aid Society of the First Universalist Church of Englewood. (Chicago: C. H. Morgan Co., printers, 1891). 95p. frontis, portrait. Ads.

561 Shutt, Mrs. William E. The Exchange Cook Book . . . Springfield: Phillips Bros., printers and binders, 1892. 114p.

562 Patented Methods of Canning Fruits and Vegetables. By Hot Air and Steam. Recipes for the family. Lacks title page. Decorative end papers. Illinois, 1893. 523p.

563 Shuman, Carrie V. Favorite Dishes. A Columbian autograph souvenir. 23 portraits contributed by the Board of Lady Managers. Illus. by May Root-Kern, Mellie Ingels Julian, Louis Braunhold, George Wharton Edwards. Recipes for snipe, woodcock, prairie chicken, etc. Chicago: R. R. Donnelley & Sons Co., 1893. 221p.

564 Armstrong, Kathryn (editor). The White Ribbon Cook Book. Original and revised recipes. Chicago: The Woman's Temperance Pub. Assoc. (1894). 274p.

565 Home Remedies for Man & Beast & Family Receipts (cover title). Title page reads: The Household Guide; Or, Practical Helps Book by Mrs. J. L. Nichols & Anna for Every Home . . . by Prof. B. G. Jefferies. Also A Complete Cook Holverson. 12th ed. Profusely illus. A quaint compilation of American home and health recipes. Pub. by J. L. Nichols, Napersville, 1894. 410p.

566 McClure, Mrs. J. C. Gathered Crumbs. Peoria: Transcript Pub. Co., 1894. 245p. illus.

567 The Woman's Exchange Cook Book. Compiled by The Woman's Exchange of Chicago . . . Chicago: Monarch Book Co. (1894). 527p. illus.

568 Delicate Dishes. A cook book. Compiled by ladies of St. Paul's Church. Chicago: E. B. Smith, 1896. 186p. and ads. Wraps.

569 Warsaw's Choice Recipes. Compiled for the benefit of the Warsaw Free Public Reading Room by the Woman's Club. Pub. under management of Donna M. Parker, Pres. Warsaw: Nov. 1897. Autographed recipes. 71p. and ads.

570 The Home Queen Cook Book. 2000 valuable recipes contributed by over 200 World's Fair Lady Managers, and other ladies of position. Autographed receipts. Fort Dearborn Publishing Co., Chicago, 1898. 608p.

571 The East St. Louis Cook Book. Compiled by the Ladies' Literary Circle of Summit Ave. M.

E. Church Unusual ads and printer's devices. 24 photos of the lady compilers. East St. Louis, 1899. 272p.

572 New Century Cook Book; compiled from recipes contributed by ladies of Chicago and other cities and towns . . . Chicago: Wesley Hospital Bazaar Committee, 1899. 317p.

573 Warsaw's Choice Recipes. Autographed recipes; compiled for the benefit of the free public reading room by The Woman's Club. Donna M. Parker, Pres. Warsaw, 1899. 178p.

574 Detlefs, Edward. A Little Book of Practical Cookery . . . Danville, n. pub., 1900. 72p.

575 The Hyde Park Cuisine. Pub. by the Women of the Hyde Park Baptist Church, 1900. Chicago. 93p.

576 Palmer, Minnie. The Woman's Exchange Cook Book. A new and complete American culinary encyclopedia. By Mrs. Palmer, with the approval of Mrs. J. B. Lyon. Chicago: W. B. Conkey Co. (c. 1901). 527p. Frontis., illus.

577 Sackett, Anna K. and Mills, Fannie F. Recipes. 'Old and New, Tried and True.' (Half-title: Margaret Etter Creche Cook Book). Chicago: Libby & Sherwood Printing Co., 1901. 26p. Wraps.

578 King, Mrs. J. La Forest. The King's Own Cook Book. Springfield, The H. W. Rokker Co., 1903. 336, 4, 17p.

579 The Service Club Cook Book. . . Compiled by The Service Club. (Chicago: E. Keog Print. Co., 1904). 81p.

580 The North End Club Cook Book. A collection of choice and tested recipes, compiled and arranged by Ladies of the Club. Autographed recipes. Chicago: Stevens, Maloney, 1905. 144p. and ads.

581 Sexton, Marian B. The Monmouth Baptist Ladies' Cook Book. Choice and tested recipes contributed by the ladies of Monmouth, and elsewhere. 3rd ed., 1907. 298p. and 12 index.

582 Twentieth Century Cook Book. A feast of good things; a careful compilation. The Ladies Aid Society of the Baptist Church, Plano, 1907. 160p.

583 A New (picture of key) To The Cupboard. Picture of First Christian Church. Society of Christian Church Workers, Barry, 1908. 111p.

584 The Mendelssohn Club Cook Book. 1394 valuable recipes for cooking, and serving instructions. Also menus. Autographed recipes. Compiled by the Active Members. Mendelssohn Club: Rockford, 1909. 339p.

585 Winship, L. H. Fireless Cooker Recipes. Winnetka: No pub., 1909. 24p. Wraps.

586 The Economy Cook Book. Printed by the Inter Aid Bureau, Streator, 1910. 127p.

587 Glen Ellyn Cook Book. Pub. by the Ladies Sewing Circle of the Congregational Church. Autographed recipes. Glen Ellyn: 1911. 110p. and ads.

588 The Inglenook Cook Book. New and rev. ed. Choice recipes contributed by sisters of the Church of the Brethren, subscribers and friends of the Inglenook Magazine. Elgin: Brethren Pub. House, 1911. 416p.

589 The New Home Cook Book. Compiled from recipes contributed by Ladies of Chicago and other cities and towns. Originally for the benefit of the Home for the Friendless. Chicago: A. C. McClurg, 1911. 406p. (See No. 546).

590 1912 Cook Book, compiled by members of St. Elizabeth's Day Nursery, Catholic Woman's League. Chicago: (Press of the Mayer & Miller Co., 1911). 94p.

591 Queen Esther Cook Book. Compiled by the Queen Esther Circle of the First Methodist Episcopal Church. (Evanston: The Index Pub. Co., 1911.) 161p.

592 The Bethany Union Cook Book. By Womans' Society of Bethany Union Church. (Chicago: H. G. Adair Prtg. Co., 1912). 224p.

593 Christopher House Guild Cook Book. Compiled by the Guild of the First Presbyterian Church, Evanston: (1912). 212p. and ads.

594 The Cook County Cook Book, Compiled by Associated College Women Workers, Chicago: Press of McElroy Pub. Co. (1912). 574p.

595 Good Luck Cook Book. St. Paul's Episcopal Church: Week End Club. 3rd ed. (DeKalb: The Chronicle Press, 1912). 106p.

596 Maquon Cook Book. 3 ed. rev. Compiled by Maquon Ladies Cemetery Association. (Maquon: Maquon Tomahawk Print.) 1912. 78p.

597 Van Galder, Anna Claire. Modern Women of America Cook Book. Recipes contributed by women who use them every day. Rock Island. The Modern Woodman Press (1912). 281p.

598 A Book of Cookery. Compiled by St. Mary's Guild, Emanuel Church, La Grange, 1916. 124p.

599 Centralia Cook Book. Prepared by the Ladies' Aid Society of the M. E. Church. Autographed recipes. Cover photo of church. Centralia: Dec., 1916. 157p. and ads.

600 The Methodist Cook Book—A Selection of Tested Recipes. Prepared by the Members of the Ladies' Aid Society of the Methodist Church. Garden Prairie: 1916. Autographed recipes. 55p. and ads.

601 Balanced Meals with Recipes. Pub. by the Lake View Woman's Club. Chicago (1917). 189p.

602 Queen Esther Chapter Cook Book. Favorite, Tried Recipes, autographed. Illinois: 1917. 109p. and ads.

603 The Woodstock Woman's Club Cook Book. Compiled by the Members of the Club. Signed recipes. Contemporary ads. Woodstock, 1917. 207p.

604 AUNT BETTY'S COOK BOOK. Sold by Le Cercle Francais of the American Fund for French Wounded for the benefit of the *Chicago Branch.* Cincinnati: 1918. 97p.

605 FAVORITE RECIPES. Humboldt Park Chapter O.E.S. Compiled by Dagmar Stevens, Mabel Baker and Esther Stevens. Recipes for Cadillac Crab Meat, Hutzel Bread. Wraps. Chicago, 1918. 116p. and ads.

606 OFFICIAL RECIPE BOOK. Containing all demonstrations given during patriotic food show. Chicago: Jan. 13, 1918. 72p. Pict. cover.

607 COOK BOOK. Compiled and published by the Board of Directors of the Larkin Home for Children (photo as frontis.). Autographed recipes. Elgin: Willson Press, 1919. Rev. ed. 160p. and ads.

608 FAVORITE RECIPES compiled by the Woman's Guild of St. Peter's Church (Episcopal). Chicago: Woman's Guild of St. Peter's Church, 1919. 128p. and ads. Paper.

609 STEVENSON MEMORIAL COOK BOOK. Pub. by the Sarah Hackett Stevenson Memorial Lodging House Association. Chicago: The association (1919). 197p. and ads.

610 YE OAKTON COOKERIE. A BOOK OF UNUSUAL RECIPES for the members of the PTA. Autographed recipes. Oakton School, Evanston. n.d. (1920's). 127p.

611 THE COOK BOOK OF LEFT-OVERS. By the More Nurses in Training Movement; from recipes contributed by Illinois Ladies. Rochelle, 1920. 183p.

612 RECIPES compiled by the members of St. Frances' Guild for the benefit of St. Mary's Home for Girls. Chicago: 1920. 153p.

613 ZETA TAU ALPHA COOK BOOK. Compiled by Ruth Hodgson Lang; assisted by Joy B. Sabli, Esther C. Evans and Verna V. Welch for Alpha Phi Chapter House Fund. 2nd ed. Northwestern University, Evanston, 286p. (c. 1920's).

614 FAVORITE RECIPES OF GOOD THINGS TO EAT. P.T.A. of Niles Center, Ill., Dist. 69. Autographed recipes. Evanston: Mumm Print, 1921. 331p. and ads.

615 HOME BUREAU AND COMMUNITY COOK BOOK. Danvers Township Home Bureau Unit. Danvers, 1921. 164p.

616 ILLINOIS STATE FAIR, School of Domestic Science. Wraps. Springfield, 1921. 80p.

617 PENNYMITE COOK BOOK. Compiled by the Ladies of the Penny Mite Society. Autographed recipes. Woodstock, 1921. 187p.

618 THE PILGRIM COOK BOOK. Published by the Ladies' Aid Society of Pilgrim Ev. Lutheran Church. Chicago: 1921. Some autographed. 148p. Wraps.

619 PRESBYTERIAN COOK BOOK, 4th ed. Ladies Aid Society, First Presbyterian Church, Chester, Ill. Chester: Printed by Chester Herald (1921). 84p.

620 TRIED AND TESTED RECIPES. Daughters of Union Veterans of the Civil War.—Department of Illinois: Ida McKinley Tent No. 21. (Oak Park: Pioneer Pub. Co.), 1921. 59p. illus.

621 PAIDER, MARIE AND KAMMERER, BLANCHE. Prague Chapter Book of Recpies, 1922 . . . 3rd ed. enl. and rev. Chicago: Herschman & Cardy (c. 1922). 116p. Wraps. Autographed recipes.

622 THE P.E.O. COOK BOOK. Chapter Z. of Harrisburg, Ill. Autographed recipes. Danville: Illinois Printing Co., 1922. 212p.

623 THE STAR COOK BOOK. 3rd ed., compiled by the ladies of the "Star Society" of the Grace M. E. Church, Pekin, Illinois . . . Pekin: "Star Society" (1922). 276p. illus.

624 BAILEY, N. BETH. MEAL PLANNING AND TABLE SERVICE. Menus, and table service etiquette. Illus. Preface by Florence E. Busse. Manual Arts Press, Peoria (1923). 1st ed. 128p.

625 THE COLLEGE WOMAN'S COOK BOOK. 1st ed. Evanston: The College Woman's Cook-book (c. 1923). 96p.

626 COOK BOOK. Compiled by the Ladies' Aid Society of the Redeemer English Evangelical Lutheran Church. Autographed recipes. Photo of church as frontis. Chicago: 1923. 152p. and ads.

627 COOK BOOK. Autographed recipes compiled by the Epworth League, Niedringhaus Memorial M. E. Church. Granite City: 1923. 196p. and ads. 1st ed.

628 THE NEW HOME COOK BOOK. Prepared by Ladies Club in friendly rivalry for best recipes. Booklet; wraps. Illinois State Register, Springfield, 1923. 128p.

629 FAVORITE RECIPES. Compiled by the Young Woman's Auxiliary of the Congregational Church. Autographed recipes. La Grange: Citizen Publishing Co., 1923. 162p. Ads.

630 2ND BAPTIST CHURCH COOK BOOK. Recipes by Members of the Second Baptist Church, compiled by The Steadfast Circle of the King's Daughters. Chicago, 1923. 104p. and ads.

631 BARNUM, MRS. RICHARD S. (ed). Recipes, contributed by the Presbyterian ladies of Waukegan and their friends . . . (Waukegan, 1924). 191p.

632 GIRLS' WORK COMMITTEE. Community Service Cook Book compiled by the Home Economic Committee. Autographed Recipes: n.p. 1924-1925. 190p. and ads.

633 INGLENOOK COOK BOOK. New and rev. ed. Choice recipes contributed by Sisters of the Church of the Brethren, subscribers and friends of the Inglenook magazine. Autographed recipes. Elgin: Brethren Pub. House, 1924. 416p.

634 TOPPAN, FAETTE S. National Park Seminary (alumnae) Cook Book. Favorite and tested recipes

submitted by former students. Chicago: The Chicago Chapter, 1924. 245p. and ads.

635 ANDERSON, MRS. ADELLA B. (Compiler). YE KIRKE COOKERY. Compiled for The Women's Union. First Methodist Church. Autographed recipes. Evanston: Mumm Print Shop (c. 1925). 250p. and ads.

636 CHI OMEGA COOK BOOK. Edited by the North Shore Alumnae for Xi Chapter House Fund, Northwestern University. Autographed recipes. Evanston. n.d. (ca 1925). 244p.

637 COOK BOOK. Compiled by the Ladies of the First Presbyterian Church of Virden, Ill. Autographed recipes. Springfield: Schnepp & Barnes, 1925. 154p. and ads. 3rd ed. rev.

638 LEBO, NETTIE M. The New American Beauty Cook Book. A collection of recipes for use in the American kitchen. Clinton: The author (c. 1925). 176p.

639 MIDLOTHIAN WOMAN'S COOK BOOK. Tested recipes. Pub. by Woman's Society of St. Luke's Union Church. Midlothian: 1925. 128p.

640 THE NEW HOME COOK BOOK. Ladies' Club rivalry for best recipes. Booklet. Wraps. Illinois State Register, Springfield, 1925. 128p.

641 SELECTED RECIPES. Compiled by Young Woman's Auxiliary, St. Mark's Church. Evanston: no pub. (c. 1925). 95p. and ads. Illus. title page.

642 SWEETS & MEATS. Directory. Woman's Guild. Wraps. First Presbyterian Church, Quincy (c. 1925). 48p.

643 SWEET SIXTEEN. Compiled by the Panadelphian Class of The Western Avenue Baptist Church. 18 signed recipes in booklet tied by ribbon. Chicago, n.d. (c. 1925). 36p.

644 THE RECIPE BOOK FOR CLUB ALUMINUM WARE WITH PERSONAL SERVICE. Ill.: 1926. 32p. advertising booklet, col. pict. cover.

645 MRS. DEGRAF'S COOK BOOK. St. Charles: Universal Press, 1927. 372p.

646 HOSTESS REFERENCE BOOK. Business and Professional Women's Circle, First Presbyterian Church. Directory of members with addresses. Springfield: 1927. 56p. and ads.

647 KINDERHEIM KOOKBOOK. Autographed recipes published by the Ladies' Auxiliary for the benefit of the Kinderheim. Photo on cover. Addison: 1927. 166p. and ads.

648 SELECTED RECIPES. Chosen by the Woman's Board of the Jackson Park Sanitarium stock yards day nursery. Chicago: S. D. Childs, 1927. 250p.

649 NOTES ON COOKERY. Compiled by Mrs. Leonard Vaughan, Mrs. Thomas Harwood, Mrs. Horace E. Collom. Signed recipes. Private printing, 1928. n.p. Illinois. 84p.

650 BOOKMEYER, MARY B. CANDY AND CANDY-MAKING. Well illustra-

ted. The Manual Arts Press: Peoria (1929). 127p.

651 COOK BOOK. Standard and Special Recipes. Autographed recipes compiled by Arcadia Women's Union of Arcadia Ave. Presbyterian Church. Drawing of church on cover. Peoria: Bush Print., 1929. 74p. and ads.

652 DECATUR WOMAN'S CLUB COOK BOOK. Mendota: The Hope Press (c. 1929). Loose-leaf book.

653 KENILWORTH COOKERY. Selected Recipes by The Wilmette Women's Exchange of the Wilmette Parish Methodist Episcopal Church. Oilcloth. Wilmette (1929). 199p.

653a RECIPES FROM HERE AND THERE. Compiled by The Thirty Group, Bethany Union Church. Foreword by Ruth J. Menees. Signed recipes. Chicago, n.d. (c. 1929). 160p.

654 SELECTED RECIPES. Wilmette Woman's Exchange. First M. E. Church (pict. as frontis.). Autographed recipes. Wilmette: Printing Studio, 1929. 200p. and ads.

655 1929 COOK BOOK. Paul Revere Chapter No. 855, Order of the Eastern Star. Autographed recipes. Chicago: W. H. Wilton, 1929. 103p. and ads.

656 THE CHICAGO JEWISH YEAR BOOK, 1930. (see Foreign sec.)

657 THE MOTHERS' ROUND TABLE COOK BOOK. Tested Recipes. Wraps. Compiled by Members of the Mothers' Round Table of Woodlawn. Chicago (c.1930). 112p.

658 DISTINGUISHED HOSTESSES. Signed recipes. Wraps. Woman's National Republican Club of Chicago; (1931). 181p. ads.

659 FIRST PRESBYTERIAN CHURCH COOK BOOK. 75 Selected Recipes. By 75 Pekin Women. Compiled and Edited by 3 Married Men of the First Presbyterian Church. Autographed recipes. Pekin: Lohnes Print Shop (1931). 80p. and ads.

660 KENILWORTH RECIPES. Signed by members Women's Guild of Kenilworth Union Church. Halftone photo. Kenilworth, 1932. 53p.

661 COOK BOOK. Winona Chapter No. 59, Order of the Eastern Star. Pub. under the auspices of the Winona Gavel Club. Autographed recipes. Winona: 1933. 49p.

662 DUNHAM, EDITH. Palatable Patter. Preface says she "begged, borrowed and inherited" the recipes; pub'd. them to secure "financial aid for Passavant Hospital, and to pay tribute to Mrs. Joseph Coleman." Chicago: n. pub., 1933. 48p.

663 COOK BOOK. Recipes Prepared, Tested & Approved by the Members of the Daughters of Indiana, Chicago, 1934. 108p.

664 CULINARY CAPERS. Autographed recipes, collected by the Evanston Junior Auxiliary of the Chicago Infant Welfare Society. Illustrated by Mrs. Joseph L. Corcoran. End paper drawings. Evanston Junior Auxiliary: Evanston, 1934. 255p.

665 COOK BOOK. Compiled by Ladies' Auxiliary. Autographed recipes. Wraps. Illinois Rural Letter Carriers Association, Ill. 1935. 83p.

666 SUMPTON, LOIS LINTNER & ASHBROOK, MARGUERITE LINTNER. COOKIES AND MORE COOKIES, Recipes from Many Nations. Peoria, 1936. 225p.

667 SOME LIKE IT HOT, SOME LIKE IT COLD. Collected recipes. Spiral binding. Winnetka Junior Auxiliary of the Cradle: Winnetka, 1938. 116p.

668 TWENTIETH ANNIVERSARY COOK BOOK. Dedicated to Miss Clara R. Brian, Home Adviser of McLean County. Favorite Recipes Compiled by Members of McLean County Home Bureau, Spiral. Bloomington, 1938. 228p.

669 PLAT, SIR HUGH. DELIGHTES FOR LADIES. Originally printed in London in 1602. Reprinted from 1627 ed., illus. from 1609 ed. collated and edited by V. & H. Trovillion, pub. privately at The Sign of the Silver Horse in Perrin, 1942. 498 copies signed by the editors. 120p.

670 HAVING A HEART FOR CHRIST'S LITTLE ONES. By the Lutheran Child Welfare Auxiliary. Recipes for: Honey Mayonnaise, Bavarian Liver Dumplings, etc. Spiral binding. Addison (c. 1943). 233p. and ads.

671 POWERS, MARGARET: The Party Table. Illus. Peoria, 1946. 167p.

672 ERMINGER, LILA W., HOPKINS, MARJORIE R. (presentation copy) FOOD AND FUN FOR DAUGHTER & SON. Illus. Published by The Illinois Children's Home & Aid Society. Chicago, 1947. 120p.

673 HOME BUREAU COOK BOOK. Prepared by La Salle County Home Bureau. Some autographed recipes. Spiral binding. Home Bureau, Ottawa, 1947. 210p. 8p. index.

673a ALUMNAE COOK BOOK. Compiled by The Alumnae Ass'n. Autographed recipes (addresses of donors). Mimeo. sheets in colored paper wraps. National College of Education, Evanston, 1948. 25p.

674 AUTOGRAPHED COOKERY. Compiled by The Highland Park Auxiliary of the Cradle. Illus. Mimeo. Spiral binding. Highland Park, 1948. 319p.

675 FAVORITE CASSEROLES & SALADS. Circle 9 Compiled Them, W. S. C. S. Members Supplied Them. Unique oblong format. Ring binder. Cover picture Christmas Tree Fare. 1st Methodist Church, Evanston, 1951. 46p.

676 HOFFMAN, FLORENCE (editor). HUMMINGBIRDS AND RADISHES. Unusual recipes, and a 14-day egg diet. Drawings. Spiral binding. Kenilworth Center of the Infant Welfare Society, Chicago (1953). 218p.

677 BAPTIST CHURCH COOK BOOK. Baptist Church, Vandalia (19-?).

678 COOK BOOK. Woman's Society of the Ravenswood Congregational

Church. Autographed recipes. Chicago: n.d. 71p. and ads.

679 COOK BOOK OF FAVORITE RECIPIES OF THE I. W. A. C. MEMBERS. Signed recipes. Compiled and Edited by the Home Economics Comm. Wraps. Illinois Women's Athletic Club, Chicago. n.d. 128p.

680 RECIPES from the Bishop Anderson Guild of the Church of the Holy Comforter. Kenilworth, Ill.

681 TRIED & TRUE RECIPES. East End Circle Women's Guild. Illus. First Congregational Church, Wilmette. n.d. 124p.

Chicago

682 ARCHDEACON, WILLIAM. Archdeacon's Kitchen Cabinet, A Book of Receipts: preserving, canning. Improvements in housekeeping. With many reliable selections from the Highest Known Authorities on a great variety of subjects. Chicago: pub. for the author, 1876. 548p.

683 THE HOME KEEPER'S GUIDE. Nearly 100 recipes and other valuable information, contributed by the lady readers of the Chicago Daily Tribune. Chicago: H. M. Wilcox, 1877. 168p. Wraps.

684 DONNELLEY, NAOMI A. (Anon.) The Lakeside Cook Books: No. 1. A Manual of palatable and healthful cookery; & No. 2. A Manual for cooking, preserving, pickling. Chicago: Donnelley, Gassette & Lloyd, 1878. 47p. and 47p.

685 HOLMES, MARION. HOW TO COOK. A literary cook book. Chicago, 1880. 351p. 1st ed.

686 PYE, JULIA A. Invalid Cookery: A manual of recipes for preparation of food for the sick and convalescent. Edited by Mrs. Eliza A. Pitkin. Chicago: no pub., 1880. 127p.

687 THE COMPLETE BREAD, CAKE AND CRACKER BAKER. The art and science of baking. Gill: Mgr. Confectioner and Baker: Chicago, 1881. 252p.

688 OWENS, FRANCES E. Mrs. Owens' Cook Book, and Useful Hints for the Household. Chicago: S. K. Reed, 1881. 364p.

689 MATTHIESSEN, ADELE GIGNOUX. Nonpareil Practical Cook Book. Chicago: Jansen, McClurg & Co., 1882. 435p.

690 WHITEHEAD, JESSUP. The Professional Cook's Own Receipt Book. Book of fine pastries: book of salads; book of breads; book of puddings. Republished from the Chicago Daily National Hotel Reporter. Rev. & corrected. Chicago: the author, 1882. 219p.

691 EWING, EMMA P. COOKING AND CASTLE-BUILDING. Entertaining discussion of period cooking. Chicago, 1883.

692 SIX LITTLE COOKS; or, Aunt Jane's Cooking Class. Chicago: Jansen, McClurg, 1883. 236p.

693 SPENCER, EDGAR L. (Anon.) The Great Rock Island Cook Book, a carefully compiled selection of

the most useful recipes . . Dedicated to the women of America by the general ticket and passenger department of the Chicago, Rock Island & Pacific Railway . . Chicago: J. M. W. Jones Stationery and Printing Company, 1883. iv, 118, 3p. and ads.

694 WHITEHEAD, JESSUP. The Chicago Herald Cooking School. A professional cook's book for household use. Chicago: the author, 1883. 126p.

695 WHITEHEAD, JESSUP. The Hotel Book of Soups and Entrees. Specimens of French, English and American menus. Chicago: 1883. 309-345p. Wraps.

696 FRYE, G. V. Frye's Practical Candy Maker. Receipts for the manufacture of Fine Hand-Made Candies, especially adapted for fine retail trade. Chicago: (1884). 96p.

697 MOODY, MARGARITE A. Moody's Household Adviser and Cook Book. Replete with practical and reliable information and advice important to every housekeeper. Chicago: J. Cashe & Co., 1884. 321, xviip.

698 JUDD, MRS. ORANGE (Anon.) The Kitchen; or, Every-day Cookery. Many useful, practical directions, recipes, etc. . . Chicago: Rand, McNally & Co., 1885. 104p. Wraps.

699 MORENCI, L. R. The French Cook. (See Foreign sec.)

700 WHITEHEAD, JESSUP. Cooking for Profit. A new American cook book adapted for use of all who serve meals for a price. In 2 parts. Chicago: the author, 1886. Illus.

701 WILLARD, HARRIET J. Familiar Lessons for Little Girls. A First Book—for industrial schools and for homes. Chicago: Geo. Sherwood, 1886. 63p.

702 CLARKE, ANNE. The Ideal Cookery Book . . . 1349 new, useful and unique recipes. Chicago: F. J. Schulte & Co. (1889). 402p. Frontis.

703 DINNEROLOGY. Our Experiments in Diet from Crankery to Common-Sense. A tale for the times. By Pan. Chicago: Belford, Clarke, 1889. 205p. Wraps. Ads.

704 FRYE, G. V. The Housewife's Practical Candy Maker. Receipts for the finest candy adapted for the American Kitchen. Chicago: Belford, Clarke & Co., 1889. 169p.

705 GILLETTE, MRS. FANNY LEMIRA. The American Cook Book. A Selection of Choice Recipes, collected during 40 years. Chicago, 1889. 521p.

706 KRAMER, BERTHA F. (Anon.) "AUNT BABETTE'S" COOKBOOK. Foreign and Domestic Recipes for the Household. Chicago: The Bloch Publishing & Printing Co. (1889). 520p.

707 WHITEHEAD, JESSUP. THE STEWARD'S HANDBOOK and Guide to Party Catering in hotels, restaurants, for private parties. Some handwritten recipes. Chicago, 1889. 464p. Appendix on How to Fold

Napkins, description and diagrams, Chicago, 1888. 29p. 6pages adv.

708 NEILL, MISS E. THE EVERY-DAY COOK BOOK. Encyclopedia of Practical Recipes for Family Use. Donohue: Chicago, n.d. (late 1880's) 316p.

709 BLAKESLEE, MRS. E. C. AND LESLIE, EMMA, AND HUGHES, S. H. The Compendium of Cookery and Reliable Recipes. Two vols. in one: cooking, confectionery, Book of Knowledge or 1000 ways of getting rich. Rev. & enl. Chicago: The Merchants' Specialty Co., 1890. 309 plus 103p.

710 THE COMPLETE PRACTICAL CONFECTIONER. In 8 parts: and it's really complete. Chicago: J. Thompson Gill; 1890. 557p.

711 GATES, S. M. Mother's Cook Book for Every Day in the Week. And kitchen encyclopedia, Chicago: L. Benham & Co., 1890. 315p. Frontis.

712 LEE, LESLIE, HEDGES. Complete Library of Cookery. Illus. Chicago, 1890. 300p.

713 SHIELDS, G. C. CAMPING AND CAMP OUTFITS. A manual of Instruction, including food. Illustrated—advertisements. Rand, McNally: Chicago, 1890. 169p.

714 TOWNSEND, MRS. GRACE. IMPERIAL COOK BOOK. A Monitor for the American Housewife; the choicest original and selected recipes. Frontispiece photograph. Monarch Book Co., Chicago, (1890). 527p.

715 BUCKEYE COOKERY. With hints on practical housekeeping. Some handwritten recipes. H. J. Smith & Co., Chicago, 1891. 536p.

716 ELLIS, WILLIS ARNOLD. The Acme Cook Book and Housekeeper's Guide. A complete encyclopaedia of cookery and household matters. Chicago: The Enterprise Pub. Co., 1891. 216p.

717 KIRKLAND, MISS E. S. Dora's House-keeping. A story of Dora, her learning to house-keep and cook. Chicago: A. C. McClurg & Co., 1891. 275p. and ads.

718 SIX LITTLE COOKS, OR AUNT JANE'S COOKING CLASS. Chicago: A. C. McClurg, 1891. 236p. 8th ed.

719 WHITEHEAD, JESSUP. Family Cook Book and Book of Breads and Cakes (originally titled Herald Cooking School). Rev. and improved. Chicago: Whitehead & Co., 1891. 128p. plus 4p. illus.

720 GILLETT, EGBERT W. Gillett's Magic Cook Book . . . Chicago: E. W. Gillett (1892). 283p. Wraps.

721 MARTHA WASHINGTON COOK BOOK. A Compendium of Cookery and Reliable Recipes. Chicago: F. Tennyson Neely, 1892. 315p. illus. Ads. Pict. cover.

722 600 SELECTED RECIPES. By well known authorities on cooking. Booklet: wraps. Fairbank: Chicago (c. 1892). 131p.

723 STIEFEL, IFA (editor). St. Paul's Bazaar Kochbuch und Geschaeftsfuehrer . . . (see Foreign sec.)

724 America's Cereal Foods and How to Cook Them. Souvenir booklet of Chicago World's Fair. Chicago: American Cereal Co., 1893. 68p. illus. Adv'g. booklet. 2nd ed. Col. pict. cover.

725 Kramer, Bertha F. (Anon.) "Aunt Babette's" Home Confectionery. Bloch Publishing & Printing Co., Chicago, 1893. 38p.

726 Parloa, M. Choice Receipts. Specially prepared for Exhibit at World's Columbian Exposition. Chicago: Walter Baker & Co., 1893. Col. pict. cover. Frontis. of Walter Baker & Co. Exhibition Building. 32p. advertising booklet.

727 Practical Cookery by an Epicure. A choice selection. Chicago: Fred. Klein, 1893. 436p.

728 Rorer, Sarah T. Columbian Exposition. Recipes used in Illinois Corn Exhibit Model Kitchen. Booklet, wraps. Illinois Women's Exposition Board, Chicago, 1893. 16p.

729 Walton, Izaak & Cotton, Charles. The Compleat Angler. Marginal illus. on every page. Ref. to cooking the catch. Edward Gilpin Johnson (ed.). Ltd. ed. of 500. Pict. cloth. A. C. McClurg, Chicago, 1893. 287p.

730 Whitehead, Jessup. Hotel Meat Cooking. 6th ed. Comprising Fish & Oyster Cooking. Chicago: author, 1893. 229-397p.

731 Hansey, Jennie A. The Century Cook Book. A carefully selected list of recipes. Also Dr. Oliver's Treasured Secrets. 301 illustrations. Laird & Lee, Chicago, 1894. 353p.

732 Townsend, Mrs. Grace. Dining Room and Kitchen (rev. ed.), an economical guide in practical housekeeping, cooking, & special articles on nursery, dining room & laundry. Illus. Home Publishing Co. (1894). Chicago. 527p.

733 Whitehead, Jessup. The American Pastry Cook. For Hotel and Steamboat use, for Cafes and Fine Bakeries. 7th ed. Chicago: the author, 1894. 225p.

734 Green, Mary E., M.D. Food Products of the World. Intro. by Juliet Corson. Edited & illus. by Grace Green Bohn. Chicago; The Hotel World, 1895. 249p.

735 Swedish-English Cook Book. (see Foreign sec.)

736 Boyd, Mrs. William Hart. The Queen Cook Book . . . Chicago: F. H. Revell Co.: (1896). 328p.

737 Chesbrough, Mrs. Mary Mott (ed.) The Chicago Record Cook Book. Inexpensive Bills of Fare . . contributed by the Women of America to the daily contest for Menus for a Day. Autographed recipes. Chicago: Chicago Record, 1896. 607p. Col. pict. cover.

738 The Daily News Cook Book. Same contents as Chicago Record Cook book. Chicago, 1896. 607p.

739 Tschirky, Oscar. The Cook Book by "Oscar" of the Waldorf. Its Maitre d'Hotel for so many

years that the two are almost synonymous. Chicago: The Werner Company (1896). xxii, 907p. Frontis. port. of the author.

740 Fletcher, Horace. Menticulture, or The A-B-C of True Living. By the originator of the system of "Fletcherizing" - i.e., chewing food thoroughly for better digestion. Chicago: A. C. McClurg, 1897. 141p.

741 Svensk-Amerikansk Kokbok. (see Foreign sec.)

742 Cozart, W. Forrest. The Waiters' Manual. A Technical Treatise on Dining-Room Service. The Hotel World, Chicago (1898). 116p.

743 Chidlow, Garrett, Vail & Others: The American Pure Food Cook Book & Household Economist. Wraps. Turkey-Pilgrim cover. Illus. Geo. M. Hill Co., Chicago, 1st ed. (1899). 508p.

744 Hemmets Drottning Kokbok. (see Foreign sec.)

745 Our Chef's Best Receipts. A practical cook book for people who like good things to eat. Chicago: Rand, McNally (c. 1899). 122p. and ads.

746 Cooke, Maude C. Three Meals a Day. Chicago: The Educational Co., 189?. 576p. illus.

747 Cotton, Olive A. Cake and Bread Recipes. Everykind, with and without frostings. Chicago: R. R. Donnelley & Sons Co., 1900. 176p.

747a Dr. King's New Guide to Health. Household Instructor and Family Prize Cook Book. Advertises the "Electric Bitters" for consumption, coughs & colds. Chicago: H. E. Buchlen, 1900. 32p.

748 Receipts. For a few soups and sauces which can be made with Armour's beef extract. Small booklet, wraps. Armour: Illinois, c. 1900. 31p.

749 Smiley's Cook Book and universal household guide. Chicago: Smiley Pub., 1901. 990p. illus. Col. pl.

750 "That Full Dinner Pail." What to put in it. Also suggestions for home meals. Chicago: W. B. Conkey (1901). 238p.

751 Lees-Dods, Matilda. My Mother's Cook Book. Practical lessons. Edited by Henriette de Conde Sherman. Chicago: Thompson and Thomas (1902). 240p.

752 Quin, Charles W. Handbook of Universal Information and Encylopedia of practical recipes. Chicago: M. A. Donohue & Co., 1903. 192p.

753 Vachon, Joseph. Vachon's Book of Economical Soups and Entrees. Chicago: The Hotel Monthly Press, 1903. 96p.

754 Whitehead, Jessup. The Steward's Handbook. Guide to Party Catering; menus, catering, service, dictionary. Whitehead: Chicago, 1903. 464p. and ads.

755 Young, Anne M. Bills of Fare. Chicago: Rogers & Wells, 1903. 35p. illus. Wraps.

756 Fellows, Charles. The Culinary Handbook. "Most complete" culinary reference book. Chicago: The Hotel Monthly, 1904. Frontis. port. of author. 186p.

757 Encyclopedia of Mother's Advice. By a Thousand American Mothers. How to Cook Everything. Photographs of Mrs. William McKinley and James A. Garfield. Bible House, Chicago, 1905. 315p.

758 Ny Norsk-Dansk og Amerikansk Kogebog. (See Foreign sec.)

759 Palmer, Ida M. Culinary Wrinkles. Practical recipes for using Armour's extract of beef. Chicago: Armour & Co. (1905). 47p. Wraps.

760 Barnet, Daisy Wilson. Tested Recipes for the Modern Hostess. Choice recipes from various sources. . . Chicago: Regan Printing House (1906). 52p. Wraps.

761 Baxter, Richard. Baxter's Practical Up-to-date Receipt Book for Bakers. Rev. and enl. ed. Chicago: Laird & Lee, 1906. 100p. and frontis. port. of author.

762 Carruthers, Mrs. Francis. Twentieth Century Home Cook Book. Chicago: Thompson & Thomas (1906). 491p.

763 Cooking, Housekeeping, Care of the Sick. The Encyclopedia of Mother's Advice. (see No. 757). Illus. Chicago, 1906. 315p.

764 Friedman, Jacob. Friedman's Common-Sense Candy Teacher. Complete Formulas, for both steam and open fire work, for manufacturer or beginner. Frontis. port. of the author. Chicago: Jonas N. Bell, (1906). 359p.

765 Kientz, Leon. The Fish and Oyster Book by the chef of Rector's. Chicago: The Hotel Monthly, 1906. 157p.

766 Moore, Charles G. The Vest Pocket Vegetable Book. Not a "vegetarian" book. Just how to use more vegetables in a more appetizing way. Chicago: The Chicago Monthly, 1906. 126p. Frontis. of author.

767 Barrows, Anna. Principles of Cookery. From the Library of Home Economics, prepared by Teachers of Recognized Authority. Chicago: American School of Home Economics, 1907. 200p. illus.

768 Pierce, Paul. Dinners and Luncheons. Unusual material. Chicago: Brewer, Barse, 1907. 96p.

769 Richards, Paul. Book of Breads, Cakes, Pastries, Ices and Sweetmeats. Especially adapted for Hotel and Catering Trades. Frontispiece photograph. The Hotel Monthly: Chicago, 1907. 172p. and ads.

770 Davenport, Laura (Selected by) The Bride's Cook Book. A superior collection of thoroughly tested practical recipes. Some handwritten recipes in back pages. Decorations. Thumb index. Reilly & Britton: Chicago (1908). 265p.

771 LEE, WILLIAM HENRY AND HANSEY, JENNIE A. The Standard Domestic Science Cook Book . . 1400 famous recipes . . French terms used in cookery with English equivalents. 135 special drawings, 15 full page pl. Chicago: Laird & Lee (c. 1908). 522p.

772 FELLOWS, CHARLES. A SELECTION OF DISHES AND THE CHEF'S REMINDER. A high class culinary text book. Pocket size book. The Hotel Monthly, Chicago, 1909. 220p. and ads.

773 FULLER, EVA GREENE. The Up-To-Date Sandwich Book. 400 ways to do it. Chicago: McClurg & Co., 1909. 180p. and 7 index.

774 GLOVER, ELLYE HOWELL. "DAME CURTSEY'S" BOOK OF RECIPES. Practicability is the focus. Numerous illustrations. McClurg & Co.: Chicago, 1909. 1st Amer. ed. 484p.

775 HOWLAND, MARION R. Woman's World Cook Book. Hundreds of invaluable recipes. Illus. by Mary Woleben Sackett. Chicago: Currier Pub. Co., 1909. 128p. Plates.

775a DR. KING'S NEW GUIDE TO HEALTH. (see No. 747a). Chicago: 1909. 32p. Pict. cover.

776 MILLER, VAL. STANDARD RECIPES FOR ICE CREAM MAKERS. Wholesale and retail. Copyright William H. Lee, 1909. 138p. (Chicago).

777 BLACKSTONE, ELLA M.: THE AMERICAN WOMAN'S COOKBOOK. Quaint frontis., pict. cover. Wraps. Chicago, 1910. Laird & Lee. 384p. illus.

778 FELLOWS, CHARLES. The Menu Maker. Suggestions for Menus for Hotels & Restaurants. A chapter about the most popular soups, fish, boiled meats, roasts & entrees. Decorative end papers. The Hotel Monthly, Chicago, 1910. 64 pages and Appendix 110 pages.

779 HULSE, OLIVE M. 200 Recipes for Making Salads with 30 Recipes for Dressings and Sauces. Chicago: The Hopewell Press, 1910. 94p.

780 1910 SODA WATER GUIDE AND BOOK OF RECIPES. Chicago: Liquid Carbonic Co., 1910. 192p. and ads.

781 PUBLOW, CHARLES A. Fancy Cheese in America. From the milk of cows, sheep and goats. Chicago: American Sheep Breeder Co., 1910. 96p. illus. ads.

782 A PURE FOOD COOK BOOK. Home Helps. Lincoln, Rorer, Harland et al. Chicago, 1910. 80p.

783 WILKINSON, MARY E. (Anon.) A Cook Book for the poor, rich, sick, well. An economy book. Chicago: W. B. Conkey (1910). 328p. illus.

784 THE COOK'S BOOK. Chicago: 1911. 64p. advertising booklet, col. illus.

785 DAVENPORT, LAURA. The Small Family Cook Book. Economy in the kitchen. Chicago: The Reilly and Britton Co. (1911). 256p. Frontis. plates.

786 ESTES, RUFUS. GOOD THINGS TO EAT. Unusual. Author born a slave, entered Pullman Co. Service, became chef of subsidiary of U. S. Steel Corp. in Chicago. Private printing: Chicago, 1911. Frontis. portrait. 142p.

787 FIELD, RUTH ALDEN. The Corona Cook Book. A collection of choice recipes, with expansible device for keeping personal cooking rules. Chicago: The Abbey Co., 1911.

788 PARSONS, FLORENCE CROSBY. Every Woman's Cook Book. An economical, practical guide for the 20th century housekeeper. Chicago: L. W. Walter Co., n.d. (1911). 224p.

789 THE PROGRESS MEATLESS COOK BOOK. Also suggestions for all kinds of cleaning and helps for the household. Chicago: Progress Co. (1911). 272p.

790 RICE, LOUISE. Dainty Dishes from Foreign Lands. Chicago: A. C. McClurg & Co., 1911. 58p.

791 THOMSON, HELEN MAR. Oysters in a Hundred Ways. Wraps. Chicago, Ill. Booth Fisheries, 1911. 103p.

792 GLOVER, ELLYE H.: "Dame Curtsey's" Book of Novel Entertainments for Every Day of the Year. McClurg & Co.: Chicago, 1912. 269p.

793 HANSEY, JENNIE. THE HOUSEHOLD COOK-BOOK. The Century Cook Book. Selected recipes. Title page and meat chart not included in binding. 200 illustrations. Laird & Lee, Chicago (1912). 266p.

794 HULSE, OLIVE M. 200 RECIPES FOR MAKING DESSERTS, Including French Pastries. Chicago, 1912. 1st ed. 154p.

795 KIMBALL, CLAUDE EUGENE (Anon.) The Young Bride's Household Guide. Chicago: The Household Guide Corp. (1912). 207p.

796 MENDELSOHN, FELIX. The Cook Book de luxe. Over 600 recipes of "quality." Chicago: F. Mendelsohn, (c. 1912). 224p.

797 ROBINSON, EVA ROBERTA AND HAMMEL, HELEN GUNN. Lessons in Cooking through preparation of meals. A correspondence course to teach the art of cooking in the home. Chicago: American School of Home Economics, 1912. 467p. Frontis. illus.

798 TEETSHORN, KATE S. THE CALENDAR OF DINNERS. A Daily Blessing to the housekeeper. Dinner menus with recipes. Chicago, Sullivan & Blakely Printing Co., 1912. 52p.

799 THOMAS, CARROLL HOYT (Anon.) Home Helps. A guide to the new Housewife. Chicago: The Thomas Advertising Co. (1912). 152p.

800 BRADT, CECILIA K. (Anon). Cooking Hints and Helps to Reduce the Cost of Living. Chicago: The Northern Trust-Company-Bank (1913). 66p. Wraps.

801 DAVENPORT, LAURA. The Ideal Home Cook Book. Designed for the inexperienced housekeeper. Chicago: The Reilly and Britton Co. (1913). 256p.

802 DAVIS, ELDENE. A Table for Two. Good Things to Eat. Chicago: Forbes & Co., 1913. 217p.

803 GLOVER, ELLYE HOWELL. "Dame Curtsey's" Book of Candy Making. A little book about 'the gentle art.' A. C. McClurg & Co., Chicago, 1913. 110p.

804 HARRIS, ETHEL (LONGLEY). Wholesome Cooking, a practical book for a practical cook; 200 recipes. Chicago: Rand, McNally & Co. (1913). 32p.

805 HEMMETS KOKBOK. (see Foreign sec.)

806 HILLER, MRS. ELIZABETH O. FIFTY-TWO SUNDAY DINNERS. Menus and recipes for each. N. K. Fairbank Co.: Chicago, 1913. The last gasp of the old fashioned Sunday dinner. 192p.

807 TELLMAN, JOHN: The Practical Hotel Steward—Revised to Incorporate Both American & European Plans. Interesting menus, some illus. Chicago, 1913. 248p.

808 AUSTIN, BERTHA J. Domestic Science Book One. Material from teachers from different sections of the country. The editor of Andrews Institute for Girls. Willoughby, O. Chicago: Lyons & Carnaham (1914). 205p.

809 BOSSE, SARA AND WATANNA, ONOTO. Chinese-Japanese Cook Book. (see Foreign sec.)

810 CONGRESS HOTEL—HOME OF A THOUSAND HOMES. Rare and Piquant Dishes of Historic Interest. Charming illustrations. A small book, beautifully printed. M. M. Kaufman, Chicago, 1914. 51p.

811 GOESSLING, ADELINE O. The Orange Judd Cook Book. Tested recipes for practical housekeepers. Chicago: Orange Judd Co., 1914. 4, 276p. illus. Frontis.

812 HERRICK, CHRISTINE TERHUNE. Candy Making in the Home. Color cover. Chicago, 1914. 130p.

813 HULSE, OLIVE M. TWO HUNDRED RECIPES FOR COOKING IN CASSEROLES. History of casseroles and recipes. The Hopewell Press, Chicago (1914). 1st ed. 97p.

814 RICHARDS, PAUL. Pastry for the Restaurant. Recipes especially adapted for hotels of the European Plan. Chicago: The Hotel Monthly Press (1914). 144p.

815 RIESENBERG, EMILY. Preserving and Canning. A Book for the Economist. The author is a special writer for the Chicago Record-Herald. Chicago: Rand McNally & Co., 1914. 104p.

816 FARMER, FANNIE MERRITT. PASTRY WRINKLES. Pies and cakes. Small booklet; wraps; color illustrations. Armour: 1915. 16p.

817 FRIES, ALFRED. Amerikanische Gerichte. (See Foreign sec.)

818 HILLER, ELIZABETH O. The Calendar of Dinners. 365 answers to the question, What Shall we Have for Dinner." Chicago, 1915.

819 MCCREA, R. M. My Own Recipes. Chicago: 1915. 157p.

820 SENN, C. HERMAN. THE BOOK OF SAUCES. Pocketbook size handbook for chefs. Decorative end papers. Hotel Monthly Press, Chicago, 1915. 128p. and ads.

820a THE COOK'S BOOK. Baking Powder and how to use it. Collection of choice recipes edited by Mrs. J. M. Hill. Wraps. Illus. in color. Jaques Mfg. Co., Chicago, 1916. 64p.

821 HULSE, OLIVE. 200 Recipes for Making Salads with 30 Recipes for Dressings and Sauces. Chicago: Hopewell Press, 1916. 94p.

822 RICHARDS, PAUL. The Lunch Room. Plans, equipment, management, accounting, food and drink sales, bills of fare, receipts. The economical operation and quick service of wholesome foods and drinks. Chicago: The Hotel Monthly Press (1916). 238p.

823 SECRETS OF MEAT CURING AND SAUSAGE MAKING. How to cure hams, bacon, corned beef, etc. and how to make all kinds of sausage to comply with the pure food laws. Chicago: B. Heller, 1916. 286p. illus. Ads. 3rd ed.

824 ADAMS, JEAN PRESCOTT. (editor). The Business Of Being A Housewife. A manual to promote household efficiency and economy. Chicago: Armour and Co., 1917. 60p. Wraps.

825 BEEZLEY, RUTH ALLEN AND GREGORY, ANNIE R. The National Course in Home Economics. Contains more than 1000 tested recipes, including modern dishes. Chicago National School of Home Economics (1917). 578p.

826 FOOD AND LIFE. Diet for Fat & Lean; Many special recipes. Nile C. Smith: Chicago, 1917. 123p. and ads.

827 LEE'S PRICELESS RECIPES. Collection of Famous Formulas. Chicago, 1917. 368p.

828 MEYER, ADOLPHE. Eggs in a Thousand Ways. The title speaks for itself. Chicago: The Hotel Monthly Press (1917). 140p.

829 NESBITT, FLORENCE. LOW COST COOKING. A manual of cooking, diet, home management. American School of Home Economics, Chicago, 1917. 127p.

830 PARLOA, MARIA. Canned Fruit, Preserves and Jellies. Household Methods of Preparation. Chicago: The Saalfield Publishing Co. (1917). 101p.

831 ROBERTSON, JOHN DILL. SPEND LESS AND EAT MORE COOK BOOK. How to Combat the High Cost of Living. Records of Economic Diet Squad. Wraps. M. A. Donohue & Co., Chicago (1917). 64p.

832 WADE, MRS. MARY L. The Book of Corn Cookery. 150 recipes

showing how to use this nutritious cereal. A. C. McClurg & Co., Chicago, 1917. 105p.

833 WAR TIME COOKERY. Recipes to reduce the high cost of living, adapted to wheatless and meatless days. Compiled and published by the Club Messenger. Chicago: 1917. 16p. Paper.

834 BARTLETT, MARIE MUNN. Conservation Menus and Recipes. Chicago: Barnard & Miller, 1918. 34p. Wraps.

835 HAYWARD, AGNES CARROLL. Yacht Club Manual of Salads. Chicago: Tildesley & Co. Yacht Club Food Products, 1918. 32p. advertising booklet. Col. pict. cover. 4th ed.

836 HILLER, MRS. ELIZABETH O. (compiler). THE CORN COOK BOOK. War Edition. Chicago: P. F. Volland Co. (1918). 127p.

837 LINDLAHR, MRS. ANNA & HENRY. THE NATURE CURE COOK BOOK and A B C of Natural Dietetics. Recipes and menus. Nature Cure Publishing Co., Chicago (1918). 484p.

838 MORTON, LILLIAN. Thrift Cook Book. A conservation cook book for the economical housewife. Chicago: Shrewesbury Publishing Co. (c. 1918). 142p. Wraps.

839 RICHARDS, PAUL. BAKERS' BREAD. Not for the home; for the bakery. The Bakers' Helper Company, Chicago, 1918. 143p.

840 STEWART, FRANCES ELIZABETH. Lessons in Cookery. Book I. Food Economy. The author, an instructor in Murray F. Tuley H. S. Chicago: Rand McNally & Co., 1918. 250p.

841 COATES, HARRIET ELLSWORTH. Unusual Meats. Chicago: Swift & Co., 1919. 24p. Wraps. Illus. in color.

842 DONNELLY, ALICE M. AND CRAMP, HELEN. Practical Home Economics. 1245 scientific recipes. Fully illus. Col. pl. Chicago: D. E. Cunningham & Co. (1919). 507p.

843 HIRTZLER, VICTOR: THE HOTEL ST. FRANCIS COOKBOOK. Menus and recipes. Chicago, 1919. 1st ed. 431p.

844 ROZNER, JAN F. Dyeta Domowa i Kuchnia Ekonomiczna, (See Foreign sec.)

845 WRIGHT, ELEANOR LEE. Wilson's Meat Cookery. Chicago: Wilson & Co. (1919). 49p. illus. in col. Wraps.

846 APPERT, NICOLAS. The Book for all Households, or the Art of Preserving Animal and Vegetable Substances for Many Years. Trans. by K. G. Bitting, M.S., bacteriologist, Chicago, 1920. 133p.

847 GRAY, GRACE VIALL. EVERY STEP IN CANNING. The cold pack method. Forbes & Co., Chicago, 1920. 253p.

848 KIRKLAND, MISS E. S. Six Little Cooks, or Aunt Jane's Cooking

Class. 14th ed. Chicago: A. C. McClurg & Co., 1920. 236p.

849 Murphy, Bessie R. Peanuts for Breakfast, Dinner, Supper. A Southern food expert shows how to use them. Chicago: Rand McNally and Co. (1920). 18p. Wraps.

850 Sonia's Cook Book. A Cook Book De Luxe of Tested and Selected Recipes. Presentation copy from the Publisher. Felix Mendelsohn, Chicago, 1920. 336p.

851 Hinkle, Thomas Clark, M.D. How to Eat—A Cure for "Nerves." Chicago, 1921. 128p.

852 Loeb, Carl. The Black Art of Cooking. Illus. by Dr. Harlan Tarbell. The author likes "unfired" foods and honey as the only "natural" sugar. Chicago: Chicago Labor Printing Co., 1921. 127p. illus.

853 The New Dr. Price Cook Book. For use with Dr. Price's Phosphate Baking Powder. Ill.: 1921. 49p. Col. pict. cover.

854 Twentieth Century Cook Book. An Up-to-Date and Skillful Preparation on the Art of Cooking and Modern Candy Making . . Compiled and Pub. by The Geographical Pub. Co. Chicago: 1921. Copyright by John Thomas. 182p. illus.

855 Woman's World Cookery Calendar. Recipes, and menus for each day in the year. Published by Woman's World Magazine Co., Chicago (1921). 67p.

856 Barrows, Anna. Principles of Cookery. By a teacher at Teachers College, Columbia Univ. Illustrated. American School of Home Economics, Chicago, 1922. 234p.

857 Bradley, Alice. Cooking for Profit. Catering and Food Service Management. Illustrated. American School of Home Economics, Chicago, 1922. 285p.

858 Brebner, Gertrude Frelove (compiler). The All-American Cook Book. The Favorite Dishes of Famous Americans: beginning with Warren G. Harding, thru generals & admirals & senators etc. Chicago: Judy Pub. Co., 1922. 185p.

859 Lindlahr, Anna and Henry. The Lindlahr Vegetarian Cook Book, and ABC of natural dietetics. 15th ed. rev. and enl. Chicago: The Lindlahr Pub. Co. (1922). 535p.

860 Raskin, Xavier. The French Chef in Private American Families. (See Foreign sec.)

861 Recipes for Institutions. Collected and edited by The Chicago Dietetic Association, Inc., in the interest of better food for the institution. New York: Macmillan Co., 1922. 163p.

862 Carney, Cleve. Cakes and Pastries. 3rd ed. Chicago: Calumet Baking Powder Co. (1923). 64p. Col. plates.

863 Delicious Desserts and Candies. Chicago: Price Flavoring Extract Co., 1923. 3rd ed. Col. pict. cover. 24p. advertising booklet.

864 Donahey, Mary Dickerson. The Calorie Cook Book. Economical recipes giving values of foods. Reilly & Lee Co., Chicago (1923). 1st ed. 250p.

865 Quinlan, Mary Ellen. The Universal Cook Book. From government bulletins. Universal Press, Chicago (c. 1923). 735, 7p.

866 Reynolds, Mary R. The Farm and Home Cook Book. A compilation of tested recipes. Chicago: Phelps Publishing Company, 1923. 162p. Wraps. Illus.

867 Walli, Mina. Keittokirja, Kolmas, Korjattu ja Laajennettu Painos Cook Book. (See Foreign sec.)

868 Bradley, Alice. Jams, Jellies and Marmalades Made with Certo. Ill.: 1924. Color illus. 24p. advertising booklet.

869 Drews, Dr. George J. Unfired Food and Tropho-Therapy. Designed for mothers, students and doctors. 360 recipes for health foods and drinks: such as flower salads and brawn foods, unfired pies and wedding cakes. Chicago: The Apyrtropher Pub. House, 1924. 9th ed. 337p.

870 The Fifty-Two Sunday Dinners. A selection of tested and balanced menus, easily prepared. Chicago: Woman's World Magazine Co. (1924). 64p.

871 Peterson, Anna Josephine and Badenoch, Nena N. Mrs. Anna J. Peterson's simplified cooking. Handbook of everyday meal preparation. Chicago: American School of Home Economics, 1924. 255p. Frontis. port. of author.

872 Baker, W. C. Mastercraft in Cakes and Decorating. Instructions, recipes and methods. Chicago: Bakers' Helpers Co., 1925. 194p. illus.

873 De Both, Jessie Marie. Home Makers' Cooking School Cook Book. From the Home Makers' School. Chicago, 1925. 319p.

874 Foods from Twenty Lands. Favorite recipes of women living in 20 countries, contributed in a spirit of good will. Chicago: Popular Mechanics Press, 1925. 172p.

875 Peters, Lulu Hunt. Diet and Health with Key to the Calories. Illus. by the author's small nephew, Dawson Hunt Perkins. Reilly & Lee Co., Chicago (1925). 127p.

876 Carruthers, Zilpha. The Path of the Gopatis. A story of the historic and symbolic records relating to the dairy cow. Illus. by Jessie Gillespie. Chicago: National Dairy Council (1926). 100p.

877 Fries, Alfred. The Blue Book of American Dishes. Illus. Approved recipes of professional cooks, compiled by the Chef of Pompeian Rooms, Congress Hotel. Chicago: the author (1926). 201p.

878 Morton, Lillian. Mrs. Morton's Cook Book for the Economical Housewife. Wraps. Chicago, 1926. 142p.

879 MY MEAT RECIPES. 103 Prize Winning Recipes. Meat charts. Wraps. National Live Stock and Meat Board, Chicago, 1926. 48p.

880 SHIRCLIFF, ARNOLD. The Edgewater Beach Hotel Salad Book. Unusual book on salads; beautiful illus. Chicago: Hotel Monthly Press: 1926. 265p.

881 TEN LESSONS ON MEAT. For H. S. Prepared by the National Live Stock and Meat Board Dept. of Home Econ. Chicago: National Live Stock and Meat Board, 1926. 79p. illus. Paper.

882 TODOROFF, ALEXANDER. What Is What In Groceries. Chicago: The Grocery Trade Publishing House (1926). 208p. illus.

883 WINDSOR COOK BOOK. Tested recipes from Pictorial Review—for the Windsor Range. Booklet. Montgomery Ward: Chicago, 1926. 48p.

884 CAKES AND DESSERTS. 150 tested recipes arranged by months. Booklet. Wraps. Illustrated. Woman's World Magazine: Chicago, 1927. 50p.

885 CHASE, A. W., M.D. Dr. Chase's New Receipt Book and Medical Advisor—or Information for Everybody. Naturally recipes, too. Chicago: M. A. Donohue, (1927). 366p.

885a THE COOKERY CALENDAR. Selected recipes for every month & balanced menus. Illus. Wraps. Woman's World Magazine Co., Chicago (1927). 50p.

886 DARRAH, JUANITA E. (compiled by) MODERN BAKING POWDER. An effective, healthful leavening agent. The occurrence of aluminum in foods and their effect on health. Illustrated. Calumet Baking Powder Co., Chicago, 1927. 125p.

886a THE FIFTY TWO SUNDAY DINNERS. For all the year. Menus and recipes. Illus. Wraps. Woman's World Magazine Co., Inc., Chicago, 1927. 66p.

887 LEITER, JOSEPH. Favorite Old Recipes. A comprehensive and diverse collection gathered from many sources. Chicago: Privately printed, 1927. Limited ed. of 1000 copies.

888 PARKER, MARIAN JANE. Selected Recipes and Menus for Parties, Holidays and Special Occasions. Chicago: Calumet Baking Powder Co., 1927. 40p. illus. Col. pict. cover.

888a SALADS AND SANDWICHES. 150 tested recipes, arranged by months. Illus. Wraps. Woman's World Magazine Co., Inc., Chicago, 1927. 50p.

889 TWENTY-FIRST YEAR BOOK AND CULINARY ALAMANAC, INTERNATIONAL COOKS ASS'N. INC. Chicago Branch, Chicago, 1927. 100p. and ads. Paper.

890 CHEESE, THE IDEAL FOOD. Many Delicious Ways to Serve It. Prepared by the Home Economics Dept. Chicago: Kraft-Phenix Cheese Co., 1928. 32p. illus. Col. pict. cover. Adv'g. booklet.

891 THE FISH BOOK. Recipes of fresh and salt water fish. Booklet, wraps. Illustrated. Woman's World Magazine: Chicago, 1928. 50p.

892 IDEAS FOR REFRESHMENT ROOMS, hotel restaurant, tea room, coffee shop, etc. A ready reference catering. Chicago: Hotel Monthly Press, 1928. 376p. illus.

893 MANDARIN CHOP SUEY COOK BOOK. (See Foreign sec.)

894 RECTOR, GEORGE. THE RECTOR COOK BOOK. World Famous Recipes, specialties from Noted Restaurants. Frontispiece of the old Rectors. Rector Publishing Co., Chicago (1928). 173p.

895 VAN WYCK, CAROLYN (ed.) PHOTOPLAY'S COOK BOOK. 150 Favorite Recipes of the Stars. Wraps. 3rd ed. Each recipe signed by a movie star. Chicago: W. F. Hall Printing Co., 1928. 64p.

896 VAUGHAN, ANITA GERTRUDE (compiler). With Mrs. Thomas Harwood, Mrs. Horace E. Collom. Notes on Cookery. Chicago: n. pub., 1928. Some recipes signed. 83p.

897 THE BEEF COOK BOOK. A collection of Attractive Recipes. Chicago: National Live Stock and Meat Board, 1929. 20p. advertising booklet. Pict. cover.

898 DE BOTH, JESSIE MARIE (Presentation copy) Modernistic Recipe—Menu Book. From the Home Makers' Schools. Chicago, 1929. 318p.

899 HALLIDAY, EVELYN G. AND NOBLE, ISABEL T. HOWS AND WHYS OF COOKING. Factors which contribute to success in preparation of foods. With illustrative recipes. Illustrated. University of Chicago: Illinois, 1929. 179p.

900 HALLOCK, GRACE T. Grain Through the Ages. With Thomas D. Wood, M.D. Prof. of Health Educ., Teachers College, Columbia Univ. Illus. by Jessie Gillespie. Chicago: The Quaker Oats Co., 1929. 95p.

901 HALLOCK, GRACE T. Hob o' the Mill. With Julia Wade Abbot, Dir. of Kindergartens, Phila. Pub. Schools. Chicago: The Quaker Oats Co., 1929. 111p.

902 MOWAT, JEAN. MEALS FOR SMALL FAMILIES. Recipes, and ideas for smart serving. Decorative end papers. Drawings. Laidlaw Brothers, Chicago (1929). 188p.

903 FISCHER, ESTHER ACKERSON. THE BOOK OF WEIGHT CONTROL. 20 practical Menus for daily guidance. Also Exercises. Hanson Scale Co., Chicago, 1930. 48p.

904 HERMAN THE HEALTH CHEF'S OWN MENU AND RECIPE BOOK. Picture of Herman on cover. Chicago (c. 1930). Spiral bdg. 89p. and ads.

905 HUGHES, WALTER C. The Story of Candy. The author, Secretary of The National Confectioners' Association of the United States. Chicago: (1930). Sewed. 30p.

906 The Master Baker's Manual. For Bakeries, Hotels, Restaurants, etc. Illus. Calumet Baking Powder Co., Chicago (1930). 127p.

907 The Menu Book of the American Housewife. Chicago: Manning Publishing, 1930. 57p. illus. Col. plates. Wraps.

908 Shircliffe, Arnold. The Edgewater Sandwich Book, with chapters on Supremes, Hors d'Oeuvres, Garnitures, Relishes & Flavored Butters. Plates. John Wiley, Inc., Chicago (1930). 260p.

909 Shuck, Edith G. (editor of cookery) and Bundesen, Dr. Herman N. (editor of special dietetics.) The Chicago Daily News Cook Book. A practical guide on menus and recipes. (Chicago:) Chicago Daily News (1930). 363p. illus. col'd pl., portraits.

910 The Story of Evaporated Milk. A study topic. Chicago: Evaporated Milk Ass'n (1930). 32p. illus.

911 Adams, Jean Prescott (Leona Malek) Meatless Meals. Decorative end papers. Laidlaw Bros.: Chicago (1931). 192p.

912 Drury, John. Dining in Chicago. Foreword by Carl Sandburg. John Day: New York, 1931. 274p.

913 Hallock, Grace T. Around the World with Hob. Illus. by Electra Papadopoulos. Chicago: The Quaker Oats Co., 1931. 44p. illus. Col. frontis. Wraps.

914 Hallock, Grace T. Travels of a Rolled Oat. Illus. by Jessie Gillespie. Chicago: The Quaker Oats Co., 1931. 78p.

915 Loudon, Dorothy Ayers (Editor) The Majestic Recipe Book. Refrigerator recipes. Wraps. Grigsby Grunow, Chicago, 1931. 40p.

916 Reeves, Grace G., Trilling, Mabel B., Williams, Florence. Problems in Food and the Family. Home Economics Text. Illus. J. B. Lippincott Co., Chicago (1931). 350p.

917 Sampson, Mrs. Emma (Speed). Miss Minerva's Cook Book. Reilly & Lee Co.: Chicago (1931). Illus. 280p.

918 Wallace, Lily Haxworth. The Woman's World Cook Book. A comprehensive manual of cookery. Illustrated. Extra large plates. Reilly & Lee Co., Chicago (1931). 468p.

919 International Cooks' Association Section Chicago. 26th Year Book and Culinary Almanac. Portraits. Herbs, spices, condiments; national dishes. Chicago: 1932. 104p. Wraps.

920 Richards, Paul. Cakes for Bakers. Frontis. port. of author. Chicago: Bakers' Helper Co., 1932. 638p. illus.

921 The Cook's Book. A talk on Baking Powder, collection of choice recipes by Mrs. Janet Hill. Illustrated. Wraps. Jaques Mfg. Co., Chicago, 1933. 48p.

922 Halliday, Evelyn G. and Noble, Isabel T. Hows and Whys

of Cooking. Rev. ed. 1933. 252p. (See No. 899).

923 International Cooks' Association Section Chicago. Brief encyclopedia of foods, historical data. Chicago: 1933.

924 Mandeville, Paul. Eggs. Two vols. treating of the history of the hen; the hen as food (with recipes). Prepared by a staff of specialists. Chicago: Progress Publications (1933). 304p. illus.; 323-631p.

925 May, Madeline. The International Cook Book. Wilcox & Follett Co., Chicago (1933). Looseleaf. Obl. 91p.

926 The Modern Way of Canning and Cooking. Chicago: Burpee Can Sealer Co. (1933). 77p. illus. Ads. Wraps.

927 New Salads, Bridge Luncheons, Canned Meals. From the Women's Pages. Illustrated. The Chicago Daily News, Chicago (1933). 400p.

928 The Palmer House Cook Book. 1022 Original Recipes for Home Use. Created and tested by Ernest E. Amiet, Exec. Chef. Intro. by Walter L. Gregory, Mgr. Pub. Chicago: Palmer House. Printed Idianapolis, Ind., 1933. 310p. 1st ed.

929 Bauer, Fred. The Baker's Library. Cook-Art-Craft. Complete book on cake ornamenting designs & instructions. Chicago: Fred Bauer, 1934. Ilus.

930 Calkins, Myrtle. The Home Menu Cook Book. Including recipes for popular mixed drinks. Chicago, Goldsmith Pub. (1934). 253p.

931 DeBoth, Jessie Marie. The Fashion Book of Recipes. Plain and fancy recipes. Dinette cookery. Chicago, 1934. 316p.

932 Martin, Mary Hale. My Best Recipes. Chicago: Libby, McNeill & Libby, 1934. 87p. illus.

933 A Modern Kitchen Guide. A complete book of up-to-date recipes & drinks. Wraps. Sears, Roebuck & Co., Chicago, 1934. 255p.

934 Osborn, Marjorie Noble. Jolly Times Cook Book. Simple Recipes for Young Beginners. Illus. by Clarence Biers. Small book, large print. Rand McNally & Co., Chicago (1934). 64p.

935 Shircliffe, Arnold. The Edgewater Beach Hotel Salad Book. Chicago: Hotel Monthly Press, 1934. 5th printing. Many col. plates. 306p.

936 Aunt Jemima's Album of Secret Recipes. All about waffles and pancakes and what to serve with them. Booklet, wraps. Colorful illustrations. Aunt Jemima Pancake Flour: Chicago, 1935. 33p.

937 Rivers, Frank. The Hotel Butcher, Garde Manger and Carver. Meat for Hotels, Restaurants, Clubs & Institutions. Profusely illustrated. Decorative end papers. Hotel Monthly Press, Chicago, 1935. 128p.

938 Favorite Recipes of Famous People. Chicago: Felix Mendel-

sohn, Auditorium Hotel (c. 1936). 232p. Paper, metal binder.

939 VEHLING, JOSEPH DOMMERS. Apicius. Cookery and Dining in Imperial Rome. Subscription ed. First trans. into English. Chicago: Walter M. Hill, 1936. 301p.

940 KINYON, KATE W., HOPKINS, THOMAS. JUNIOR FOODS (revised) For boys and girls. Drawings by C. E. B. Bernard. Benj. H. Sanborn & Co., Chicago (1937). 1st ed. 362p.

941 SEXTON, SHERMAN. THE SEXTON COOK BOOK. Institutional cooking. Published by Sexton, Chicago (1937). 1st ed. 442p.

942 CALENDAR OF MEAT RECIPES. Illus. Wraps. Chicago, 1938. 40p.

943 SONDHEIM, S. CLAIRE. My Favorite Recipe by 500 of the World's Best Cooks. Consolidated Book Pub., Chicago; 1938. 244p.

944 THOUGHTS FOR FOOD, A Menu Aid. Chicago: Institute Publishing Co., 1938. 323p.

945 ACCEPTED FOODS and Their Nutritional Significance. Descriptions of Products. American Medical Ass'n., Chicago, 1939. 492p.

946 GAIGE, CROSBY (editor). Season To Taste—Spices, and How to Use Them. Dishes of glamour and how to prepare them, with accent on spice. Chicago: Griffith Laboratories, 1939. Copyright, American Spice Trade Assoc. Map of world as end papers. 48p. adv'g. booklet. Col. pict. cover.

947 THE VITAMINS. A Symposium under the auspices of the Council on Pharmacy & Chemistry and the Council on Foods of the A.M.A. American Medical Ass'n. Chicago, 1939. 637p.

947a BEROLZHEIMER, RUTH (edited by). COOKIE BOOK. All kinds of cookies-baked and refrigerator. 250 recipes. Illus. Wraps. Culinary Arts Institute, Chicago, 1940. 48p.

947b BEROLZHEIMER, RUTH (edited by). DAIRY DISHES. 300 Tasty, Healthful recipes. Illus. Wraps. Culinary Arts Institute, Chicago, 1940. 48p.

947c BEROLZHEIMER, RUTH (edited by) 500 DELICIOUS DISHES FROM LEFTOVERS. To get the most from the food you buy. Illus. Wraps. Culinary Arts Institute, Chicago, 1940. 48p.

947d BEROLZHEIMER, RUTH (edited by) 500 SNACKS. Bright ideas for entertaining. Illus. Wraps. Culinary Arts Institute, Chicago, 1940. 48p.

947e BEROLZHEIMER, RUTH (edited by) 500 Tasty Sandwiches. Especially for parties. Illus. Wraps. Culinary Arts Institute, Chicago, 1941. 48p.

947f BEROLZHEIMER, RUTH (edited by) 300 TASTY, HEALTHFUL DAIRY DISHES. Economical recipes. Illus. Wraps. Culinary Arts Institute, Chicago, 1940. 48p.

947g BEROLZHEIMER, RUTH (edited by) 250 DELECTABLE DESSERTS. Custards, souffles, sauces, puddings, cakes. Illus. Wraps. Culinary Arts Institute, Chicago, 1940. 48p.

947h Berolzheimer, Ruth (edited by) 250 Refrigerator Desserts. Lucious recipes. Illus. Wraps. Culinary Arts Institute, Chicago, 1941. 48p.

947i Berolzheimer, Ruth (edited by) 250 Ways to Prepare Poultry and Game Birds. Your grandmother's way, and yours. Illus. Wraps. Culinary Arts Institute, Chicago, 1940. 48p.

948 Den Dooven, K. Camille. Modern Cook Book. The art of cooking and baking for the housewife. Hamilton Ross, Chicago (1940). 238p.

948a Recipes for Modern Menus . . Cakes. Wraps. Reprinted from The Woman's Pages. The Chicago Daily News (1940). 32p.

948b Recipes for Modern Menus . . Cookies. Reprinted from The Woman's Pages. Wraps. The Chicago Daily News (1940). 32p.

948c Recipes for Modern Menus . . Meats. Reprinted from The Woman's Pages. Wraps. The Chicago Daily News (1940). 32p.

948d Recipes for Modern Menus . . Party Desserts. Reprinted from The Woman's Pages. Wraps. The Chicago Daily News (1940). 32p.

948e Recipes for Modern Menus . . Salads. Reprinted from The Woman's Pages. Wraps. The Chicago Daily News (1940). 32p.

948f Recipes for Modern Menus . . Vegetables. Reprinted from The Woman's Pages. Wraps. The Chicago Daily News (1940). 32p.

948g Time for a Party. A Hostess Book of Baking Recipes. Illus. Wraps. General Foods Corp., Chicago, 1940. 38p.

949 A Treasury of Meat Recipes. Well illustrated booklet. Wraps. National Live Stock and Meat Board: Chicago, 1940. 40p.

950 Berolzheimer, Ruth (Edited by) The Dairy Cook Book. All about the use of milk and milk products. Illustrated. End paper photographs. Culinary Arts Institute, Chicago (1941). 256p.

951 Berolzheimer, Ruth (editor) Breakfast & Brunch Cookbook. Pamphlet. Illus. Chicago, 1942. 48p.

952 Hinman, Robert B., Harris, Robert B. The Story of Meat. History of and information about the industry. Foreword by Jacob Simonson. Illus. Decorative end papers. Swift & Co., Chicago (1942). 291p.

953 Berolzheimer, Ruth (Edited & Revised by) Victory Cook Book. Wartime Edition with Victory Substitutes and Economical Recipes. From the Delineator Cook Book. Profusely illustrated. Decorative end papers. Thumb index. Consolidated Book Publishers, Chicago, 1944. 816p. and 64p.

954 Creamer, Jack B. The Handy Household Manual. Answers lots

of 'how to' questions. Illustrated. Ziff-Davis, Chicago, 1946. 190p.

955 Berolzheimer, Ruth (Ed.) The United States Regional Cook Book. Illus. by Albert H. Winkler. Culinary Arts Institute, Chicago, 1947. Thumb index. Col. end papers. 752p.

956 Halliday, Evelyn G. and Noble, Isabel T. Hows and Whys of Cooking. Rev. ed. (1947). 328p. (See No. 899).

957 Eskew, Garnett L. Salt, The Fifth Element. Illus. by Mary Enslow. Chicago: J. G. Ferguson & Assoc., 1948. 239p.

958 Ald, Roy. Favorite Recipes of Famous Men. Mouth-watering cookery; not for the calorie-conscious. Foreword by Eddie Cantor. Illustrated by the author. Ziff-Davis Publishing Co., Chicago (1949). 1st ed. 105p.

959 Indorante & De Weese. Delightful Recipes from the Four Corners of the World, by the "Recipe Kings." 36 countries. Wraps. Chicago, 1949. 124p.

960 Berolzheimer, Ruth. Encyclopedic Cookbook. Cooking instructions and variations in recipes. Illustrated. Thumb index. Culinary Arts Institute, Chicago, 1950. 974p. lxvi p. index.

961 Vehling, Joseph D. America's Table. Dictionary form. 10,000 descriptions and explanations. Most complete. Chicago, 1950. 882p.

962 Berolzheimer, Ruth (ed) 500 Tasty Snacks. Ideas for entertaining. Pamphlet. Illus. Chicago, 1952. 48p.

963 Berolzheimer, Ruth (edited by) 200 Ways to Prepare Meat. Illustrated. Booklet, wraps. Culinary Arts Institute, Chicago, 1952. 48p.

964 Given, Meta. Modern Encyclopedia of Cooking. Complete; for the beginner and the expert. Illustrated; colorful end papers. G Ferguson and Associates, Chicago, 1952. 1699p.

965 Harvey, Peggy. When the Cook's Away. Wonderfully simple recipes for sophisticated entertaining. Foreword by Moss Hart. Decorations by Franklin McMahon. Henry Regnery Co., Chicago, 1952. 159p.

966 Stearns, Osborne Putnam. Paris Is A Nice Dish. (See Foreign sec.)

967 Berolzheimer, Ruth (edited by) 300 Ways to Serve Eggs. Entrees, main dishes, salads. Booklet, wraps, illustrations. Culinary Arts Institute, Chicago, 1953. 48p.

968 Berolzheimer, Ruth (edited by) 250 Refrigerator Desserts. Illustrated. Booklet, wraps. Culinary Arts Institute, Chicago, 1953. 48p.

969 Berolzheimer, Ruth. 250 Ways to Prepare Meat. Illustrated. Booklet: wraps—back cover missing. Consolidated Book Publishers. Chicago, 1953. 48p.

970 BEROLZHEIMER, RUTH (ed.) 2000 USEFUL FACTS ABOUT FOOD. Pamphlet. Illus. Chicago, 1953. 48p.

971 McDERMOTT, IRENE E. AND TRILLING, MABEL B. AND NICHOLAS, FLORENCE WILLIAMS. Food for Better Living. Rev. Ed. Profusely illus. Chicago: J. B. Lippincott Co. (1954). 581p.

972 BROBECK, FLORENCE (Compiled & edited) The "Best-of-All!" Cook Book. A library of great cook books. Beautifully illus. Kingston House: Chicago (1960). 1st ed. 512p.

973 THE ART OF MAKING BREAD. Bread and rolls. Pamphlet. wraps. Northwestern Yeast Co. Chicago, n.d. 20p.

974 A BOOK OF PRACTICAL RECIPES FOR THE HOUSEWIFE. Chicago: Chicago Evening American, n.d. 244p.

975 GIFFORD, MARIE. 69 Ration Recipes for Meat From Marie Gifford's Kitchen. Illus. booklet. Chicago: Armour and Co., n.d. (World War II). 30p.

976 ICE CREAM, Retail and Wholesale Manufacturing. Booklet. Chicago, n.d. 24p.

977 THE LITTLE TREASURE CHEST. Recipes and household hints, games & puzzles. Ads for Dr. Peter's Gomozo. Wraps. Pub. by Dr. Peter Fahrney & Sons, Chicago, n.d. 38p.

978 MATA SKRZYNKA SKARBOW. (See Foreign sec.)

979 MEAT COOKERY. Chicago: Institute of American Meat Packers, n.d. 24p. Wraps.

980 NATIONAL HOME COOK BOOK. Chicago: National Cloak and Mfg. Co., n.d. 191p.

981 PERRETT, LOUISE. Recipes, My Friends' and My Own. Designed and illustrated by the author. Chicago: Reilly and Britton Co., n.d. Blank pages, not numbered.

982 60 WAYS TO SERVE HAM. Pamphlet, Armour & Co. Illus. Chicago. n.d. 28p.

983 69 RATION RECIPES FOR MEAT. Armour & Co. Wraps. n.d. Chicago

984 THE STORY OF MEAT. A brief history of the live stock and meat industry . . from farm to table. Chicago: Institute of American Meat Packers, n.d. 48p. illus.

985 VEST POCKET PASTRY BOOK. 200 receipts from the magazine, and adapted to the use of hotels, etc. 6th ed. Chicago: The Hotel Monthly Press, n.d. 90p.

986 WEEDMAN, F. ELECTRIC COOKERY. Pamphlet. Hotpoint, Chicago. 72p.

Indiana

987 EDIBILIA. ABC OF VALUABLE PRIVATE RECEIPTS. Pub. by Ladies of Christ Church, Indianapolis, 1873. Illus.

988 KIMBALL, LAURA A. (Anon.) Manual of Practical Housekeeping. The household treasure, compiled from recipes of ladies of Fort Wayne and other places, printed

for benefit of Plymouth Congregational Church. Fort Wayne: Gazette Book Printing House, 1873. 128p. and ads.

989 THE HOUSEKEEPER'S HELP: A book of tested recipes. The proceeds from the sale are to be devoted to "Foreign Missions," as connected with the "Woman's Board." Indianapolis: Baker, Schmidlap, 1876. 139p.

990 JENNINGS, MRS. S. C. The Household Friend; a practical domestic guide for home comfort. Lafayette, Septimus Vater, printer, 1876. 246p.

991 INDIANAPOLIS COOK BOOK, compiled by the ladies of the Pattison Methodist Episcopal Church. Indianapolis: Hasselman-Journal Co., 1883. 191p. Signed recipes.

992 THE PERFECT COOK. Improved edition. Pub. by the Ladies of the St. Paul's Episcopal Church, Evansville, Ind. . . Evansville: Journal Co., 1885. 81p. and ads.

993 THE PUREST AND BEST. Booklet of recipes using cornstarch. Wraps. Muzzy Starch Co., Elkhart, 1885. 16p.

994 REAMY, MRS. L. B. L. Tried Recipes. A valuable collection of tested recipes and useful suggestions, gathered from various sources. Richmond: the author, 1888. 609p.

995 HAMILTON, MYRTA. Helpful Hints to Housekeepers. Collected and compiled by the Young People's Circle of Plymouth Church, Indianapolis, Ind. . . . Indianapolis, W. B. Burford, 1890. 117p.

996 KEESLING, B. F. Keesling's Book of Recipes and Household Hints. Logansport: B. F. Keesling, 1890. 328, xvi p. and ads.

997 PRAIRIE CITY COOK BOOK. 500 tested recipes for the preparation of daily and occasional dishes. Recommended by experienced housekeepers. Compiled by the ladies of Centenary M. E. Church. Terre Haute: Moore & Langen, 1891. 134p.

998 HARLAND, MARION. MARION HARLAND'S COMPLETE COOKBOOK. A great book in a lavish culinary period. Illus. Pict. cover. Indianapolis: Bobbs-Merrill Co., 1903. 1st ed. 780p.

999 COOKING CLUB. Pictorial wraps. Illus. The Practical Culinary Magazine, Goshen, 1906. 62p.

1000 DAINTIES. Wraps. The Home Missionary Society of the Friends Church, Portland (c. 1907). 40p. and ads.

1001 FIRST BAPTIST CHURCH COOK BOOK. Issued as feature of the Christmas Fair; compiled by the Ladies of the Church. Wraps. Pub. in book form by Irvington Print Shop, Indianapolis, 1907. 168p. and ads.

1002 20TH CENTURY COOK BOOK. A feast of Good Things. The Mite Society of the Presbyterian Church, Bristol, 1907. 159p.

1003 The Otterbein Cook Book. Published by the Ladies' Aid Society of the United Brethren Church, Honey Creek, Ind. . . Middletown: Press of the Middletown News (1908). 160p. illus. Ads.

1004 Cook Book. By the ladies of the Presbyterian Church (Fowler), 1909. 190p. and ads.

1005 Princeton Cook Book. First Presbyterian Church, Princeton, Ind. (Evansville: Printed by Keller-Crescent Prtg. & Eng. Co., 1909.) 205p.

1006 Barfield, Mrs. D. R. (editor). Our Girl's Cook Book. Pub. by the Working Girls' Association, Evansville, Indiana. (Evansville: Journal Job Printing Co.), 1910. 107p.

1007 Hiller, Elizabeth O. Leftover Foods and How to Use Them. Suggestions regarding the preservation of foods in the home. Written for the McCray Refrigerator Co. Kendalville, 1910. 32p. illus. Col. frontis.

1008 Ware, Clara Priscilla Buckland. The Ideal Cook Book. Marion: Commercial Printing Co. (1912). 233p. and ads. Portrait.

1009 Hough, Charlotte Amelia. Willy Lou's House Book; a collection of proved recipes, hints and suggestions for practical cooking, housekeeping and housewifery. Indianapolis; The Bobbs-Merrill Company (1913). 175p.

1010 Rhodes, Susie Root and Hopkins, Grace Porter. The Ecoomy Administration Cook Book. Hammond: W. B. Conkey Co. (1913). 696p. illus.

1011 Frich, Lilla P. Cooking. Book One . . Illustrated. From the Extension Department of Muncie Normal Institute. Muncie, 1914. 271p.

1012 Metcalf, Martha L. Food and Cookery. Student's Manual in household Arts. Industrial Education Co., Indianapolis, 1915. 299p. illus. and Index.

1013 A Collection of Rare, Original, Tested Recipes for Cooking and Baking. Autographed recipes. Ladies of Lutheran Church, Portland (before 1918). 83p. and ads.

1014 Foods, Their Preparation and Serving. Public Schools of Indianapolis, Ind. No pub. (1919). 170p. Copyright by Russell C. Lowell.

1015 Philathea Class Cook Book. Westminster Presbyterian Church, South Bend (c. 1920). 64p. and ads.

1016 Presbyterian Cook Book, 4th ed. Autographed recipes. Oilcloth covers. First Presbyterian Church, Huntington, 1921. 87p.

1017 Market Basket Recipes. Comprehensive recipes contributed to the market basket pages of the Richmond Item by its patrons. Richmond: The Item Newspaper Co., 1923. 232p. Wraps. Ads.

1018 COOK BOOK. Autographed recipes. Compiled and published by the Members of the Day Nursery Association, Richmond, 1924. 171p. and ads.

1019 A BOOK OF RECIPES. Autographed recipes. Wraps. Compiled and edited by the young women of the "Truth Seekers" class of Zion Evangelical Sunday School, Indianapolis, 1925. 66p.

1020 COOK BOOK. Of the Home Economics Clubs of Cass County. Autographed recipes. Wraps. (Churubusco: Gray Press, 1926). 256p.

1021 DOMESTIC SCIENCE COOK BOOK. For the use of the Public Schools. Revised edition. Board of Education, South Bend, 1926. 212p.

1022 SHANKS, LAURA E. The Farmer's Guide Cook Book. Tested recipes contributed by readers. Huntington: The Farmer's Guide (1927). 192p.

1023 THE SWANS DOWN WAY TO PERFECT CAKES. Wraps. Igleheart Brothers, Inc., Evansville, 1928. 12p.

1024 QUAKER COOK BOOK FROM QUAKER KITCHENS. Autographed recipes. Oilcloth covers. Calendar Club of First Friends Church, Indianapolis, 1930. 175p.

1025 WILSON, ROBERT FORREST. How to Wine and Dine in Paris. Indianapolis: Bobbs-Merrill (1930). 122p.

1026 THE VITAMINS. A Symposium on the Present Status of the Knowledge of Vitamins. Special edition. Mead Johnson & Co., Evansville, 1932.

1027 AMIET, ERNEST E. THE PALMER HOUSE COOK BOOK. 1022 original recipes for home use. Bobbs-Merrill Co., Indianapolis (1933) 1st ed. 310p.

1028 EASTERN STAR COOK BOOK. Compiled by the Nettie Ransford Chapter, No. 464, Order of the Eastern Star, Indianapolis. Indianapolis: Nettie Ransford Chapter, No. 464 (1933). 104p.

1029 A COOK BOOK. Compiled by the Teachers of Home Economics. Plaid oilcloth covers. Board of Education, School City of South Bend, 1921, revised 1936. 288p.

1030 HILLIS, MARJORIE AND FOLTZ, BERTINA. CORNED BEEF AND CAVIAR. For the live-aloner. Drawings by Cipé Pineles. Bobbs-Merrill, Indianapolis, 1937. 1st ed. 195p.

1031 HILLIS, MARJORIE. ORCHIDS ON YOUR BUDGET, or Live Smartly on What Have You. Illus. Indianapolis, 1937. 1st ed. 171p.

1032 PRICE, LITA AND BONNET, HARRIET. MAIDCRAFT. A Guide for the One-Maid Household. Illustrated. Bobbs-Merrill: Indianapolis, 1937. 1st ed. 216p.

1033 CANNING. The Ball Blue Book of Canning and Preserving Recipes. Well illus. Muncie: Ball Brothers, 1938. 56p. and ads. Wraps.

1034 COOK BOOK. Wraps. Women's Auxiliary, Westminster Presbyterian Church. South Bend, 1930's 64p. and ads.

1035 CENTENNIAL COOK BOOK 1840-1940. Compiled by the Missionary Society. Autographed recipes. First Presbyterian Church, Warsaw, 1940. 75p. and ads.

1036 GAMBLE, MARGARET TURNER AND PORTER, MARGARET CHANDLER. To MARKET TO MARKET. A complete practical guide to the selection of staples, meat, poultry, eggs, dairy products. Illustrated. Bobbs-Merrill Co.: Indianapolis, 1940. 1st ed. 279p.

1037 PRICE, LITA; BONNET, HARRIET. How to Manage without a Maid. A complete and practical guide. Illustrated by Elizabeth Dodds. Bobbs-Merrill; Indianapolis (1942). 1st ed. 220p.

1038 ROMBAUER, IRMA S., BECKER, MARION ROMBAUER. The Joy of Cooking. Bobbs-Merrill: Indianapolis, 1951. 1011p (see No. 1963).

1039 JOHNNY APPLESEED, ORCHARDIST. A life of John Chapman. Prepared by the staff of the Public Library of Fort Wayne and Allen County. Illus. Pictorial wraps. Private printing. Indiana, November, 1952. Unnumbered p.

1040 TRACY, MARIAN (Selected by) COAST TO COAST COOKERY. Recipes selected by America's food editors from Alabama to Wyoming —some about Canada, too. Indiana University: Bloomington, 1952. 1st ed. 318p.

1041 TRACY, MARIAN. Marian Tracy's Complete Chicken Cookery. Illus. by Marguerite Burgess. Bobbs-Merrill Co., Indianapolis, 1953. 1st ed. Illus. on title. 234p.

1042 FRICH, LILLA P. Basic Principles of Domestic Science. A course of 72 illus. lessons. Author, of Minneapolis P.S. Muncie: Muncie Normal Institute, n.d. 200, 6p.

Iowa

1043 COOK BOOK OF THE NORTHWEST. Written for the Ladies of the Westminster Presbyterian Church. Cloth. Quaint ads. Perhaps the first printed in Iowa. Keokuk, 1875. 156p.

1044 SHANKLAND, MRS. EDWARD R. The Matron's Household Manual. Dubuque: Palmer, Winall & Co., 1875. 117p.

1045 "76" A Cook book edited by the ladies of Plymouth Church. Des Moines: Mills & Co., 1876. 278p.

1046 SHANKLAND, MRS. EDWARD R. The Matron's Household Manual. New and improved ed. for the "Centennial." Assisted by Sue W. Hetherington. Dubuque: Palmer, Winall (1876). 137p.

1047 WELCH, MARY B. Mrs. Welch's Cook Book. The author, instructor in domestic economy, Iowa Agric. College. Des Moines: Mills & Co., 1884. 279p. illus.

1048 POWERS, KATE. Best Receipts. Containing thoroughly tested and reliable receipts for cooking, home remedies, and general information, contributed especially for this work. Sheldon (c. 1900). 132p. Autographed recipes. Wraps.

1049 PROTEUS CLUB COOK BOOK. . . (Des Moines:) The G. A. Miller Prtg. Co. (1900). 83p.

1050 ALLYN, ANGIE M. (compiler). The Mt. Ayr. Cook Book . . . Mt. Ayr: H. J. Reger, 1901. 184p. and ads.

1051 BURLINGTON LADIES COOK BOOK, and 25 secrets of success; how to make a fortune. Burlington: G. Bree (1901). 92p.

1052 THE PELLA COOK BOOK. Choice and Tested Recipes Contributed by Pella's Dutch and American Housekeepers. Pella, 1901. 125p. and ads.

1053 TRIED AND TRUE RECIPES. Autographed recipes. Cloth. Quaint ads. Compiled and published by the Choir Guild of St. John's Episcopal Church, Dubuque, 1903. 158p.

1054 BOYS' AND GIRLS' HOME COOK BOOK. Published and put on sale at the annual fair, Nov. 23 and 24, 1906. (Sioux City). 111p. and ads.

1055 THE W.R.C. COOK BOOK AND USEFUL HINTS FOR THE HOUSEHOLD. Autographed recipes. Pictorial wraps. The Guardsman Printing Co., Red Oak, 1906. 256p.

1056 ST. ANDREW'S GUILD COOK BOOK. Chariton, Iowa. Signed recipes. Frontispiece photograph of church. Ads. Knoxville, 1907. 198p.

1057 THE NINETEEN TEN FRIDAY CLUB COOK BOOK. Oilcloth wraps. Denison, 1910. 101p.

1058 SPIRIT LAKE COOK BOOK. Autographed recipes. Ads. Compiled and published by the Ladies' Aid Society of the M. E. Church, Spirit Lake, Beacon Point, 1910. 95p.

1059 WILSON, LUCY ELIZABETH. A Practical Cook Book. Cedar Rapids: Torch Press, 1912. 210p.

1060 PARSONS, MRS. CHARLES F. Reliable Cook Book. Tried and Approved Recipes. Cedar Rapids: Commercial Art Printing Co., 1913. 195p.

1061 RECIPES FOR LUNCHEONS, DESSERTS AND BEVERAGES. Contributed by famous cooks. Sioux Rapids: Plager & Nelson, 1913. 48p.

1062 CONGREGATIONAL COOK BOOK. —Ladies of the Congregational Church, Marshalltown, Ia. . . Marshalltown: Herald Print. Co., 1914. 228p. and ads.

1063 THE BEST OF THE WEST. Our Friends' Recipes Compiled by Several Ladies. Cloth pictorial covers. Many interesting ads. Sioux City (c. 1915). 102p.

1064 THE RELIABLE COOK BOOK. A collection of choice and tried recipes by the Ladies' Society of the Congregational Church. . . Eldora, 1917. 197p. illus. 3rd ed. rev. and enl.

1065 OUR FRIENDS' RECIPES. Compiled by Mrs. Benjamin Davidson, Mrs. Isaac G. Trauerman, Mrs.

Herman Galinsky, Mrs. Emil Marx. Assisted by Mrs. Walter Franc, Mrs. Benjamin Shufein, Mrs. Joseph Bolstein. Sioux City, Davidson Bros. Co. (1918). 134p.

1066 "QVINNAN OCH HEMMETS" NYA KOKBOK. (See Foreign sec.)

1067 THE HOSTESS COOK BOOK. Written by Iowa women. Des Moines: Women's and Children's Ass'n. (1923). 287p. and ads. Ports. of recipe donors.

1068 WALLACE, JOSEPHINE M. Aunt Josephine's Book of Recipes. Des Moines: Wallace Publishing Co., 1923. 71p. Wraps.

1069 HAGGART, MARGARET H. Foods and Cookery. A handbook for homemakers and teachers of home economics, compiled for Dept. of Foods and Nutrition, Div. Home Econ., Iowa State College. Ames: The Collegiate Press, Inc., 1926. 254p. Frontis., illus.

1070 AMES WOMAN'S CLUB COOK BOOK, compiled by club members. Ames (1930). 262p.

1071 WYLIE, JOSEPHINE. (Compiler). My Better Homes & Gardens Cook Book. Designed by Rex F. Stark. Des Moines, Meredith Pub. Co. (1930). Illus.

1072 WYLIE, JOSEPHINE (compiler) MY BETTER HOMES & GARDENS LIFETIME COOKBOOK. Looseleaf book with tabs; blank pages for additions. Better Homes & Gardens: Des Moines, 1931. 177p.

1073 STOVALL, WILLIAM G. Jean's Junior Cook Book. Monroe: Mirror Publishing Co. (1932). 95p. illus.

1074 WAITT, CLARA FARMER. Clara Waitt's Cook Book. Sioux City, Verstegen Printing Co. (1933). 108p. and ads. Wraps.

1075 IOWA BLUE CHEESE. Pictorial Wraps. Agricultural Experiment Station, Iowa State College of Agriculture and Mechanic Arts. Ames, Feb. 1935. p. 253 to 277.

1076 PERSIS PANTRY. 3rd ed. by the Ladies of First Presbyterian Church, Fairfield. Ads. Wraps. Plastic spiral binding. Printed by Lockridge Times, Lockridge, 1946. 609p.

1077 NAUVOO DISTRICT, THE REORGANIZED CHURCH OF JESUS CHRIST OF LATTER DAY SAINTS COOK BOOK. 236 Favorite Tested Recipes. 72 Household hints. Autographed recipes. Illus. Mimeographed. Wraps. Sponsored by the Women's Department. Compiled and printed by Shirley S. Howard, Fort Madison, July, 1948.

1078 NEW SWEDEN CENTERMAID COOK BOOK. Recipes by Members and Friends of the First Augustana Evangelical Lutheran Church. Ads. Autographed recipes. Wraps. Spiral binding. Lockridge, 1948. 98p.

1079 BERGER, FLORENCE E. (Sudhoff) Cooking for Christ, the liturgical year in the kitchen. Des Moines, National Catholic Rural Life Conference (1949). 127p.

1080 COOKING ROUND THE WORLD AND AT HOME. Plastic bdg. Pub. by The Mashaka County King's Daughters & Sons. Oskaloosa, 1949. 104p.

1081 WHAT'S COOKIN' IN HARCOURT, IOWA. Autographed recipes. Photo of Harcourt School Gymnasium. Photo of Church on title page. Pictorial wraps. Spiral plastic binding. Illus. Ads. The Harcourt Lutheran Ladies Aid. Harcourt, 1950. 165p.

1082 NICHOLS, NELL B. GOOD HOME COOKING ACROSS THE U.S.A. A Source Book of American Foods. Illustrated by Ray Irwin. Decorative end papers. Iowa State College Press: Ames, 1952. 1st ed. 560p.

1083 THE CANDY BOOK. Booklet. Pictorial wraps. Woolverton Printing and Publishing Co., Osage. 24p.

1084 GOOD THINGS YOU HAVE EATEN IN WATERLOO HOMES. Over 200 Choice Recipes from the Waterloo Daily Reporter. Autographed recipes, giving address of contributors. Cloth. Matt Parrott & Sons: Waterloo. n.d.

Kansas

1085 THE LADIES' FLORAL CALENDAR AND HOUSEHOLD RECEIPT BOOK. Lawrence: B. W. Woodward (1868). 32p. Wraps.

1086 THE KANSAS HOME COOK-BOOK: consisting of recipes contributed by ladies of Leavenworth and other towns and cities for the Kansas Home for the Friendless. Leavenworth: J. C. Ketcheson, book and job printer, 1874. 264p. and ads.

1087 THE KANSAS HOME COOK BOOK. Leavenworth: 1881 (See No. 1086).

1088 SCOTT, ANNA M. The U.S.C. Cook Book, compiled for the Universalist Social Circle of Junction City, Kansas . . . Junction City: Tribune Job Print, 1895. 91p.

1089 KANSAS KOOK-BOOK FOR KANSAS KOOKS . . . Topeka, 1900. 84p.. illus.

1090 GIST, ELIZABETH. The Gist of Domestic Science . . . Topeka: F. M. Stevens & Sons, 1905. 128p. and ads.

1091 PRESYTERIAN COOK BOOK. Emporia: The Aid Society of the First Presbyterian Church (1906). 240p., illus. Ads.

1092 CENTRAL CONGREGATIONAL CHURCH COOK BOOK . . . Topeka: Press of the Trapp Print-Shop (1913). 126p. incl. front., plates, portraits. Ads.

1093 GOOD THINGS TO EAT. Ladies Society of the First Presbyterian Church. Hutchinson: Sixth Division of the Ladies Society, First Presbyterian Church, 1913. 248p.

1094 PRACTICAL COOKERY. A compilation of principles of cookery and recipes, and the etiquette and service of the table. Dept. of Food Econ. and Nutrition, Kansas State Agric. College. 4th ed. rev. Manhattan: Dept. of Printing, Kansas

State Agric. College. 250p. illus. Frontis., 1920.

1095 Twentieth Century Cook Book. An up-to-date and skillful preparation on the Art of Cooking, candy-making, drying fruits and vegetables, and butchering. Girard: Appeal Pub. (1921). 182p., diagrams, frontis.

1096 Good Things to Eat. Compiled by the Daughters of the First Presbyterian Church—Signed recipes. Wraps. Ads. Salina, 1922. 184p.

1097 The Thursday Afternoon Cooking Club's Cook Book. (Wichita Cooking Club Cook Book). Signed recipes. Wichita: Thursday Afternoon Cooking Club (c. 1922). 360p.

1098 Meuser, Mary Louise. What to Cook and How to Cook It . . . Paola: no pub., 1926. 127, 5p. Wraps.

1099 Fredericks, Anderson. 100 Cocktails. How to Make Them and What to Eat with Them. Little Blue Book No. 1688. Haldeman-Julius, Girard (1931). Wraps. 32p.

1100 The Household Searchlight Recipe Book . . . Topeka: The Household Magazine, 1931. 304p.

1101 The Household Searchlight Recipe Book. Compiled and edited by Ida Migliario, Harriet W. Allard, Zorado Z. Titus, Irene Westbrook. Topeka: The Household Magazine, 1932. 304p. (See No. 1100).

1102 A Collection of Proved Recipes. Compiled by the Junior and Senior League. Atchison: Press of Burbank's Print Shop, 1933. 132p.

1103 The Household Searchlight Recipe Book. Compiled and edited by Ida Migliario, Harriet Allard, Zorada Titus, Irene Nunemaker. Thumb index. Colorful end papers. The Household Magazine, Topeka, 1937. 320p.

1104 Favorite Recipe Cook Book. Ladies Aid of Trousdale Methodist Church. Trousdale, 1939. 72p.

1105 Justin, Margaret M.; Rust, Lucille Osborn; Vail, Gladys E. Foods. An Introductory college course at Kansas State College. Illus. Houghton Mifflin Co., Boston (1948). 723p.

1106 The 20th Century Club Cook Book. Plastic bdg., many ads. Compiled by the 20th Century Club, Wichita, 1949. 216p.

1107 The Presbyterian Cook Book. Published by the Ladies of the Presbyterian Church. Atchison: n.d. 114p.

Kentucky

1108 Housekeeping in the Blue Grass. A new and practical Cook Book; nearly 1000 recipes such as have been used by the best housekeepers of Kentucky and other states. Edited by the ladies of the Presbyterian Church, Paris, Ky. Cincinnati, Geo. E. Stevens, 1875. 168p.

1109 Housekeeping in the Blue Grass. A New and Practical Cook Book; nearly 1000 recipes . . New and enlarged edition—10th. Many interesting ads. The Ladies of the Presbyterian Church, Paris, Ky.: 1879. 190p.

1110 The New Kentucky Home Cook Book. Compiled by the ladies of the Methodist Episcopal Church, South, Maysville, Ky. . . Nashville, Tenn.: Southern Methodist Pub. House, 1884. 392p. Ads.

1111 White, Mrs. Peter A. The Kentucky Housewife. A collection of recipes for cooking. Chicago: Bedford, Clarke & Co., 1885. 316p.

1112 Louisville Cook Book. Louisville: Guide, 1890.

1113 Woman's Wisdom. A collection of choice recipes. Published by the Ladies' Society of the First Presbyterian Church. Owensboro: O. T. Kendall, 1890. 54p.

1114 Carlisle, Mary Jane. Mrs. John G. Carlisle's Kentucky Cook Book. With original recipes. Neely: Chicago, 1893. 249p.

1115 Carlisle, Mary Jane. Mrs. Carlisle's Kentucky Cook Book. Edition de luxe. Chicago: Neely, 1894. (See No. 1114).

1116 Housekeeping in the Blue Grass. New and enl. Cincinnati, O.: Robt. Clarke, 1896. (See No. 1108).

1117 The Way to a Man's Heart—A Cook Book. Bibliography of cookbooks is included. The Ladies' Aid Society of the Hill Street Methodist Church, Lexington, 1897. 160p. and ads.

1118 Bowling Green Cook Book. By the Ladies' Bible Class of Bowling Green. 1898.

1119 Johnson, Nannie Talbot. What to Cook, and How to Cook It. Nearly a thousand recipes . . . Louisville: Pentecostal Herald Press (1899). xiii, 3-114, 13, 115-239p.

1120 Carlton, Helen T. The Practical and Fancy Cook Book. Courier Journal, Job Printing Co. Louisville, 18(?). 95p.

1121 Favorite Food of Famous Folk. With directions for preparation, given for the most part by the famous folk themselves. Ladies of the Guild of St. James' parish church. J. P. Morton: Louisville, 1900. 86p.

1122 Frazer, Mrs. Mary Harris. Kentucky Receipt Book. (Louisville: Press of the Bradley & Gilbert Co., 1903.) 365p.

1123 Benedict, Jennie Carter. The Blue Ribbon Cook Book. A second pub. of "One Hundred Tested Receipts" together with others which have been found valuable. Louisville; J. P. Morton & Co., 1904. 143p.

1124 Fox, Minerva C. (Compiled by) The Blue Grass Cook Book. List of contributors—mostly from Kentucky and Virginia. Introduction by John Fox, Jr. Illus. with photographs. Kentucky, 1904. 350p.

1125 DUNLAP, LINA. Candlelight Tea; a book of recipes. "Treats" for beverages, salads, sandwiches. Lexington: Transylvania Printing Co., 1910. 52p. Wraps.

1126 DUNLAP, LINA. Heart of the Wheat; a book of recipes. Breads, cakes, pies . . . Lexington: 1910. Transylvania Printing Co., 45p. Wraps.

1127 DUNLAP, LINA. Out of the Blue Grass; Soups, meats, vegetables. . . Lexington: Transylvania Printing Co., 1910. 48p. Wraps.

1128 SMITH, ELIZABETH W. The Model Housekeeper. Thousands of Best Receipts. Louisville: Pentecostal Pub., 1911. 416p.

1129 COLVILLE, JESSIE HENDERSON. A Kentucky Woman's Handy Cook Book. (Cincinnati:) the author (1912). 134p.

1130 HAYES, MRS. W. T. Kentucky Cook Book; easy and simple for any cook, by a colored woman (i-e., Mrs. W. T. Hayes). St. Louis: J. H. Tomkins Prtg. Co., 1912. 45p.

1131 JOHNSON, NANNIE TALBOT. Cake, Candy and Culinary Crinkles: Louisville: Pentecostal Publishing Co., 1912. 222p.

1132 THE LAWRENCEBURG BAPTIST COOK BOOK. Compiled by the Ladies' Aid Society, Baptist Church of Lawrenceburg, Ky. . . Louisville: Pentecostal Pub. Co. (1913). 193p.

1133 MAURY, SARAH WEBB AND TACHAN, LENA L. A Penny Lunch. Its equipment, menus and management. With an endorsement by E. O. Holland, Supt. of P. S., Louisville. Copyright, 1915. 61p. Wraps.

1134 FOX, MINNIE C. (Compiler). The Blue Grass Cook Book. New ed. Kentucky, 1918. (See No. 1124).

1135 NAZARETH ALUMNAE COOK BOOK, 1923. Louisville: Slater Printing Co., 1923. 112p.

1136 COBB, IRVIN S. IRVIN S. COBB'S OWN RECIPE BOOK. Essays and anecdotes about drinks; how to make them. Illustrations. Booklet: wraps. Frankfort Distilleries: Louisville, 1936. 52p.

1137 HINES, DUNCAN. ADVENTURES IN GOOD COOKING. Illustrated. 466 recipes plus chapt. on carving. Wraps. Adventures in Good Eating, Inc. Ky. 1939.

1138 HINES, DUNCAN. ADVENTURES IN GOOD EATING. Along the Highways of America. Wraps. Illus. Adventures in Good Eating, Inc. Ky. (1939). 271p.

1139 D.A.R. FAVORITE RECIPES of members of Poage Chapter. . . . Ashland (193-?). 55p.

1140 HINES, DUNCAN. ADVENTURES IN GOOD EATING. Along the Highways, and in Cities of America. Wraps. Illus. Adventures in Good Eating, Inc., Ky. (1947). 303p.

1141 FLEXNER, MARION. Title: OUT OF KENTUCKY KITCHENS. Preface by Duncan Hines. Published by Franklin Watts, Inc. New York, 1949. 319p.

1142 HINES, DUNCAN. FOOD ODYSSEY. About restaurants and recipes in the U.S.A. with a few from abroad. Colored end papers. Crowell; New York, 1955. 1st ed. 274p.

1143 FAMOUS KENTUCKY RECIPES. Compiled by Cabbage Patch Circle, Louisville. Decorated with charming sketches. Spiral binding. Cabbage Patch Circle, Kentucky, 1956. 216p.

1144 SOUTHERN KENTUCKY COOK BOOK. 3rd ed. Presbyterian Woman's Missionary Society, Smiths Grove, Kentucky. n.d.

Louisiana

1145 THE CREOLE COOKERY BOOK. Edited by the Christian Woman's Exchange of New Orleans. To provide funds for a new building. Recipes contributed by experienced housekeepers. New Orleans: T. H. Thomason, 1885. 216p.

1146 HEARN, LAFCADIO. (Compiler). La Cuisine Creole. A collection of culinary recipes from leading chefs and noted Creole housewives, who have made New Orleans famous for its cuisine. W. H. Coleman: New York (1885). 268p. Intro. 2p.

1147 HEARN, LAFCADIO (Anon.) La Cuisine Creole. (See No. 1146). A rare book, as Hearn's work is a collector's item first for its literary value, and second for its culinary importance. This copy has a gorgeous colored bookplate. New Orleans: F. F. Hansell & Bro. Ltd. (copyright 1885). 268p. Intro. 1p.

1148 JAMES, VIRGINIA E. A (Key) to Good Cooking and Useful Household Hints. New Orleans: L. Graham & Son, 1890. 509p.

1149 DIXIE PASTRY COOK BOOK. Gulf Manufacturing Co., New Orleans, 1896. 23p.

1150 NEW ORLEANS COOK BOOK. Compiled by the Woman's Parsonage and Home Mission Society of the Parker Memorial Methodist Episcopal Church, South. (New Orleans), 1898. 95p. and ads.

1151 THE PICAYUNE'S CREOLE COOK BOOK . . . The Picayune: New Orleans, 1900. 352p.

1152 THE PICAYUNE'S CREOLE COOK Book. Picayune Publishing Co., New Orleans, 1901. 2nd ed. Illus. 462p.

1153 EUSTIS, CELESTINE. COOKING IN OLD CREOLE DAYS. Intro. by S. Weir Mitchell. Illus. by Harper Pennington with period characters and snatches of folk songs with the music. Louisiana, 1903. 1st ed. 129p.

1155 STANFORD, MARTHA PRITCHARD. A cook book of old and new recipes. Learey; New Orleans, 1904. 24p.

1156 THE PICAYUNE'S CREOLE COOK BOOK. 3rd ed. The Picayune, 1906. 418p. illus. (See No. 1151).

1157 COOK BOOK. Order of Eastern Star, Rob Morris Chapter No. 1. New Orleans, 1909. 130p.

1158 THE PICAYUNE'S CREOLE COOK BOOK. La.: The Picayune, 1910. 410p. 4th ed. (See No. 1151).

1159 BOYER, HARRIET AMELIA. Notes and Recipes, Freshman Domestic Science at Newcomb College. Illus. by S. A. E. Irvine and Mary McNaughton of the School of Art. New Orleans: Tulane Univ. Press (1915). 95p. plus 96-192 blank. Wraps.

1160 THE PICAYUNE'S CREOLE COOK BOOK. Times-Picayune Pub. Co., New Orleans, 5th ed. (1916). 302p.

1161 THE NEW ORLEANS FEDERATION OF CLUBS COOK BOOK . . . New Orleans: (Louisiana Prtg. Co., Book Dept.), 1917. 861p.

1162 THE PICAYUNE'S CREOLE COOK BOOK. 6th ed. New Orleans: Times—Picayune, 1922. 390p. col'd frontis. (See No. 1151).

1163 NOTT, GEORGE WILLIAM. A tour of the Vieux Carré, with intro. by Grace King. Illus. folding plan. Tropical Printing Co.: New Orleans, 1928. 63p.

1164 THE PICAYUNE'S CREOLE COOK BOOK. 7th ed. New Orleans: Times-Picayune, 1928. 390p. Col'd frontis. (See No. 1151).

1165 SCOTT, NATALIE. MIRATIONS AND MIRACLES OF MANDY. Some favorite Louisiana recipes. Wraps. (Robt. H. True: New Orleans, 1929). 61p.

1166 A BOOK OF FAMOUS OLD NEW ORLEANS RECIPES. Used in the South for more than 200 years. Rice Journal Pub. Co.: Lake Charles (1930). Illus. (32)p.

1167 SCOTT, NATALIE. 200 Years of New Orleans Cooking. Decorations by William Spratling. New Orleans, 1931. 1st ed.

1168 FISHES AND FISHING IN LOUISIANA, including recipes for the preparation of seafoods. Bulletin No. 23 of Louisiana Dept. of Conservation. New Orleans, 1932. 638p.

1169 SEA FISHES AND SEA FISHING IN LOUISIANA, including recipes for sea foods. Bulletin No. 21 of Louisiana State Conservation Dept. New Orleans, 1932. 186p.

1170 GRISWOLD, FRANK GRAY. The Gourmet. Limited signed ed. 200 copies. Creole cooking. The Provinces of France, Original & zesty. Duttons, Inc.: New York, 1933. 121p.

1171 SCOTT, NATALIE & JONES, CAROLINE MERRICK. Gourmet's Guide to New Orleans. Many signed recipes. Wraps. New Orleans, 1933. 96p.

1172 FROG RECIPE BOOK. Pamphlet Pub. by American Frog Canning Co. New Orleans, 1934. 24p.

1173 NEW ORLEANS RECIPES. A book of famous old recipes used in the South for more than 200 years. 4 plates-drawings by H. F. Castleden incl. The Courtyard of Mme. John's Legacy. New Orleans: Peerless Pub. (c. 1935). 44p. Ads.

1174 MME. BÉGUÉ'S RECIPES OF OLD NEW ORLEANS CREOLE COOKERY. Mme.'s restaurant was celebrated in the 90's. Wraps. Harmanson, New Orleans (1937). 64p.

1175 OTT, ELEANOR. Plantation Cookery of Old Louisiana. Page decorations by Mary Evans Isom. New Orleans: Harmanson, 1938. 1st ed. 96p. Wraps.

1176 A BOOK OF FAMOUS OLD NEW ORLEANS RECIPES. Used in the South for More Than 200 Years. Illus. pict. bds. Plastic binding. Reprinted for the Free French Movement World War II. Copyright 1900. (c. 1940). 62p.

1177 RICHARD, LENA. New Orleans Cook Book. Intro. by Gwen Bristow. 333 of the most successful creole recipes. Houghton Mifflin Co., Boston, Mass. (1940). 146p.

1178 SCOTT, NATALIE, AND JONES, CAROLINE MERRICK. GOURMET'S GUIDE TO NEW ORLEANS. Many signed recipes. Wraps. (Scott & Jones: New Orleans, 1941). 118p.

1179 THE ORIGINAL PICAYUNE CREOLE COOK BOOK. A compilation of the many excellent and matchless recipes of the New Orleans cuisine. Times-Picayune Publishing Co., New Orleans, 1942. 438p.

1180 BREMER, MARY MOORE. NEW ORLEANS RECIPES. Old recipes and New. Spiral binding. Copyright 1932. Published by Dorothea Forshee, New Orleans (1944). 10ed. 86p. 5 Index.

1181 COOPER, VIRGINIA M. Creole Kitchen Cook Book. Famous New Orleans Recipes. New Orleans, 1946. 248p.

1182 OTT, ELEANOR. Plantation Cookery of Old Louisiana. 2nd ed., 1949. (See No. 1175).

1183 TABASCO. A gay little booklet, color illus. Principally New Orleans recipes. Avery Island: McIlhenny Co., 1951. 24p.

1184 MONTEGUT, CARMEN BULLIARD. LE PETIT PARIS DE L'AMERIQUE. From the files of the Old Castillo Hotel, and from friends and relatives. Wraps. St. Martinville, 1955. 20p.

1185 MIGNON, FRANCOIS AND HUNTER, CLEMENTINE. MELROSE PLANTATION COOKBOOK. Some very old, very unusual French-African recipes. Photographs by Carolyn Ramsey. Spiral binding. Private printing, New Orleans (1956). 1st ed. 31p.

1186 TO A KING'S TASTE. Collected by the National Society of the Colonial Dames of America. Autographed recipes. Illus. Wraps. New Orleans, 1957. 196p.

1187 RECIPES FROM AUDUBON'S HAPPY LAND. Feliciana Recipes, Audubon wild turkey on cover. Wraps. Receipts of Cookery from the day books of the great-grandmothers of West Feliciana Parish. Louisiana, 24p.

1188 SMITHERMAN, MRS. JAMES E. The Louisiana Plantation Cook Book — Shreveport, Louisiana,

Brookwood, East Feliciana Parish, Glenco Plantation: Ina Scott Thompson, n.d. 274p. Pictures, poems, ads.

1189 The Up-To-Date Cook Book. Rev. ed. Ladies Aid and Sewing Society of New Orleans. New Orleans, n.d. 160p.

1190 Weiss, Caroline D. A Collection of Creole Recipes as Used in New Orleans. Prepared for use with Herbs & Seasonings of New Orleans, Accurate recipes and regional chatter. Spiral. Kiskaton Farm, Mandeville, 50p.

Maine

1194 Sorosis Receipt Book. Ladies of the Unitarian Society, Waterville: 1878. 100p.

1195 Ladies Handbook and Household Assistant. Congregational Society, Rockland: 1886. 76p.

1196 Ladies' Handbook and Household Assistant. By the Ladies Circle of the Chestnut Street Church. Pine Point, Me. . . . Claremont, N.H.: Cooperative Pub. Co. (1886). 76p. illus.

1197 Fish, Flesh and Fowl. A cook book of valuable recipes. Compiled by ladies of State Street Parish. Enl. ed. Portland: Transcript Printing House, 1894. 112p.

1198 Cook Book, containing tested and proved recipes furnished by the ladies of Pine Point.—Ladies of the First Christian Church, Pine Point. n.p., 1902. 48p. illus.

1199 Cook Book. St. Jude's Guild, Seal Harbor (c. 1910). Mimeo. Ring book. 45p.

1200 Cook Book, compiled by members of the Woman's Club of Damariscotta and Newcastle, Me. Damariscotta: 1910. 86p.

1201 Wiggin, Kate Douglas (editor). Dorcas Dishes. A Little Book of Country Cooking. Introduction by Kate Douglas Wiggin. Family recipes contributed by the Dorcas Society of Hollis and Buxton: privately printed, 1911. 96p. Photo of the old Congregational Church at Buxton Lower Corner. 1st ed.

1202 Meserve, Mary Ann (Anon.) These receipts are guaranteed to be strictly original with the Songo cook, and have in past years met with approval by the guests of the house . . . Portland: Smith & Sale, printers, 1914. 66p. frontis. and 1 pl.

1203 Collection of Recipes . . . contributed by the Ladies of the Congregational Church and their Friends. Rockland, 1915. 124p. illus.

1204 Comfort's Home-Makers' Help and Family Guide, in best methods of housekeeping and cooking, canning and preserving; also for improving and beautifying the home. Augusta: W. H. Gannett, (c. 1919). 192p. illus.

1205 Kendall, Ellen B. (compiler). Choice and Tested Recipes, contributed by the women of Bar Harbor . . . Bar Harbor: Sherman Pub. Co., 191-?). 119p.

1206 DORCAS DISHES. A Little Book of Country Cooking. Intro. Kate Douglas Wiggin. Centennial ed. Family Recipes contributed by the Dorcas Society. Bds. 5000 privately printed. Hollis & Buxton (1922).

1207 TESTED RECIPES.—Ladies Circle of the Congregational Church, Fryeburg, Maine. (North Conway, N.H.: Reporter Press, 192?). 58p. and ads.

1208 THE DAILY KENNEBEC JOURNAL HOME CORNER COOK BOOK, contributed by the members and assembled by the editors of the Home Corner Department. Augusta: Daily Kennebec Journal, 1932. 248p. incl. plates.

1209 MOSSER, MARJORIE. GOOD MAINE FOOD. With introduction by Kenneth Roberts. Doubleday, Doran, New York, 1939. 1st ed. 381p.

1210 ISLEFORD CHURCH CLUB. The Island Cook Book. Isleford: 1940. 76p.

1211 COFFIN, ROBERT P. TRISTRAM egged on by RUTH P. COFFIN. MAINSTAYS OF MAINE. About Maine and people. Not a cook-book though there are a lot of good Maine dishes in it. Macmillan: New York, 1944. 185p.

1212 BEAN, L. L. HUNTING-FISHING & CAMPING. How to use Reflector Baker, Grub Lists, Recipes and Hints. Lavishly illus. Pub. by the author, Freeport, 1947. 104p.

1213 KITCHEN SECRETS. St. Savior's Episcopal Church. Reprinted from 1914 ed. Plastic bdg. Oilcloth. Maine, 1954. 62p.

1214 A BOOK OF SELECTED RECIPES BY THE LADIES OF THE CHRISTIAN CIRCLE AT LOVELL CENTER, MAINE . . . (poem). 55p. and ads.

1215 COOK BOOK. Compiled by the Alumni Ass'n. of Porter High School. Kezar Falls: (n.d.) 28p.

1216 RELIABLE RECIPES. Business and Professional Women's Club, Portland: n.d. 72p.

Maryland

1217 MONCURE, MRS. M. B. The Art of Good Living. Baltimore: William K. Boyle, 1870. 228p.

1218 HOWARD, MRS. B. C. Fifty Years in a Maryland Kitchen. Baltimore: Turnbull Brothers: 1873. xvi, 378p.

1219 LEA, ELIZABETH. Domestic Cookery and Hints to Young Housekeepers. Baltimore: Cushing & Bailey, 1873. 293p.

1220 HOUSEKEEPER'S FRIEND. A Collection of New and Valuable Recipes compiled by Smith, Hanway & Co., Baltimore (1879). Pictorial wraps. 88p.

1221 HOUSEKEEPER'S FRIEND. A Collection of New and Valuable Recipes compiled by Smith, Hanway & Co., Baltimore, Pictorial wraps. 1880 ed. 88p.

1222 CHOICE RECIPES AND SPECIMEN PAGES FROM MISS PARLOA'S NEW COOK BOOK. Interesting illus.

Pictorial wraps. Presented by the Baltimore News Co., Baltimore, 1881. 16p.

1223 HOLLYDAY, MRS. R. C. Domestic Economy, A New Cookery Book containing numerous valuable receipts for aid in housekeeping. Baltimore: John Murphy & Co., 1882. 263p. illus.

1224 SHRIVER, FANNY. Every-day Cookery. A collection of new and reliable recipes. Cumberland: The Daily News job office and book bindery. 1883. 49p.

1225 FAVORITE RECEIPT BOOK. Ladies Aid Society of Church of Holy Comforter, Baltimore, 1884. 28 leaves, Ads.

1226 GIESE, MRS. J. H. Over 300 Well Tried Recipes. And where to buy almost everything pertaining to Housekeeping from well established firms. Baltimore: Hanziche & Co., 1888. 139p. and ads.

1227 FILIPPINI, ALESSANDRO. THE TABLE. How to Buy Food, How to Cook It, and How to Serve It. Illus. Revised edition with supplements. Charles L. Webster & Co., Baltimore, 1891. 432p. and ads.

1228 MOREHOUSE, ARTHUR G. (Anon.) The Lucille Cook Book. Baltimore; n. pub., 1892. 279p. and ads.

1229 GIBSON, MARIETTA FAUNTLEROY (POWELL) HOLLYDAY. Mrs. Charles H. Gibson's Maryland and Virginia Cook Book. J. Murphy & Co., Baltimore, 1894. 323p.

1230 GOOD THINGS. A cookery book and book of comfort & health. Advertising St. Jacobs Oil. Baltimore: Charles A. Vogeler Co., 1897. 32p. Wraps.

1231 WATKINS, MRS. SPENCER AND FIELD, MRS. FRANCIS F. The Up-to-Date Cook Book of Tested Recipes. Compiled and published for the benefit of St. John's Church, Montgomery Co., Md. Washington, D. C., National Publishing Co., 1897. 150p. and ads. Signed recipes.

1232 MARSHALL, MRS. CHARLES. Recipes Old and New. Collected for the benefit of the Confederate Relief Bazaar. Baltimore, Guggenheimer, Weill & Co. (1898). 74p. Wraps.

1233 MARYLAND RECIPES. Autographed recipes. Selected and Compiled by the Ladies' Aid Society of the Methodist Episcopal Church. Wraps. North East. Tried and True. 1901. 114p.

1234 PICKENPAUGH, MRS. LAURA DEARING. New-Old Southern Cookery. L. D. Pickenpaugh, Baltimore (1902). 276p.

1235 SMEDLEY, EMMA. INSTITUTION RECIPES. In use at the Johns Hopkins Hospital and Drexel Institute Lunch Room. Boards. Maryland (1904). 121p.

1236 BOMBERGER, MAUD ADA. Colonial Recipes, from Old Virginia and Maryland Manors . . . New York and Washington: The Neale Pub. Co., 1907. 107p.

1237 HARLAND, MARION. MARION HARLAND'S COOK BOOK. Bread Sponge and Breakfast Breads; general recipes. Wraps. Ottenheimer: Baltimore, 1907. 157p.

1238 THE CHURCH COOK BOOK; published for the benefit of church work and charity. Baltimore: Wilkins Co., 1908. 180p. illus.

1239 MCCORMICK'S MANUAL OF COOKERY. Tried and tested recipes. Baltimore: McCormick & Co. (c. 1912). 160p. and ads.

1240 BEE BRAND MANUAL OF COOKERY. The Blue Book of the Culinary Art. Baltimore: McCormick (c. 1913). 192p. and ads. Wraps.

1241 HOWARD, MRS. B. C. Fifty Years in a Maryland Kitchen. New and rev. ed. Baltimore: Norman, Remington Co., 1913. 419p. 5th ed. (See No. 1218).

1242 HARCUM, CORNELIA GASKINS. Roman Cooks. A dissertation by a Wellesley College instructor in Greek; to the board of Johns Hopkins Univ.; for degree of doctor of philosophy. Baltimore: J. H. Furst Co., 1914. 85p. Wraps.

1243 THE WASHINGTON COUNTY HOSPITAL "BENEFIT" COOK BOOK OF PRICELESS "TRIED AND TESTED" WASHINGTON COUNTY RECIPES. Issued by The Ladies' Auxiliary and sold for the benefit of the Washington County Hospital, Hagerstown (1914?). 160p. Paper.

1244 MACKAY, L. GERTRUDE. HOUSEKEEPER'S APPLE BOOK. 197 Delicious health giving apple recipes, tested by an expert in domestic economy. Pictorial wraps. Advertising Committee, International Apple Shippers' Ass'n., Baltimore (c. 1915). 40p.

1245 MEDDERS, MRS. WILLIAM. The Eastern Shore Cook Book, of Maryland recipes. Signed and tested recipes by the Epworth League of the Still Pond Methodist Episcopal Church. Pub. 1916. Revised, 1919. Wilmington, Del.: H. A. Roop, printer, 1919. 98, 2p. Wraps.

1246 EDDY, WALTER H. The Vitamine Manual. Illus. Baltimore, 1921. 121p.

1247 MCNALLY, CLARA LOUISE (HUMPHREY), Chevy Chase Cook Book, compiled and published by Mrs. William J. McNally, Mrs. Thomas F. Keane . . . Washington, D.C.: Press of C. H. Potter and Co., Inc. (1926). 119p.

1248 CRUMBINE, SAMUEL J. AND TOBEY, JAMES A. THE MOST NEARLY PERFECT FOOD. The Story of Milk—with some recipes. Williams & Wilkins: Baltimore, 1929. 292p.

1249 PURCELL, ELEANOR. Aunt Priscilla in the Kitchen. A collection of winter-time recipes, menus, and suggestions for afternoon teas and special holiday parties. Baltimore: Aunt Priscilla Publishing Co. (c. 1929). 176p. illus.

1250 STIEFF, FREDERICK PHILIP (presentation copy) EAT, DRINK & BE MERRY IN MARYLAND. An anthology from a great tradition of excellent cuisine. Illustrated by Edwin Tunis. End papers of a food map of Maryland. Putnam: New York, 1932. 1st ed. 326p.

1251 WINE AND DINE WITH THE LAKE ROLAND GARDEN CLUB. Each section edited by a different Club member. Illus. Map of "Whereabouts of the Lake Roland Garden Club" as end papers. Spiral. Baltimore, 1935. 235p.

1252 HOWARD, MRS. BENJAMIN CHEW. (1801-1890). Fifty Years in a Maryland Kitchen. Completely revised by Florence Brobeck. Fabulous dinners and cookery. M. Barrows: New York, 1944. 1st printing, rev. ed. 234p.

1253 BELL, LOUISE PRICE. KITCHEN FUN. Teaches children to cook successfully. Illus. . . . . . Wraps. Perks: Silver Spring, 1946. 31p.

1253a MARYLAND COOKERY. Reproduced handwritten recipes with appropriate illus. by friends of the association. Maryland Home Economics Assoc., 1948. 309p.

1254 LET'S COOK. Favorite Recipes. Illus. Plastic bdg. Bethel Class of Bell's Methodist Church, Camp Springs, 1952. 148p.

1255 OUR BEST RECIPES. Collected by the Rector's Guild. Illus. Autographed recipes. Photo of church on title. Plastic spiral binding. Wraps. Trinity Church, Towsontown, 1952. 147p.

1256 PERSONAL RECIPES. Compiled by the Esther Circle. Autographed recipes. Ads. Plastic spiral binding. Photo of church on front cover. St. Timothy's Church, Catonsville (1954). 48p.

1257 A COOK'S TOUR OF THE EASTERN SHORE OF MARYLAND. Autographed recipes reproduced in the handwriting of contributor. Plastic spiral binding. Pictorial wraps. Illus. Eastern Maryland Memorial Hospital Junior Auxiliary, (1955). 1st ed. 6th printing. 360p.

1258 NEWMAN, HAROLD. Newman's European Restaurant Guide. List of 1235 restaurants in over 500 cities & towns. Wraps. I. & M. Ottenheimer: Baltimore (1955). 94p.

1259 WHITE, FAIRY MAPP. FOOLPROOF COOK BOOK (autographed). Monumental Press, Baltimore, 1958. 1st ed. 232p.

1260 BROWN, DELANE. DELANE BROWN'S COOK BOOK. Good Things to Eat and How to Serve Them. Wraps. Baltimore, n.d. 54p.

1261 SMORGASBORD COOK BOOK. (See Foreign sec.)

Massachusetts

1262 HUTCHINS' RECEIPT BOOK. Springfield, 1860. 26p.

1263 HOWLAND, MRS. ESTHER ALLEN. The American Economical Housekeeper and Family Receipt Book, Worcester, Mass. . . . Boston: G. W. Cottrell (1867). 138p. illus. Pict. wraps.

1264 NANTUCKET RECEIPTS. Ninety receipts collected chiefly from Nantucket sources. Boston: Robert Bros., 1874. 40p.

1265 In the Kitchen. This book is respectfully dedicated to the "cooking class" of the Young Ladies' Saturday Morning Club of Boston, Mass. Foreword by Elizabeth S. Miller. New York; Lee & Shepard & Dillingham, 1875. 568p.

1266 Walter Baker & Co. An account of the Manufacture and Use of Cocoa and Chocolate in Ancient and Modern Times, together with Copious Receipts for their preparation for domestic use. Dorchester: (1876). 24p. Col. pict. wraps.

1267 Hood's Cook Book. Number One. Advertising booklet reprinted. Lowell: C. I. Hood & Co., 1877. 32p.

1268 Massachusetts Woman's Christian Temperance Union Cuisine. Recipes known to be reliable; together with reports, constitution, by-laws, etc. Published by the ladies of the M.W.C.T.U. in aid of the fair in Horticultural Hall, April 22, 1878. Boston: E. B. Stillings, 1878. 128p. and ads.

1269 The Pet Cook Book. A help to young housekeepers. By a practical cook. Melrose: no pub. (c. 1878). 32p. Wraps.

1270 Domestic Receipt Book and Business Directory. Natick: 1880. 48p. Wraps.

1271 Colton, J. W. Choice Recipes, presented by Brooks & Sears. Athol: Calendar for 1881. 30p. Wraps.

1272 Hood's Cook Book. Number One. Advertising booklet reprinted. Lowell: C. I. Hood & Co., n.d. (c. 1881). 32p. and ads. (See No. 1267).

1273 The Housekeeper's Friend. Published by the Ladies of the Methodist Episcopal Church, in connection with their Annual Fair and Festival, Dec. 12 and 13, Dorchester Lower Mills, 1882. 36p. Ads. wraps.

1274 The Pentucket Housewife. Whittier's birthplace; many of the recipes are signed by ladies of the Whittier Family. Cookbook compiled by Ladies of the First Baptist Church. Haverhill, 1882. 136p. and ads.

1275 "Helping Hands" Cook Book. Compiled by the Young Ladies of the First Unitarian Church. Autographed recipes. Worcester: Press of F. S. Blanchard & Co., 1883. 35p. Wraps.

1276 Pabke, Marie. Mrs. A. Pabke's One Hundred Recipes For Dishes both Wholesome and Palatable . . . Wholly without the use of baking powders, saleratus and soda. Springfield: M. C. Stebbins & Co., 1883. ix, 11-43p. Wraps.

1277 Squire, Miss Emily E. (editor). Culinary Gems—A Collection of Choice Recipes Gathered with Care from the Treasures of Culinary Experts. Autographed recipes. Westfield: J. D. Cadle & Co., Printers, 1884. 147p. Ads. 2nd edition.

1278 AYER'S PRESERVE BOOK. Pub. by Dr. J. C. Ayer & Co., Lowell (c. 1885). 24p. illus. Pict. wraps.

1279 THE HIGH-STREET COOK BOOK. The collection of the Ladies of High-Street Church, Lowell, Mass. Booklet—wraps. Hood's Sarsaparilla: Lowell, 1885. 32p.

1280 OUR COOK BOOK, Explains How to Make from Glen Mills Breadstuffs Bread, Biscuit, Rolls, Muffins, etc. Glen Mills, Rowley: Pub. by N. N. Dummer, 1885. Picture of Glen Mills as frontis. 76p. pict. wraps.

1281 RECIPES FOR COOKING GLEN MILLS BREAD-STUFFS. Advertising leaflet presented by N. N. Dummer. Rowley: Economy Printing Co. of Newburyport (c. 1885). 8p. Pictorial wraps with picture of Indians grinding corn.

1282 BURR, HATTIE A. (editor) The Woman Suffrage Cook Book. Recipes, Directions for Care of the Sick, Practical Suggestions. Boston: Pub. in aid of the festival & bazaar, 1886. 148p.

1283 THE HOUSEKEEPER'S FRIEND. Lawrence: Kiley Brothers (1886). Unnumbered pages, illus. Ads. Pictorial wraps in color.

1284 625 CHOICE RECIPES from the Ladies of the Second Congregational Church, of Holyoke, Mass. Autographed recipes. Holyoke: Transcript Pub. Co., 1886. 108p.

1285 FLETCHER, MRS. J. M. Mrs. Fletcher's Common Sense Cook Book . . . Lowell: Marden & Rowell, 1887. 53p. and ads. Wraps.

1286 HANDY HOUSEHOLD HINTS. Lowell: H. V. Huse, 1887. 31p. and ads.

1287 LOCAL RECEIPT BOOK. South Framingham: 1887. 136p.

1288 COOKING RECEIPTS—First Universalist Church Fair. Proved and Tested Cooking Receipts compiled by the Pickle and Preserve Committee, First Universalist Church Fair, Somerville, Mass. Boston: Press of Coburn Brothers, 1888. 73p. Boards. Autographed recipes.

1289 CRUMBS OF COMFORT—A Collection of Tried and True Recipes, pub. by the Ladies of the Housekeeper's Table at a Fair Held in Aid of the First Universalist Church, of Charlestown, Nov. 13 and 14, and 15. Autographed recipes. Boston: H. E. Browne, Printer, 1888. 124p. Ads.

1290 HOOD'S BOOK OF HOME-MADE CANDIES. Lowell: C. I. Hood & Co.: 1888. 16p. advertising booklet.

1291 THE MIDDLESEX MIRROR. Contains column called "Dining Room and Kitchen." Many food ads. Cambridgeport: Pub. monthly by Fred J. Row & Co., issue of November 1888. 8p.

1292 OUR COOK BOOK—By the Ladies' Aid Society of the Fifth Street Baptist Church . . . Lowell: Press of Adams & Farley, 1888. 88p. and ads.

1293 THE PENTUCKET HOUSEWIFE —A Manual for Housekeepers, and Collection of Recipes, contributed by the Ladies of the First Baptist Church, Haverhill, Mass. Autographed recipes. Haverhill: Press of Chase Brothers, 1888. 3rd ed. 144p. Ads.

1294 OUR VILLAGE COOK-BOOK. Pub. for the Festival of Days, Nov. 12 and 13, 1889. Boston: Avery L. Hand, Printer, 1889. 104p. Ads. Pictorial cloth cover.

1295 HOOD'S COOK BOOK. Number Two. Lowell: C. I. Hood & Co. (1880's). 16p. advertising booklet.

1296 HOOD'S COOK BOOK. Number Three. Respectfully dedicated to the Ladies of the United States. Pub. in response to the desires of thousands who have used, with preeminent success and entire satisfaction, the receipts pub. in Hood's Cook Book No. One and Two. Lowell: C. I. Hood & Co., Apothecaries (late 1880's). 32p. advertising booklet.

1297 CURTISS, FRED H. The Berkshire News Comic Cook Book and Dyspeptic's Guide to the Grave. Great Barrington: Douglas Brothers, Publishers, 1890. 70p.

1298 HOME COOKERY No. 2. A Collection of Tried Receipts from Many Households. Selected by the Ladies of the Newton Universalist Church. Autographed recipes. Newtonville: 1890. 202p. Ads. Picture of church on front cover.

1299 THE WELLESLEY COOK BOOK. Prepared by ladies of the Congregational Society, Parlor Fund Committee, Congregational Church of Wellesley, Mass. Boston: C. J. Peters & Son, 1890. 184p. and ads.

1300 BEST OF ALL. The cook book of the South Salem Congregational Church. South Salem: 1891. 20p. Wraps.

1301 THE CHOCOLATE - PLANT (Theobroma Cacao) and Its Products. A few culinary relations. Delightful illustrations. Walter Baker and Co: Dorchester, 1891. 40p.

1302 J. W. COLTON'S SELECT FLAVORS OF CHOICEST FRUITS AND OTHER SPECIALTIES WITH CHOICE COOKING RECIPES. Small booklet, wraps. Westfield, 1891. 32p.

1303 STANDARD COLLECTION OF TESTED RECIPES FROM MANY HOUSEHOLDS, Selected by the Ladies of the First Universalist Church, Fitchburg. Autographed recipes. Many interesting ads. "Home Gleanings." Fitchburg: 1891. 100p. Rev. Ed.

1304 AYER'S BOOK OF PIES AND PUDDINGS. Booklet; wraps. Dr. J. C. Ayer: Lowell, 1892. 24p.

1305 AYER'S HOME ECONOMIES. Odds and Ends from Table and Market, and How to Use Them. Lowell: J. C. Ayer & Co., 1892. 32p. illus. Pictorial wraps.

1306 HOOD'S GOOD PIE. Recipes and testimonials. Lowell: C. I. Hood & Co., 1892. 16p. Illus. ads.

1307 Parloa, Maria. Choice Receipts. Specially prepared for Walter Baker & Co., Ltd. Dorchester: 1892. 40p.

1308 Ayer's American Almanac, 1894. Remedies, not recipes. Lowell: Dr. J. C. Ayer & Co., 1893. Unnumbered pages, illus. Pictorial wraps.

1309 Burr, Mrs. Clarence I. What Shall We Have To Eat? A bill of fare for every day in the year . . with some receipts. South Framingham: Lakeview Press, 1893. 111p.

1310 The Egremont Cook Book. Compiled by the Ladies of the Baptist Society, North Egremont, Mass. Autographed recipes. Pittsfield: Press of the Eagle Pub. Co., 1893. 79p. Oilcloth wraps.

1311 Estabrook, Mrs. Sarah B. The Appetizer. A Thoroughly Reliable Cook Book, Every recipe having been tested by experienced Cooks. Worcester: Lucius P. Goddard, 1894. 54p. Ads.

1312 Carr, Lucien. The Food of Certain American Indians and Their Methods of Preparing It. From proceedings of the American Antiquarian Society, April, 1895. Worcester: Charles Hamilton, printer. 38p. sewed.

1313 Cook Book—Of the Women's Auxiliary of the Young Men's Christian Association, Malden . . . Malden: Calumet Press, 1895. 97p.

1314 Hood's High Street Cook Book. By the Ladies of High-Street Church. Picture of cooking lesson on front cover. Lowell: C. I. Hood & Co., 1895. 32p. booklet.

1315 Thurston, Rev. Wm. A. (editor), Pastor of the Avenue M. E. Church. The Beverly Cook Book and Housewife's Companion —A Collection of Tested Recipes for the Kitchen and Useful Information. Autographed Recipes. Beverly: Printed at the Citizen Office, 1895. 103p. and ads.

1316 Worcester Family Cook Book. Recipes of the Worcester cooking schools to which are appended other choice recipes. (Worcester? 1895?) 138p. and ads.

1317 Dorchester Woman's Club Cook-Book. Published for the Bazaar, Nov. 4th, 5th, 6th, Norfolk Hall, Dorchester. Autographed recipes. Boston: Press of Mills, Knight & Co. (see p. 12 for date, 1897). 146p. and ads.

1318 Hood's Practical Cook's Book for the Average Household. Lowell: C. I. Hood Co., 1897. 6th ed. 349p.

1319 The Up To Date Cook Book. Compiled by the Thought and Work Club. Salem: 1897. 160p.

1320 Choice Receipts, contributed by the Ladies of the First Universalist Society, Haverhill. Autographed recipes. Haverhill: Printery of Franklin P. Stiles, 1897-1898. 131p. Ads.

1321 Bearse, Alice (Anon.) Ladies' P.M. Cook Book, for the

benefit of the Cotuit Library . . . Hyannis: F. B. & F. P. Goss, 1899. 46p.

1322 Cook Book of Reliable Recipes.—Ladies of the Universalist Church, Brookline, Mass. . . Brookline: Riverdale Press, 1899. 64p. and ads.

1323 Harrigan, Mrs. George M. Colonial Cook Book. Issued for St. John's Hospital . . . Lowell: Lawler & Co., 1899. 142p. and ads. Signed recipes. Poem on food and diet by Pope Leo XIII.

1324 The Hatfield Cook Book. Plain and fancy recipes, arranged by the "real folks" of the Congregational Church. Hatfield, Mass. Holyoke: Hubbard & Taber Printing, 1899. 157p. Paper.

1325 The Iyanough Cook Book. 2nd ed. enl. and improved. Published by the ladies of the Hyannis Public Library Association . . . Hyannis: F. B. & F. P. Goss, 1899. 96p. and ads.

1326 Cook Book of the Ladies Aid Society of the Congregational Church, of Middlefield, Mass. Pr. Pittsfield (18-?). 74p.

1327 Hood's Cook Book. No. 2 Lowell (1890's). (See No. 1295).

1328 Temperance Cook Book.—International Order of Good Templars, Fraternal Order No. 24. Brockton . . . n.p. (189-?). 24p.

1329 The American Kitchen Magazine. Pub. monthly by the Home Science Pub. Co., Mass. Feb. 1900, pages 163-200. Many interesting ads. Wraps.

1330 Autographed Cook Book. Choice recipes. Ladies of First Congregational Church, Lowell, 1900. 127p.

1331 Good Bread. Bread, soup sticks, buns. Booklet, wraps. Hood's Sarsaparilla; Lowell (c. 1900). 16p.

1332 King's Daughters' Cook Book, containing 500 Favorite Recipes collected and published by Whatsoever Circle of King's Daughters of Clarendon St. Baptist Church. Autographed recipes. Boston: 1st ed. (date 1900 on Walter Baker ad). Ads.

1333 Receipts for cakes, creams, custards, candies. Small booklet, wraps. Baker Extract Co. Mass. c. 1900. 24p.

1334 Dorcas Cook Book of Tested Recipes. Autographed recipes published by the Ladies' Sewing Society of the First Baptist Church. Athol: 1901. 64p. Wraps.

1335 Choice Recipes. By Miss Parloa and other Noted Teachers. Dorchester: Walter Baker & Co., Ltd., 1902. 76p. illus. Col. pictorial wrappers.

1336 Kings Daughters Cook Book. Valuable recipes contributed by the Charity Circle, autographed. Small booklet, wraps. New Bedford, 1902. 24p.

1337 Christie, George Allan. Tried and True Cook Book; published in connection with the fair in aid of the building fund of the Free Congregational Church, Andover, 1903.

1338 FIFTY PERFECT RECEIPTS FOR DAINTY TABLES. Issued by the Buffalo Colony of the National Society of New England Women, for the benefit of the "Home Fund." These receipts are used through the courtesy of the Girls' Friendly Society. Beverly: (c. 1903). 32p. Ads. Wraps.

1339 TOWNE, ELIZABETH. Just How to Cook Meals Without Meat. Holyoke: 1903. 24 unnumbered pages. Wraps.

1340 THE FIRST PARISH COOK BOOK. Tested and Approved Recipes by Ladies of the First Congregational Church. Autographed recipes. Interesting local ads. Picture of church on front wrap. Woburn, 1904. 96p.

1341 THE REBEKAH COOK BOOK. Autographed recipes. Pub. in connection with the Annual Carnival of Vass River Lodge No. 141, I.O. O.F., Beverly: The Citizen Printing Co., 1904. 55p. and ads.

1342 CHOICE RECEIPTS—A Compilation by the Professional and Business Woman's Club. Boston, 1905. 91p.

1343 COOK BOOK. Autographed recipes compiled by the New Bedford Mothers' Club. New Bedford: A. E. Coffin Press, 1905. 32p.

1344 WOODSIDE COOK BOOK . . . Framingham, 1905. 106p.

1345 CHOICE RECIPES. Dorcester: 1906. 64p. (See No. 1335). (Walter Baker Co.)

1346 HOUSEHOLD RECEIPTS that have been tried and found good. Autographed. Compiled by the Ladies of the Board of Managers of the Baptist Home. Cambridge (c. 1906). 110p.

1347 BELLOWS, MRS. A. S. (compiler). Brampton Cook Book. Composed of autographed recipes contributed by the Members and Friends of St. Paul's Parish, Hopkinton, Mass. The Compiler of Ashland (1907). 82p. Bds.

1348 THE ELMHURST COOK BOOK. Autographed recipes. Boston: The Angel Guardian Press, 1907. 59p. and ads. Wraps.

1349 THE FIRST NANTUCKET TEA PARTY. Illus. Decorated and Illuminated by Walter Tuttle. Mass., 1907. Col. illus. unnumbered pages. 1st ed. Col. pictorial cloth cover.

1350 GOESSLING, ADELINE O. The Farm and Home Cook Book and Housekepeer's Assistant. Springfield: The Phelps Publishing Co. (1907). 320p. Frontis. and illus.

1351 CHOICE RECEIPTS. Compiled by the Ladies' Benevolent Society of the Second Congregational Church. Autographed recipes. Many interesting ads. Holyoke, 1908. 113p. Bds.

1352 SHARPE, M. R. L. (collected by) THE GOLDEN RULE COOK-BOOK. 600 recipes for meatless dishes. Illustrated. University Press, Cambridge, 1908. 323p.

1353 "OLD NEWBERRY" COOK BOOK, of True and Tried Recipes. Pub. for the benefit of the Ladies' Benevolent Society, First Church. Newbury, 1909. 54p. Oilcloth wraps.

1354 PARLOA, MISS. Chocolate and Cocoa Recipes. (and) HILL, MRS. JANET MCKENZIE . . Home Made Candy Recipes. Dorchester: Walter Baker & Co. Ltd., 1909. 62p. illus. Col. pictorial wraps. Col. plate.

1355 PHILLIPS, FANNIE FRANK AND LEVY, REEVA HUSON. The Universal Cook Book. A collection of tried and tested home receipts. Issued by the Boston section, Council of Jewish Women. Boston: Daniels Printing Co., 1909. 163p. and ads.

1356 A BOOK OF RELIABLE RECIPES. Autographed recipes, by members of the First Parish of Weston, for the Annual Fair. Weston: 1910. 145p.

1357 THE BROCKTON HOSPITAL COOK BOOK . . . (1910 edition.) Contains over 600 valuable local cooking recipes not in the 1906 edition. Autographed recipes. Ads. Picture of Hospital on title. Bds. Brockton: The Brockton Hospital Ladies' Aid Association, 1910. 239p.

1358 CHAPMAN, MRS. ANNA S. Mrs. Chapman's Cook Book. Autographed recipes. Pub. by the author. Hyde Park: J. Morton Binkly, Boston. (c. 1910). 89p. Ads. Wraps.

1359 THE COMET 1910 RECEIPTS. Dedicated to the National League by the Massachusetts Association of Women Workers . . . (West Roxbury?), 1910. 3-92p.

1360 COOK BOOK. Wraps. Ladies' Social Circle, Church of Our Saviour, Universalist. Waltham (1910). 28p.

1361 GOESSLING, ADELINE O. Housekeeper's Reference Book & Domestic Counselor. Illus. Wraps. Springfield, 1910. 156p.

1362 THE MELROSE WOMAN'S CLUB COOK BOOK. Autographed recipes published by the Household Table Committee of the Harvest Festival held in Melrose, Mass., Nov. 8, 9, 10, 1910. 255p. and ads.

1363 OUR COOK BOOK. Recipes printed, signed; some handwritten. Molly Varnum Chapter, D.A.R. Lowell, 1910. 131p.

1364 VARNUM, MOLLIE. MOLLIE VARNUM COOK BOOK. Autographed recipes. Lowell, 1910. 131p.

1365 WHAT SALEM DAMES COOKED IN 1700, 1800, AND 1900. Being a Choice Collection of Recipes. Compiled and pub. by the Board of Managers of the School, with a cover design by Ross Turner. Salem: Printed by the Stetson Press of Boston for the Esther C. Mack Industrial School, 1910. 40p. Wraps.

1366 YE COOK BOOK OF YE FIRST PARISH ALLIANCE. Autographed recipes. Waltham (1910). Ads. Wraps. 106p.

1367 HANDY, AMY L. (compiler). WHAT WE COOK ON CAPE COD. Foreword by Joseph C. Lincoln. Pub. by the Village Improvement Society, Barnstable, Mass. Autographed recipes. Hyannis: F. B. and F. P. Goss, 1911. 82p.

1368 PERKINS, EVORA BUCKNUM. THE LAUREL HEALTH COOKERY. Practical Suggestions and recipes for the preparation of non-flesh foods. Illustrations. Laurel Publishing Co.: Melrose, 1911. 525p.

1369 ST. PAUL'S GUILD COOK BOOK. Tested Recipes, autographed. St. Paul's Episcopal Mission. Millis, 1911. 99p. and ads. Wraps.

1370 WOMEN'S EXCHANGE COOK BOOK. 264 Tested Recipes. Issued by the Inquirer and Mirror. Nantucket: W. C. and F. D. Burgess Co., 1911. 32p. Wraps.

1371 WOODSIDE COOK BOOK. 2nd ed. Framingham: 1911. 99p. (See No. 1344).

1372 BROOKLINE PUBLIC SCHOOLS. Text-book for cooking classes. Ring binding. Boards. Brookline: (c. 1912). 52p.

1373 THE FRIDAY CLUB MENUS; a Cape Cod Cook Book. The Friday Club, Yarmouth, 1912. 95p.

1374 CHRISTIE, GEORGE ALLAN. Tried and True Cook Book. 2nd ed. 1913. Andover. 94p. Wraps. (See No. 1337).

1375 KIMBALL CLASS COOK BOOK. Pub. by The Kimball Class of Dudley St. Baptist Church. Boston, 1913. 86p. Autographed recipes.

1376 A PRACTICAL COOK BOOK compiled by the Ladies of the Congregational Church. Autographed recipes. Shelburne Falls, 1913. 123p. and ads. Wraps.

1377 TESTED RECIPES. By the Ladies of the Universalist Church. Autographed recipes. Photo of church on front wrap. South Weymouth. 40p. and ads. (c. 1913).

1378 THE ETA COOK BOOK. Boston Alumnae Chapter of Alpha Phi . . . Brookline: Huntington Art Press, 1914. 18-173p.

1379 FOLIN, OTTO, PH.D. PRESERVATIVES AND OTHER CHEMICALS IN FOODS: THEIR USE AND ABUSE. From Harvard Health Talks. Harvard Univ. Press, Cambridge, 1914. 60p.

1380 GOOD LUCK IN PRESERVING—A Booklet of Recipes and Suggestions. Set of fruit labels included. The secret of successful preserving—use Good Luck Rings. Col. pictorial wraps. Mass.: (c. 1914).

1381 THE HOME COOK BOOK. Autographed recipes, compiled by the Ladies Aid Society of the First Presbyterian Church. South Framingham (c. 1914). 11p. of recipes and the same number of pages of interesting local ads. Wraps.

1382 HOUSEHOLD RECIPES. Autographed recipes compiled by the Ladies of the First Baptist Church. Interesting local ads. Watertown, 1914. 216p.

1383 THE LOYAL WORKERS COOK BOOK. Autographed recipes compiled and issued by the Loyal Workers Society of the Advent Christian Church. Contains Nearly 400 Tested Recipes contributed by Many Good Cooks. Springfield, June 1914. 2nd ed. 98p. Photo of Church on title page.

1384 MEDFORD WOMEN'S CLUB COOK BOOK. (Medford), 1914. 95p.

1385 A PRACTICAL COOK BOOK. By Ladies of the Eastern Hampden Medical Association. Springfield: Daily News & Job Print (c. 1914). 55p.

1386 PRACTICAL COOKING RECIPES, together with Health Suggestions concerning the Use of Lydia E. Pinkham's Vegetable Compound . . . Lynn: Lydia E. Pinkham Medicine Co. (c. 1914). 32p. advertising booklet. Illus. Pictorial wraps.

1387 WETHERED, FLORA A. The Worcester Domestic Science School's One Year's Course Laboratory Cook Book. Worcester: Worcester Domestic Science School, 1914. 249p. Frontis.

1388 BISCUIT AND CAKES. Success Assured. Mass., 1915. 59p. (An earlier edition of this advertising booklet was published in 1913.)

1389 BOWLES, MRS. A. LINCOLN AND FOSSETT, MISS MARGARET P. (compilers). Cook Book. Woman's Alliance, Roslindale Unitarian Church. Boston, 1915. 75p. and Ads. Wraps.

1390 GOOD BREAD. This Book Tells How To Make Good Bread. Presented with the Compliments of E. W. Keyes, Druggist of Auburndale. 32p. advertising booklet, pictorial wraps. (c. 1915).

1391 HOOD'S COOK BOOK. No. 2. Lowell (c. 1915). (See No. 1295).

1392 MINUTE COOK BOOK. Orange: Minute Tapioca Co. (1915). 32p. illus. advertising booklet.

1393 QUINCY WOMEN'S CLUB COOK BOOK. Pub. by the Home Economics Committee 1915-1916. Quincy: The Spargo Print, 1915. 175p. and ads.

1394 SWEETS. Herein is contained a collection for home candy making and we believe everyone who tests their merits will find them good. Lynn: Lydia E. Pinkham (c. 1915). 22p. illus. Pictorial wraps.

1395 THE TADMUCK CLUB COOK BOOK OF WESTFORD, MASS. Autographed recipes. For friends who excel in the great art of cooking. Wraps. Ayer: News Printing Co., 1916. 97p. and ads.

1396 BRADLEY, MRS. ROBERT S. (compiler). Cook Book—Helpful Recipes for War Time. For the benefit of the Red Cross and American Fund for French Wounded. Pride's Crossing, Mass. Pictorial wraps. Manchester-by-the-Sea: North Shore Breeze, 1917. 1st ed. 51p.

1397 WAR-TIME COOK AND HEALTH BOOK. An advertising booklet.

Lynn: Lydia E. Pinkham Medicine Co., 1917. 32p. Pictorial wraps.

1398 Cramp, Helen. The Institute Cook Book—Food Economy and War-Time Recipes, prepared in co-operation with the U.S. Food Administration. Springfield: Merriam, 1918. 486p. col. plates. Illus.

1399 Liberty Cook Book. A Manual of Tested, Palatable and Economical Recipes. Pub. by the North Adams Branch, Berkshire County Chapter, American Red Cross. North Adams: Excelsior Printing Co., 1918. 178p.

1400 Rush, Jane. The Cook Book. Dorchester: J. J. McSweeney (1918). 192p.

1401 Webber, Carolyn Putnam. Two Hundred and Seventy-five Wartime Recipes . . Bedford: The Bedford Print Shop, 1918. 73p.

1402 McCormick, Mary Lillian (Anon.). "Victory" Cook Book . . Boston: Mission Church Press (c. 1919). 59p. Wraps. Autographed recipes.

1403 The Lynn Bride . . . 500 Ways to Please a Husband. Compliments of the leading merchants of Lynn, 1920. cover-title, 96p. and ads.

1404 192 Old-Time Concord Recipes. Compiled by the Church Aid Society, Trinity Church. Many recipes attributed to local residents. Concord: (c. 1920). 28p. Spiral.

1405 Tabernacle Church Cook Book. Salem: 1920. 97p.

1406 Cook Book of the Second Congregational Church, West Newton, Mass. Recipes tested by the families of the parish . . . West Newton: Press of E. F. Dow, 1921. 108p. and ads.

1407 Lawrence City Mission Cook Book—Favorite Recipes of the Women of Greater Lawrence, signed by them. Interesting local ads. Lawrence: (c. 1921). 164p.

1408 108 Sensible Recipes. Compliments of Baker Extract Co. Springfield (1921). 32p. folder. Pictorial envelope.

1409 Recipes. Compiled by the Women's Guild of the Second Church of West Newton, Mass. Tested by the families of the parish . . . West Newton: Press of E. F. Dow, 1921. 108p. and ads.

1410 Barry, Rena Elizabeth and Mansfield, Agnes H. How to Cook It. Springfield: authors, 1922. 97p. Wraps.

1411 The Center ..Table. (See Foreign sec.)

1412 Grace House Cook Book. Tested Recipes contributed by the Women of Grace Church. New Bedford: 1922. 64 unnumbered p. Ads. Wraps.

1413 The Philathea Cook Book, Trinity Methodist Episcopal Church. Autographed recipes. Worcester, 1922. 96p. Ads. Wraps.

1414 The West Acton Woman's Club Cook Book. Selection of Tested Recipes. Signed. West Acton, 1923-24. 96p. Wraps.

1415 The Cantabrigia Club Cook Book, containing favorite and tried recipes solicited from Club Members by the Home Economics Committee of 1923-1924. Cambridge: Cambridge Publishing Co., 1924. 192p. and Ads.

1416 Choice Recipes. Compliments of Walter Baker & Co., Ltd. Dorchester, 1924. Pictorial wraps in color. 64p. illus. with color plates.

1417 Cook Book.—Unitarian Woman's League, Gardner, 1924. 67p.

1418 Greenwood Cook Book. Pub. by the Ladies' Circle of the Greenwood Union Church. Autographed recipes. Many fascinating local ads. Mass., 1924. 53p. Wraps.

1419 The Homemaker's Cook Book.—Women's Missionary Society of the Congregational Church of Tewksbury, Mass . . . (Andover: Andover Press, 1924.) 14-178p.

1420 The Kensington Avenue School Mother's Club Cook Book. A collection of tried recipes from "Our Mother" and their friends. Autographed recipes. Many ads. Wraps. Springfield: 1924. 64p.

1421 Cook Book. Compiled and arranged by the Choir of the First Baptist Church. Autographed recipes. Danvers: (c. 1925). 116p., ads., wraps.

1422 The Pocumtuc Housewife. A Guide to Domestic Cookery. A Choice Conserve. By Several Ladies. Deerfield, 1925. 54p.

1423 Sea Foods with the Tang O'The Sea. How to Prepare and Serve Them. From the Gloucester fishermen. Gloucester: Frank E. Davis Fish Co. (c. 1925). 32p. Pictorial wraps. Col. illus.

1424 Cook Book of the First Methodist Episcopal Church. Autographed recipes published by the Woman's Council. Pittsfield: Dec. 1, 1926. 62p. Ads. Wraps.

1425 Gottfried, Ruth A. Jeremiah. The Questing Cook. A Bundle of Good Recipes from Foreign Kitchens. Washburn & Thomas, Cambridge, 1927. 1st ed. 380p.

1426 The Household Digest and Directory—Ladies' Aid Society of the First Methodist Episcopal Church, Waltham, Mass. (Waltham, 1927?). 40p.

1427 Turner, Harry Baker. (Edited by) Nantucket Cook Book. One Hundred Recipes collected from Nantucket Housewives Past and Present. Nantucket Island: Inquirer and Mirror Press, 1927. 40p. Wraps.

1428 Famous Recipes for Baker's Chocolate and Breakfast Cocoa. Principally beverages and desserts. Booklet: Wraps. Colorful illustrations. Baker: Dorchester, 1928. 64p.

1429 Wilson, Mrs. George H. (compiler). The Community Cook Book. Pub. for the benefit of the

Reed Community House and Kingston Playground. Kingston: 1928. 232p.

1430 COOK BOOK. Autographed recipes pub. by New Bedford Business and Professional Women's Club. Oilcloth wraps. New Bedford: Nov. 1929. 166p.

1431 FLANDERS, MRS. LYDA (editor). Worcester Evening Post Prize Cook Book . . . Worcester: Worcester Post Co., 1929. 498p. incl. frontis.

1432 FOUR HUNDRED FAVORITE RECIPES. Autographed recipes pub. by the Home Economics Committee of the Plymouth Woman's Club. Plymouth: The Memorial Press, 1929. 141p. Wraps.

1433 CHOICE RECIPES.—Women's Association of the Eliot Union Church, Lowell, Mass. (Lowell, 192-?) 68p.

1434 COOK BOOK. Undine Chapter No. 120. Order of the Eastern Star. Revere: (c. 1930). 64p. illus. Wraps.

1435 GRUVER, MRS. SUZANNE CARY. The Cape Cod Cook Book. Little, Brown, & Co., Boston, 1930. 214p. Illus.

1436 NEW BEDFORD TIMES HOMEMAKERS' COOK BOOK. Over 1000 prize recipes selected from innumerable contributions by the women of New Bedford and Cape Cod. New Bedford Times, New Bedford, 1930. 369p.

1437 A PRESIDENTS' COOK BOOK, 1880-1930. Recipes contributed by presidents of women's clubs and other women of note thruout the U.S. Compiled by the West Newton Women's Educational Club. Brookline: 79p. and ads. Paper.

1438 TRIED AND TRUE. Autographed recipes compiled by the Ladies of the First Baptist Church. Malden, 1930. 34p. Ads. Wraps.

1439 BARRY, ALICE LYNN. The Home Kitchen. Springfield: McLoughlin Bros., Inc. (1932). 124p.

1440 OLD GLOUCESTER SEA FOOD RECIPES. From Frank E. Davis, the Gloucester Fisherman. Gloucester: 1932. 32p. Col. plates. Col. pictorial wraps.

1441 FLANDERS, LYDA (Edited by) PRIZE COOK BOOK. Household Encyclopedia; 1411 Home-Tested Recipes selected from 33,000 contributions. Contest by the Worcester Evening Post. Worcester Post Co., Worcester, 1933. 288p.

1442 WARNER, VICTORIA. Glenwood Cook Book . . Some selected recipes and suggestions for better home menus. Taunton: Glenwood Range Company (1933). 72p. illus. Wraps.

1443 A CONCORD COOK BOOK.—Church Aid Society of Trinity Church, Concord, Mass . . . Concord: (Printed by the Concord Pub. Co.) 1934. 76p.

1444 FROM CAPE COD KITCHENS. Offset printing from handwritten recipes. Harwich Port Library Assn., Harwich Port, Cape Cod, 1934. 239p.

1445 THE GRANGE COOK BOOK. Souvenir of the 25th Anniversary of East Bridgewater Grange, No. 284. Autographed recipes. Mass.: 1909-1934. 56p. Ads. Wraps.

1446 THE ROAD TO GOOD FOOD. For the benefit of the Franklin County Public Hospital at Greenfield, Mass. Autographed recipes reproduced in handwriting of contributor. Spiral, oilcloth boards. Greenfield: 1935. 276p. plus xii p. illus.

1447 COOK BOOK. "The Recipes in this book have all been tried and found not wanting, but wanted." Pub. by the Prudential Committee of the Tyngsboro Evangelical Church. Mass.: May 1936. 68p. Ads. Autographed recipes. Pict. wraps.

1448 GRUVER, SUZANNE CARY. Title: THE CAPE COD COOK BOOK. Illus. Published by Little, Brown, and Company, Boston, 1936. 214p.

1449 SOUTHBORO RECIPES OLD AND NEW . . . Contributed by members & friends of the village society. (Boston: Merrymount Press, 1936?). 85p.

1450 THE GREENWOOD COOK BOOK. Tasty Echoes from Friends of the Greenwood Union Church. Autographed recipes. Greenwood: (Nov. 1937). 96p. Ads. Wraps.

1451 HOSMER, GLADYS E. H. AND WINNEK, MARIAN F. (compilers). A Cookery Book. Distinctive American and Foreign Recipes. Radcliffe: 1937. 44p. Wraps.

1452 THREE HUNDRED FAVORITE RECIPES (TRIED AND TESTED). Autographed recipes. Pub. by the Cook Book Committee of the Bridgewater Visiting Nurse Assoc. Mass.: (1937-1938). 104p. Ads. Ring bdg. Col. pictorial wraps.

1453 WESTFIELD WOMAN'S CLUB COOK BOOK. Autographed recipes. Westfield: 1937. 70p. Spiral bdg. Wraps. Ads.

1454 AS THE WORLD COOKS. Recipes from Many Lands. Autographed recipes, reproduced in the handwriting of the contributor. Profusely illus. by artist of the community. Spiral. Pict. wraps. Lowell: May, 1938. 266p. plus x p.

1455 FAVORITE RECIPES. Compiled by the Women's Guild and the Young People's Society of Park Congregational Church. Autographed recipes. Worcester: 1938. 106p. mimeographed. Pict. wraps. Photo of church on front wrap.

1456 INTERNATIONAL INSTITUTE COOK BOOK. Illus. by Annette A. Bernadin. Hand lettered by Lillian Bruce. Lawrence: Merrimac Printing Co. (1938).

1457 LONGMEADOW COOK BOOK. More than 400 recipes. Some date back over 100 years. Autographed recipes. Charming decorations. Spiral binding. Longmeadow, 1938. 264p. and ads.

1458 WEBBER, ELIZABETH E. (compiler). Dinner Is Served Cook Book. Autographed recipes. Cambridge: (1938). 86p. Ads. Spiral bdg. Pict. wraps in color.

1459 A COLLECTION OF SELECTED RECIPES. Pub. by The Martha Club, First Congregational Church. West Brookfield: Ware River News Print, 1940. 70p. and ads. Autographed recipes. Wraps.

1460 SCAMMON, MRS. ROSE A. Technique New England Cook Book . . . (So. Lancaster: College Press, c. 1940). 101p.

1461 SIPPICAN SAVORIES. Compiled by the Marion Milk Fund Committee. Autographed recipes. Boston: Industrial School for Crippled and Deformed Children, 1940. 107p. Spiral.

1462 WOMEN'S CHRISTIAN TEMPERANCE UNION COOK BOOK. Autographed recipes. Mass.: Dartmouth Women's Christian Temperance Union. Group 5, Dec. 1940. 56p. illus. Wraps.

1463 CAPE COD'S FAMOUS CRANBERRY RECIPES. Hanson: 1941. 28p. illus. Wraps.

1464 RECIPES. First Congregational Church Unitarian. A Cook Book by the Evening Alliance of the Unitarian Church. Autographed recipes. Drawing of church on cover. Chelmsford: 1943. 105p. illus. Spiral.

1465 WAKEFIELD, RUTH GRAVES. RUTH WAKEFIELD'S TOLL HOUSE. Tried and True Recipes. Illustrations, decorations. Barrows, New York, 1943. 275p.

1466 THE HARMONY GUILD COOK BOOK. Compiled by the Members of Harmony Guild of the Orthodox Congregational Church, Manchester-by-the-Sea, Mass. Spiral binding. Cricket Press, 1944. 104p.

1467 MCCUE, DORIS M. (compiler). Recipes from a Cape Cod Kitchen. Pub. by James Westaway McCue. Silver Lake Post Office: New England Book Co. (1946). 1st ed. 72p.

1468 WAKEFIELD, RUTH GRAVES (autographed) Ruth Wakefield's Toll House. Tried & True Recipes from a famed New England Inn—the 23rd printing of this book. Illus. M. Barrows; New York, 1946. 275p.

1469 COOK BOOK R.F.D. Compiled by the Ladies Auxiliary of South Salem Presbyterian Church. Sketch of South Salem on front cover. South Salem: 1948. 144p. Spiral binding.

1470 RECIPES FROM NEAR AND FAR. Autographed recipes and local ads. Westfield: Westfield Women's Club, 1948. 138p. Spiral.

1471 JUST TOPS! Some Recipes used by members of St. Michael's Church. Plastic bdg. Milton, 1949. 20p.

1472 POT LUCK. Compiled by Wednesday Informal Group of the Women's Fellowship, First Church in Cambridge, Congregational. Drawings by Florence J. Grant. Autographed recipes reproduced in handwriting of contributor. Spiral, pict. wraps. Cambridge: Marian T. Blake, 1951. 220p.

1473 PRINCE GOLDEN MACARONI RECIPES. Advertising pamphlet, col. plates, col. pict. wraps. Mass.: (1951). 30p.

1474 THE OLD COLONY CLUB COOK BOOK. Autographed recipes, wraps. South Weymouth: 1952. 53p.

1475 FROST, HELOISE. Early American Recipes. Traditional Recipes from New England Kitchens. Illus. by Barbara Corrigan. Newton: Phillips Publishers, Inc. (1953). 112p. Spiral bdg., col. pict. wraps, boxed.

1476 HUNT, PETER: CAPE COD COOKBOOK. Illus. by the author. Hawthorne Books, New York (1954). 1st ed. 181p.

1477 "THE BEST IN COOKING" IN CROTON. First Parish Church, Unitarian. Autographed recipes. Pictures of church on front cover. Spiral bdg. Croton: (1955). 30p.

1478 FAVORITE RECIPES. Brooks School Children. Cover by Josie Cole. Illus. by Bud Cross. Autographed recipes. Concord: E. V. Sherwin for the Brooks School of Concord (1956). 51p. Spiral bdg.

1479 FAVORITE RECIPES. Autographed recipes. Harvard Church Woman's Guild. Brookline, Mass.: (1950's). 110p. Spiral, pict. wraps.

1480 WHAT'S COOKIN'? in Ayer & Croton, Forge Village & Harvard. Compiled by St. Andrew's Parish. Autographed recipes. Photo of Church on fly. Mass.: 1960. 44p. Ads. Pict. boards.

1481 AS YOU LIKE IT RECEIPTS. Autographed recipes. Compiled by Women of St. Chrysostom's Parish. Wollaston. n.d. 75p. and ads.

1482 BROOKLINE GRAMMAR SCHOOLS Text-book for cooking classes. Bound with string. 48p.

1483 COOK BOOK. A collection of signed recipes. Wraps. Philathea Class of the South Congregational Church. Brockton. n.d. 32p. & ads.

1484 COOK BOOK. Signed recipes. The Ladies' Aid Society of Epworth M. E. Church. Cambridge, n.d. 85p. & ads.

1485 FLAVORS AND SAVORS. Contains some very good hints on herb cookery and amusing quotations, besides varied and well-selected recipes. Boston: The New England Unit of the Herb Society of America. Wraps.

1486 LADIES' AID COOK BOOK OF THE BAPTIST CHURCH. Autographed recipes. Lanesboro, 76p. and ads. Wraps.

1487 MASSACHUSETTS COOKING RULES, OLD AND NEW. Women's Republican Club of Mass. Autographed recipes reproduced in handwriting of contributor. Boston: 316p. Plastic bdg. Wraps.

1488 OVER 250 WAYS TO COOK AND SERVE FISH AND OTHER PRODUCTIONS OF THE SEA. A choice collection of recipes, representing the latest and most approved methods of cooking. Gloucester: Shute and Merchant, n.d. 35p. and ads. Wraps.

1489 ROUND ROBIN OF RECIPES. The pet recipes of several good cooks —signed. Circle Six of Belmont, n.d. 128p.

1490 TRIED AND TRUE COOK BOOK. Compiled and published for the Ladies Aid Society, Asbury Methodist Episcopal Church, Springfield. n.d. 40p. Many ads.

Boston, Mass.

1491 CORNELIUS, MRS. M. H. THE YOUNG HOUSEKEEPER'S FRIEND. (Rev. and enlarged) Brown & Taggard, Boston: 1860. 254p.

1492 HOSKINS, THOMAS H., M.D. What We Eat. An account of the most common adulterations of Food and Drink. Boston: Burnham, 1861. 218p.

1493 PUTNAM, MRS. A PRIMARY COOK BOOK for Beginners in Housekeeping. Receipts suited to the times. Loring: Boston, 1862. 84p.

1494 BURR, FEARING. The Field and Garden Vegetables of America; desc., directions for propagation, culture, and use. Boston: Crosby & Nichols, 1863. 674p. illus.

1495 KNIGHT, MRS. S. G. TIT-BITS; How to Prepare a Nice Dish at a Moderate Expense. Crosby and Nichols, Boston, 1864. 124p.

1496 THE ART OF CONFECTIONERY: Preserving fruits and juices; jams and jellies; summer beverages, dessert cakes. From the best New York, Philadelphia, Boston confectioners, and many foreign recipes. Boston: J. E. Tilton, 1866. 346p.

1497 BARRINGER, MARIA MASSEY. Dixie Cookery: or How I Managed My Table For Twelve Years. . . Boston: Loring, 1867. 121p.

1498 MRS. CORNELIUS. THE YOUNG HOUSEKEEPER'S FRIEND. Revised and enlarged. Taggard and Thompson, Boston, 1868. 254p.

1499 BELLOWS, ALBERT J., M.D. THE PHILOSOPHY OF EATING. Lectures of Physiology, Chemistry and Hygiene. Houghton Mifflin Co., Boston (1870). 426p.

1500 CORNELIUS, MRS. M. H. THE YOUNG HOUSEKEEPER'S FRIEND. Furnish the best aid to young housekeepers. Recipes and household suggestions. Colored end papers. Thompson, Bigelow & Brown: Boston, 1871. 312p.

1501 DEDHAM RECEIPTS, prepared by a Practical Housekeeper. 2nd ed. Boston: A. Williams & Co., 1871. 33p. wraps.

1502 THE CUISINE. 2nd Edition containing Household Cooking Recipes, prepared under the supervision of an Eminent Caterer. Boston: Fox & Co., 1872. 120p. Ads. Wraps.

1503 THE DESSERT BOOK: A complete manual from the best American and foreign authorities. Economical recipes. By a Boston lady. Boston: J. E. Tilton, 1872. 202p.

1504 PARLOA, MARIA. The Appledore Cook Book, containing practical receipts for plain and rich cooking. Boston: Graves and Ellis, 1872. 204p.

1505 CORNELIUS, MRS. M. H. THE YOUNG HOUSEKEEPER'S FRIEND. Colored end papers. Thompson, Brown: Boston, 1873. 312p.

1506 SUGGESTIONS IN CULINARY CHEMISTRY . . Boston: Rockwell & Churchill, 1874. 63p. Paper. (Copyright by E. A. Clarke).

1507 WOODMAN, MISS M. S. Choice Receipts. Boston: J. R. Osgood, 1875. 200p.

1508 FARMAN, ELLA. The Cooking Club of In-Whit Hollow. Boston: D. Lothrop & Co. (c. 1876). 223p.

1509 FAY, CLARA C. Boston Receipts. Over 200 commonsense receipts. Boston: A. Williams & Co.: 1876. 48p. 2nd ed.

1510 A FEW GLEANINGS FOR HOUSEKEEPERS. Compiled by Mrs. J. B. W. Boston: Franklin Press; Rand, Avery & Co., 1876. 47p. wraps.

1511 MATHEWS, HENRY M. (Anon.) The Housewife's Companion: presented with the compliments of A. Shuman & Co. . . Boston: Lockwood, Brooks & Co., 1878. 96p.

1512 PARLOA, MARIA. THE APPLEDORE COOK BOOK. Graves, Locke: Boston, 1878. 234p.

1513 PARLOA, MARIA. Camp Cookery. How to live in camp. Boston: Estes and Lauriat (1878). 91p.

1514 RICE, MRS. E. H. Comforts of Home. A book of tested receipts. Boston: Rand, Avery & Co., 1878. 63p. Wraps.

1515 PARLOA, MARIA. First Principles of Household Management and Cookery. A text-book for schools and families. Boston: Houghton, Osgood and Co., 1879. 133p.

1516 WHITNEY. Just How: A Key to the Cook-books. Boston: Houghton, Osgood & Co., 1879. 311p.

1517 PARLOA, MARIA (presentation copy) New Cook Book and Marketing Guide. Illustrated. Estes and Lauriat, Boston, 1880. 1st ed. 430p.

1518 BREWER, MRS. WILLIAM H. (Anon.) Aunt Mary's New England Cook Book. A collection of useful cooking receipts, tested. By a New England mother. Boston: Lockwood, Brooks & Co., 1881. 72.

1519 PARLOA, MARIA. MISS PARLOA'S NEW COOK BOOK. A Guide to Marketing and Cooking. Illustrated, Estes and Lauriat, Boston, 1881. 430p.

1520 KINGSTON, MAY. That Wonderful Cousin Sarah, and Her Receipts. Boston: Howard Gannett, 1883. 116p. Wraps. Book ads.

1521 WILLIAMS, HENRY T. AND "DAISY EYEBRIGHT." Household Hints and Recipes. (No recipes.) Boston: Peoples Publishing Co., 1884.

1522 BROWN, SUSAN ANNA. In Bridget's Vacation . . . Boston: J. R. Osgood & Co., 1885. 3, 42p. Wraps.

1523 DANIELL, OLIVE C. The Dedham Cook Book. A Practical Housekeeper's Collection of Tested and Valuable Receipts for Cake. Boston: (1885). 47p.

1524 BRAXTON, GEORGE F. Braxton's Practical Cook Book. Boston: Walker, Young & Co., 1886. 96p.

1525 COLBRATH, M. TARBOX: WHAT TO GET FOR BREAKFAST; with more than 100 different Breakfasts & Full Directions for Each. Interleaved. Boston, 1886. 268p.

1526 HOUSEHOLD RECEIPTS.—Valuable Receipts for those who regard Economy as well as Excellence. Boston: Joseph Burnett & Co., 1886. 4th ed. 68p. Wraps.

1527 THE LADIES' DELIGHT COOK BOOK. Number One. Boston: A. P. Ordway & Co., Publishers, 1886. 32p. Pict. wraps.

1528 LINCOLN, MARY JOHNSON (Mrs. D. A. Lincoln). The Peerless Cook-Book. Valuable receipts for cooking. Compact and practical. Boston: Redding & Co., 1886. 128p. and ads. Wraps.

1529 BENTON, J. ROSALIE. How To Cook Well . . . Boston: D. Lothrop & Co. (1887). 9-425p.

1530 GRIER, SARAH A. A Few Hints About Cooking with Remarks on Many Other Subjects. Boston: Wright & Potter Printing Co., Portrait of Author as frontis. 321p.

1531 LINCOLN, MRS. D. A. Boston Cooking School Kitchen Text-Book—Lessons in Cooking for the use of classes in public and industrial schools. Boston: Roberts Brothers, 1887. 237p. Pictorial boards, book ads. 1st ed.

1532 PARLOA, MARIA. Miss Parloa's Kitchen Companion. A Guide for All Who Would Be Good Housekeepers. Illus. 20th ed. (1887). Estes and Lauriat, Boston, 966p. Ads.

1533 LINCOLN, MRS. D. A. BOSTON COOK BOOK. What to do and what not to do in cooking. Illus. Roberts Brothers: Boston, 1888. 536p., ads. and handwritten recipes.

1534 STONE, ELIZABETH. The New Helping Hand. A collection of family receipts. Boston: Smith and Porter (1888). 45p. Wraps.

1535 WHITE, SALLIE JOY. Housekeepers and Home-Makers. Boston: Jordan, Marsh & Co., 1888. 260p.

1536 THE LADIES' DELIGHT COOK BOOK. No. 2. Boston: A. P. Ordway & Co., 1889. (See No. 1527).

1537 HERRICK, CHRISTINE TERHUNE. Liberal Living Upon Narrow Means. Boston: Houghton, Mifflin and Co., 1890. 275p.

1538 LINCOLN, MRS. D. A. MRS. LINCOLN'S BOSTON COOK BOOK. What to do and what not to do in cooking. Roberts: Boston, 1891. 539p.

1539 STROHM, GERTRUDE (compiler) THE UNIVERSAL COMMON SENSE COOKERY BOOK. Practical Recipes for Household Use. By Mrs. D. A. Lincoln, Miss M. Parloa, Marion Harland, Mrs. Washington, Thomas Murrey and Others. Boston: Charles E. Brown & Co. (1892). 236p.

1540 WHITCOMB, M. HOUGHTON. "Souvenir" Cook Book. Tried and

approved recipes. Boston: Beacon Press, 1892. 72p. Wraps.

1541 CAMPBELL, HELEN (STUART). In Foreign Kitchens; with choice recipes from England, France, Germany, Italy, and the North. Boston: Roberts Brothers, 1893. 116p.

1542 MCBRIDE, MARION A. (arranged by) BURNETT'S STANDARD COLOR PASTES. For frostings, desserts. Wraps. Joseph Burnett & Co. Boston, at the Columbian Exposition, 1893. 10p.

1543 PARLOA, MARIA. Miss Parloa's Young Housekeeper. Designed Especially to Aid Beginners. Economical receipts for small families. Illus. Boston: Dana Estes and Co., 1893. 405p. 1st ed.

1544 ATKINSON, EDWARD. The Science of Nutrition. With reference to the use of the Alladin Oven. Diet and food charts. Diagrams. Boston: Damrell & Upham, 1894. 179, 111, 111p.

1545 THE CONGRESS COOK BOOK. A choice collection of receipts and practical suggestions on every day cooking. Boston: D. & L. Slade Co., 1894. 2nd ed. 72p.

1546 THE NEW ENGLAND KITCHEN MAGAZINE. A Domestic Science Monthly. Vol II. Oct. 1894—Mar. 1895. Boston: Press of Carl H. Heintzemann. 308 (2)p. illus.

1547 ATKINSON, EDWARD. SCIENCE OF NUTRITION. Damrell & Upham, Boston, 1896. 246p.

1548 100 DAINTY DESSERTS. A dainty little booklet pub. in Boston: Frostlene Manufacturing Co., 1898. 32p. illus.

1549 WALTON, IZAAK & COTTON, CHARLES. THE COMPLETE ANGLER. Plates and other illus. Ref. to cooking the catch. 6th Lowell ed. with intro. by James Russell Lowell. Boston, 1898.

1550 HILL, JANET MACKENZIE. Salads, Sandwiches, and Chafing-dish Dainties, with 32 illustrations of original dishes . . . Boston: Little, Brown & Co., 1899. 250p.

1551 COLT, J. N. (compiler). Choice Recipes from Miss Farmer's Slips. 1890's. 43p. Wraps.

1552 HOW TO COOK ATWOOD'S HAMBURGER STEAK. 20p. advertising booklet, pub. by A. H. Atwood, Boston. Pictorial wraps. (c. 1900).

1553 LINCOLN, MRS. D. A. Mrs. Lincoln's Boston Cook Book. Rev. ed. Boston: 578p. and ads. 1900. (See No. 1538).

1554 SOWLE, HENRIETTA. I Go A-Marketing. Boston: Little, Brown and Company, 1900. 237p.

1555 LINCOLN, MARY JOHNSON. The Peerless Cook-Book. New and enl. with recipes for the chafing dish. Boston: Little, Brown & Co.: (c. 1901). 140p. and wraps.

1556 RECEIPTS FOR HOME-MADE BONBONS. Boston: The Walter M. Lowney Co., 1902. 16p. illus. Wraps.

1557 RELIABLE RECEIPTS. Boston: Reliable Flour Co. (1902). 32p. Wraps.

1557a SLADE'S GUIDE TO GOOD COOKING. Title page covered with cooking clippings. Boston: D. & L. Slade, 1902. Booklet. 64p. illus.

1558 BURRELL, CAROLINE BENEDICT. A Little Cook Book for a Little Girl. Boston: Dana Estes & Co. (1905). 179p.

1559 THE CARE AND FEEDING OF INFANTS. From the suggestions of many doctors. Interesting photographs of babies and young children. Mellin's Food Company: Boston, 1905. 62p.

1560 HEARD, MARY A. The Hygeia Cook Book. Cooking for Health. Boston: Press of the South End Industrial School, 1905. 43p.

1561 SLOAN'S COOK BOOK AND ADVICE TO HOUSEKEEPERS. Boston: Dr. Earl S. Sloan, 1905. 32p. illus. Pictorial wraps.

1562 TURNER, ALICE M. (compiled by). The New England Cook Book; the latest and the best methods for economy and luxury at home. Illus. C. E. Brown Pub. Co.: Boston (1905). 286p.

1563 HILL, JANET MCKENZIE. THE UP-TO-DATE WAITRESS. Illustrated with half-tone Engravings of Tables, Prepared Dishes, Appliances. Little, Brown; Boston, 1906, 1st ed. 148p.

1564 LINCOLN, MRS. D. A. CARVING AND SERVING. Instructions by an expert. Little, Brown and Co.: Boston, 1906. 52p. and ads.

1565 PHILLIPS, A. LYMAN. A Bachelor's Cupboard. Crumbs from the cupboards of the great unwedded. Drawings by Will Jenkins. John W. Luce & Co.; Boston, 1906. 210p.

1566 FARMER, FANNIE MERRITT. FOOD AND COOKERY FOR THE SICK AND CONVALESCENT. By the principal of the Boston Cooking School. Illustrated. Little, Brown, and Co., Boston, 1907. 289p. and ads.

1567 HERRICK, CHRISTINE TERHUNE. Sunday Night Suppers. Boston: Dana Estes & Co., 1907. 126p.

1568 SLADE'S GUIDE TO GOOD COOKING. A compilation of household hints and reliable recipes prepared by well known cooking experts. Boston; D. & L. Slade Co., 1907. 2nd ed. 64p. illus. Pictorial wraps.

1569 BENTON, C. F. Living on a Little. A book of household directions written like a novel. Dana Estes & Co., Boston, 1908. 264p.

1570 THE BOSTON COOKING-SCHOOL MAGAZINE. Culinary Science and Domestic Economics. Vol. XII. Illus. June-July, 1907—May, 1908. Boston Cooking-School Magazine: Boston. 484p. and ads.

1571 HOWARD, MARIA W. Lowney's Cook Book. Recipes for beginners and accomplished cooks. Col. illus. Boston: Walter M. Lowney Co., 1908. 1st ed. rev. 410p.

1572 LINCOLN, MARY J. AND BARROWS, ANNA. THE HOME SCIENCE

COOK BOOK. Recipes for breakfast, luncheon and dinner. Whitcomb & Barrows, Boston, 1908. 281p.

1573 PARLOA, MARIA. MISS PARLOA'S NEW COOKBOOK and Marketing Guide. Rev. ed. of 1908. Illustrated. Dana Estes and Co., Boston (1908). 430p.

1574 BOSTON SCHOOL KITCHEN TEXT-BOOK. (Earlier ed. with similar title pub. in 1887). Mass., 1909. 237p.

1575 FARMER, FANNIE MERRITT. Food and Cookery for the Sick and Convalescent. Boston, 1909. (See No. 1566).

1576 HILL, JANET MCKENZIE. COOKING FOR TWO. A handbook for young housekeepers. Illus. Little, Brown & Co., Boston, 1909. 1st ed. 407p.

1577 SLADE'S COOKING SCHOOL RECIPES. By 25 Cooking School Teachers. Together with a collection of household and health hints. Autographed recipes. Illus. Pictorial wraps. Boston; D. & L. Slade Co., 1909. 1st ed.

1578 WRIGHT, HELEN S. (compiler). Old-Time Recipes for Home Made Wines, Cordials and Liqueurs from Fruits, Flowers, Vegetables, and Shrubs. Boston: (1909). 156p.

1579 KEEN, ADELAIDE. WITH A SAUCEPAN OVER THE SEA. Quaint & Delicious Recipes from Kitchens of Foreign Lands. Boston: Little, Brown & Co., 265p. Illus.

1580 LINCOLN, MARY J. AND BARROWS, ANNA. The Home Science Cook Book. Boston: 1910. (See No. 1572).

1581 MUCKENSTRUM, LOUIS. Louis' Every Woman's Cook Book. Boston: H. M. Caldwell Co. (1910). 88p. Frontis. portrait of author.

1582 BENTON, CAROLINE FRENCH. Easy Entertaining. Boston: Dana Estes Co., 1911. 251p.

1583 FARMER, FANNIE MERRITT. CHAFING DISH POSSIBILITIES. Little, Brown: Boston, 1911. 161p.

1584 OLSEN, JOHN C., A.M., PH.D. PURE FOODS. Their Adulteration, Nutritive Value, and Cost. Illus. Ginn and Co., Boston (1911). 210p. and ads.

1585 CLARKE, IMOGENE. RHYMED RECIPES. Cucumber boats jingle etc. with blanks for culinary rhymes by others. Pict. cover. H. M. Caldwell Co., Boston, 1912. 87p.

1586 FALES, WINIFRED AND NORTHEND, MARY H. The Party Book. Illus. Boston: Little, Brown, and Co., 1912. 354p.

1587 FARMER, FANNIE MERRITT. A NEW BOOK OF COOKERY. 860 recipes by the Boston Cooking School. Illustrated. Little, Brown; Boston, 1912. 1st. 440p.

1588 FLAGG, ETTA PROCTOR. A Handbook of Home Economics. Author, supervisor of domestic science in Los Angeles P.S. Boston: Little, Brown and Co., 1912. 98p.

1589 HERRICK, CHRISTINE TERHUNE. LIKE MOTHER USED TO MAKE. Dana Estes & Co., Boston (1912). 1st ed. 220p.

1590 HOWARD, MARIA WILLETT. LOWNEY'S COOK BOOK. (revised) A new guide for the housekeeper. Walter M. Lowney Co.: Boston, 1912. 421p. and ads.

1591 JONES, MARY CHANDLER. Lessons in Elementary Cooking. Illus. Boston, 1912. 266p.

1592 BAXTER, LUCIA ALLEN (MILLETT). Housekeepers Handy Book. Illus. by Mary H. Northend. Boston: Houghton Mifflin Co., 1913. 270p. frontis., plates.

1593 BENTON, CAROLINE FRENCH. Easy Meals. Illus. Dana Estes: (1913). Boston. 325p.

1594 BISCUIT AND CAKES. The "Reliable" Method. Boston; Reliable Flour Co., 1913. 64p. Pictorial wraps.

1595 MORRIS, JOSEPHINE. Household Science and Arts for Elementary Schools. By the supervisor of household science in the Boston P.S. New York: American Book Co. (1913). 248p. illus.

1596 SEA FOOD RECIPES. How to Prepare & Serve Fish, Oysters, clams, scallops, lobsters, crabs and shrimp. Boston, 1913. 147p.

1597 HILL, JANET MCKENZIE. THE AMERICAN COOK BOOK. Recipes for Everyday Use. Illustrated. Boston Cooking-School Magazine, 1914. 1st ed. 255p.

1598 WARDALL, RUTH A. AND WHITE, EDNA NOBLE. A Study of Foods. The authors, professors at, respectively, Iowa and Ohio State Univ. Boston: Ginn & Co. (1914). 174p. Frontis.

1599 GREER, CARLOTTA C. A TEXT-BOOK OF COOKING. From the Technical High School. Illustrated. Allyn and Bacon; Boston, 1915. 431p.

1600 HILL, JANET MCKENZIE. Canning, Preserving & Jelly Making. Little, Brown & Co., Boston, 1915. Illus. 189p. & ads.

1601 ALLEN, IDA C. BAILEY. Mrs. Allen's Cook Book. Intro. by Professor Lewis B. Allyn. Illus. with photographs by T. L. Allen and A. E. Sproul. Boston: Small, Maynard & Co., 1917. 756p.

1601a DRAKE, SAMUEL ADAMS. Old Boston Taverns and Tavern Clubs. With account by Walter K. Watkins. Boston: Butterfield, 1917. 124p. and map.

1602 EAST, ANNA MERRITT. KITCHENETTE COOKERY. Practical plans and foods. Illustrated. Little, Brown: Boston, 1917. 112p.

1603 HANDY, AMY L. WAR. FOOD. Practical & Economical Methods of Keeping Vegetables, Fruits, and Meats. Houghton Mifflin, Boston, 1917. 76p. illus.

1604 HOWARD, M. W. THE PRACTICAL COOKBOOK—A Book of Economical Recipes. Ginn Co.: Boston, 1917. 152p.

1605 KIRK, ALICE GITCHELL. PRACTICAL FOOD ECONOMY. With illustrations. Little, Brown, and Company, Boston, 1917. 246p.

1606 LINCOLN, MARY J. The School Kitchen Textbook. Illus. Boston: Little, Brown, and Company, 1917. 308p.

1607 O'BRIEN, CHARLES. Food Preparedness for the United States. Boston: Little, Brown, and Company, 1917. 118p.

1608 SABIN, EDWIN L. How Are You Feeling Now? Includes chapter "On a diet." Illus. by Tony Sarg. Little, Brown & Co., Boston, 1917. 1st ed. 97p.

1609 STERN, FRANCES AND SPITZ, GERTRUDE T. Food for the Worker. Food values, costs and recipes for 7 weeks. Foreword by Lafayette B. Mendel, Professor of Psysiological Chemistry, Yale Univ. Boston: Whitcomb & Barrows, 1917. 131p.

1610 WELLMAN, MABEL THACHER. Food Study. A textbook in home economics for high schools. The author, assistant professor in Indiana University. Boston: Little, Brown and Company, 1917. 324p. illus.

1611 ALLEN, IDA BAILEY. Mrs. Allen's Book of Sugar Substitutes. Boston: Small, Maynard & Co., 1918. 92p.

1612 ALLEN, IDA BAILEY. Mrs. Allen's Book of Wheat Substitutes. Boston: Small, Maynard & Co., 1918. 80p.

1613 BRADLEY, ALICE. Wheatless and Meatless Menus and Recipes. Boston: B. B. Nichols, printer, 1918. 35p.

1614 BREWSTER, EDWIN TENNEY AND LILIAN. THE NUTRITION OF A HOUSEHOLD. House Beautiful Publishing Co., Boston, 1918. 208p.

1615 DAVIS, MARY C. The Cook's Economical Book. Boston, W. A. Butterfield (1918). 104p. plus 2p. illus.

1616 DONHAM, S. AGNES. MARKETING AND HOUSEWORK MANUAL. Menu making. Little, Brown, and Co., Boston, 1918. 241p.

1617 HUGHES, MARY B. EVERYWOMAN'S CANNING BOOK. The A B C of Safe Home Canning and Preserving. Whitcomb & Barrows, Boston, 1918. 96p.

1618 KEENE, SALLY. Eat To Live. The Problem of Food Values Reduced to Simple Terms. Boylston Publishing Co., Boston, 1918. 47p.

1619 KING, CAROLINE BLANCHE. Caroline King's Cook Book. Foundation principles of good cookery, with recipes. Illus. from photos. Boston: Little, Brown and Co., 1918. 275p.

1620 NEIL, MARION HARRIS. ECONOMICAL COOKERY. How to choose foods, plan and prepare meals. With illustrations from photographs. Little, Brown and Co.: Boston, 1918. 346p.

1621 SMITH, FRANCES LOWE. More Recipes for Fifty. Boston: Whitcomb and Barrows, 1918. 225p.

1622 Bergengren. The Comforts of Home. Concerning Kitchens. Boston, 1919. 107p.

1623 Farmer, Fannie Merritt. The Boston Cooking School Cook Book. Illus. Little, Brown, Boston, 1919. 656p. and ads. (Note: 1st ed. 1896).

1624 Andrea, A. Louise. Dehydrating Foods. Fruits, Vegetables, Fish and Meats. Illustrated. Cornhill: Boston, 1920. 206p.

1625 Greer, Carlotta C. School and Home Cooking. Illus. Boston: Allyn & Bacon (1920). 530p.

1626 Harvey, Lucile Stimson. Food Facts for the Home-Maker. Town Dietitian, Brookline, Mass. Boston: Houghton Mifflin Co., 1920. 314p. 4 col. pl.

1627 Hunt, Laura A. (Editor). The Housekeeper. Boston: The H. Lee Company (1920). 680p. Ads.

1628 Howard, Maria Willett. Lowney's Cook Book. A full record of delicious dishes. Col. illus. Boston: Lowney, 1921. 395p., bibliography, glossary, index and ads.

1629 Matthews, Mary Lockwood. Foods and Cookery and the Care of the House. First lessons for elementary schools. The author, a professor of home economics in Purdue Univ. Boston: Little, Brown, & Co., 1921. 189p. illus.

1630 Spencer, Evelene and Cobb, John N. Fish Cookery. 600 recipes for the preparation of all kinds of fish; with accompanying sauces, seasonings, dressings and forcemeats. Authors respectively of the U. S. Bureau of Fisheries, and the Univ. of Washington. Boston: Little, Brown, and Co., 1921. 364p.

1631 Bradley, Alice. For Luncheon and Supper Guests. 10 menus; more than 100 recipes. Illustrated. Whitcomb & Barrows: Boston, 1922. 1st ed. 96p.

1632 Richards, Lenore and Treat, Nola. Quantity Cookery. Menu planning and cookery for large numbers. The authors, assistant professors of institution management, Univ. of Minn. Boston: Little, Brown & Co., 1922. 200p.

1633 Chambers, Mary D. A Book of Unusual Soups. Boston: Little, Brown, and Co., 1923. 162p. illus.

1634 Fox, Fannie Ferber and Schwartz, Lavinia S. Fannie Fox's Cook Book. Illus. from photographs. Boston: Little, Brown and Co., 1923. 535p.

1635 Hill, Janet McKenzie. Cooking for two. A Handbook for Young Housekeepers. Illustrated. Little, Brown: Boston, 1923. 406p.

1636 Hill, Janet McKenzie. Salads, Sandwiches and Chafing-Dish Dainties. 54 illustrations of original dishes. Little, Brown: Boston, 1923. 231p.

1637 McKenny, Ella Clark. Cooking Problems of the Community Group and Formulas Standardized for Quantity Work.

The author, instructor at the Univ. of Chicago. Boston: Whitcomb & Barrows, 1923. 169p.

1638 ALLEN, LUCY G. CHOICE RECIPES FOR CLEVER COOKS. Recipes carefully selected and tested at the Boston Cooking School. Illustrated from photographs. Little, Brown; Boston, 1924. 1st ed. 282p.

1639 ALLEN, LUCY G. TABLE SERVICE. For Students of the cooking school. Illustrated. Little, Brown: Boston, 1924. 128p.

1640 BRADLEY, ALICE. The Candy Cook Book. Illus. Boston, 1924. 222p.

1641 CHAMBERS, MARY D. One-Piece Dinners. Short and/or long cooking. Frontispiece. Little, Brown & Co., Boston, 1924. 188p.

1642 MODERN PRISCILLA COOK BOOK. 1000 recipes tested and proved at the Priscilla Proving Plant. Special subscription edition. Priscilla: Boston, 1924. Illus. 352p.

1643 CHAMBERS, MARY D. ONE-PIECE DINNERS. Illustrations from photographs. Little, Brown; Boston, 1925. 188p.

1644 ALDRICH, MRS. THOMAS BAILEY. CHOICE RECEIPTS. Boston, 1925. 1st ed. 219p.

1645 FARMER, FANNIE MERRITT. THE BOSTON COOKING-SCHOOL COOK BOOK. Illustrated. Little, Brown, and Co., Boston, 1925. 806 p. ads missing.

1646 JACQUES, MARIE. COLETTE'S BEST RECIPES. (See Foreign sec.)

1647 RICHARDS, LENORE AND TREAT, NOLA. Tea-Room Recipes. A book for home makers and tea-room managers. Boston: Little, Brown, and Co., 1925. 147p.

1648 ROGERSON, JESSIE B. A CAKE MANUAL. Classification of cakes—, and recipes. M. Barrows: Boston, 1925. 113p.

1649 ALLEN, LUCY G. TABLE SERVICE. Table service for all occasions. Illustrated. Little, Brown; Boston, 1926. 128p.

1650 BRADLEY, ALICE. Salads Alluring and New. Discoveries in color, rare new flavor and zest. Boston (1926). 12p. booklet.

1651 HAINES, EDITH. TRIED TEMPTATIONS. Todd Press, Boston: 1926. 71p.

1652 HILL—JANET MCKENZIE. THE AMERICAN COOK BOOK. Recipes for Everyday Use. Illustrated. Boston Cooking-School Magazine Co., Boston, 1926. 263p.

1653 MILLEN, ROSE. Light on Dietetics, Menus to reduce, or to gain weight. Boston: The Four Seas Co., (c. 1927). 88p. illus. Frontis. portrait.

1654 PICKETT, MARY C. (Edited and Tested by) HOME BEAUTIFUL EXPOSITION BOOK. Prize recipes. Campbell: Boston (1927). 1st ed. 64p.

1655 SPRING, JAMES W. BOSTON AND THE PARKER HOUSE. About the people who lived on that historic spot. Old menus, and one new one.

Illustrated: colored end papers. Privately printed. J. R. Shipple Corp., Boston, 1927. 230p.

1656 ALLEN, LUCY G. A BOOK OF HORS D'OEUVRES. Relishes and appetizers. Profusely illustrated. Little, Brown; Boston, 1928. 119p.

1657 BIXBY, CAROLYN WEBBER. The Glenwood Cook Book . . . Boston: Glenwood Home Service Department (1928). 106p., illus.

1658 CHAMBERS, MARY D. BREAKFASTS, LUNCHEONS AND DINNERS. How to plan, serve, and how to behave at them. A book for school and home. Illustrated. Boston Cooking-School Magazine: Boston, 1928. 151p.

1659 COWLES, FLORENCE A. (Compiled by) SEVEN HUNDRED SANDWICHES. Little, Brown; Boston, 1928. 1st ed. 246p.

1660 DEN DOOVEN, K. CAMILLE. The Modern Cook Book . . . Original photos. Boston: The Colonial Press (1928). 224p.

1661 HARRISON, MARIE. Cook and Be Cool. A book for hotweather housekeeping. Boston: Houghton Mifflin Co., 1928. 150p.

1662 MACDOUGALL, ALICE FOOTE. The Autobiography of a Business Woman. Illus. Boston, 1928. 205p.

1663 SMITH, FRANCES LOWE. Recipes and Menus for Fifty as used in the School of Domestic Science of the Boston Y.W.C.A. Boston: M. Barrows & Co., 1928. 246p.

1664 TALCOTT, MELINDA E. (director). Tested Recipes, compiled by Houghton & Dutton's Modern Methods Kitchen. Ring binder. Mass., 1928.

1665 ALLEN, LUCY G. A BOOK OF HORS D'OEUVERS. Relishes and appetizers and foods. Illustrated. Little, Brown: Boston, 1929. 119p.

1666 LA GANKE, FLORENCE. Patty Pans. A cookbook for beginners. Illus. by W. Prentice Phillips. Boston: Little, Brown, and Company, 1929. 268p.

1667 RUDY, ABRAHAM. Practical Handbook for Diabetic Patients. With 180 international recipes (American, Jewish, French, German, Italian, Armenian, etc.) Intro. by Dr. Frederick M. Allen. Boston: M. Barrows & Co., 1929. 180p. illus.

1668 BRADLEY, ALICE. DESSERTS. Including layer cakes and pies. Illustrated. Barrows: Boston, 1930. 270p.

1669 COME INTO THE KITCHEN. 32p. illus. Pictorial wraps. Mass., 1930.

1670 BBADLEY, ALICE. DESSERTS including LAYER CAKES AND PIES. Hot desserts, and frozen desserts; by a Principal of Miss Farmer's School of Cookery. M. Barrows, Boston, 1931. 270p.

1671 FEICHELT, MELANIE. Two Hundred Famous Viennese Recipes. (See Foreign sec.)

1672 HEYWOOD, MARGARET WEIMER. In cooperation with World Famous Chefs. THE INTERNATIONAL COOK BOOK. With photographs of

48 chefs who contributed to the volume. No publisher, no date. Boston (c. 1931). 383p.

1673 MEAD, WILLIAM EDWARD. The English Medieval Feast. Describes food and drink, their preparation, service and setting. Boston: Houghton Mifflin Co., 1931. 272p.

1674 LUTES, DELLA THOMPSON. BRIDGE FOOD FOR BRIDGE FANS. M. Barrows & Co., Boston, 1932. 1st ed. 70p.

1675 ALLEN, LUCY G. TABLE SERVICE. With illustrations. Little, Brown: Boston, 1933. 174p.

1676 HARRIS, JESSIE W.; SPEER, ELISABETH LACEY. EVERYDAY FOODS. Values of foods, menus, recipes. Houghton Mifflin, Boston (1933). 1st ed. 550p.

1677 HESELTINE, MARJORIE AND DOW, ULA M. Good Cooking Made Easy and Economical. Boston: Houghton Mifflin Co., 1933. 507p. illus.

1678 HILL, SARAH C. A Cook Book for Nurses. 5th ed. rev. Boston, 1933. 76p.

1679 THE MODERN HOME. Compiled by expert economists. Boston: Modern Home Publishing, 1933. 337p. Wraps.

1680 ALLEN, LUCY G. MODERN MENUS AND RECIPES. Little, Brown; Boston, 1935. 1st ed. 335p.

1681 CODMAN, THEODORA LAROCQUE. Was It a Holiday? Illus. Boston, 1935. 1st ed. 235p.

1682 MACDOUGALL, ALICE FOOTE. COOK BOOK. A cookbook for the home maker, and for the woman in business. Photographs from the restaurants by F. S. Lincoln Lothrop, Lee and Shepard Co., Boston, 1935. 292p.

1683 PLATT, JUNE. Party Cookbook. How to cook for friendly or elegant parties. Houghton Mifflin, Boston (1936). 277p.

1684 FARMER, FANNIE MERRITT. THE BOSTON COOKING-SCHOOL COOK BOOK. Illus. 6th ed. completely revised. Little, Brown and Co., Boston, 1937. 838p. and ads.

1685 GREER, CARLOTTA C. FOODS AND HOME MAKING. A text book. Illus. Decorative end papers. Allyn and Bacon, Boston, 1937. 635p.

1686 EL COCINERO ESPANOL. Tested Recipes of Famous Spanish Dishes. (See Foreign sec.)

1687 HARRIS, FLORENCE LA GANKE. The Home Economics Omnibus. For the well-fed family. Illus. Little, Brown & Co., Boston, 1938. 617p.

1688 HILL, JANET MCKENZIE. COOKING FOR TWO. Special plans for the small family. Illustrations. Little, Brown: Boston, 1938. 362p.

1689 ANDRESS, GOLDBERGER, AND DOLCH. Growing Big and Strong. A child's book. Col. illus. Boston, 1939. 237p.

1690 LANG, GLADYS T. THE COMPLETE MENU BOOK. Menus and recipes for all occasions. Houghton Mifflin: Boston, 1939. 1st ed. 399p.

1691 OWEN, JEAN Z. IT'S MORE FUN TO BE THIN. Things to do to get that way. Line drawings. Marshall Jones Co.: Boston (1939). 181p.

1692 ALLEN, LUCY G. TABLE SERVICE. A guide to the teacher and the waitress, and a reference book for the hostess. New edition, completely revised. With illustrations. Little, Brown & Co.: Boston, 1940. 203p.

1693 EARLY, ELEANOR. She knew what he wanted. Stories about what men like, including food. Drawings by Jane Miller. Waverly House, Boston, 1941. 1st ed. 190p.

1694 FOWLER. Food. A weapon for Victory. Boston, 1942. 185p.

1695 KENT, LOUISE ANDREWS. MRS. APPLEYARD'S KITCHEN. A reading cook book about good food and people. Houghton Mifflin: Boston, 1942. 1st ed. 319p.

1696 MILLS, MARJORIE. COOKING ON A RATION. Food is Still Fun. Houghton Mifflin: Boston, 1943. 190p.

1697 PERKINS, WILMA LORD. The Fannie Farmer Junior Cook Book. Fun cookery for junior miss. Illus. by Martha Powell Setchell. Little, Brown: Boston, 1943. 208p.

1698 BROWN: CORA, ROSE AND BOB. THE WINE COOK BOOK. Incomparable Recipes from France, the Far East, South and Elsewhere. A section on wine. Little, Brown, Boston (1944). 462p.

1699 COWLES, FLORENCE A. (compiled by) 1001 SANDWICHES. Hot and cold and every which way. Little, Brown, and Co., Boston, 1944. 288p.

1700 HIBBEN, SHEILA. AMERICAN REGIONAL COOKERY. Recipes from your favorite region. Little, Brown: Boston, 1946. 1st ed. 354p.

1701 RASMUSSEN, MRS. MRS. RASMUSSEN'S Book of One-Arm Cookery. Pict. end papers. Boston, 1946. 101p.

1702 LUCAS, DIONE. THE CORDON BLEU COOK BOOK. (See Foreign sec.)

1703 MCCARTHY, MARGUERITE GILBERT. THE COOK IS IN THE PARLOR. Delicious recipes that are economical. Little, Brown and Co., Boston, 1947. 1st ed. 310p.

1704 MCCARTHY, MARGUERITE GILBERT. Aunt Ella's Cook Book. Atlantic Monthly Press Book. Little, Brown & Co., Boston, 1949. 205p.

1705 MORRISSEY, LOUISE LANE AND SWEENEY, MARION LANE. AN ODD VOLUME OF COOKERY. From the collection of the Club of Odd Volumes. Decorations by John V. Morris. Mifflin: Boston, 1949. 215p.

1706 PASLEY, VIRGINIA. THE CHRISTMAS COOKIE BOOK. DRAWings by Barbara Corrigan. Colored, cookie end papers. An Atlantic Monthly Press Book. Little, Brown, Boston, 1949. 1st ed. 147p.

1707 VERRILL, A. HYATT AND BARNETT, OTIS W. Foods America Gave the World. Illus. by the author. A fascinating book. Appendix I gives list of American Food Plants, and Nuts. Appendix II a list of American Food Animals and edible Insects. Boston: L. C. Page & Co., 1937. 5th impression, 1950. 289p.

1708 MARVEL, ELINORE J. Cook It Ahead. Houghton Mifflin: Boston (1951). 243p.

1709 MACLAREN, HALE. Be Your Own Guest. Once-a-Week Cooking with Section on Wines by Emerson Wirt Axe. Houghton Mifflin, Boston, 1952. 178p.

1710 EWELL, RAYMOND. DINING OUT IN AMERICA'S CITIES. Listings with comments. Little, Brown and Co., Boston, 1954. 1st ed. 226p.

1711 LUCAS, DIONE AND ROBBINS, ANN ROE. THE DIONE LUCAS MEAT AND POULTRY COOK BOOK. Drawings by Phoebe Nicol. Little, Brown & Co., Boston, 1955. 1st ed. 324p.

1712 SOME PUDDINGS. Boston: Reliable Flour Co. n.d. Tiny, 16p. advertising booklet.

Michigan

1713 THE HEALTH REFORMER'S PROGRESSIVE COOK BOOK AND KITCHEN GUIDE, comprising recipes for the preparation of hygienic food, directions for canning fruit, etc. Battle Creek: Health Reform Institute, 1870. 76p. pamphlet. Ads.

1714 DUFFIELD, MARY B. AND STEWART G. D. The Home Messenger Book of Tested Receipts. Respectfully dedicated to the friends and patrons of the Detroit Home of the Friendless . . . Detroit; E. B. Smith and Co., 1873. 137p.

1715 GRAND RAPIDS RECEIPT BOOK, compiled by the Ladies of the Congregational Church, for the Ladies' Fair, held at Luce's Hall, May, 1871. New ed. rev. and enl. Grand Rapids: H. M. Hinsdell, 1873. 51p.

1716 A CHOICE FRAGMENT of what mother-in-law knows about cooking; or, Many a dime saved. Compiled by two ladies of much experience both in cooking and economy. Detroit: W. A. Scripps, 1875. 24p. Wraps.

1717 THE HOUSEHOLD MANUAL OF DOMESTIC HYGIENE; Foods and Drinks, Common Diseases, Accidents and Emergencies, and Useful Hints and Recipes. Battle Creek: Office of the Health Reformer, 1875. 1st ed. 124p. (Bound with: The Health and Diseases of Woman, by R. T. Trall, M.D., Battle Creek 1873, 60p. and An Essay on Tobacco-Using by R. T. Trall, M.D., Battle Creek, 1872. 62p. and ads.)

1718 KELLOGG, J. H., M.D. THE HOUSEHOLD MANUAL. Hygiene, Food and Diet. The Office of the Health Reformer, Battle Creek, 1877. 1st ed. 172p. and ads.

1719 THE AMERICAN HOME COOK BOOK. By ladies of Detroit and other cities. Detroit & Chicago: Rose-Belfore Pub., 1878. 386p.

1720 ATKINS, BARBARA M. (pub. anon.) The Temperance Cook

Book: plain or fancy cookery without use of wine, cider or alcoholic liquors. Detroit: Herald Pub. House (1878). 376p.

1721 Kellogg, J. H., M.D. The Household Manual. 2nd ed. Mich., 1878. (See No. 1718).

1722 Stewart, Isabella G.D., Sill, Sally B. and Duffield, Mary B. The Home Messenger Book of Tested Receipts. Total abstinence. Respectfully dedicated to the patrons and friends of the Detroit Home of the Friendless. 2nd ed. Detroit: E. B. Smith & Company, 1878. 287p.

1723 Scripps, J. Annie. Our Daily Bread, as prepared at Dr. Fairchild's Hygiene Home, Quincy, Illinois. Detroit: W. A. Scripps, Printer, 1879. 63p. Wraps.

1724 The Successful Housekeeper. A Manual of Universal Application, dedicated to Those Housewives who delight in making home a place of peace, comfort and enjoyment. Detroit: M. W. Ellsworth, 1882. 608p. illus. with col. plates and black & white cuts.

1725 Trinity Church Cook Book. By the Ladies of St. Mary's Society. Bay City: 1887. 104p. Many ads.

1726 The Successful Housekeeper. A Manual of Universal Application. Several thousand recipes. Frontispiece in color, many illus. Frank S. Burton: Detroit, 1888. 608p.

1727 Darling, Edgar S. (Anon.) Our Home Cyclopedia . . . Cookery and Housekeeping. Detroit: The Mercantile Publishing Co., 1889. 400p. illus.

1728 Bush, B. . . Fields' Busy Bee-Hive Economy Cook Book. Jackson: Published expressly for the Dry Goods House of L. H. Fields (Jackson, Mich.) (Late 1880's). This is one of the most curious of early American regionals, because actually it is the same *Every-day Cook-Book* by Miss E. Neill, under another name—obviously a nom de plume, B. Bush suggesting Busy B. Although the text is the same, and the true title "Every-day Cook-book" is carried at the top of every page, there are 316 pages instead of 315 as in the Neill copy, so the books were printed from different plates.

1729 Neill, Miss E. The Every-Day Cook-Book. Encyclopedia of Practical Recipes for Family Use. Economical, reliable and excellent. Decorative end papers. Busy Bee Hive, Jackson. no date (late 1880's). 315p. & viii pages Index.

1730 A Collection of Tested Recipes.—Compiled by the Ladies' Aid Society of the First Methodist Episcopal Church; Albion: Albion Recorder Book and Job Print, 1890. 148p. and frontis. Ads.

1731 Ellsworth, Milon W. and Tinnie. The Queen of the Household. "Thoroughly Practical, Rigidly Economical and in Every Way Reliable." Detroit: Ellsworth & Brey, 1890. 166p. illus.

1732 F. P. W. (compiler). Hints for the Table—A Collection of recipes from Many Sources. Detroit: Dec. 8 to 13, 1890. 97p. and ads. Wraps.

1733 THE MUSKEGON COOK BOOK OF TESTED RECEIPTS (total abstinence). Ladies' Society of the First Baptist Church . . . (Muskegon:) Wanty & Manning, 1890. 128p. and ads.

1734 KELLOGG, MRS. E. E. SCIENCE IN THE KITCHEN. A scientific treatise on food, principles of healthful cookery, large number of wholesome recipes. Illustrated. Health Publishing Co., Battle Creek, 1892. 1st ed. 573p.

1735 ELLSWORTH, MILON W. AND TINNIE. The Home Economist. A manual for the people. Frontis. and illus. Detroit: F. B. Dickerson Co., 1895. 473p.

1736 THE ANN ARBOR COOK BOOK. Compiled by the Ladies' Aid Society of the Congregational Church. Ann Arbor: 264p. and ads. 1899.

1737 LAMBERT, ALMEDA. Guide for Nut Cookery. With a brief history of nuts and their food values. Illus. Battle Creek: Joseph Lambert & Co., 1899. 451p.

1738 SELECTION OF CHOICE RECEIPTS. Compiled by St. Paul's Guild of the Episcopal Church, Cover-title, "Lansing Cook-Book." Lansing: (early 1900's). 100p. and ads. Wraps.

1739 SOUVENIR COOK BOOK. Published by A. B. Watson Women's Relief Corps, No. 171. With list of members and officers of W.R.C., Auxiliary to the Grand Army of the Republic. Grand Rapids: (early 1900's). 64p., wraps, many ads.

1740 THE LEONARD COOK BOOK. Compiled expressly for 'our' many customers. Recipes contributed by the ladies of Grand Rapids. H. Leonard & Sons: Grand Rapids (1901-1902). 248p.

1741 CHASE, ALVIN WOOD. Dr. Chase's Recipes or Information for Everybody, an invaluable collection of practical recipes, occupational, medical, household. (Thompson & Thomas, 1902). Ann Arbor, 601p.

1742 BROOKS, CHARLES JOSEPH. Marine Stewards and Cooks' Guide and Manual of Cooking . . . Port Huron: C. J. Brooks, 1903. 128p.

1743 MOTHER HUBBARD'S MODERN CUPBOARD. "This book is never sold but is given away with $1.00 worth of extracts." Battle Creek: R. W. Snyder (1903.) 170p.

1744 THE ANN ARBOR COOK BOOK. Compiled by the Ladies' Aid Society of the Congregational Church. Menus and signed recipes. Handwritten recipes & clippings added. Second ed. George Wahr, Ann Arbor, 1904. 607p.

1745 LANDAU, ELIZA. The Four World's Fairs' Cook Books of Philadelphia, Chicago, Buffalo and St. Louis. Nothing omitted in the way of good things to eat. Detroit: Griswold Press (1904). 287p.

1746 Old Recipes for New Housekeepers and New Recipes for Old Housekeepers. Published by the Ladies of Trinity Episcopal Church. Grand Lodge: (c. 1905). 103p. and ads. Wraps.

1747 Superior Cook Book. Grace Church. (Ishpeming: Press of the Peninsular Record Pub. Co., 1905.) 5ed. 78p. and ads.

1748 Kellogg, Mrs. E. E., A.M. Healthful Cookery. A collection of choice recipes, with special reference to health. Wraps. Kellogg Food Company, Battle Creek, 1908. 314p.

1749 Michigan State Federation Cook Book. Recipes contributed by Women's Club members from places all over the state of Michigan. 1909. 135p. and ads.

1750 Every-Day Cooking Cards. Detroit: no pub., 1911. 20 leaves. Copyright by M. E. Trowbridge.

1751 Nolton, Jessie Louise. Chinese Cookery in the Home Kitchen. (See Foreign sec.)

1752 Muskegon Woman's Club Cook Book. A Collection of Choice Tested Recipes compiled and arranged by the Social Department of the Club. Muskegon: 1912. 129p. and ads.

1753 Cooper, Lenna Frances. The New Cookery. A book of recipes, most of which are in use at the Battle Creek Sanitarium. Illus. Good Health Publishing Co.; Battle Creek (1914). 301p. and ads.

1754 Hoover, Ruth H. Honey Flavor Harmonies. Extension Bulletin 213. Illus. Michigan State College, East Lansing, 1914. 36p.

1755 The Housewife's Kitchen Companion Cook Book and Book of 1000 Facts. Buying, cooking and medical remedies. Detroit: Oldor Publ. (1915). 111p. Paper.

1756 Meyer, Virginia M. Simple Menus for Informal Affairs. Detroit: (1916). 19p. Wraps.

1757 Warner, Harriet. Attractive Menus. Bay City: A. E. Ripley, 1916. 28p. Wraps.

1758 Blackman, Edith. War-time Cookery. Practical recipes to aid in the conservation movement. Ypsilanti: The Ypsilanti Press (1917). 55p. Wraps.

1759 Cooper, Lenna Frances, B.S. How to Cut Food Costs. Low cost recipes; good bibliography, index. Good Health Publishing: Battle Creek, 1917. 128p.

1760 Hegner, Jane Zabriskie. The Nellie Custis Cook Book . . . (By Jane Z. Hegner.) (Ann Arbor: Ann Arbor Press, 1917.) 78p. 5th ed.

1761 Cook Book. Compiled by Fassett Mother's Club of Parma, Mich. This is almost as much a joke book as a cook book—about 40p. have jokes between the ads. Mich.: (c. 1920). 98p. and ads.

1762 Favorite Recipes. Prepared by the Woman's Guild. Signed by the contributors. Wraps. St. Paul's Episcopal Church, Lansing, 1920. 106p.

1763 McCollum, Elmer Verner, and Simmonds, Nina. The American Home Diet. Illus. F. G. Mathews Co. Detroit. 1920. 237p.

1764 Book of Recipes. Woman's Association, Brewster-Congregational Church. Detroit, 1921. 193p. illus. 2nd ed. ads.

1765 Copely, Lu Vada. Copely's Recipes of Good Things To Eat. 89 recipes. Kalamazoo: Merchants Pub. Co., 1921. 60p. Port. on title p.

1766 Recipes for Instruction in Domestic Science, elementary and intermediate grades. Published by the authority of the Board of Education. City of Detroit. Detroit, 1921. 72p.

1767 The Battle Creek Cook Book. First Congregational Church, Battle Creek, Mich. . . Battle Creek: Ellis Pub. Co., 1922. 163p. (Lettered on cover, 3rd ed.)

1768 Stevens, Mary. The Easy Way in Cookery. A modern book of tested and tried recipes for these days of light housekeeping and kitchenettes. Bay City: Snover & Laframboise, 1922. 280p.

1769 A Collection of Recipes. Compiled by The Negaunee Woman's Club. Autographed. Negaunee Woman's Club, Negaunee (1923.) 127p. and ads.

1770 Leonard, Mrs. C. H. and Whittier, Mrs. W. H. Mrs. Leonard's Cookbook. Grand Rapids: Grand Rapids Refrigerator Company (c. 1923). 253p.

1771 McCollum, E. V., and Simmonds, Nina. The American Home Diet. An answer to 'What Shall We Have for Dinner.' Illus. Frederick C. Mathews: Detroit, 1920. (1923). 237p.

1772 The Yellow and Blue Cook Book. Women's Auxiliary to the University of Michigan Presbyterian Corporation. The First Presbyterian Church, Ann Arbor, Mich. . . (Milan: Printed by the Milan Leader), 1923. 160p. and ads.

1773 Old and New Tested Recipes. Compiled by the Ladies' Aid Society of the Scandinavian M.E. Church. Wraps. Ludington, 1924. 81p.

1774 Rockford Congregational Church Cook Book. (Rockford), 1924. 56p. and ads.

1775 The Trinity Community Church Cook Book. Published by the Ladies' Aid Society. Grand Rapids: 1924. 140p. and ads. Wraps.

1776 King, Helen Gleason. Some Things in Good Taste . . Bay City: (1925). 85p. Wraps.

1777 A Collection of Recipes. Negaunee: 1926. 2nd ed. (See No. 1769).

1778 Cook Book. League of Cathedral Women of St. Paul's Cathedral. Detroit: (1926). 121p. Ads.

1779 The Road to Wellville. Use of cereals as food—or drink.

Frontispiece. Postum Cereal Co.: Battle Creek, 1926. 103p.

1780 Williams, Myrtle Dyer. The Y.W.C.A. Blue Book of Menus. Grand Rapids: Caroline W. Putnam Training School, YWCA (1926). 46p. Wraps.

1781 A Collection of Recipes. Compiled by the Presbyterian Ladies' Aid, Presbyterian Church, Bessemer, Mich. . . Bessemer: The Herald Pub. Co., 1929. 224p.

1782 Good Will Cook Book. Published by Good Will Circle, King's Daughters, Ann Arbor: 1929. 120p. and ads.

1783 Plymouth Ten Cook Book. Park Congregational Church. Signed recipes. Grand Rapids: 1929. 120p.

1784 What to Eat and How to Cook It. A book of tested recipes by the Ladies' Aid Society of the Baptist Church. Nashville: 1929. 53p.

1785 Cook Book. Compiled by The Mayflower Guild, 1st Congregational Church. Kalamazoo, 1930. 222p.

1786 Munising's Tried and True Cook Book. Compiled and arranged by the Ladies' Aid Society of the First Presbyterian Church, Munising: 1930. 120p.

1787 The New Idea Cook Book. Women's Missionary Society, First United Presbyterian Church. Detroit: (c. 1930). 65p. and many ads.

1788 Saunders, Mrs. Carrie Ives. Bread-Winner's Smiles, or Choice Recipes for the Modern Home-Maker. Recipes for Political Potpourri, Jack Straw Salad, Bancroft Hash (Noted from Shore to Shore.) Saginaw: n.d. (c. 1930). 20p. wraps.

1789 Thompson, Anna. The Anna Thompson Cook Book. My many years experience as a cook. Detroit; C. Burris, printer, (1931). 138p. Wraps.

1790 Calkins, Myrtle. The Detroit News Menu Cook Book. Detroit: The Detroit News, 1933. 256p.

1791 A Book of Practical Recipes for the Housewife. Cover-title "Detroit Times Cook Book, 1934 Edition." Detroit: Detroit Times, 1934. 309p.

1792 The Calumet Book of Oven Triumphs! Calumet: General Foods Corp. (1934). 32p. illus. Col'd. covers.

1793 Dwyer, Eleanor and Vincent. Caviar to Cordial. A book of recipes. Detroit: Sign of the Mermaid, 1935. 129p.

1794 Lutes, Della T. The Country Kitchen. Stories of cookery at home, with some family recipes. Country nostalgia, from Michigan of the '80's. Little, Brown; Boston, 1936. 261p.

1795 Cooking With Cold. Practical Recipes . . . Detroit: Norge Rollator Refrigerator Co. (1937). 22p. illus. with photographs. Wraps.

1796 SWEENY, MARY E. AND BUCK, DOROTHY CURTS. How to Feed Young Children in the Home. Detroit: The Merrill-Palmer School, 1937. 68p. illus. with photographs. Wraps.

1797 COOK BOOK. Compiled by the Mayflower Guild of the First Congregational Church. Kalamazoo: 1941. 219p. and ads.

1798 WHITFIELD, MILDRED G. & HORNBACHER, MARIE & PEARSON, RUTH. The Fine Art of Cooking. Recipes without meat. Unusual color plates & good printing. White Brothers' Graphic Arts Center, Berrien Springs. (1941). 175p.

1799 CORBETT, LUCY AND SIDNEY. TESTED RECIPES. Hope Church 60th Anniversary Cook Book 1862-1942. Published by the Women's Aid Society of Hope Church. Holland: 1942. 112p., plastic bdg. Ads. Frontis. photo of church.—same as above with pictorial dust wrapper, "Tulip Time Recipes."

1800 HOUGH, STELLA V. AND KOPERA, KAY. Woman's Exchange Recipes—Fifty Years of Good Cooking. Detroit: (1946). 189p. Photo. of Woman's Exchange on dust wrapper. Ads.

1801 ANGELS IN THE KITCHEN "FAVORITE RECIPES." Compiled and published by the Marygrove College Alumnae Association. (Detroit: 1947). 154p., spiral bdg., ads.

1802 CORBETT, LUCY AND SIDNEY. POT SHOTS FROM A GROSSE ILE KITCHEN. About life and philosophy and food. Decorative end papers. Illustrated by William Thomas Woodward. Harper: New York, 1947. 214p.

1803 CORBETT, LUCY AND SIDNEY. FRENCH COOKING IN OLD DETROIT SINCE 1701. (See Foreign sec.)

1804 KITCHEN KAPERS. Sponsored by the Women of the Neese Chapter No. 401. List of Officers for 1954-1955. Fremont: (c. 1955). 60p. illus. Ads.

1805 ADVENTURES IN COOKING. Women's Guild of the Episcopal Church, Ironwood, n.d. 106p. and ads.

1806 ALLEN, ANNE. LUNCHEON IS SERVED. Jenny Wren's favorite recipes. Wraps. Jenny Wren Tea & Gift Shop, Pentwater, n.d. 102p.

1807 CHOICE RECIPES. Young Ladies Sodality of St. Adalbert's Parish. Ring binder, light cardboard pages, replete with ads. Grand Rapids, n.d. (before 1920?). 95p.

1808 FAVORITE RECIPES AND DIRECTORY. Traverse City: Central M. E. Church. 32p. wraps. Many ads.

1809 MCGUIRE, LELIA M. Old World Foods for New World Families. A handbook. Detroit: Merrill-Palmer School, n.d. 74p. Wraps. Frontispiece.

1810 SELECTED RECIPES. St. James Church, Grosse Ile: n.d. 174p. Oilcloth hard cover.

1811 SUCCESSFUL COOKING PRIMER. Ten lessons, illustrated by menus and recipes. Detroit: The Detroit Free Press, n.d. 66p. Wraps.

1812 VEGETARIAN COOK BOOK. The principles of vegetarianism from a scriptural standpoint. Benton Harbor: Published by House of David, n.d. 175p.

Midwest

1813 SAFFORD, VIRGINIA. FOOD OF MY FRIENDS. The specialties of food served by friends; it is preponderantly from the Mid-West. Illustrations by Grace Keen. University of Minnesota: Minn., 1944. 1st ed. 300p.

1814 LOTHE, ADA B. AND GRIEM, BRETA L. AND KEATING, ETHEL M. THE BEST FROM MIDWEST KITCHENS. Menus and recipes and table settings for holidays. M. S. Mill Co.: New York, 1946. 1st ed. 284p.

1815 CLARK, GRACE GROSVENOR. THE BEST IN COOKERY IN THE MIDDLE WEST. Principally regional cookery; warm & friendly notes telling the background of the recipe. Decorative end papers. Doubleday & Co., Inc., New York, 1956. 1st ed. 355p.

Minnesota

1816 BUCKEYE COOKERY AND PRACTICAL HOUSEKEEPING. Tried and approved, original recipes. Buckeye Publishing: Minneapolis, 1877. 464p.

1817 PRACTICAL HOUSEKEEPING. A Careful compilation of tried and approved recipes. Buckeye Publishing Co.: Minneapolis, 1881. 670p.

1818 BEECHER, MRS. HENRY WARD. The Home: How to make and keep it. Minneapolis: Buckeye Publishing Co., 1883. 598p. Frontis. port. of the author.

1819 PRACTICAL HOUSEKEEPING, a Careful Compilation of Tried and Approved Recipes. Frontis: "Love in a Cottage" engraved by Willard from a drawing by Sol Eytinge, Jr. Minneapolis: Buckeye Publishing Co., 1883. 672p.

1820 KLEIN, NORA C. (Anon.) The Golden Mean in Cookery. Minneapolis: W. L. Klein & Co., 1884. 144p.

1821 PRACTICAL HOUSEKEEPING. A careful compilation of Tried and Approved Recipes. Illustrated. Buckeye Publishing. Minneapolis, 1884. 688p.

1822 SIDLE, FLETCHER, HOLMES COMPANY'S COOK BOOK. For housewives everywhere. With the compliments of the proprietors of the celebrated North Western & Zenith Mills. A booklet. Minneapolis, 1885. 45p.

1823 (WILCOX, ESTELLE WOODS). The Buckeye Cook Book. A careful compilation of tried and approved recipes for all departments of the household. Subsc. ed. Minneapolis: Buckeye Pub. Co., 1887. 1288p. illus.

1824 VALLENTIN, C. A. Praktisk Illustrerad Kok-Bok for Svenskarne Amerika. (See Foreign sec.)

1825 BARNES, AMY (compiler). Cooking School Recipes . . . Minneapolis: A. Roper, 1890. 106p.

1826 Wilcox, E. W. (Anon.) The New Practical Housekeeping. A compilation of new, choice and carefully tested recipes. Minneapolis: Home Pub. Co., 1890. 689p. illus.

1827 Chauven, Jane Putnam. The Columbian Cook Book. Plain and fancy cookery, carefully tested. St. Paul: J. W. Cunningham & Co., 1892. 107p.

1828 The Country Kitchen. The Northwestern farmer recipe book. Every recipe contributed by a farmer's wife, mother, or daughter. St. Paul: E. A. Webb, 1894. 136p. illus.

1829 Masterman, Lillian C. The Common Sense Cook Book. A volume of practical recipes . . presented with compliments of the Weinhold Drug Co. Minneapolis: The Swinburne Printing Co., 1894. 160p. and ads. Wraps.

1830 Washburn, Crosby Co.'s New Cook Book. Minneapolis: Washburn, Crosby, 1894. 72p. illus. Paper.

1831 Wilcox, E. W. (Anon.) The Housekeeper Cook Book. Published to meet the sustained demand for Buckeye Cook Books. Minneapolis: Housekeeper Pub. Co., 1894. 759p. illus.

1832 Snapp, Suzan Sweeny. Salads: Sauces & Savory Sundries. St. Paul: Wm. E. Banning, 1895. 62p. illus. Hard cover.

1833 Marshall Ladies' Choicest and Best. Compiled by the Ladies of St. Cecelia Guild. Marshall: no pub., 1898. 133p. and ads.

1834 Schaeffer, Jennie (Anon.) Metropolitan Club Cook Book. New York City. Minneapolis: Augsburg Publishing House Print (1901). 224p.

1835 Shepperd, Juniata L. Handbook of Household Science. Author's edition. St. Paul: Webb Publishing Co., 1902. 593p. illus.

1836 The New Buckeye Cook Book. Revised and enl. ed. of Practical Housekeeping. 9th ed. St. Paul: Webb, 1904. 1288p. illus. Portrait.

1837 Langdon, Amelie. Dainty Drinks and Sherbets. A little booklet of recipes. Wraps. 1906. (The Great Western Printing, Minneapolis), 72p.

1838 Daniel Webster Cook Book. New Ulm: Eagle Roller Mill Co. (c. 1907). 105p. illus. Wraps.

1839 Gregory, Annie R. Woman's Favorite Cook Book. Author assisted by 1000 homekeepers. Embellished with col. and photo engravings. Autographed recipes. (Minneapolis: 1907). 610p.

1840 Langdon, Amelie (compiler). Just For Two. 4th ed. rev. & enl. Minneapolis: H. W. Wilson Co., 1909. 223p.

1841 Lyndale Cook Book. Compiled by The Ladies' Aid Society of Lyndale Congregational Church. Minneapolis, 1910. 142p.

1842 TRIED AND TRUE COOK BOOK. Compiled by THE WILLING WORKERS of The Incarnation Parish. Minneapolis, 1910. 151p.

1843 CLUB WOMAN'S COOK BOOK. Signed recipes. Wraps. The Ramblers Club, Minneapolis, 1911. 1st ed. 166p. and ads.

1844 THE PILLSBURY COOK BOOK. A new edition. More than 300 recipes compiled by Mrs. Nellie D. Gans . . with 70 original drawings picturing the process of flour milling. Designed by Geo. J. Lewis. Minneapolis: 1911. 125p. Paper.

1845 WHEELOCK, MRS. T. B. MY NEW RECIPE BOOK. Privately printed. St. Paul, 1912. 310p. and ads.

1846 THE PILLSBURY COOK BOOK. Pamphlet. Illus. 300 Recipes with menus. 70 original drawings of flour milling. Pillsbury Flour Mill: Minneapolis (1914). 126p. Wraps.

1847 BROTHERS, MINNIE E. Bread Making and Bread Baking Embracing Selections in Pastry, General Cooking, Canning, Preserving, Jelly Making and Candy Making. Minneapolis, no pub., 1915. 128p.

1848 HOUSEWIVES' FAVORITE RECIPES for cold dishes, dainties, chilled drinks, etc. Compiled by White Enamel Refrigerator Co. St. Paul: Louis F. Dow, 1916. 126p. and ads. Signed recipes.

1849 SAUER, ELFRIEDA VON ROHR. The Wingold Cook Book. Compiled for St. Martin's sewing circle. Winona: Jones & Kroeger Co. (1916). 217p.

1850 FRICH, LILLA P. The Housewife's Cook Book . . . Minneapolis: Augsburg Pub. Co., 1917. 3, 297p.

1851 COOKING FOR THE JOYFUL EATER. A cook book of 800 tried recipes. Compiled by The Second Division of the First Presbyterian Church. Mankato. n.d. 192p. and ads. pict. wraps. Signed recipes. (c. 1919).

1852 THE CLUB WOMAN'S COOK BOOK. Autographed recipes. Minneapolis, 1920. A. M. Chesher Ptg. Co., 238p. and ads.

1853 LYNHURST CONGREGATIONAL CHURCH COOK BOOK. Tested recipes. Minneapolis, 1920. 215p.

1854 DELTA GAMMA COOK BOOK. For National Scholarship Fund. Lambda Nu Chapter, Minneapolis, 1922. 271p.

1855 THE COMMISSION SHOP COOK BOOK. Published by the Commission Shop of Minneapolis (1923). 184p.

1856 OIE, HELMINA. Recipe Book, with household hints and diet suggestions for the sick. Minneapolis: Augsburg Publishing House (1923). 100p.

1857 RELIABLE RECIPES. Prepared by the Rector's Guild, St. John's Church, St. Paul, Minn. . . St. Paul: Griggs, Cooper & Co. (1923). 191p. and ads.

1858 BAILEY, PEARL L. Foods, Preparation and Serving. St. Paul: Webb Pub. Co., 1924. 486p. illus.

1859 ABBOTT HOSPITAL ALUMNAE DIETS AND RECIPES. Nurses Alumnae Association of Abbott Hospital. (Minneapolis), 1925. 251p. incl. frontis.

1860 BAILEY, PEARL L. Domestic Science, Principles and Application. A textbook for public schools. St. Paul: Webb Pub. Co., 1926. Rev. ed. 375p. illus.

1861 DIAMOND JUBILEE RECIPES. The Sisters of Saint Joseph, St. Paul, 1851-1926. 181p. and ads.

1862 FISHER, MARIAN COLE. Marian Cole Fisher handbook of cookery. St. Paul, n. pub., 1927. 814p. illus. Ads. Frontis. port. of author, col. plates.

1863 THE BRIDE'S BOOK OF RECIPES AND HOUSEHOLD HINTS. St. Paul: C. J. West (c. 1928). 122p. illus. Ads.

1864 BATES, GEORGE M., World War Veteran. Select Recipes of Prominent Ladies. Autographed recipes in a little book. St. Paul: Pub. by the author (1929). 72p. 3p. Index.

1865 CHRISTIANSON, LOUISE C. Tested Recipes with practical references, my friends' favorite recipes. Tintah: L. C. Christianson, 1931. 128p. and ads. Wraps.

1866 BUSINESS WOMAN'S CLUB COOK BOOK. Compiled by Ways and Means Committee. Autographed recipes, favorites of members. Minneapolis: The Business Women's Club, March, 1932. 127p. Ring book, wraps.

1867 BALANCED RECIPES. Prepared under the personal direction of Mary Ellis Ames, Head of Staff of the Cooking Service. Looseleaf book with indexed recipes; in metal cover for moisture proofing. Pillsbury Flour Mills Co., Minneapolis, 1933. 224p. and blank note p.

1868 COOK BOOK BY THE ST. PAUL'S CHURCH GUILD. Wraps. St. Paul's Episcopal Church, Minneapolis, 1934. 166p.

1869 CROCKER, BETTY. Vitality Demands Energy. 109 smart new ways to serve bread. (Minneapolis). General Mills, Inc. (1934). Sewed. 54p. illus.

1870 DIET MANUAL. Hospital nutrition. St. Mary's Hospital, Rochester (1934). 191p.

1871 WILLIAMS, MIRIAM J. The Country Kitchen Cook Book. Rev. by Farmer's Wife Magazine. St. Paul: Webb Book Pub., 1934. 183p. illus. Wraps.

1872 KELLOGG P.T.A. COOK BOOK. Recipes collected and signed. Looseleaf booklet. Contemporary and local ads. Kellogg, 1935. 80p.

1873 THE GOLD MEDAL RYE DICTIONARY. For bakers. Illus. Spiral binding. Gold Medal Rye Flours, General Mills, Minneapolis (1936). 93p.

1874 ST. ELIZABETH'S GUILD COOK BOOK. St. Paul, 1936. 72p.

1875 WATKINS COOK BOOK. A spicy collection of recipes. Watkins: Winona, 1936. Spiral binding . . 192p.

1876 MADISON, WILLIAM. MA-NO-MIN (WILD RICE). Ojibway's Native Food Recipes. Booklet. Private printing. Minneapolis, 1940. 16p.

1877 FRIENDSHIP LEAGUE'S BOOK OF TESTED RECIPES. Collected among the friends of the Swedish Tabernacle Church, Spiral binding. Independent Press, Minneapolis, 1944. 250p.

1878 VICTORY COOK BOOK. Recipes, autographed, compiled by The Ladies' Aid of Victory Lutheran Church. Here's a Lazy Daisy Cake. Names & addresses of the Committee. Minneapolis: (Osterhus Pub. Co., 1947). 196p. Photo of church. Spiral. Wraps.

1879 THE MARIETTA CIRCLE. By the Reorganized Church of Jesus Christ of Latter Day Saints. A home made job, mimeo, many unnumbered pp. Oilcloth ring bdg. Minneapolis, 1947-8.

1880 WILLIAMS, CAROLINE D. THE JUNIOR COOK. For students of H. S. age; beginners in cooking. Spiral binding, mimeographed pages. Burgess Publishing Co., Minneapolis, 1948. 116p.

1881 CROCKER, BETTY. BETTY CROCKER'S PICTURE COOK BOOK. Recipes with pictures. Colored end papers with lists of measures, contents of cans, temperature chart. General Mills, Minneapolis, 1950. 1st ed. 449p.

1882 THE METHODIST COOK BOOK. Spiral. Ellendale, 1950. 67p.

1883 ENCORE. A Cookbook of the Favorite Dishes of the World's Most Famous Musicians. Introduction by Francis Robinson. Illustrations by Antal Dorati. Compiled by Women's Assoc. of Minneapolis Symphony Orchestra. End paper charts and measures. Random House: New York 1958. 310p.

1884 COOK BOOK . . Women's Guild of Hennepin Avenue Church. Heavy looseleaf paper book. n.d. 144p.

1885 COOK TO PLEASE. Autographed recipes from friends & members. Casseroles, salads & desserts. Cover drawing by Mr. Mart Fowler; Division page drawings by Mrs. Brewster Hanson. Minneapolis: The Junior Board of Northwestern Hospital. 127p. n.d.

1886 MILLS, RUTH ELIZABETH. DELICIOUS COOKIE RECIPES. Guaranteed 100 per cent perfect in every respect. Wraps—advertising Gettelman Milwaukee Beer. Frederick H. Girnau Creations, Minneapolis, no date. 64p.

1887 MILLS, RUTH ELIZABETH. FAMOUS INTERNATIONAL RECIPES. From all over the world. Wraps. Frederick H. Girnau Creations, Minneapolis. n.d. 96p.

1888 THE MINNEAPOLIS JUNIOR LEAGUE COOK BOOK. Foreword by Louise Andrews, Pres. Illus. by Mrs. J. D. Holtzermann. Reproduced handwritten & signed recipes of members. Minn.: 398p. n.d.

1889 RECIPE FOR MAKING BREAD. By Merchant Millers. Washburn,

Crosby Co., Minneapolis, n.d. folder.

1890 THE ROBBINSDALE LIBRARY CLUB COOK BOOK. Autographed recipes. Compiled by the Cook Book Committee. Photo of library. Robbinsdale: Osterhus Pub. Co. n.d. Unnumbered pages. Ring book. Stiff paper.

Mississippi

1891 WARREN, MARY ELIZABETH (CARSON), "Mrs. E. F. Warren." Cook Book. New southern recipes. Yazoo City Herald Print., Yazoo City, 1922. 115p.

1892 HENDERSON, MINNIE. Selected recipes used by Mrs. H. Gulfport: no. pub. (1924). 32p. (Recipes from the Gulf Coast).

1893 THE LAUREL COOK BOOK. Compiled by the Women of St. John's Guild in the year 1900. Revised and reprinted 1914. Revised and reprinted 1933. Edited by Mrs. George Gardiner and Mrs. McWhorter Beers. Nine-page story of Laurel by Harriet Stark Gibbons. Autographed recipes. Interesting ads. Boards. Laurel, 1933. 331p.

1894 WATTS, EDITH BALLARD WITH JOHN WATTS. Jesse's Book of Creole and Deep South Recipes. Special recipes from the Bay St. Louis, Miss. and New Orleans. Viking: New York, 1954. 1st ed. 184p.

1895 COOKING 'ROUND THE WORLD. Southern Recipes. Ads. Brookhaven. n.d. 88p.

Missouri

1896 THE GRANITE IRON WARE COOK BOOK, cover-title "How to Cook." Booklet 3½ x 5 in. St. Louis Stamping Co., St. Louis, 64p. Date (c. 1878) deduced from testimonials. 80 illus.: Batter buckets, special broilers, Oval Butter Kettle, an Oyster Stand. Of importance because it set the style of kitchen utensils country-wide.

1897 MY MOTHER'S COOK BOOK. Compiled by Ladies of St. Louis, for the benefit of the Women's Christian Home. St. Louis: Hugh R. Hildreth Printing Co., 1880. 244p.

1898 THE HAND AND CORNUCOPIA FULL OF GOOD THINGS FOR EVERYBODY. Price Baking Powder Co., St. Louis and Chicago. 80p. booklet, col. pict. covers. Copyright 1878, Steele & Price; reprinted in (1883)—deduced from added, dated testimonials.

1899 SUDDOTH, HARRIET ALMARIA BAKER. The American Pictorial Home Book; or, Housekeeper's Encyclopedia. For the special use of families and nurses. St. Louis: Historical Publishing Co., 1883. 606p. Frontis. port. of author. Col. plates.

1900 THE PILGRIM HOUSEKEEPER; a collection of tried recipes. Ladies of the Pilgrim Church, St. Louis, Mo. . . St. Louis: R. P. Studley & Co., 1886. 298p. illus. Ads.

1901 THE GRANITE IRON WARE COOK BOOK. Booklet (see No. 1896). Slight variations but printed from same plates. Mo.: (1887).

1902 The Missouri Cook Book. Proved recipes, collected and arranged by the ladies of the Baptist Church, Fayette, Mo. St. Louis: Farris, Smith & Co. (1887). 163p.

1903 Willis, Mrs. Thomas F. (editor). Housekeeping and Dinner Giving in Kansas City . . . Kansas City: Press of Ramsey, Millet & Hudson, 1887. 299p.

1904 Tanty, Francois. French Cookery for Every Home. (See Foreign sec.)

1905 Laughlin, Helen M. The Journal of Agriculture Cook Book. A new, complete and specially practical and economical kitchen guide . . principally original receipts submitted in competition. St. Louis: Journal of Agriculture Co., 1894. 328p. Frontis. portraits.

1906 Yanner, Fred M. The Modern Cake Baker, Pastry Cook and Confectioner; French, German and American. For largest establishments, and private families. Kansas City: Hudson-Kimberly, 1894. 250p.

1907 Williams, Martha M. The Capital Cook Book. Compiled from original and tested recipes. Monroe City: F. L. Link, 1895. 302p. Frontis. port.

1908 Gladfelter, Lisbeth M. An outline of Domestic Science embracing 80 lessons. Designed for the P.S. St. Louis: 1898. 23p. Wraps. Frontis. practice schoolroom. Bibliography.

1909 The Canton Cook Book. Compiled from Recipes Contributed by the Ladies of Canton. Published by the Ladies of the Baptist Church. 133p. and ads. 2nd ed., 1900.

1910 Dainty Fruit Recipes. Loose leaf booklet. Coast Products Co. St. Louis (c. 1900). 92p.

1911 Jones, Mrs. Paul. Choice Recipes by Famous Cooks and Housekeepers. For benefit of Immanuel Baptist Church. St. Louis, A. R. Fleming Printing Co., 1900. 71p. and ads.

1912 Dodds, Susanna W. Health in the Household; or Hygienic Cookery. 6th ed. St. Louis: S. W. and M. Dodds, 1901. 603p.

1913 Economy Cook Book, edited by Presbyterian Ladies, Liberty, Missouri. Tried and found good. Revised ed. Liberty: Press of the Liberty Tribune, 1903. 87p. and ads.

1914 Choice and Tested Recipes. Collected and signed by the ladies. Wraps. Ladies of the Fifth Presbyterian Church of Kansas City (c. 1905). 62p.

1915 The Wilson Range Complete Cook Book. 2000 original tested recipes. St. Louis: Simmons Hardware Co. (c. 1905). 200p. illus. Paper.

1916 Harland, Marion. Marion Harland's Complete Cook Book. New ed., revised and enlarged. Thousands of carefully proved recipes. Illus. Marion Co., St. Louis (1906). 781p.

1917 St. Louis Cook Book . . . Missouri Baptist Sanitarium, St. Louis. (St. Louis: Press of Buschart Bros. Print. Co., 1908). 241p. and ads.

1918 Cook Book compiled by Ladies Aid Society of Calvary Presbyterian Church, Springfield, Mo. Rev. edition. 1909, 3rd ed. 198p. and ads.

1919 Outline of Lessons in Cooking. For the district schools. St. Louis: 1909. 61p. Wraps.

1920 Webb City Cook Book. Compiled and published by Ladies' Aid Society, Central Methodist Church. Webb City, 1909. 72p., many ads, wraps.

1921 Coppin, Charles Arthur. Mamma's Hints to Housekeepers. 4th ed. St. Louis: The F. B. Chamberlain Co., 1910. 64p. and ads.

1922 Laskowski, P. E. The Art of Baking. 3rd ed. rev. Kansas City: The Laskowski Publishing Co. (1910). 232p.

1923 National Calendar or Herrick's Almanac for the Year of our Lord 1910. Missouri.

1924 Bridal Chef. Suggestions and practical recipes for the new housekeeper. St. Louis: Brandt & Cordes, 1911. 312p. illus.

1925 Dearth, Nellie D. Food for Thought; 375 Guaranteed Recipes. Cover design and illus. by C. Forbes Baker. St. Louis: Louis F. Dow Co. (1911). 128p.

1926 Mrs. Dwelle's Cook Book. A Manual of Practical Recipes. St. Louis, 1911. 174p. and ads.

1927 Hamel, G. T. Modern Practice of Canning Meats. St. Louis: The Brecht Co. (1911). 93p. illus.

1928 Johnson, Gertrude I. Domestic Science. A text in cooking and syllabus in sewing. For use in the Kansas City Elementary Schools. 3rd rev. ed. Mo.: the author, publisher, 1912. 153p.

1929 Cook, Isaac T. (presentation copy) Food Preparation and Combination. St. Louis, 1914. 72p.

1930 Dutaud, Hannah Caren. Practical Cookery; for school and home. St. Louis: The Author, 1914. 167 plus 111p.

1931 Mission Circle Cook Book. Young Ladies Mission Circle, Christian Church. Liberty: Printed at the Advance Office, 1915. 88p.

1932 O'Bryan, Marie J. Recipes for Cooking in Casseroles. St. Louis: Daro Publishing Co., 1915. 93p.

1933 O'Bryan, Marie J. Recipes for Salads, Dressings, Sauces and Sandwiches. St. Louis: Daro Publishing Co. (1915). 93p. Portrait.

1934 Osthaus, Leo (Anon.) The Red Cook Book of Treasured Recipes and Diet Kitchen. A compilation of rare family recipes . . not heretofore published. 1st ed. St. Louis: L. Osthaus, 1915. 212p. Wraps. Signed recipes and ads.

1935 St. Mary's Guild Cook Book. A Collection of Tested Recipes. Compiled by St. Mary's Guild of St. Peter's Episcopal Church, St. Louis. Revised ed.—September 1915. 132p.

1936 Lute, Isabel M. Klever Kinks in Kookery. Kansas City: Missouri Dairy Co. (c. 1916). Wraps.

1937 Bullock, Tom. The Ideal Bartender. Tried, tested at the St. Louis Country Club. St. Louis, 1917. 53p.

1938 The Handy Cook Book. Kansas City: Neel & Son, 1917. 143p. Paper.

1939 Kansas City Conservation Cook Book. Tried Recipes, suggestions for menu making, the principles underlying balanced meals. Wraps. Kansas City Food Conservation Board, Mo. 1918. 92p.

1940 Lynch, Reah Jeannette (compiler). "Win the War" Cook Book. Published by St. Louis County Unit, Woman's Committee Council of National Defense, Missouri Division. Frontis. portrait of Mrs. B. F. Bush, Chairman of the Committee. Cartoon from St. Louis Times: "Her 1918 Cook Book" Greater Conservation of Foodstuffs Will Help Win the War. Cover decorated with American Flag. Missouri, 1918. 168p. and ads.

1941 Allen, Ida Bailey. Tempting Recipes. St. Louis: Temtor Corn and Fruit Products Refining Co. (1920). 110p. and ads. Wraps.

1942 Dixie Cook Book. Tried and Tested Recipes. Kansas City Business Woman's Club, Kansas City (c. 1921-22). 160p. and charming ads.

1943 Lynn, Alma W. Helpful Hints for the Young Wife. Kansas City: The Western Baptist Pub. Co., 1922. 146p. Wraps.

1944 Recipes from Boonville. Business and Professional Women's Club, Boonville, 1st ed., Aug. 1923. 145p.

1945 Silvernail, Lulu Thompson. Nine Hundred Successful Recipes. Kansas City: "S and H. Cook Book," (1923). 288p. Frontis. portrait.

1946 The Unity Inn Vegetarian Cookbook. A collection of Practical Suggestions and Receipts for the Preparation of Non-Flesh Foods in Palatable and Attractive Ways. Kansas City: Unity School of Christianity, 1923. 339p.

1947 Cook Book. Cavalry Presbyterian Church, Springfield: 1924. 4th ed. 24p. Wraps. (See No. 1918).

1948 Recipes from Boonville. Mo.: 2nd ed. July, 1924. (See No. 1944).

1949 Time and Temperature Oven Cooking. Col. illus. Research Kitchens of American Stove Co., St. Louis (1924). 125p. and blanks for recipes.

1950 Vegetarian Cook Book. The Unity Inn. A Collection of Practical suggestions and receipts. Pub. by the United School of Christianity, Kansas City, 1924. 339p.

1951 SILVERNAIL, LULU THOMPSON. MY MOST SUCCESSFUL RECIPES. Tested recipes by the Domestic Science Teacher for the Southwestern Milling Co. Some handwritten recipes. S. & H. Cook Book: Kansas City (c. 1925). 175p. and index.

1952 SILVERNAIL, LULU THOMPSON. One Thousand Successful Recipes. Kansas City: "S. and H. Cook Book," (1926). 366p. Frontis. portrait.

1953 COOK BOOK OF THE WOMAN'S ASSOCIATION OF THE SECOND PRESBYTERIAN CHURCH. St. Louis, 1927. 256p. and ads.

1954 MENUS AND RECIPES FROM ABROAD. St. Louis: International Institute, 1927. 68p.

1955 SANSUM, W. D., M.S., M.D., F.A.C.P. THE NORMAL DIET. A Simple Statement of the Fundamental Principles of Diet for the Mutual Use of Physicians and Patients. C. V. Mosby Co., St. Louis, 1927. 136p.

1956 BRADBURY, MARION (compiler). Cook Book, Kansas City Chapter, of Soroptimist Clubs of America. Kansas City: Kellogg-Baxter Prtg. Co., 1930. 163p.

1957 GILLUM, LULU WILLIAMS. Modern Food Studies. Kansas City: The Gillum Publishing Co., 1930. 319p. illus.

1958 LANG, GLADYS T. Choice Menus for Luncheons and Dinners. 3rd ed. St. Louis: 1930. 135p.

1959 PET MILK COOK BOOK. Col. illus. Ring bdg. Wraps. St. Louis, 1930. 80p.

1960 REMSBURG, G. W. THE PAN-AMERICAN DIET BOOK. Scientific Eating by drugless physician. Nazarene Publishing: Kansas City, 1930. 320p.

1961 SANSUM, W. D. THE NORMAL DIET. Nutrition book with some diet menus. Mosby, St. Louis, 1930. 134p.

1962 THE S.E.A. COOK BOOK. Compiled for Use in the St. Elizabeth Academy Conducted by the Sisters of the Precious Blood from O'Fallon, 1930. 193p. Wraps.

1963 ROMBAUER, IRMA S. The Joy of Cooking. A compilation of reliable recipes with a casual culinary chat. Illus. by Marion Rombauer. St. Louis: A. C. Clayton Printing Co. (1931). 395p.

1964 SHANK, DOROTHY E. (Director) LORAIN COOKING. From the research kitchens of the company. Colored plates. American Stove Co.: St. Louis, 1931. 186p.

1965 BOYNTON, LOUISE; & CHILD, GEORGIE BOYNTON. Golden Grains. Cereals and how to use them in cooking. Clark-Sprague Co., St. Louis, 1932. 1st ed. 216p.

1966 LIVINGSTON, LORRAINE (compiler). Approved Enduring Favorites . . . Illustrated by Edna Brown . . . (St. Louis:) St. Louis, Mo.

Unit, Women's Overseas Service League (1932). 170p.

1967 KITCHENOLOGY WITH PRINCIPIA FRIENDS. Issued by the Principia Mothers' Club. St. Louis, 1933. 251p. illus.

1968 LANG, GLADYS T. Choice Menus for Luncheons and Dinners. 5th ed. Mo.: 1933. (See No. 1958).

1969 OUR READERS' COOK BOOK AND HOMEMAKERS' GUIDE. . . . Kansas City: Kansas City Journal-Post (1933). 191p. illus. Ads.

1970 CO-OPERETTES' CLUB COOK BOOK, compiled by the members of the club. Kansas City, 1934. 46p.

1971 MARIANNE. My Very Best Recipes. St. Louis: 28p., 1st ed., Wraps. 1934.

1972 RICHARDSON, MYRTLE. Genuine Mexican & Spanish Cookery Recipes for American Homes. (See Foreign sec.)

1973 SPRINGTIME MENUS AND RECIPES. St. Louis. Pet Milk Co., 1935. 32p. illus. Wraps.

1974 SHANK, DOROTHY E. MAGIC CHEF COOKING. From the Research Kitchen of the Co. American Stove Co., St. Louis, 1936. 294p.

1975 SHANK, DOROTHY E. (Director). MAGIC CHEF COOKING. Prepared and Tested in the Research Kitchen of American Stove Co. End paper drawings. American Stove Co.: Mo., 1937. 199p.

1976 YOUR FAVORITE RECIPES. By the Women's Council of the Country Club Christian Church. Kansas City: 1937. 153p.

1977 COOK BOOK. Compiled by the Woman's Society of St. John's Methodist Episcopal Church, South. St. Louis: April, 1938. 72p.

1978 LEMON PIES OR WASH TUBS—HOME COMFORT COOK BOOK. Dedicated to the Greatest of American Institutions, the American Housewife, by the Wrought Iron Range Co. of St. Louis, Builders of Home Comfort Ranges Since 1864. St. Louis: 1938. 132p. col. illus. Wire binding, wraps.

1979 COOK BOOK. Methodist Church, Rothville: June 1940. 80p. mimeographed. Wraps, spiral bdg.

1980 GARY, LAMORA SAUVINET. RHYTHM IN FOODS. A harmony between fine cooking and scientific food values. Colored end papers. Decorations. Spiral binding. Brown-White-Lowell: Kansas City, 1942. 1st ed. 157p.

1981 WESTPORT VICTORY COOK BOOK. O.E.S. Missouri: 1942. Wraps. 96p.

1982 CAMPBELL, VIRGINIA. Virginia Campbell's Cook Book. Favorite recipes as served in the 1850's at the Campbell House, 20 Lucas Place. Beautifully illustrated, reproduced handwritten recipes. Wraps. The Campbell House Foundation, St. Louis, 1943. 1st ed. 33p.

1983 MARVIN, ISABEL B. BON APPETIT—THE ST. LOUIS COOK BOOK. Food in the Mississippi River Tradition. Mifflin: Boston, Mass. 1947. 1st ed. 269p.

1984 McDonald, Virginia. How I Cook It (Edited by Eleanor Richey Johnston). Missouri and Southern cooking. Introduction by Duncan Hines. Glenn: Kansas City, 1949. 256p.

1985 Bulletin Number Four. Herbs and their use in old recipes. Wraps. Herb Society of America, St. Louis, 1954. 14p.

1986 Newton, Mrs. J. Eldred (Compiled by) Symphony of Cooking. Musical notes and autographed recipes. Cover by Rudolph Czufin. Illustrations by Aurelia Gerhard and Ganz Propper. Women's Association of the St. Louis Symphony Society; St. Louis, 1954. 472p. 16p. Index & Membership.

1987 Guia Para El Cuidado Prenatal. (See Foreign sec.)

1988 Eat Your Way to Glowing Health. 16p. folder advertising Good Life Publications. Afton: 1957. Illus.

1989 Hosford, Mary. The Missouri Traveler Cookbook. Memoirs and recipes. Foreword by Max Lief. Pastel paper; decorative end paper. Illustrated by Betty Crumley. Farrar, Straus and Cudahy; New York, 1958. 200p.

1990 O'Brien, Marian Maeve. The Bible Cookbook. Recipes directly related to a place or person in the Bible. Illustrated by Doris Hallas. Bethany Press: St. Louis, 1958. 350p.

1991 Pinkley-Call, Cora. From My Ozark Cupboard. A basic Ozark cook book with 200 tasty original recipes such as My Heritage Soup, Ozark One Pot Dinner, etc. Private printing, Missouri: 1959.

1992 The Granite Iron Ware Cook Book. Smaller booklet (see No. 1896). Mo.: n.d. 16p.

1993 Pealer, Don F. The Old Tavern Book of Recipes. Pub. by the Arrow Rock Chapter of the Daughters of the American Revolution. Mo. 128p.

1994 Taylor, Caroline N. French Sauces and Entrees. (See Foreign sec.)

Montana

1995 Royal Milling Co.'s New Cook Book. Great Falls, Royal Milling Co. (c. 1894). 72p. and ads. Wraps.

1996 Johnstone, May Searles. Mrs. Johnstone's Cook Book. A collection of her own recipes, faithfully tested. Butte: Butte Miner, 1905. 73p.

1997 Johnstone, May Searles. Mrs. Johnstone's Cook Book of Tested Recipes. Butte: Miner Publishing Co. (1911). 154p.

1998 The Bozeman Woman's Club Cook Book. Oilcloth. Bozeman. n.d. 208p.

Nebraska

1999 Universalist Cook Book, published by the Ladies Aid Society of the Universalist Church, Lincoln, Neb. Lincoln: State Journal Co., 1885. 47p. and ads. Wraps.

2000 St. Cecilia's Crumbs of Comfort, compiled by The Married Ladies' Sodality of the St. Cecilia's Cathedral Parish. Omaha: The J. H. Roberts Printing Company, 1909. 256p. and ads. Autographed recipes.

2001 York Cook Book . . . Arranged by ladies of the Presbyterian Church . . . (York? 1911.) 111p.

2002 Pfuhl, Alexis Constantin Carl. Science of Health. (See Foreign sec.)

2003 Arnbrecht, Jacob. Hygienic Cook Book. Healthful cookery, nutrition. College View: International Pub. Assoc. (1914). 318p.

2004 Benson Woman's Club Cook Book . . . Omaha: Douglas Print. Co., 1915. 176p. and ads.

2005 Rosicky, Mary. Bohemian-American Cook Book. (See Foreign sec.)

2006 The Greater Omaha Cook Book. Compiled by the Sisterhood of Temple Israel . . . Omaha: The Barkley Print. Co., 1916. 249p. and ads.

2007 Harrison, Robert Addison. The National Food and Health Book, . . Lincoln: The National Publishing Company (1917). 103p. Wraps.

2008 Lynch, Carrie Pauline. Pauline's Practical Book of the Culinary Art, for clubs, homes or hotels. Omaha: 1919. 112p. illus.

2009 Ley, Mrs. Henry. Wayne Community House Cook Book. Edited by Mrs. Ley; committee: Mrs. McEachen, Mrs. Lou Owen, Mrs. Homer Scase, Miss Margaret Pryor. Wayne: 1920. 137p. Wraps. Illus. Ads.

2010 Tried and Tested Recipes contributed by members and friends of the Methodist Episcopal Church, Wayne, Nebr. Cedar Rapids, Ia.: Laurance Press, 1926. 228p. and ads. Signed recipes.

2011 Munsell, J. Guy. The Language of Nature, Simplified Form. A nature food book. Published by Munsell's Mineral Food Co., Lincoln (1928). 3rd ed. 78p. Wraps.

2012 Humphrey, Frederick Blaine Know Your Groceries. This book might be called the Natural Science of the Bible Applied to the Practice and Philosophy of Youth and Health. Lincoln, 1939. Wraps. 103p.

2013 Leverton, Ruth M., Ph.D. Food Becomes You. Discussing diet. Illustrated by David W. Seyler. Univ. Nebraska Press: Lincoln, 1952. 192p.

2014 Instructions and Recipes. For making Ice Cream. Auto Vaccuum Freezer Co., Omaha. n.d. 24p. Pict. wraps.

2015 Woodmen Circle Cook Book. Compiled by Larocca-Talley Guards, Aksarben Grove No. 1, Omaha. 136p.

Nevada

2016 Brown, Helen Evans (ed.) The Virginia City Cook Book. Hundreds of receipts contributed by residents past & present. Engravings by Harry O. Diamond. Foreword by Lucius Beebe. Richie Press of Los Angeles (1953). 148p.

2017 BOULDER DAM SOUVENIR & COOK BOOK. Ring binding. Boulder City. 76p.

New England

2018 SWETT, LUCIE GRAY. New England Breakfast Breads, Luncheon and Tea Biscuits. Illus. Lee & Shepard, Boston, 1891. 129p.

2019 STROHM, GERTRUDE (compiled by). New England Cook Book. By Mrs. Lincoln, Parloa and others. C. E. Brown: Boston (1894). 245p.

2020 THE NEW ENGLAND COOK BOOK. The latest and best methods for economy and luxury at home. Nearly 1000 receipts. Decorations, advertisements. Charles E. Brown: Boston, 1905. 286p.

2021 THE NEW ENGLAND COOK BOOK. Latest and best methods for economy and luxury at home. Nearly 1000 recipes. Chas. E. Brown Publishing Co., Boston, 1906. 296p. and ads.

2022 GOOLD, MARY. The New England Cook Book. Milne Printery, Newport, R. I., 1909. 180p.

2023 PATTEN, MRS. FRANCIS JARVIS (compiler). Our New England Family Recipes. National Society New England Women, New York, 1910. Illus. 134p.

2024 WRIGHT, HELEN SAUNDERS SMITHE. The New England Cook Book. Duffield: New York, 1912. 327p. 1st ed.

2025 MORTON, LILLIAN. MRS. MORTON'S COOK BOOK. Proven Recipes of Delicious Foods Aided by New England and other home cooks. Wraps. Shrewesbury Publishing Co., Chicago, Ill. (1926). 160p.

2026 NEW ENGLAND FARM & GARDEN ASSN. 161 Unusual Recipes. Thumb indexed, oilcloth with pockets for more recipes. Ring binder. n.p. 1931. 62p.

2027 THE NEW ENGLAND HOTEL WOMEN'S COOKBOOK. An unusual book of choice and practical recipes contributed by the N.E. hotel women and chefs. The New England Hotel Women's Relief Association, Inc.: Boston, 1933. 131p.

2028 THE NEW ENGLAND COOK BOOK. Fine Old Recipes. Compiled and Edited by Kay Morrow: Assisted by Pauline Dubin. Decorations by Florence Bowe. Wraps. Culinary Arts Press, Reading, Pa., 1936. 48p.

2029 BROWN, MRS. NELLIE I. Recipes from Old Hundred; 200 years of New England cooking. New York: M. Barrows, 1939. 255p. incl. frontis.

2030 WOLCOTT, IMOGENE. THE YANKEE COOK BOOK. An Anthology of Incomparable Recipes from the Six New England States. Decoration by Edwin Earle and Alanson B. Hewes. End papers of State

Seals. Coward-McCann, New York (1939). 398p.

2031 MITCHELL, EDWIN VALENTINE. IT'S AN OLD NEW ENGLAND CUSTOM. Illustrated with prints of old New England. Not about recipes, about eating. Vanguard Press, New York, 1946. 1st ed. 277p.

2032 BOWLES, ELLA SHANNON AND TOWLES, DOROTHY S. SECRETS OF NEW ENGLAND COOKING. Many recipes from the descendants of cooks who made them famous. Drawings by P. Wenderoth Saunders. M. Barrows: New York, 1947. 327p.

2033 ORTON, ELLEN AND VREST. COOKING WITH WHOLEGRAINS. A New England cookbook containing many old-fashioned recipes. Illustrated. Farrar, Straus & Young: New York, 1951. 64p.

2034 FROST, HELOISE. EARLY AMERICAN RECIPES. A Collection of New England Family-Favorite "Rules." Old-Time Food, flavored with nostalgia, inviting as the author's 1809 Farm Kitchen at Moultonboro, N. H. Illustrated by Barbara Corrigan. Spiral binding. Boxed. Phillips Publishers, Inc.; Newton, Mass., 1953. 112p.

2035 EARLY, ELEANOR. NEW ENGLAND COOKBOOK. The food that made New England famous. Anecdotes. Charming old engravings. Random House; New York, 1954. 1st ed. 236p.

2036 MOSSER, MARJORIE. FOODS OF OLD NEW ENGLAND. Concise, detailed recipes. Introduction and notes by Kenneth Roberts. Doubleday & Co., New York, 1957. Original edition entitled GOOD MAINE FOOD. 428p.

2037 THE NEW ENGLAND COOK BOOK. With instructions on marketing and the choice of articles for food. The Benedict Popular Pub. Co., New York, n.d. 64p.

New Hampshire

2038 THE MANCHESTER COOKERY BOOK. Autographed recipes. Pub. for the benefit of the Y.W.C.A. Wraps. John B. Clarke's Mirror Steam Printing Establishment. Manchester, 1877. 65p.

2039 CONGREGATIONAL COOK BOOK. RECEIPTS FOR PICKLES, DESSERTS AND TEAS. Compiled by the Ladies of the Congregational Society of Atkinson, 1879. Printed, by Stiles, at Haverhill, Mass. 48p. and ads.

2040 JOY IN THE KITCHEN. Choice Receipts published by the Ladies of the Universalist Society. Interesting local ads. Wraps. East Jaffrey, N.H., Printed at The Courier Office, Winchendon, 1883. 48p.

2041 THE LADY'S FRIEND. Containing Valuable Receipts . . . Presented with the compliments of the J. A. Hoitt Company. Col. pictorial wraps. Quaint advertisements. Nashua, 1883. 48 unnumbered pages.

2042 JOHNSON, ELLEN TERRY. Hartford Election Cake and other receipts chiefly from manuscript sources. Published for the benefit of St. Peter's in-the-Mount, Holderness, N.H. Hartford, Conn.: The Fowler & Miller Co., 1889. 123p.

2043 LINCOLN, MRS. D. A. FROZEN DAINTIES. Fifty Choice Receipts for Ice Creams, Frozen Puddings, Frozen Fruits, Frozen Beverages, Sherbets and Water Ices. Prepared for The White Mountain Freezer Company. Pictorial wraps. Pub. by The White Mountain Freezer Comany, Nashua, 1895. 32p.

2043a THE BONNIE COOK BOOK. Published by the Ladies' Aid Society of the M. E. Church. Gold & silver cake & Providence River chowder. Hudson (c. 1900). 24p. booklet with ads of the era.

2044 LINCOLN, MRS. D. A. Frozen Dainties. Revised edition, 1902. (see No. 2043).

2045 OUR ALMA MATER COOK BOOK . . . By the Alumni of Dow Academy, Franconia, N.H. (Littleton: The Buffington Press), 1903. 124p. illus. Ads.

2046 THE NORTH CONWAY COOK BOOK . . . By the Ladies' Social Circle of the Methodist Episcopal Church, North Conway: Reporter Press (192-?). 159p. illus. Ads.

2047 NORTH CONWAY COOK BOOK. (North Conway, Reporter Press, 19-?) 126p. and ads. 2nd ed.

2048 HOFFMAN, MAY FISKE. Favorite Recipes of Celebrated People; Florence Crittenton League of Compassion Cook Book, compiled for the 20th annual bazaar. Peterborough: (1931). Looseleaf book.

2049 NUTTER HOUSE RECIPES. Thomas Bailey Aldrich Memorial. Photograph of Nutter House on front wrap. Recipes connected with the Aldrich family. Portsmouth (1941). 32p.

2050 FAVORITE RECIPES. Compiled by Bradford Women's Club. Autographed recipes. Plastic binding, wraps. Bradford, 1943. 143p. Ads.

2051 ADAMS, HELEN WARD (Edited by) SWANZEY KITCHENS. Revised. Favorite Foods of Familiar Folks including Selected Recipes from the original Swanzey Kitchens. Favorite recipes of Swanzey men serving their country in World War II, and also favorite dishes of members of the all-Swanzey cast of Denman Thompson's "The Old Homestead." Pictorial cover, plastic ring binding. (c. 1945). Swanzey,N.H. 73p.

2052 HOGAN, SYBIL NASH (Editor) WHAT'S COOKIN'—IN NEW HAMPSHIRE. Autograph recipes from Women's Clubs all over the state of New Hampshire. Plastic binding. Pictorial cover designed by Priscilla Lunderville. Pub. by Workshop Cards, Littleton, 1945. 39p.

2053 PEARSON, HAYDN S. THE COUNTRYMAN'S COOKBOOK. Country recipes with names like Hopping John Pea Soup, Blushing Bunny, Sisickquatash. Photographs. Whittlesey House, McGraw-Hill Book Co., New York, 1946. 311p.

2054 Cooley, Donald G. Eat and Get Slim. The New 9-Day Diet. Takes pounds away. Wraps. Your Health Publications, Concord, 1947. 64p.

2055 Deerfield Cook Book. The Ladies' Aid Society of Deerfield Church—Their Cookery Book. Some autographed recipes. Pictorial wraps. Deerfield, 1949. 52p. Ads.

2056 Progressive Club's "Husband Tested" Recipes. Autographed recipes. Wraps. Plastic binding. Many local ads. First Parish Church, Somersworth, 1949. 116p.

2057 Contoocook's Treasure of Personal Recipes. Autographed recipes, compiled by the W.S.C.S. of the Contoocook Methodist Church. Illus. wraps. Plastic binding. Local ads. Contoocook (1952). 38p. plus 22 unnumbered pages.

2058 Pearson, Haydn Sanborn. Country Flavor Cookbook. Recipes and essays. Rev. ed (Greenfield: the author, c. 1956). 236p.

2059 Farmer, Gertrude S. J. Applecrest Farm Cook Book. Favorite farm recipes. Wraps. Gertrude S. J. Farmer; Hampton Falls, n.d. 108p.

2060 Thursday Circle Cook Book. Congregational Church, Exeter, N. H. (1940's). Plastic binding, wraps. Autographed recipes. Designed and Printed by The Hampton Publishing Co., Hampton, n.d. 77p. and colored ads.

2061 The Watatic Grange Tried and True Cook Book. Autographed recipes. Local ads. Mirror Press, Manchester, n.d. Wraps. 44p.

New Jersey

2062 Hoyt, J. K. Romance of the Table. Breakfast, Dinner, Tea. Times Pub. Co.: New Brunswick, 1872. 445p.

2063 Lafayette Reformed Church —Old Dutch Receipts. (See Foreign sec.)

2064 Table Talk. A collection of tried and approved recipes. Pub. by the Young People's Association, Second Reformed Church, Hackensack, N.J. (Hackensack: Democrat Print, 1886.), 68p.

2065 Cooks in Clover . . . Compiled by the ladies of the North Reformed Church, Passaic, N.J. (Passaic: Thurston & Barker, 1889). xx, 114p.

2066 Tried and True Recipes. The Home Cook Book compiled by Chapter 14, "St. Thecla," of Christ Church, East Orange, . . . (n.p., 1889). 206p. and ads.

2067 Rolfe, Mrs. John Henry (compiler) . . . Receipt Book. Published and sold by the Improvement Society of the Second Reformed Church, New Brunswick, N.J. . . New Brunswick: The Improvement Society of the Second Reformed Church, 1890. 60p.

2068 Ludlum, Mrs. L. M. The New and the Old in Cookery. Paterson: Craig, Beckmeyer & Co., 1891. 2, 66, vii p.

2069 Y's Cook-Book for Wise Cooks. Published by the Young Women's Christian Temperance Union of Salem. 3rd ed. Salem: 1893. 53p.

2070 A Friend in Need. A cook book compiled by the Ladies of Park Avenue Methodist Episcopal Chapel, East Orange, 1894. 74p. and ads.

2071 Crinkles from Competent Cooks. A collection of tested recipes compiled by the Young Ladies Home Missionary Circle of the Woodbury Presbyterian Church. Woodbury; no pub., 1899. 61p.

2072 Biardot, A. Franco-American Soups and Other Specialties. A description of each variety. Jersey City Hts.: Franco-American Food Co., 1900. 32 unnumbered p. Col. illus. Col. pict. wraps.

2073 The Morristown Cook Book. Morristown: Vogt Bros. (1900). 110p.

2074 Woodbridge Cook Book . . . Woodbridge, N.J., 1903. 226p. and ads. Delicated to the Ladies of Woodbridge. Copyrighted by the Ladies' Association of the First Congregational Church, Woodbridge. Many interesting ads, oilcloth boards, autographed recipes.

2075 Keen, Georgia Harmony. Some Famous Old Recipes. Printed for the author by Journal Press, Elizabeth, 1904. 120p. Wraps.

2076 The Practical Cook Book. Selected Recipes from New Jersey. Compiled by The Women's Aid Society of St. Mark's P.E. Church. Wraps. Press Printing: Paterson, 1906. 128p. and ads.

2077 Kirmess Cook Book: A collection of well tested recipes from the best housekeepers of Jersey City and elsewhere . . . (Jersey City? 1907). 519p.

2078 Neil, Marion Harris. Alcono Cook Book . . . Newark: J. M. Pitkin & Co., 1909. 56p. Wraps.

2079 Selected Southern Recipes. Compiled by the Colonial Villa and dedicated to Cosmovilla. Given for the benefit of Orange Memorial Hospital. Autographed recipes. Orange: Press of the Chronicle Publishing Co., 1909. 101p. and ads.

2080 Andrews, Alfred. What Shall We Eat? Food Question from standpoint of Health, Strength & Economy. The Health Culture Co., Passaic, 1910. 131p. and ads.

2081 The Palisades Cook Book. . . Compiled and published by the Ladies Aid Society, Tenafly Presbyterian Church. Tenafly (1910). 265p. and ads.

2082 Prudential Cook Book. First Aid Hints. Care of the Baby. Pict. wraps in color. (N.J.?). Calendars for 1910 and 1911. 32p.

2083 Book of Choice Recipes, compiled and published by Auxiliary No. 1 of Monmouth Memorial Hospital, Long Branch, N.J.; and

Asbury Park Auxiliary of Ann May Memorial Hospital. (Newark), 1913. 164p. and ads.

2084 THE "DAISY" COOK BOOK. First Methodist Episcopal Church. Sold under the auspices of the Ladies' Aid Society. West Orange: (c. 1913). Unnumbered pages, Ads.

2085 THE METHODIST EPISCOPAL CHURCH COOK BOOK. Pub. under the direction of Mrs. M. Wayne Womer. Englewood: (c. 1913). 65p. and ads.

2086 THE WATCHUNG COOK BOOK. Tested recipes compiled by the Woman's Society of the Watchung Ave. Congregational Church, Montclair. Autographed recipes. Montclair: Italian Mission Printing Club, Nov. 21, 1913. 62p.

2087 THE HOME COMFORT COOK BOOK, containing over 400 selected recipes. Pub. for the Rosemary Club of the Sunday School, Congregational Church. Plainfield: W. Nichols Press, 1914. 102p. and ads.

2088 UP-TO-DATE COOK BOOK. Ladies' Aid of South Park Presbyterian Church. Newark, 1914. 164p. and ads.

2089 THE CHURCH WOMAN'S HOUSEKEEPER. Compiled and published by the Koinonia Society of the Calvary Presbyterian Church. Autographed recipes. Newark: 1915. 148p.

2090 THE "HOME" COOK BOOK. For the benefit of the Children's Summer Home of Cinnaminson, N. J. Autographed recipes. 2nd ed., 1915. 165p.

2091 WHITE, MRS. ALMA. WHY I DO NOT EAT MEAT. 30 of the most unusual, fanatical & repulsive illus. ever published in a vegetarian or other cookbook, such as Devouring Decaying Flesh, "The Flesh of all Kinds of Animals is on Sale in the Markets," showing reptiles, vermin etc. under the counter. Pub. by The Pentecostal Union (Pillar of Fire), Zarephath, 1915. 213p. and ads.

2092 HELPS FOR THE HOSTESS, Including 48 original and inviting menus . . . Camden: Joseph Campbell, 1916. 64p. Col. illus. Col. pict. wraps.

2093 VICTORY COOK BOOK. Compiled by the Ladies of the First Congregational Church. Autographed recipes. Jersey City: 1919. 128p. and ads.

2094 GILLIS, MARY M. Food Efficiency; or, the best food for the least money. Jersey City: International Letter Club (1920). 264p.

2095 SHAFTESBURY, EDMUND (Interpreted by). Life Building Method of the Ralston Health Club. "All Nature" Course. Ralston Health Club, Hopewell (1920). 240p.

2096 DAVIS BAKING POWDER RECIPES. Pamphlet, col. pl. Hoboken, 1922. 48p.

2097 FAVORITE RECIPES. Calvary M.E. Church. East Orange, 1923. 143p.

2098 KITCHEN KRAFT. Autographed recipes. Montclair Women's Club. Montclair, n.d. (c. 1932). 219p. and ads. Title page picture of Club House.

2099 THE GLEN RIDGE COOK BOOK. Autographed recipes reproduced in handwriting of contributor. Sponsored by the women's association of the Glen Ridge Congregational Church. Glen Ridge: 1936. 336p. illus. pict. wraps, spiral bdg.

2099a MATTINSON, EUSTACE R., N.D., D.O. PERFECT HEALTH. How to Regain and Maintain It by Alkalizing the Body. Menus and recipes. Wraps. Mattinson Health Foundation, Inc. Pompton Lakes, 1936. 93p. and ads.

2100 FRANCIS, CLARENCE. A History of Food and Its Preservation. A contribution to Civilization. Address delivered before Princeton University. Subject is Birds Eye Foods development. The Guild of Brackett Lecturers, New Jersey, 1937. 1st ed. 45p.

2101 MODERN FOOD MERCHANDISING. Practical Suggestions for Profitable Operation of the Complete Food Market; with emphasis on refrigeration. Profusely illustrated. C. V. Hill: Trenton, 1938. 241p. & ads.

2101a FROM RIDGEWOOD KITCHENS. Autographed recipes in reproduced handwriting. Sponsored by the Woman's Guild of the West Side Presbyterian Church. Ridgewood: 1941. 2nd ed. 400p. and ads.

2102 THE VILLAGE COOK BOOK. Illus. Ring binding, offset. Methodist Church, South Orange, 1947. 290p. and ads.

2103 MORRISTOWN COOK BOOK. Morristown, 1948. 248p.

2104 OLD AND NEW RECIPES from the Ladies of St. John's Church. Autographed recipes. Collected and arranged by Helen H. Pyne for the benefit of the Organ Fund. Elizabeth: 1948. 42p. cover pict. of church in 1840. Wraps.

2105 SOUVENIR PROGRAM. First Presbyterian Church, Wood Ridge, Ads and a few recipes. 36p. Spiral bdg. wraps. 1949.

2106 ROBERSON, JOHN & MARIE. THE COMPLETE BARBECUE BOOK. Two vols. in one handbook. Building fireplaces, menus and recipes. Illus. by Doremus. Prentice-Hall, Inc., New Jersey, 1951.

2107 COGGINS, CAROLYN. FABULOUS FOODS FOR PEOPLE YOU LOVE. Famous meals and recipes from Europe, mingled with our own, to make practical and delicious American menus. Decorations by Dave Lyons. Measurements, temperatures, quantity equivalents on end papers. Prentice-Hall: Englewood Cliffs, 1955. 1st ed. 308p.

2108 MCCARTHY, JOSIE. Josie McCarthy's Favorite TV Recipes. The most requested recipes, complete with loads of special cooking hints. Englewood Cliffs: Prentice-Hall, Inc., 1958. 256p.

2109 PICTURE COOK BOOK. By the Editors of LIFE. Over 250 full color photographs. Suggestions for meals both simple and exotic . . . 600 recipes. Waterproof, Premium Recipe File Box and set of all the recipes additionally provided. Englewood Cliffs: 1958. Prentice-Hall, Inc., 300p.

2110 ROBERSON, JOHN AND MARIE. The Casserole Cookbook. How to be kitchen-free when the guests arrive. Englewood Cliffs: Prentice-Hall, Inc., 1958. 240p. illus. 5th printing.

2111 SMITH, KATE. The Kate Smith "Company's Coming" Cookbook. Her most sumptuous recipes for guests. Englewood Cliffs: Prentice-Hall, Inc., 1958. 312p.

2112 ZELAYETA, ELENA. Elena's Secrets of Mexican Cooking. (See Foreign sec.)

2113 ROBERSON, JOHN & MARIE. THE CHAFING DISH COOKBOOK. Simple & savory food served with a spark of drama. Illus. Prentice-Hall, Englewood Cliffs, 1959. 288p.

2114 WHITE, RUTH B. You and Your Food. How to plan good meals and make the best use of time and money. Englewood Cliffs: Prentice-Hall, Inc., 1961. 500p.

2115 DE WILDT, MRS. SELECTED INDONESIAN RECIPES. Booklet. Javanese Rice-table, etc. Paterson, n.d. 12p.

2116 GOOD THINGS FOR EVERY DAY OF THE YEAR. Autographed recipes. East Orange, n.d. 80p.

2117 HALE. It's Smart To Cook with Beer. Over 200 recipes. Belleville, n.d. 120p.

2118 MARSHALL, ANNE. COOKING WITH CONDENSED SOUPS. Pamphlet. illus. Campbell Soup Co., Camden. n.d. 48p.

2119 MOTHER'S COOKING RECIPES. Autographed recipes. Pub. by Woman's Aid of Mercer Hospital. Trenton: n.d. 110p.

New Mexico

2120 NEW MEXICO COOKERY; Some products of the state and how to prepare them . . . Sante Fe: State Land Office, 1916. 64p.

2121 LONG, GRACE B. Cooking Club; first year. (Mesilla Park? New Mex.), 1932. 19p. (New Mexico College of Agriculture and Mechanic Arts, Mesilla Park. Extension Service. Extension circular no. 111).

2122 LONG, GRACE B. Cooking club; third year. (Mesilla Park), 1932. (New Mexico College of A. & M. Extension Service circular no. 113).

2123 LONG, GRACE B. Home baking. (Mesilla Park), 1932. 47p. (New Mexico College of A. & M. Extension Service circular no. 115).

2124 STRONG, VEDA A. Home canning. (Mesilla Park), 1932. 31p. (New Mexico College of Agriculture and Mechanic Arts, Mesilla Park. Extension Service. Extension circular no. 120.)

2125 FERGUSON, ERNA. MEXICAN COOKBOOK. (See Foreign sec.)

2126 COMPERE, OLGA C. (Presentation copy). KOCH CANCER COOK BOOK. Menus and recipes. Wraps. Albuquerque (1935). 1st ed. 81p.

2127 KITCHEN KAPERS. The Santa Fe Women's Club and Library Association presents this collection of Community Recipes, compiled by Members. Santa Fe: 1951. Pictorial wraps. Spiral bdg.

2128 GILBERT, FABRIOLA CABEZA DE BACA. THE GOOD LIFE. New Mexican Food. Drawings. Merle Armitage: Santa Fe, 95p.

New York

2129 WARREN, NATHAN B. CHRISTMAS IN THE OLDEN TIMES, Its Carols & Customs, Together with the Celebrated Boar's Head Song (from Queen's College, Oxford). Also banqueting. Troy, 1866.

2130 THE AMERICAN COOK BOOK FOR 1868. For gratuitous distribution. Wraps. Dr. Herrick & Co., Albany, 32p. and ads.

2131 THE CHAMPLAIN VALLEY BOOK OF RECIPES. Collected by Young Ladies of Trinity Church. Autographed recipes; some handwritten recipes. Munro and Warren: Plattsburg, 1875. 185p.

2132 PLATT, FRANCES E. What We Know About Cooking. Compiled from tested recipes of the ladies of Bath. Bath: Steuben Courier Print, 1875. 48p.

2133 EVERY DAY'S NEED. Collection of well proven recipes, furnished by the ladies of the Business Woman's Union. Brooklyn: Union Steam Printing Est., 1876. 100p.

2134 SCHLICKEYSEN, GUSTAV. Fruit and Bread. (See Foreign sec.)

2135 ADAMS, ABBY MERRILL. Sense in the Kitchen: a manual of the art and science of cooking. The effects of different foods on the system. Recipes. Syracuse: A. S. Hunter, 1878. 338p.

2136 THE LADIES' COOK BOOK OF WATERVILLE, N. Y. Each recipe simply written and signed, one dated 1848. Indian Bread, Cider Jelly etc. On last two pages remedies such as Hope Yeast, Cure for Felon & Lip Salve. Published by The Ladies' Aid Society of the Presbyterian Society, Waterville, 1878.

2137 MOTHER HUBBARD'S CUPBOARD. First Baptist Church, Rochester: 1878. 94p. Wraps.

2138 PRACTICAL RECIPE BOOK. Emanuel Church, Norwich, New York. Pub. in Claremont: 1878. 100p. and ads.

2139 RANSOM'S FAMILY RECEIPT BOOK. Cooking, Coloring, Painting & Misc. A Calendar. New Every Year.; free to everyone. Wraps. Advertises Dr. Ransom's Hive Syrup and Tolu, Dr. Trask's Magnetic Ointment, Dr. Miller's Magnetic Balm, and Prof. Anderson's Dermador. D. Ransom, Son: Buffalo, 1878. 32p.

2140 Ransom's Family Receipt Book. Buffalo: 1879. (See No. 2139).

2141 M., Mrs. R. V. and C., Mrs. D. C. The Tested Cook Book, Containing over 1200 recipes and general directions. Syracuse: C. L. Rhoades, 1879. 247p.

2142 "Mother Hubbard's Cupboard." Published by the Young Ladies' Society, First Baptist Church. Rochester: E. R. Andrews, 1880. 84p. Paper.

2143 True Blue Cook Book. Choice and Tested Receipts. By the Ladies of the Presbyterian Church, Gloversville, N. Y. Autographed recipes. Doeringer & Kirchner, Brooklyn (c. 1880). 115p.

2144 The Epicure's Cook Book, translated and arranged by "One of Them." Rochester: Union and Advertiser Co., 1881. 261p.

2144a The Household Gem. A collection of valuable recipes. Ads. Dr. Traver's Cough Syrup, Thankful Coon's Indian Tooth Powder, etc. Small booklet. Perry Medical Company, Perry (c. 1881). 16p.

2145 Knight, Mrs. H. L. Breakfast, Dessert, and Supper. 275 practical recipes, the result of long experience. . . Auburn, The author, 1881. 87p. Wraps.

2146 Parloa, Maria. New Cookbook, A Guide to Marketing & Cooking. Gay colored frontis. Blank pages with contemporary recipes. Troy, 1881. 430p.

2147 Ransom's Family Receipt Book. Buffalo: 1881. (See No. 2139).

2148 Cosmopolitan Cook and Receipt Book. Rochester: Moore and Cole Co., 1882. 410p.

2149 Dingens Brothers. The Cosmopolitan Cook and Recipe Book. Recipes for dishes from many lands . . . Buffalo: Printing House of E. H. Hutchinson, 1882. 410p. Ads.

2150 The Ladies' Note-Book and Calendar. With select receipts and household information. Engravings of old Buffalo buildings. World's Dispensary Medical Assn., Buffalo, 1882. 24p. and ads. of Dr. Pierce's Extract of Smart-weed.

2151 "Our Home Favorite." Published by the Young Women's Home Mission Circle of the First Baptist Church, Saratoga Springs: Daily Saratogian Steam Job Print, 1882. 125p. and ads. Autographed recipes.

2152 The Practical Recipe Book. Compiled by the Ladies of the Episcopal Missionary Society for the benefit of Emmanuel Church. Norwich: Norwich Post Steam Print., 1883. 90p. 2nd ed.

2153 Ransom's Family Receipt Book. Buffalo: 1883. (See No. 2139).

2154 House, Mrs. E. O. (compiler). Chop-sticks. A collection of tried recipes . . . Troy: C. L. Martin, book and job printer, 1884. 158p. and ads.

2155 RANSOM'S FAMILY RECEIPT BOOK. Buffalo: 1884. (See No. 2139).

2156 WILLEY, FRANCES. The Model Cook Book. 1000 tested, economic recipes for private families. Troy: E. H. List, 1884. 398p. Frontis.

2157 SHILLABER, LYDIA. A New Daily Food. A collection of tried and reliable recipes, brought forth from the storehouse of things new and old, by the ladies of St. Paul's Church, Morrisania, New York. New York: Bedell & Brother, 1885. 128p.

2158 BROOKLYN NURSERY & INFANTS' HOSPITAL SCHOOL COOK BOOK. Pratt & Son, New York, 1886. Illus. 112p.

2159 RANSOM'S FAMILY RECEIPT BOOK. Buffalo: 1886. (See No. 2139).

2160 "THE SARATOGA FAVORITE," published by the Young Women's Mission Circle of the First Baptist Church. Saratoga Springs: Daily Saratogian Steam Book and Job Print., 1886. 160p. and ads.

2161 STEVENS, MRS. E. (compiled by). Home Dissertations: an Offering to the Household, for Economical . . Cookery . . The author illustrated it, too. Tilton: Hunter & Beach, 1886. 175p. and ads. Illus. Embossed Pict. cover.

2162 BOSTWICK, LUCY W. Margery Daw in the Kitchen and What She Learned There. Pub. by the author. Auburn: Knapp, Peck & Thomson, 1887. 4, 100p.

2163 MOTHER HUBBARD'S CUPBOARD. Young Ladies' Society of the First Baptist Church. 4th ed. Rochester: Scranton, Wetmore & Co., 1887. 87p.

2164 PRESBYTERIAN COOK BOOK. What the Brethren Eat and How the Sisters Prepare it. Signed recipes. Troy (c. 1888). 103p. Ads.

2165 RANSOM'S FAMILY RECEIPT BOOK. Buffalo: 1880. (See No. 2139).

2166 SELECT COOKING RECIPES. A pocket size little book of special recipes. For Premium Fruit Flavors. McMonagle & Rogers, Middletown, 1888. 48p.

2167 CULINARY NUGGETS. Lafayette Street Presbyterian Church. Buffalo: 1889. 168p.

2168 THE LEROY RECEIPT BOOK. Contributed Receipts, signed by donors. The Library Association, LeRoy, 1889. 116p. and Index.

2169 MOHAWK VALLEY COOK BOOK. Ladies' Society of St. Mark's Lutheran Church of Canajoharie, N. Y. Utica: Press of I. C. Childs and Son, 1889. 89p. 1st ed.

2170 PRESCOTT, AUGUSTA S. (editor). Journal Cook Book. . . Albany: The Albany Journal, 1889. 64p.

2171 WORDS OF HELP FOR KITCHEN AND PANTRY. A collection of choice recipes, contributed and endorsed. With clippings, and handwritten recipes. Ladies of the Remsen St.

M. E. Church, Cohoes, E. H. Foster, 1889. 91p. and ads.

2172 ABEL, MRS. MARY HINMAN. Practical Sanitary and Economic Cooking adapted to Persons of Moderate and Small Means. The Lomb Prize Essay. American Public Health Ass'n., Rochester, 1890. 190p.

2173 COOK BOOK. From Rochester, New York, 1890. Includes local and contemporary ads. Blank pages have a few handwritten recipes. 159p.

2174 PATENTED AND IMPROVED METHODS OF PRESERVING AND CANNING. With cook book of over 400p. with recipes from celebrated chefs of the country and Europe. Roundout: Northwestern Publishers and Patent Rights Specialists, 1890. 523p.

2175 RIVERSIDE RECIPE BOOK. This recipe book has been compiled and edited . . . Rutgers Riverside Presbyterian Church. New York: 1890. Autographed recipes. Ads. 61p.

2176 205 RECIPES TRIED AND PROVEN BY TRINITY'S LADIES. Rochester: The St. Paul's Branch of the M.C.L. of Trinity Parish, 1890. 94p.

2177 CUTTER, SARAH J. Palatable Dishes. Buffalo: Peter Paul & Bro., 1891. ix, 910p. and ads.

2178 FLOWER CITY COOK BOOK. Published by the ladies of the Lake Avenue Memorial Baptist Church. Rochester: Post-Express Printing Co., 1891. 100p. and ads.

2179 RANSOM'S FAMILY RECEIPT BOOK. Buffalo: 1891. (See No. 2139).

2180 WARNER'S SAFE COOK BOOK. Compiled for Warner's Safe Baking Powder and Yeast Co., Illus. Wraps. H. H. Warner & Co., Rochester, 1892. 465p. & 32p. ads.

2181 CRUIKSHANK, A. C. The Young Cook's Guide. Prepared for the Young Women's Christian Assoc. of Brooklyn. Brooklyn: Collins & Day, 1893. 283p.

2182 GLENS FALLS COOKERY BOOK. —Aid Society of the First Presbyterian Church, Glens Falls, 1893. 2nd ed. 338p.

2183 THE ORACLE; receipts, rare, rich and reliable . . . Parish Aid Society, of Christ Church, Tarrytown, N.Y. New York: Republic Press, 1894. 122p. and ads.

2184 RANSOM'S ..FAMILY RECEIPT BOOK. Buffalo: 1894. (See No. 2139).

2185 THE GENEVA COOK BOOK. Compiled by the Woman's Board of the Medical and Surgical Hospital. Autographed recipes. Geneva: 1895. 240p. and ads.

2186 MOTHER HUBBARD'S CUPBOARD. 5th ed. Rochester: 1895. (See No. 2163).

2187 ORLEANS COUNTY COOK BOOK. Medina: 1895. 90p. plus 12p. ads.

2188 RANSOM'S FAMILY RECEIPT BOOK. Buffalo: 1895. (See No. 2139).

2189 WINSTON, MRS. E. C. The Dining Room and the Table. Rochester: Genesee Candy Co., 1895. 64p. Wraps.

2190 COOK BOOK. Compiled by the Ladies' Village Improvement Society of East Hampton, L.I. (1896). Autographed recipes. 96p. and ads.

2191 THE INDUSTRIAL SCHOOL COOK BOOK. Compiled for the benefit of the Industrial School Ass'n., Elmira. Buffalo: (Peter Paul Book Co.), 1896. 160p. and ads.

2192 RANSOM'S FAMILY RECEIPT BOOK. Buffalo: 1896. (See No. 2139).

2193 ROBERTSON, SARA T. AND CALDWELL, SARAH S. The Economist. A practical common sense cook book. Published for the benefit of the New Universalist Church, Canton: Plaindealer Presses, 1896. 111p. and ads. Wraps.

2194 ALBION COOK BOOK. Pub. by the ladies of the Methodist Episcopal Church, Albion, 1897. 44p. and local ads. Wraps.

2195 COOK BOOK. Compiled by the Ladies' Village Improvement Society of East Hampton, L.I., 1896. autographed recipes. Winsted, Conn.: Dowd Printing Co., 1897. 100p. and ads.

2196 FIRST METHODIST EPISCOPAL CHURCH COOK BOOK. Autographed recipes. Edmeston: Edmeston Local Print., 1897. 76p.

2197 RANSOM'S FAMILY RECEIPT BOOK. Buffalo: 1897. (See No. 2139).

2198 CHOICE RECEIPTS selected and edited by the Guild-House Committee of All Saints' Cathedral . . . Albany (Albania Press), 1898. 95p.

2199 KENDALL, B. J., MD. Kendall's Perfected Receipt Book. Recipes for diseases of man & animals, Cooking, too. Wraps. illus. Kendall Pub. Co., Saratoga Spgs., 1898. 210p. and ads.

2200 PENNELL, MRS. ALVIN ROSS. The Housewife's Helper. 500 helps by 500 wives; each one tried and thoroughly reliable. Cato: (c. 1898). 144p. Wraps.

2201 RANSOM'S FAMILY RECEIPT BOOK. Buffalo: 1898. (See No. 2139).

2202 "TRIED AND TRUE" COOK BOOK. Prepared by the Cook Book Committee of the Ladies Aid Society, Park Avenue Baptist Church. Rochester, 1898. 169p.

2203 THE FREDONIA COOK BOOK. Compiled by the Trinity Parish Guild, Fredonia, N.Y. . . Fredonia: Fredonia Censor Print., 1899. 10-112p.

2204 SNAP SHOTS AT COOKERY. Pub. by the Ladies of the Church of the Ascension. Paul Book Co., Buffalo, 1899. 174p.

2205 COOK BOOK and Experiences in Original Verse. Choice Recipes. Prepared by the Ladies of the Presbyterian Church. Wraps. Enterprise Steam Print, Afton (bef. 1900). 84p.

2206 DIRECTIONS FOR USING THE PEERLESS STEAM COOKER and Special Recipes for Cooking by Steam. Some autographed recipes. Booklet, Wraps. Peerless Cooker Co. Buffalo (bef. 1900). 32p.

2207 COOK BOOK. Arranged by the Ladies' Missionary and Benevolent Society of the North Presbyterian Church. Wraps. Binghamton, circa 1900. 94p.

2208 THE COOK'S COUNSELLOR. Ladies Aid Society of the Methodist Episcopal Church, Monroe, N.Y. . . . (Newburgh:) Journal Print, 1900. Contains ads.

2209 GIRARD, EUGENE. Practical and Artistic Cookery. Part I. Soups, fish, game poultry, meats. Part II. Entrees, salads, eggs, vegetables. Part III. Bread and cakes etc. Part IV. Desserts and candy making. Part V. Ornamental cookery, wine. Massena: The Massena Observer Printing House (1900). 272p. Frontis. of author.

2210 RELIABLE RECIPES. Compiled by One Wells Girl and Contributed by Many Wells College Women. New York State: (c. 1900). Autographed recipes. 150p. Ads.

2211 DAVENPORT, FLORA LUFKIN. Hand Book of Choice Receipts; sold for the benefit of the Brooklyn Home for Consumptives. Flatbush: 1901. 85p.

2212 RANSOM'S FAMILY RECEIPT BOOK. Buffalo: 1901. (See No. 2139).

2213 THE FIRST REFORMED CHURCH COOK BOOK.—Ladies' Aid Society. (Schenectady:) Daily Union, 1903. 160p. and ads.

2214 HAWKINS, MRS. GEORGE, et al. The Malone Cook Book. Recipes contributed by ladies of Malone and published by the Woman's Aid Society of the First Congregational Church, Malone, N.Y. 4th ed. Rutland, Vt.: The Tuttle Co. (1903), 254p. Frontis. Ads.

2215 EVERY-DAY COOK BOOK. Pub. by the Ladies Aid Society of the First Baptist Church. Livonia: 1904. 72p. Wraps.

2216 FAVORITE RECEIPTS. Contributed by the Ladies of the Congregational Church, and edited by the Ever Ready Club. Autographed recipes. Photo of church as frontis. Elizabethtown: 1904. 80p. and ads.

2217 A VOLUME OF DEPENDABLE RECIPES. Compiled by the Ladies of the Presbyterian Church. Highland: 1904. 84p. and ads.

2218 CHAFING DISH SUGGESTIONS. Illustrated. Wraps. Rochester Stamping Co., Rochester (c. 1905). 62p.

2219 COOK BOOK. East Hampton: Star Press, 1905 (See No. 2190).

2220 DAINTY AND DELICIOUS DISHES. 374 Contributed Recipes sold for the benefit of The Yonkers Homeopathic Hospital and

Maternity. Yonkers: Yonkers Herald Print, 1905. 132p. and ads.

2221 Everybody's Cook Book. Compiled by the Young Women's Sewing Circle of the Fourth Presbyterian Church. Autographed recipes. New York City: (1905). Ads. 75p.

2222 Glens Falls Cookery Book. 3rd ed. Glens Falls: 1905. (See No. 2182).

2223 Hurd, Sophie B. Recipes and Suggestions for the use of canned fruits and vegetables. Wraps. Burt Olney: Oneida, 1905. 32p.

2224 Mumford, Angelina Jenkins. The Genesee Valley Cook Book. (Boston:) Privately printed (The Fort Hill Press), 1905. 110, iii p.

2225 Practical Cookery. Compiled by the Ladies of Chapter No. 4 of the Parish Aid Society of Christ Church. Rochester: 1905. 208p.

2226 The Tried and True. Published by The Women's Auxiliary of the Bedford Branch Y.M.C.A. Brooklyn: Brooklyn Eagle Book Printing Dept., 1905. 86p. and ads.

2227 Cook Book of the First Methodist Church. Rochester: 1907. 97p. Wraps.

2228 The Rural Cook Book. Some old recipes and many new ones—being the collected wisdom of a legion of home cooks. New York: Rural New-Yorker (c. 1907). 192p. Wraps.

2229 Choice and Tried Recipes. Compiled by the Young Women's Home Missionary Society of the Delaware Ave. Methodist Episcopal Church. Autographed recipes. Buffalo: Floyd-Genthner Press, 1908. 159p. and ads.

2230 Hurd, Sophie B. Soups, Salads and Desserts. Their making and serving. Wraps. Illus. Burt Olney: Oneida, 1909. 32p.

2231 Pine Hills Cook Book. Courtesies of the Ladies of Pine Hills. Compiled by the Ladies of Madison Avenue Presbyterian Church. Albany: Brandow Printing Co., 1909. Autographed recipes. 109p. and ads.

2232 Snap Shots at Cookery. Signed recipes—selected recipes. The Ladies of the Church of the Ascension, Buffalo, 1909. Ads. 205p.

2233 Souvenir Cook Cook. Published under the auspices of the Woman's Poultry Club. Saratoga Springs: (c. 1909). 29 1. illus. frontis.

2234 Chafing Dish Suggestions. Rochester: (c. 1910). (See No. 2218).

2235 Country Cookery. The members of the "Working Circle" of the Presbyterian Church. Gorham: 1910. 49p.

2236 Good Things to Eat and How to Prepare Them. More than 250 choice recipes compiled especially for customers and friends of the Larkin Co. 9th ed. rev. Buffalo: Larkin Co., 1910. 78, 2p. illus. Paper.

2237 THE HARTLEY HOUSE COOK BOOK AND HOUSEHOLD ECONOMIST. Compiled by Pierce and Noyes. New York City: Wessels & Bissell Co., 1910. 212p.

2238 HURD, SOPHIE B. Soups, Salads and Desserts. Oneida: (See No. 2230).

2239 THE IDEAL COOK BOOK. Signed recipes. Local ads. Wraps. Methodist Episcopal Church, Fayetteville (c. 1910). 48p.

2240 NEELY, FLORA. Hand-Book for the Kitchen and Housekeeper's Guide. 3rd ed. rev. New Rochelle: Paragraph Press, 1910. 364p.

2241 YOUNG WOMEN'S GUILD COOK BOOK. Fourth Presbyterian Church. Autographed recipes. Picture of church on paper cover. Albany: J. Edward Binley, 1910.

2242 THE COLONIAL COOK BOOK. Pub. by The Ladies' Union of the Flatbush Congregational Church, Brooklyn, N.Y. Autographed recipes. Decorated pages. Brooklyn: The Scientific Press, 1911. 287p. Cover sketch of church.

2243 COOK BOOK issued by Onwentsia Chapter, D.A.R. Autographed recipes. Addison: 1911. 95p. Ads.

2244 HOUSE-HOLD HINTS. Formulas, processes & recipes for cooking, candy making; for perfumes, toilet preparations, etc. Buffalo: J. M. Secord (1911). 160p.

2245 LEITER, MRS, HENRY AND VAN BERGH, MISS SARA (compiled by) THE FLOWER CITY COOK BOOK. (See Foreign sec.)

2246 RECIPES FOR FAVORITE CANDIES, Home-Made with the Taylor Home Candy Thermometer. New York State, 1911. 12p. advertising booklet. Pict. cover.

2247 HURD, SOPHIE B. Preserves and Pickles. Forty Recipes. The author a graduate of the Boston Cooking School. Oneida; The Dispatch Press, 1912. 19p.

2248 MALZBENDER'S PRACTICAL RECIPES BOOK FOR BAKERS & PASTRY COOKS. (See Foreign sec.)

2249 PINE HILLS COOK BOOK. Autographed recipes. Compiled by the Ladies of the Madison Avenue Presbyterian Church. Albany, 1912. 131p.

2250 AFTERNOON TEA DAINTIES. . . Woman's Alliance, First Baptist Church, Rochester, 1913. 44p.

2251 CARING, ELSIE GENEVIEVE. New Ways and Old; a manual of cookery esp. adapted to the gas range. Rochester: Genesee Printing Co., 1913. 19p. Wraps. Ads.

2252 THE CONGREGATIONAL CHURCH COOK BOOK. Recipes compiled by the Ladies' Mission Circle. Smyrna: 1913. Autographed recipes. 92p. ads.

2253 COOK BOOK compiled by the Earnest Workers of the First Baptist Church of Newfane, N.Y. Autographed recipes. Lockport: E. C. Haskins, 1913(?). 100p. and ads.

2254 THE EVENING RECORDER COOK BOOK. Contains favorite recipes . . by the Ladies of Amsterdam and

Vicinity, as published in the Evening Recorder. Autographed recipes. Amsterdam: Wm. J. Kline & Son, 1913. 136p. and ads.

2255 GLENS FALLS COOKERY BOOK. 4th ed. Glens Falls: 1913. (See No. 2182).

2256 "THE KIND THAT MOTHER USED TO MAKE" COOK BOOK. Compiled and issued by Ladies of the First Presbyterian Church. Autographed recipes. Ithaca: 1913. 160p. and ads.

2257 MORSE, SIDNEY; AND CURTIS, MRS. Household Discoveries & Mrs. Curtis' Cookbook. 2 vol. in one. Many illus. Petersburg, 1913. 1173p.

2258 RECIPES TRIED AND TRUE. (See Foreign sec.)

2259 SAVORY PRIZE RECIPE BOOK. Buffalo: Republic Metalware Co., 1913. 48p. illus. Ads. Col. cover.

2260 GUTTMAN, MARILLA (GOLDSTEIN), "Mrs. Adolph Guttman." The Concord Cook Book. . . 1915. 1st ed. Syracuse: The Dehler Press (1915). 339p. and ads.

2261 THE HOOSICK COOK BOOK from the Ladies' Aid Society of the First Baptist Church. Autographed recipes. Hoosick: 1915. 16p. Ads.

2262 JELLO. 3 little booklets, wraps. 1905. 1904 St. Louis Exposition award desserts. GENESEE PURE FOOD Co. Leroy: (c. 1915-1920).

2263 LARKIN HOUSEWIVES' COOK BOOK. Of the 548 recipes, 480 are prize recipes selected from more than 3000 submitted by practical housekeepers. Compiled especially for customers and friends of the Larkin Co. Buffalo: Larkin Co. (1915). 139p. illus.

2264 PATTISON: Principles of Domestic Engineering. Some chapters on food. Ltd. ed. 500 copies. Privately printed. Colonia, 1915. 310p.

2265 SOCIÉTÉ CULINAIRE PHILANTHROPIQUE. 49th Annual Ball and Grand Culinary and Alimentary Exhibition. Photographs of the master chefs, and officers of the society. Recipes. Wraps. New York, 1915. Lacks back cover. 152p.

2266 AT THE SIGN OF THE ROLLING PIN. For the Vassar College Endowment Fund. Autographed recipes. Compiled by Elizabeth Mills, Marjorie Peck, Grace Roper, Margaret Salladin, Mildred Wheeler . . Middletown: Stivers Printing Co., 1916. 227p. illus.

2267 CARRELL, THEODORA M. THE LABORATORY KITCHEN RECIPES FOR PUTTING UP FRUITS. Directions. Wraps. Contemporary and local advertisements. Benefit Vassar Endowment Fund. Poughkeepsie, 1916. 27p.

2268 JAYNES, MRS. R. T. (arranger). The Parish Cook Book. For Christ Church Guild. Warwick: Warwick Valley Dispatch, 1916. 69p. and ads.

2269 LARKIN HOUSEWIVES' COOK BOOK. Buffalo: 1916. 140p. illus. (See No. 2263).

2270 The Malone Cook Book. Signed recipes. Photograph. Woman's Aid Society of the First Congregational Church, Malone, 1917. 324p.

2271 The Sugar Plum. Issued by the Girls' Guild of the First Presbyterian Church of Brooklyn, 1917. 88p. and ads.

2272 The Sugar Plum. 2nd ed. rev. & enl. Proceeds to go to the Red Cross. (Brooklyn): 1918. 75p.

2273 Cary, Ida Lee. Cook Book of Tested Recipes by the originator of Vassar Tea Room. Poughkeepsie: A. V. Haight Co. (1920). 36p. Wraps.

2274 Cook Book. Signed recipes. Advertisements. Dome Circle of the First Congregational Church, Riverhead (before 1920). 33p.

2275 Roxbury Recipes. Collected by the Ladies' Social Society and Missionary Auxiliary of the Jay Gould Memorial Reformed Church. Roxbury: Roxbury Times Press, 1920. 60p. and ads.

2276 Thompson, Margaret J. Food for the Sick and the Well. How to Select It and How to Cook It. Yonkers-on-Hudson: World Book Company, 1920. 82p.

2277 Victory Memorial Cook Book. Published by The Women's Auxiliary, Victory Memorial Hospital, Brooklyn, 1920. Autographed recipes. 243p.

2278 Certo Makes Perfect Jams and Jellies. Small pamphlet, wraps. Pectin Sales: Rochester, 1921. 14p.

2279 Economical and Tried Recipes. Jewish Women's Relief Association, Brooklyn (1922?). 149p.

2280 Salmagundi Papers. Text and illus. by members; Col. front, signed etching. 500 copies printed. New York, 1922. 149p.

2281 The Sherwood Cook Book. Compiled by the Ladies' Aid Society of the Luther Memorial Chapel, Shorewood. Albany, no pub., 1922. 160p. and ads.

2282 Moore, Alice. Chinese Recipes. (See Foreign sec.)

2283 Plus Ultra Cook Book. Advertisements. Wraps. Barre Center, New York State, 1923. 69p.

2284 Bradley, Alice. Jams, Jellies and Marmalades made with Certo. Booklet, wraps. Douglas-Pectin Corp., Rochester, 1924. 24p.

2285 Dainty Desserts for Dainty People. Illustrated. Wraps. Knox Sparkling Granulated Gelatine, Johnstown, New York, 1924. 41p.

2286 Douglaston Cook Book. The Community Church of Douglaston, L. I., 1924. 154p. and ads. Thumb index.

2287 The Star Cook Book. Empire Chapter, No. 68 of the Order of the Eastern Star, Canton, N.Y. . . Sandy Creek: The Corse Press (1924). 207p. and ads.

2288 Book of Recipes. Ellen Hardin Walworth Chapter of the Daughters of the American Revolution, New York. Autographed recipes compiled by the committee on the Book. . . (New York), 1925. 230p. illus. Ads.

2289 Buell, Jessie Belle (Huntington), "Mrs. E. G. Buell." Community Cook Book . . . (Brooklyn: Guide Print. & Pub. Co., 1925). 128p. and ads.

2290 The Cocksure Cook Book; A collection of well tested recipes, selected by the women of the Red Circle of the First Congregational Church, Mount Vernon, N. Y. Mount Vernon, 1925. 181p. Ads.

2291 Needlework Guild Cook Book. Compiled by the guild; autographed by the members. Some recipes written in. First Presbyterian Church, Jamestown, 1925. 412p.

2292 Schwartzkopf, Mrs. L. (compiled & edited by). The Modern Cook Book. Tested recipes from many lands, adapted for the American household. United Order of True Sisters, New York, 1925. 1st ed. 276p. and ads.

2293 Souvenir Book of 35th Anniversary of Founding of D.A.R. Autographed recipes. New York, 1925. 230p. and ads.

2294 The Congregational Cook Book. Compiled by the Ladies Aid Society. Autographed recipes, Ads. The First Congregational Church, Pulaski, 1926. 112p.

2295 Lebanon Valley Cookery, including "Tried Receipts" published in 1889, by the Ladies Guild. Lebanon Springs: Church of Our Saviour, 1926. 133p., tables. Illus. plates.

2296 Pattee, Alida Frances. Practical Dietetics. With reference to diet in health and disease. A. F. Pattee, Mount Vernon, 1926. 687p.

2297 Norman, Grace F. Menus for the Busy Housewife. Syracuse: the author (c. 1927). 103p. Wraps.

2298 Ladies Aid Cook Book. A careful collection of recipes. Wraps. Ladies Aid Society, Baptist Church, West Henrietta, 1928. 155p.

2299 Silver Jubilee Cook Book of Tested Recipes. Signed recipes. Advertisements. St. Mark's M.E. Church, Brooklyn, 1928. 160p.

2300 Dainty Desserts, Candies, Salads. Small booklet, wraps. Knox Gelatine: N. Y. State, 1929. 47p.

2301 Hay, William Howard, M. D. Health Via Food. About diet and disease. Menus for 1 month. Sun-Diet Press: East Aurora, 1929. 311p.

2302 The Health Value of Knox Sparkling Gelatine. Small booklet, wraps. Knox: Johnstown, 1929. 31p.

2303 Hart, Frances Noyes. Pigs in Clover. Illus. tale of a gastronomical trip through France. End paper maps. Garden City: Doubleday, Doran, 1931. 1st ed. 297p.

2304 WESTCHESTER COOK BOOK for Westchester County Children's Assn., Rye, 1931. 168p.

2305 CANAPE PARADE. 100 Hors D'oeuvre recipes. Decorations. Wraps. Canape Parade, Scarborough (1932). 29p.

2306 ST. ANDREW'S EVENING BRANCH WOMAN'S AUXILIARY COOK BOOK. Recipes and ads. Wraps. St. Andrew's Memorial Episcopal Church, Yonkers, 1932-33. 48p.

2307 STEESE, MAUD HEATON. The Queen of Hearts' Recipe Book. New Rochelle: The Little Print, 1932. 105p. Illus. by E. Steese.

2308 THE WOMAN'S UNION COOK BOOK. Sponsored by the Trustees of the Woman's Educational and Industrial Union. Autographed recipes. Auburn: Dec., 1932. 103p. illus.

2309 "CENTRAL" COOK BOOK. Memorial Missionary Society of Central Presbyterian Church, . . Rochester (1933). 24p.

2310 SHARP, JEAN R. Let's Give a Party. Artistic and practical menus and recipes for special as well as everyday use. Elmira: Commercial Press (1933). Loose-leaf book.

2311 CHOICE RECIPES. Munsey Park Woman's Club. Munsey Park, 1935. 72p.

2312 LONG ISLAND FAVORITES. Collected, signed recipes. For the benefit of the Oyster Bay Visiting Nurse Ass'n. Looseleaf booklet, wraps. Oyster Bay Visiting Nurse Ass'n.: New York, 1935. 1st ed. 126p.

2313 TESTED RECIPES. Proportions of 50 for use in school cafeterias. Used by Board of Education. Buffalo: (1935). 155p.

2314 WINTHROP, ALBERTA SHEFFORD. Dishes with cheese. Small booklet; wraps. Shefford Cheese Co.: N. Y. State, 1935. 32p.

2315 BELLE TERRE FAVORITES. Signed recipes by members of the Garden Club. Spiral binding. Belle Terre Garden Club, Pt. Jefferson, 1936. 1st ed. 160p.

2316 CHILDREN'S HOSPITAL AID ASSOCIATION COOK BOOK. Signed recipes; menus; advertisements. Illustrations by Louisa Robins. Buffalo, 1936. 320p.

2317 AT HOME ON THE RANGE. Advertisements in color. Westchester Ladies' Auxiliary of the United Home for Aged Hebrews. New Rochelle, 1938. 105p.

2318 COOK BOOK OF TESTED RECIPES. Issued by the Women's Auxiliary to the University Hospital of the Good Shepherd. Autographed recipes. Syracuse: 1938. 256p. and many ads.

2319 PARISH COOKS of the Enfield Larger Parish, and Friends. Enfield: 1938. 100p. illus. Ring Bdg. Ads.

2320 BEROLZHEIMER, RUTH. THE UNITED STATES REGIONAL COOK-

BOOK. Decorative end papers; illustrated. Thumb index. Culinary Arts Institute, Garden City: New York, 1939. 751p.

2321 FREDERICK, J. GEORGE. LONG ISLAND SEAFOOD COOK BOOK. By the President, Gourmet Society. Recipes edited by Jean Joyce. Business Bourse, New York, 1939. 1st ed. 324p.

2322 SPAHR, MARY (Compiled by). HONOR AMONG COOKS. Some signed recipes. Book sold to aid Refugee Children. Cover by John Hartell. Illustrations. Spiral binding. Wm. A. Church Co. Ithaca, 1939. 117p.

2323 CASE, FRANK. Tales of a Wayward Inn. The Algonquin, a meeting place for celebrities. Some of the best liked recipes. Illus. with drawings. Garden City Publishing Co., New York (1940). 390p.

2324 HACKNEY, MRS. G. EDGAR (compiler). Dining for Moderns with Menus and Recipes. Wine Notes by Peter Greig. Pub. by and for the benefit of the N. Y. Exchange for Women's Work. New York: 1940. 72p. Spiral binding.

2325 RECIPES FROM HISTORIC LONG ISLAND. Autographed recipes. Ads. Illustrations. Spiral binding. Nassau County YWCA, 1940. 1st ed. 416p.

2326 GELATINE DESSERTS, SALADS, CANDIES AND FROZEN DISHES. Small booklet, wraps, color illustrations. Knox: N. Y. State, 1941. 55p.

2327 RECIPES. Autographed. Compiled by the Business and Professinal Women's Group. Wraps, mimeographed pages. St. George's Church, New York, 1941. 43p.

2328 WHERE TO EAT, SLEEP, AND PLAY IN THE U.S.A. Recommends Hotels, Restaurants with notes about things of interest. Traveler's Windfall Ass'n.: Bronxville, N.Y. (1941). 648p.

2329 MILLER, MRS. LAWRENCE MCKEEVER AND HARPER, MRS. J. HENRY. (Compiled & Edited by). POT LUCK. Recipes for ration-time. Wraps. New York City Women's Council of the Navy League of the U.S. 1942. 80p.

2330 HENDRICKSON, ROY F. Food "Crisis" account of food situation in America, past, present and future. Doubleday, Doran & Co., Garden City, 1943. 274p.

2330a KNOX GELATINE. For Salads, Desserts, Pies, Candies. Sampler cover, colored illus. Wraps. Charles B. Knox Gelatine Co. Inc., Johnstown, 1943. 40p.

2330b KNOX GELATINE. For Salads, Desserts, Pies, Candies. Sampler cover, colored illus. Wraps. Charles B. Knox Gelatine Co., Johnstown, 1945. 27p.

2331 THE NORTH AVENUE COOK BOOK. Compiled by The Women's Society of the North Avenue Presbyterian Church. Signed recipes. Illustrations by Jean Dick and others. Spiral binding. North Avenue Church Women's Society, New Rochelle, 1945. 305p.

2332 ALLEN, IDA BAILEY. Title: FOOD FOR TWO. Published by Garden City Publishing Co., Inc., Garden City, 1947. 1st ed. 339p.

2332a LANDSTAD-JENSEN, MAGNY. Norwegian Recipes. Brooklyn: 1947. 175p. Pict. cover on plastic bds.

2333 TRIED AND TRUE FROM PAINT POT KITCHENS. Compiled by the Paint Pot Guild of St. Andrew's Memorial Episcopal Church. Handwritten, autographed recipes. Yonkers: 1947. 383p. illus. Plastic spiral binding. Pict. cover.

2334 ANGELOH, FRED. YOUR JUST DESSERTS. Plain and fancy cakes baked by an expert. Illus. Private printing: (Kiamesha Lake, 1949). 256p.

2335 EVERGREEN FAVORITE RECIPES. Autographed recipes from members of the Evergreen Chapter No. 261, Order of the Eastern Star. Springfield Center: 1949. Pict. cover.

2336 FAVORITE RECIPES OF WELLESLEY ALUMNAE. Compiled by Wellesley-in-Westchester. Signed recipes. Spiral binding. Photographic end papers. Scarsdale, 1950. 144p.

2337 THE FIGURE OF HEALTH. Drawings. Wraps. New York State Department of Health, Albany: 1950. 20p.

2338 HURLEY, LOIS J. AND GROETZINGER, ISABELLE J. THE STATE FAIR BLUE RIBBON COOK BOOK. Prize winning recipes. Illustrated by H. Lawrence Hoffman. Fell: New York, 1950. 1st ed. 256p.

2339 MURGATROYD, EBENEZER. COOKING TO KILL! Comic Cannibal recipes. Sure-fire salads by ghouls. Comic drawings by Herb Roth. Peter Pauper: Mount Vernon, 1951. 47p.

2340 BEILENSON, EDNA (Compiled by). RECIPES MOTHER USED TO MAKE. Whether mother came from New England, South, West, Mid-West, or Europe. With typical menus. Decorated by Vee Guthrie; attractively presented. Colored end papers. Peter Pauper: Mt. Vernon, 1952. 1st ed. 158p.

2341 ABBOTT, ANITA. MAGIC HALF HOUR DINNERS. For the business woman, and the busy woman. Wraps. Harian: Greenlawn, 1953. 128p.

2342 THE BEDFORD COOK BOOK. Autographed recipes. Illustrated: wraps. The Bedford Garden Club: Bedford, 1953. 1st ed. 295p.

2343 BEILENSON, EDNA. Holiday Punches. Col. illus. Boxed. Peter Pauper Press, Mt. Vernon, 1953. 61p.

2344 LINDLAHR, VICTOR H. Eat and Reduce. Lose 7 lbs. in a week while eating 3 square meals a day. Wraps. Permabooks: Garden City (1953). 240p. and ads.

2345 COGGINS, CAROLYN. Carolyn Coggins' Company Cookbook. Cakes, desserts and company dinner menus & recipes. Hanover House, Garden City (1954). 1st ed. 394p.

2346 De Gouy, Louis P. The Master Chef's Best appetizers, snacks, punches and cocktails to make your party a success. Wraps. Harian Publications, New York (1954). 173p.

2347 Allen, Ida Bailey. Ida Bailey Allen's Cook Book for Two. (Rev. & enl.) Garden City: 1957. (see No. 2332).

2348 Beazley, Mrs. James V. and Stone, Miss Lucy; (compilers). Favorite Recipes. Binghamton: Monday Afternoon Club, n.d. 144p.

2349 Dibble, Edward F. Dibble on the Potato. Elements of Success in Potato Growing. (an address printed). Small booklet, no wraps. Cornell University, Ithaca, n.d. 16p.

2350 The Knox Candy and Pie Parade. A folder with pie and candy recipes. Col. illus. Johnstown: Charles B. Knox Gelatine Co., n.d.

2351 A Little Book of Recipes. Compiled by the Ladies of the Chapin Memorial Church. Autographed recipes. Oneonta: n.d. 62p. and ads.

2352 Pyrex Ovenware Booklet. Cooking school finds what baking ware gives best results . . . recipes. Wraps—cover missing. Corning Glass Works: Corning, n. d. 29p.

2352a Recipes. Frontispiece of old Norwich Church. Compiled by the Ladies' Aid Society of Emmanuel Church. Norwich. Section of contemporary and local advertisements. 123p. viii p. Index.

2353 Woodstock Cook Book. Signed recipes from New York's famed art colony. Artistic cover. 106p.

New York City

2353a Breakfast, Dinner, and Tea. Viewed Classically, Poetically and Practically. Contains curious dishes and modern receipts. New York: D. Appleton, 1860. 361p.

2354 Robinson, Solon. How to Live: Saving and Wasting, or domestic economy illustrated by the life of two families of opposite character. Full of useful lessons in housekeeping; including the story of A Dime a Day. New York: Fowler and Wells, 1860. xii, 9-343p.

2355 The American Housewife and Kitchen Directory. Most valuable & original receipts. F. A. Brady, New York. 1862. 144p.

2356 Sala, George Augustus. Breakfast in Bed: or Philosophy between the Sheets. A Series of Indigestible Discourses. New York, 1863. 1st American ed. 275p.

2357 Jones, Mattie M. The Hygienic Cook Book; recipes for making bread, pies, puddings, mushes, and soups; directions for cooking vegetables, canning. Also household suggestions. New York: Miller & Browning, 1864. 48p. illus. Wraps.

2358 Victor, Metta Victoria (Fuller). Beadle's Dime Cook Book. Embodying what is most economic, most practical, most excellent. Rev. and enl. ed. New York: Beadle and Company (1864). vii, 11-100p. illus. Wraps.

2359 BLOT, PIERRE. WHAT TO EAT AND HOW TO COOK IT. Over one thousand receipts. Appleton: New York, 1865. 259p.

2360 THE COOK'S OWN BOOK. An American Family Cook Book. More than 2500 receipts. Miss Leslie's 75 receipts for pastry, cakes and sweetmeats. This is a cookbook in dictionary form. By a Boston Housekeeper. New York: Oliver S. Felt, 1865. 300, 37p. illus. Col. frontis.

2361 WHAT TO DO WITH THE COLD MUTTON: A book of réchauffées. Many approved receipts for the kitchen of a gentleman of moderate income. New York: Bunce & Huntington, 1865. 218p.

2362 BARBER, JOSEPH: Crumbs from the Round Table. A Feast for Epicures. America's Earliest culinary rhapsodist. New York, 1866. 1st ed. 106p.

2363 CROLY, MRS. J. C. JENNIE JUNE'S AMERICAN COOKERY BOOK. Over 1200 choice recipes. American News Co., New York (1866). 379p.

2364 MACÉ, JEAN. The History of a Mouthful of Bread & Its Effect on the Organization of Men & Animals. American News Co.: New York (1866). 1st Am. ed. 399p.

2365 COMMON SENSE COOK BOOK, containing plain directions for all the dishes, from soup to dessert; with a chapter on beverages, food for infants etc. by a veteran cook. New York: J. C. Haney (1867). 113p.

2366 COZZENS, F. S.: The Sayings of Dr. Bushwhacker & other Learned Men. Early American gustatory pieces by the editor of "The Wine Press." New York, 1867. 1st ed. 213p.

2367 DE VOE, THOMAS F. The Market Assistant, Containing a Brief Description of Every Article of Human Food Sold in the Public Markets of New York, Philadelphia & Brooklyn, Including the Various Domestic & Wild Animals, etc. with Many Curious Incidents and Anecdotes. Printed for the author, 1867. 455p.

2368 HILL, A. P. House-keeping Made Easy. A receipt book particularly adapted to the South, with directions for carving and arranging the table for parties. New York: J. O. Kane, 1867. 427p. illus.

2369 PUTNAM, E. MRS. PUTNAM'S RECEIPT BOOK AND Young Housekeeper's Assistant. Oakley & Mason, New York, 1867. 228p.

2369a WHAT SHALL WE EAT? A Manual for Housekeepers. Comprising a Bill of Fare for Breakfast, Dinner, and Tea, for Every Day in the Year. Appendix contains recipes for Pickles and Sauces. New York: Putnam, 1868. 134p. and book ads.

2369b MRS. WINSLOW'S DOMESTIC RECEIPT BOOK. Cooking recipes and

Advertisements for Brown's Bronchial Troches & Mrs. Winslow's Soothing Syrup. Wraps. Copyright by Jeremiah Curtis & Sons: and John Brown & Sons: New York. Published every year. 1868. 32p.

2369c BELLOWS, ALBERT J. Philosophy of Eating. By the late professor of chemistry, physiology, and hygiene. 2nd ed. Hurd & Houghton: N.Y., 1869. 344p.

2369d HECKERS' CROTON FLOUR MILLS. For bread and griddle cakes etc. HECKERS'; New York City, 1869. 32p.

2369e PUTNAM, E. MRS. PUTNAM'S RECEIPT BOOK. Young Housekeeper's Assistant (new and enlarged). Sheldon: New York, 1869. 322p.

2369f TRALL, RUSSELL THACHER. The New Hydropathic Cook Book; with recipes for cooking on hygienic principles. Dr. Trall was the editor of medical journals and the author of many medical and diet books. New York: Samuel R. Wells, 1869. xviii, 19-226p.

2369g BEECHER, CATHERINE E. AND STOWE, HARRIET BEECHER. PRINCIPLES OF DOMESTIC SCIENCE. As applied to the Duties and Pleasures of Home. A text-book for schools. Illustrations. J. B. Ford and Co., New York, 1870. 1st ed. 390p.

2369h ELLIOTT, SARAH A. Mrs. Elliott's Housewife. Containing practical receipts in cookery. New York: Hurd & Houghton, 1870. 347p.

2369i HENDERSON, W. A. How to Cook, Carve and Eat: or, Wholesome Food, and How to Prepare It for the Table . . . New York: Leavitt & Allen Brothers (1870). 360, 3-61, xii p. Frontis., plates.

2369j TROWBRIDGE, LAURA. Excelsior Cook Book and Housekeeper's Aid: receipts for cooking, dyeing, care of the sick, gardening, care of house plants, etc. New York: Mason, Baker & Pratt (1870). 288p.

2370 BEARD, GEORGE M. Eating and Drinking; a popular manual of food and diet in health and disease. New York: G. P. Putnam & Sons, 1871. 180p.

2371 BLOT, PIERRE. Hand-book of Practical Cookery, for Ladies and Professional Cooks. New York: Appleton, 1871. 478p. and book ads.

2372 BRIDGEMAN, THOMAS. AMERICAN GARDENER'S ASSISTANT. New ed. revised, enlarged and illus. by S. Edwards Todd. Contains cooking advice, herbs, etc. New York, 1871. In 3 parts, 152p, 211p, 161p.

2373 MRS. WINSLOW'S DOMESTIC RECEIPT BOOK. (see No. 2361). New York: 1871.

2374 COMPTON, MARGARET (Mrs. Amelia Williams Harrison). Grand Union Cook Book. Recipes for hundreds of tempting dishes. New York: Grand Union Tea Co.: (1872). 318p.

2375 HARLAND, MARION (Mrs. Mary Virginia Terhune). Common Sense in the Household. A manuel of practical housewifery.

New York: C. Scribner & Co., 1872. 556p.

2376 Soyer, Alexis. The Modern Housewife or Menagère with nearly 1000 recipes. Illus. D. Appleton & Co.: New York, 1872. 364p.

2377 Beecher, Mrs. Henry Ward. Motherly Talks with Young Housekeepers. J. B. Ford & Co., New York, 1873. 492p.

2378 The Art of Dining and of Attaining High Health; with a few hints on suppers. Anecdotes of dining connected with distinguished individuals. By a Bon Vivant. New York: Robert M. De Witt (1874). 288p.

2379 Mrs. Winslow's Domestic Receipt Book. New York, 1874. (See No. 2361).

2380 Diamond Spectacle Receipt Book. A little book of recipes—including Silver Pie. Adv. the *new* diamond spectacles (New York, Diamond Spectacles c. 1875). 48p.

2381 Durkee, E. R. & Co. Practical Cook Book; with more than 250 useful and economical recipes. New York: E. R. Durkee & Co. (1875). 89p. Wraps.

2382 Harland, Marion. Breakfast, Luncheon and Tea. "Common Sense in the Household" Series. Musings, methods and recipes. Scribner's; New York, 1875. 1st ed. 459p.

2383 Trall, R. T., MD. The Hygeian Home Cook Book, or Healthful and Palatable Food Without Condiments. Stereotyped by the Orphans of the Church Charity Foundation. New York: Samuel R. Wells & Co., 1875. 70p. and book ads.

2384 Mrs. Winslow's Domestic Book. New York, 1875. (See No. 2361).

2385 Youman, A. E. A Dictionary of Every-Day Wants. 20,000 receipts in nearly every department of human effort. New York: Frank M. Reed, 1875. 539p.

2386 Corson, Juliet (edited by). American Cookery. A Monthly Cook-Book, Devoted to Reform in the Kitchen. Royal Baking Powder. Vol. 1, No. 1 to 12. New York, 1876.

2387 The Economical Cook Book; or, how to prepare nice dishes at moderate cost. Over 400 receipts, selected by a practical housekeeper. New York: Charles A. Lilley (c. 1876). 120p.

2388 Mrs. Winslow's Domestic Receipt Book. New York, 1876. (See No. 2361).

2389 Corson, Juliet. The Cooking Manual of Practical Directions for Economical Every-day Cookery. By the Supt. of the New York Cooking School. New York: Dodd, Mead, 1877. 144p.

2390 Corson, Juliet. Fifteen Cent Dinners for Families of Six. New York: The Author. 1877. vii, 8-40p. Wraps.

2391 Fruit and Bread, a Scientific Diet. Tells of a man living 40 years on apples alone. Booklet. New York, 1877. 8p.

2392 Goodholme, Todd S. (edited by). A Domestic Cyclopaedia of Practical Information. A complete book of food. Illus. Henry Holt: New York, 1877. 1st ed. 599p.

2393 Greenslade, Kate. The Young Wife's Own Cook Book. Teaching plainly how to buy, cook and serve every kind of food. New York: Hurst & Co. (1877). 8-124p. illus.

2394 Henderson, Mary F. Practical Cooking and Dinner Giving. A treatise on cooking, serving and fashionable modes of entertaining. Illus. New York: Harper & Brothers, 1877. 376p.

2395 Holbrook, M. L., MD. Eating for Strength: A Book Comprising 1. The Science of Eating. 2. Receipts for Wholesome Cookery. 3. Receipts for Wholesome Drinks. 4. Answers to Ever Recurring Questions. New York: Wood & Holbrook, 1877. 6th ed. 157p. and book ads.

2397 Mrs. Winslow's Domestic Receipt Book. New York, 1877. (See No. 2361).

2398 The Young Wife's Own Cook-Book. Teaching plainly how to buy, dress, cook, serve and carve every kind of fish, fowl, meat, game and vegetable. How to preserve fruits and vegetables; how to make pastry. By an experienced House-keeper. New York: Hurst & Co. (1877). 124p. illus.

2399 Corson, Juliet. Twenty-five Cent Dinners, for Families of Six. The author was superintendent of the New York School of Cookery. New York: The Author, 1878. ix, 10-72p.

2400 Croly, Mrs. J. C. Jennie June's American Cookery Book. New York, 1878. 399p. & ads. (See No. 2363).

2401 Felker, P. H. The Grocers' Manual. A full description of all the goods sold by the trade. Spices included. American Grocer Publishing Ass'n., New York. (1878). 312p.

2402 Harland, Marion. The Dinner Year-Book. Col. plates. New York: Charles Scribner's Sons, (1878). 713p.

2403 Macdonald, James. Food from the Far West. American Agriculture, with special reference to Beef Production & Importation. Orange Judd: New York (c. 1878). 331p. & ads.

2404 Rudmani, Guiseppi (compiled by). The Royal Baker and Pastry Cook. By professor of New York Cooking School. Wraps. Royal Baking Powder Co., New York (1878). 32p. and ads.

2405 Silleck, Miss Willie. Reliable Cook Book. Compiled in aid of Industrial School and Home for Destitute Children . . New York: D. H. Gildersleeve & Co., 1878. viii, 164p.

2406 Smith, Edward, MD., LL.B., F.R.S. Foods. Scientific treatise, and charts. D. Appleton and Co., New York, 1878. 485p.

2407 Mrs. Winslow's Domestic Receipt Book. New York, 1878. (See No. 2361).

2408 The Epicure, containing valuable original recipes contributed by the most celebrated chefs de cuisine and bon vivants in the U. S. 1st ed. New York: H. K. & F. B. Thurber, 1879. 110p. and ads.

2409 Henderson, Mrs. Mary F. Practical Cooking and Dinner Giving. Instructions in cooking, in combination and serving of dishes . . . Illustrated. Harper & Brothers, New York, 1879. 376p. 8p. book lists.

2410 Neely, Flora. Hand-book for the Kitchen and Housekeeper's Guide. Household recipes of every description — including family dyes. New York: Trow's Printing and Bookbinding Co., 1879. 358p. illus.

2411 Mrs. Winslow's Domestic Receipt Book. New York, 1879. (See No. 2361).

2412 Youmans, Eliza A. Lessons in Cookery. Hand-book, National Training School, South Kensington, London; plus Principles of Diet in Health and Disease by Thomas K. Chambers. New York: D. Appleton, 1879. 382p.

2413 Astor, Jane. The New York Cook-Book. Cook palatable, digestible meals. Serving. Useful medical receipts. New York: G. W. Carleton & Co., 1880. 337p. and Index.

2414 Carroll, George D. The Art of Dinner Giving and Usages of Polite Society. New York: Dempsey & Carroll (1880). 127p. many not num. Frontis. coat of arms of Prince Albert.

2415 Fothergill, J. Milner and Wood, Horatio C. Food for the Invalid; the Convalescent; the Dyspeptic; and the Gouty. New York: Macmillan and Co., 1880. 157p.

2416 Lees-Dods, Matilda. The Art of Cooking. A series of Practical Lessons. Edited by Henriette De Condé Sherman. New York: G. P. Putnam's Sons, 1880. 226p.

2417 Babcock, Emma Whitcomb. Household Hints. New York: D. Appleton & Co., 1881. 144p.

2418 Campbell, Helen (Stuart). The Easiest Way in Housekeeping and Cooking. For homes or classes. New York: Fords, Howard & Hulbert, 1881. 283p.

2419 The Centaur Receipt Book. Dewey & Co., New York, 1881 (?) Illus. 32p.

2420 Henry's Universal Cook-Book. New York: John F. Henry & Co., 1881. 32p. booklet advertising Dr. Hall's Balsam. Shows kitchen stove, on pict. cover.

2421 How to Cook. The housekeeper's friend. Valuable recipes for meats, fish and game. Also for bread, desserts. New York: F. Tousey (c. 1881). 60p. Wraps.

2422 OWEN, CATHERINE. CULTURE AND COOKING, Or Art in the Kitchen. The first of its kind in America. New York (1881). 1st ed. 121p.

2423 WARFORD, AARON A. (Anon.) The Gem Cook Book. No. 1. Useful recipes for cooking all kinds of meats, fish, game, bread, cake and pastry. Also for making preserves, jellies, and jams . . New York: F. Tousey, 1881. 48p.

2424 THE ART OF CANNING, SMOKING, PICKLING, DRYING, AND OTHERWISE PRESERVING MEATS, FOWL, GAME, FRUIT, AND BERRIES. Also How Pickles Are Made and The Process of Candying. New York: Hurst, 1882. 96p. Wraps.

2425 CORSON, JULIET. Meals for the Million: the People's Cook-Book. 3rd ed. New York: N. Y. School of Cookery, 1882. 84p.

2426 HENDERSON, MRS. MARY F. PRACTICAL COOKING AND DINNER GIVING. Illustrated. Harper, New York, 1882. 376p. 8p. book advertisements.

2427 HOUSEHOLD ECONOMY. A manual for use in schools. Under direction of The Kitchen-garden association. Ivison, Blakeman & Co., New York, 1882. 145p.

2428 LAIN, GEORGE T. (Anon.) The Housekeeper's Manual of Cookery and Shopping Guide. Contains 200 valuable cooking recipes, carefully selected . . Brooklyn: New York: Lain & Co., 1882. 104p. Wraps. Ads.

2429 MARTINELO, MARIE. THE NEW YORK COOK BOOK. A complete manual of cookery in all its branches. New York; James Miller, 1882. 1st part, 142p. and 2nd part, 120p.

2430 THE PRACTICAL HOME COOK-BOOK. With useful instructions on marketing. New York: N. Y. Popular Pub. Co. (c. 1882). 64p. Wraps.

2431 RUDMANI, GUISEPPI. Royal Baker and Pastry Cook. New York: Royal Baking Powder Co. (1882). 41p. illus.

2432 TAYLOR, MRS. JENNIE (compiler). The People's Cook Book. A collection of nearly 1000 Valuable Cooking Recipes . . . New York: Grand Union Tea Co., 1882 (copyright by J. S. Ogilvie). 185p.

2433 TAYLOR, MRS. JENNIE. THE POPULAR COOK BOOK. Nearly 1000 valuable cooking recipes. Col. plates. Abraham Strauss, Brooklyn (1882). 185p.

2434 WILLIAMS, HENRY LLEWELLYN (Anon.) The New Homemade Cook-book. Healthful, cheap and refined recipes. New York: M. J. Ivers (1882). 336p.

2435 BROWN, SUSAN ANNA. MRS. GILPIN'S FRUGALITIES. Scribner's: New York, 1883. 102p.

2436 HARLAND, MARION. The Cottage Kitchen. A collection of practical and inexpensive receipts. New York: C. Scribner's Sons, 1883. 276p.

2437 ICE-CREAM AND CAKES. A new collection of standard, and

original receipts for household and commercial use. By an Amercian. New York: Charles Scribner's Sons, 1883. 384p.

2438 THE NEW YORK RECEIPT BOOK. New York: Castoria Co., 1883. 36p. advertising booklet, illus., with pictorial cover.

2439 DÉLIÉE, FELIX J. The Franco-American Cookery Book. (See Foreign sec.)

2440 HARLAND, MARION. Breakfast, Luncheon and Tea. Common Sense in the Household Series. Charles Scribners: New York, 1884. 157p.

2441 THE LATEST & BEST COOK-BOOK. Over 800 valuable recipes. Ed. by a skilled corps of Practical Experts. Illus. New York, 1884. 369p.

2442 MURREY, THOMAS J. 50 SOUPS. A little book. Quaint col. cover. The author was caterer at the Astor House & proprietor of the restaurant, House of Representatives in Washington. New York: White, Stokes & Allen, 1884. 37p.

2443 "NESSMUK." Woodcraft. New York: Forest and Stream Publishing Co., 1884. 149p.

2444 THURBER, FRANCIS. Coffee from Plantation to Cup. A Brief History of Coffee Production and Consumption. With "Notes by the Way"—letters during a trip of the East. New York: American Grocer Pub. Ass'n., 1884. 9th ed. 416p. 13 illus.—2 plates. With appendix.

2445 CANOE AND CAMP COOKERY: A practical cook book for canoeists, Corinthian sailors and outers. By "Seneca." New York: Forest and Stream Pub., 1885. 96p.

2446 CORSON, JULIET. PRACTICAL AMERICAN COOKERY AND HOUSEHOLD MANAGEMENT. Oilcloth. Illus. New York (1885). 591p.

2447 DONNELLEY, NAOMI A. (Anon.) The Home Made Cook Book. A complete manual of cookery. New York: M. J. Ivers & Co. (1885). 47p.

2448 E. R. DURKEE & CO.'S PRACTICAL COOK BOOK. Nearly 300 economical, useful and tested recipes. Booklet. Wraps. E. R. Durkee: New York, 1885. 92p.

2449 HUNTINGTON, EMILY. The Cooking Garden. A course of cooking for pupils of all ages, including plan of work, bills of fare, songs and letters of information. Illus. by Jessie Shepherd. New York: J. W. Schermerhorn & Co. (1885). 199p.

2450 LYNNDE, ELMER (Mrs. J. F. Stone). The Mode Cook: or, Things Good to Eat and How to Make Them. New York: O. Judd Co., 1885. 120p.

2451 MURREY, THOMAS J. 50 SALADS. One of a collection of little books by a famous culinary authority. New York, 1885. (see No. 2442). 32p.

2452 MURREY, THOMAS J. Valuable Cooking Receipts. Good and literary. By the caterer of N. Y. Astor House & Philadelphia Continental Hotel. White, Stokes & Allen; New York, 1885. 128p.

2453 HOLLOWAY, LAURA C. The Buddhist Diet Book. No animal foods or stimulants. New York: Funk & Wagnalls, 1886. 80p. Wraps.

2454 MURREY, THOMAS J. BOOK OF ENTREES. (same format as No. 2442). New York, 1886. 83p.

2455 MURREY, THOMAS J. PUDDINGS DESSERTS. (same format as No. 2442). New York, 1886. 53p.

2456 MY FAVORITE RECEIPT. New York: Royal Baking Powder Co., 1886. 123p. (Compiled from contributions of patrons.)

2457 TILTON, MRS. E. STEVENS. HOME DISSERTATIONS: An Offering to the Household for Economical & Practical Skill in Cookery. New York, 1886. 176p. (see No. 44).

2458 WASHINGTON, MRS., pseudonym. The Unrivalled Cook-Book and Housekeeper's Guide. Harper & Bros., New York, 1886. 624p. 1st ed.

2459 WASHINGTON, MRS. The Unrivalled Cook-Book and Housekeeper's Guide. 2nd ed. Harper & Bros., New York, 1886. viii, 640p.

2460 BATTERSHALL: FOOD ADULTERATION. With Photomicrographic Plates and a Biblio Appendix. New York, 1887. 328p.

2461 BROWN, SUSAN ANNA. The Book of Forty Puddings. New York: Charles Scribner's Sons, 1887. 52p. not numbered.

2462 GILLETTE, MRS. FANNIE LEMIRA. White House Cook Book. New York, Gillette Publishing Co., 1887. 1st ed. (Same as No. 403).

2463 HARLAND, MARION. Gesunde Vernunft im Haushalte. (See Foreign sec.)

2464 MURREY, THOMAS J. COOKERY FOR INVALIDS. (Same format as No. 2442). New York, 1887. 32p.

2465 SHILLABER, LYDIA. Mrs. Shillaber's Cook-Book. A practical guide for housekeepers. Intro. by Mrs. Partington . . New York: T. J. Crowell & Co.: (1887). xviii, 265p.

2466 STROHM, GERTRUDE. The Universal Cookery Book. Practical recipes, selected from the most eminent authorities . . and original recipes. New York: White, Stokes & Allen, 1887. xx, 245p.

2467 BLOT, PIERRE. Handbook of Practical Cookery. (See No. 2371). 1888.

2468 HELLSTERN, CHARLES. KOCHBUCH. (See Foreign sec.)

2469 LOUGHEAD, FLORA APPONYI (Anon.) Quick Cooking: A book of culinary heresies for the busy wives and mothers of the land. New York: G. P. Putnam's Sons, 1888. 294p.

2470 PARKER, MRS. E. H. Mrs. Parker's Complete Housekeeper. New York: M. T. Richardson, 1888. 473p. illus. Ads.

2471 MURREY, THOMAS J. LUNCHEON. (same format as No. 2442). New York, 1888. 69p.

2472 FILIPPINI, ALESSANDRO. THE TABLE. How to Buy Food, How to

Cook It, and How to Serve It. Revised ed. Facsimile letters from Filippini and Delmonico to each other. Merriam Co., New York (1889). 505p.

2473 GUNTER, BESSIE E. Housekeeper's Companion. New York: J. B. Alden, 1889. 211p.

2474 HOW THE SHAKERS COOK. 1889. n.p. 50p. Wraps. (New York). A small almanac.

2475 THE KINGS OF THE KITCHEN. A small booklet—wraps. Vanderbilt's Candy Church, N.Y.C. 1889. 33p.

2476 LUPTON, FRANK M. (Anon.) The Modern Cook Book and Medical Guide. New York: F. M. Lupton, 1889. 128p.

2477 OGILVIE, MRS. JOHN STUART (Anon.) The "Press" prize recipes for meals. A collection furnished by the lady readers of the Press. New York: J. S. Ogilvie, 1889. 92p. Wraps.

2478 ORMISTON, HELEN F. (Anon.) The Ideal Cook Book. Compiled by a committee of ladies in the interest of Christian work. New York: J. J. Little & Co., 1889. 121p.

2479 OWEN, CATHERINE. CHOICE COOKERY. Recipes written for Harper's Bazaar, and collected into a book. Harper & Brothers: New York, 1889. 320p.

2480 RORER, MRS. S. T. GOOD WAYS IN COOKING. For the family. Wraps. Syndicate Trading Co., New York (1889). 1st ed. 202p. and ads.

2481 BLITS, PROFESSOR H. Methods of Canning. Decorative end papers. H. I. Blits, Brooklyn, N.Y., 1890. 106p., ads., & testimonials.

2482 BRUGIERE, SARAH VAN BUREN: GOOD LIVING, A Practical Cookery-Book for Town & Country. New York, 1890. 1st ed. 580p.

2483 CHILD, THEODORE. Delicate Feasting. A savory tome on the gastronomic art. New York: Harper & Bros.; 1890. 214p.

2484 FILIPPINI, ALESSANDRO. THE TABLE: How to Buy Food, How to Cook it, and How to Serve It. Revised edition with supplements. Charles L. Webster & Co., New York, 1890. 505p. and ads.

2485 GOOD FORM. DINNERS. CEREMONIOUS AND UNCEREMONIOUS . . . New York: Stokes & Brother, 1890. 80p. 4th ed.

2486 HECKER'S HOUSEHOLD RECIPES. New York: (c. 1890). 4p. advertising folder. Col. pict. cover.

2487 LATHROP, MRS. C. M. (Anon.) Riverside Recipe Book . . New York: Press of W. R. Jenkins, 1890. 64p.

2488 THE NEW YORK COOK BOOK. A Complete Manual of Cookery. New York: Worthington & Co., 1890. 142p. illus.

2489 OLCOTT, BELLE. The Kitchen, John and I. Twenty chapters from a young housekeeper's journal.

New York: Jas. McCall & Co., 1890. 132p. Wraps.

2490 ON THE CHAFING-DISH. A word for Sunday night teas. New York: G. W. Dillingham, 1890. 70p.

2491 THE PATTERN COOK-BOOK. History, chemistry, equipment, marketing. Directions for preparing food. Illustrated. Decorative end papers. Butterick Publishing Co.: New York, 1890. 1st ed. 624p.

2492 POOLE, MRS. HESTER M. Fruits and How to Use them. 700 Wholesome Recipes. Fowler & Wells; New York, 1890. 242p.

2493 SAWTELLE, H. L. WHAT ONE CAN DO WITH A CHAFING-DISH. A guide for amateur cooks. Ireland: New York, 1890. 76p. 3p. ads.

2494 SCHULTZ, PAULINE (Anon.) Grand Union Kochbuch. (See Foreign sec.)

2494a THE WASHINGTON COOK BOOK. Statesmen's Dishes, autographic receipts by Mrs. Benjamin Harrison . . . and more than 200 other prominent women. Also Mrs. H. P. Bailey's Receipts for "The Chafing Dish and Blazer." New York; G. W. Dillingham, 1890. 222p. (see No. 404).

2495 WEHMAN, HENRY J. Wehman's Cook Book. A complete collection of valuable recipes suited to every household and all tastes. New York: H. J. Wehman (1890). 100p. Wraps.

2496 WEHMAN'S DEUTSCH — AMERIKANISCHES KOCHBUCH . . in German. New York: n.d. 126p. (c. 1890). (See Foreign sec.)

2497 EVERYDAY COOK BOOK. New York: Street & Smith (1891). 64p. Paper.

2498 HANEY, JESSE. The New Family Cook Book, with recipes for breakfast, soups, gravies, roast & boiled dinners, desserts, etc., adapted to the needs of families of moderate means. Also recipes for invalid and Hebrew cookery. New York: Excelsior Publishing House, 1891. 57p. Wraps.

2499 HELLSTERN, CHARLES. DEUTSCH-AMERIKANISCHES KOCHBUCH. (See Foreign sec.)

2500 HERRICK, CHRISTINE TERHUNE. WHAT TO EAT, HOW TO SERVE IT. Menus, recipes—even flower decorations. Harper & Brothers: New York, 1891. 309p.

2501 NEILL, MISS E. The Handy Cook Book. Designed for every day use . . . New York: J. S. Ogilvie, 1891. 32p. Wraps.

2502 THEISE, WILLIAM (Anon.) Haushaltungs-Kochbuch. (See Foreign sec.)

2503 WARREN, JANE. The Ladies' Own Cook Book. A practical and economical guide to cooking, canning, curing and preserving . . New York: Hurst & Company, 1891. 120, 20, 7-96p. illus.

2504 EXTRACTS AND BEVERAGES. Preparation of cordials, syrups, beverages, colognes. Metropolitan Pamphlet Series. Butterick: New

York, Sept. 1892. 32p. iv advertisements.

2505 Filippini, Alessandro. 100 Choicest Recipes for Cooking, by the World Famous Delmonico Chef. New York: The New York Sunday Press, 1892. 30p.

2506 Filippini, Alessandro. The author was 25 years with Delmonico. Handy Volume, Culinary Series includes: I. 100 Ways of Cooking Eggs. II. 100 Recipes for Cooking and Serving Fish. III. 100 Desserts. H. M. Caldwell Co., New York, 1892. 364p.

2507 Herrick, Christine Terhune. The Little Dinner. New York: Charles Scribner & Son, 1892. 150p.

2508 Neill, Miss E. What Shall I Eat? The housewife's manual. New York: Home Life Publishing Co. (1892). 208p. Wraps. Ads. (see No. 757).

2509 Nicol, Mary E. 366 Dinners. Suggested by M.E.N. New York: G. P. Putnam's Sons, 1892. 186p.

2510 Sawtelle, H. L. What One Can Do With a Chafing-Dish. 4th ed., 1892. 78p. (See No. 2493).

2511 Sherwood, M. E. W. The Art of Entertaining. Dodd, Mead & Co., New York, 1892. 404p.

2512 Taylor: Marie Hansen-Taylor. Letters to Young Housekeepers by the wife of Bayard Taylor. C. Scribner's Sons. New York, 1892. 1st ed.

2513 Warren, Jane. The Handy Reliable Cook Book. A practical and comprehensive manual of commonsense cookery. New York: Hurst & Co. (1892). 13, 27-124, 7-100p. Wraps.

2514 Watson, Marcia L. The Reliable Cook Book. 600 tested recipes for delicious and inexpensive dishes for breakfast, dinner and supper. New York: W. N. Swett & Co., 1892. 101p.

2515 Babet. 99 Practical Methods of Utilizing Boiled Beef and the Original Recipe for Stewed Chicken. (See Foreign sec.)

2516 Beverages and Sandwiches For Your Husband's Friends. By One who knows. A solution to the problem . . . The Labyrinthian way to a man's heart. New York: (G. L. Horton, 1893.) 6-48p. (1).

2517 Boland, Mary A. A Handbook of Invalid Cooking. For the use of nurses. Century Co., New York, 1893. 1st ed. 323p.

2518 Bussing, Charles F. (Compiler). Canned Foods. How to Prepare Them for the Table. New York: Retail Grocers' Publishing Co., 1893. 192p.

2519 "Grid" Real Cookery. American dishes, unusual material. Pictures. Cassell Pub. Co. New York, 1893. 86p.

2520 Harrison, Mrs. Benjamin. The Columbian Memorial Cook Book: New York: Dillingham, 1893. (same as No. 404).

2521 "SENECA": CANOE & CAMP COOKERY, A Practical Cook Book for Canoeists, Corinthian Sailors & Outers. New York, Forest & Stream Pub. Co., 1893. 96p.

2523 THE UNIVERSAL COMMON SENSE COOK BOOK. Practical Recipes for Household Use by Corson, Lincoln, Parloa, etc. Wraps. Index tabs, The Housewife Pub. Co., New York (c. 1893). 52p.

2524 WHITE, JAMES EDSON AND WANLESS, MRS. M. L. (Anon.) The "Home Queen" World's fair souvenir cook book. 2000 valuable recipes on cookery and household economy, New York: G. F. Cram, 1893. 608p. illus.

2525 LARNED, LINDA HULL. The Little Epicure. New York: The Baker & Taylor Co. (c. 1894). 276p.

2526 RANHOFER, CHARLES. The Epicurean. (See Foreign sec.)

2527 SPRINGSTEED, ANNE FRANCES. The Expert Waitress. A manual for the pantry, kitchen, and dining room. Harper and Brothers, New York, 1894. 1st ed. 131p. and ads.

2528 GIBSON, W. HAMILTON. Our Edible Toadstools and Mushrooms and How to Distinguish Them. 30 Native Food Varieties; Simple Rules for Identification of Poisonous Species. Col. plates and other illus. New York: Harper & Brothers (1895). x, 337p. Exact and beautiful illus.

2529 KINSLEY, H. M. ONE HUNDRED RECIPES FOR THE CHAFING DISH. Illustrations of silver service. Gorham Manufacturing Co., New York, 1895. 1st ed. 183p.

2530 MY FAVORITE RECEIPT. Contributions from patrons. Colored end papers. Royal Baking Powder Co. New York, 1895. 7th ed. 126p.

2531 SWAIN, RACHEL. Swain Cookery. With health hints. New York: Fowler & Wells Co., 1895. 228p.

2532 WELCH, DESHLER. The Bachelor and the Chafing Dish. With a dissertation on chums. Drawings by Francis Day and George Halm. Devil dishes too. New York: F. Tennyson Neely (1895). 1st ed. 141p. & book ads.

2533 COMPTON, MARGARET. (editor). The Alex. Campbell prize Milk Cook Book. Brooklyn: The Alex. Campbell Milk Co., 1896. 104p. Wraps.

2534 HARLAND, MARION. The Art of Cooking by Gas. New York: American Technical Book Co., 1896. 226p.

2535 HOOKER, MARGARET HUNTINGTON. Ye Gentlewoman's Housewifery containing Scarce, Curious, and Valuable Receipts. Compiled from old and reliable sources (an imitation of an old cookery book.) New York: Dodd, Mead and Co., 1896. xxii, 227p. illus.

2536 PENNELL, ELIZABETH ROBINS (edited by) THE FEASTS OF AUTOLYCUS. The Diary of a Greedy Woman. Frontispiece engraving. The Merriam Co., New York, 1896. 1st ed. 264p.

2537 SALA, GEORGE AUGUSTUS. THE THOROUGH COOK: a Series of Chats on the Culinary Art, and 900 Recipes. New York, Brentano's, 1896. 492p.

2538 WILLIAMS, W. MATTIEU. The Chemistry of Cookery. New York: D. Appleton, 1896. 328p.

2539 YSAGUIRRE AND LA MARCA. COLD DISHES FOR HOT WEATHER. Harper & Brothers, New York, 1896. 126p.

2540 THE CHAFING DISH. Small booklet, wraps. Illustrated. S. Sternau & Co. 1897. 32p.

2541 ECCLES, ANNA K. A Manual of What To Eat and How To Cook It for Salisbury patients. New York: Kellogg & Co., 1897. 75p. illus. Ads.

2542 FRAZER, PERRY D. CANOE CRUISING & CAMPING. Illus. of original light wire range for camp cooking. New York, 1897. 87p.

2543 GALLIER, ADOLPHE. The Majestic Family Cook-Book. 1300 selected recipes, simplified for the home. A few choice bills of fare. New York: G. P. Putnam's Sons, 1897. 419p. Chapters ornamented.

2544 HARLAND, MARION. Breakfast, Dinner and Supper. Special chapter on preparation of food for infants, and advice to housekeepers. Prefatory poem by Ella Wheeler Wilcox. New York: G. J. McLeod and Co. (c. 1897). 359p.

2545 99 SALADS. And How To Make Them with Rules for Dressing and Sauce. Gorham Manufacturing Co., New York (1897). 57p.

2546 REED, VIRGINIA. The Way We Did at Cooking School. New York: John B. Alden, 1897. 272p. illus.

2547 RONALD, MARY. The Century Cook Book. Recipes from the simplest forms to high-class dishes and ornamental pieces. Illus. The Century Co., New York, 1897. 588p. & Memo. p.

2548 CUTTING, ELISABETH BROWN. Old Taverns and Posting Inns. Published in the Interest of the New York City History Club. Wraps. G. P. Putnam's Sons, New York, 1898. 282p.

2549 DWIGHT, HENRIETTA LATHAM. The Golden Age Cook Book. New York: The Alliance Publishing Co., 1898. 178p.

2550 HILL, A. P. House-keeping Made Easy. New ed., 1898. 416p. (See No. 2368).

2551 HOLT, DR. L. EMMETT. THE FEEDING OF YOUNG CHILDREN. Reprinted from 'Babyhood.' Babyhood Publishing Co., New York, 1898. 46p. and ads.

2552 JAMES, ALICE L. CATERING FOR TWO. Comfort and Economy for Small Households. G. P. Putnam's Sons, New York, 1898. 1st ed. 292p.

2553 MEYER, ADOLPHE. Eggs, and How to Use Them. Over 500 different styles, with some historical notes. By the one-time chef of the

Union Club. New York: The author, 1898. 149p.

2554 MORITZ, MRS. C. F. AND KAHN, MISS ADELE. THE TWENTIETH CENTURY COOK BOOK. Each department of cookery represented. Dillingham; New York, 1898. 5th ed. 388p.

2555 PARLOA, MARIA. Home Economics—A Practical Guide in Every Branch of Housekeeping. Illus. New York: The Century Co., 1898. 378p.

2556 SALADS. How to make and dress them. Illus. Wraps. E. R. Durkee & Co., New York, 1898. 32p.

2557 BAILEY, HARRIET P. On the Chafing-Dish. A word for Sunday Night Teas. G. W. Dillingham Co., New York, 1899. 76p.

2558 CARON, PIERRE. French Dishes for American Tables. (See Foreign sec.)

2559 GILLETTE, MRS. F. L. AND ZIEMANN, HUGO. DAS "WEISSE HAUS" KOCHBUCH. (See Foreign sec.)

2560 THE GORHAM CHAFING DISH BOOK. New York: Gorham Mfg. Co., 1899. 100p.

2561 HARLAND, MARION. Cooking Hints. A tiny booklet. From the Bits of Common Sense Series. Home Topics Pub. Co., New York, 1899. 119p.

2562 LEMCKE, GESINE. Desserts and Salads. By the principal and owner of the Brooklyn and New York Cooking Colleges. 7th ed. New York: the author, 1899. 311p.

2563 DE PUY, FRANK A. THE NEW CENTURY HOME BOOK. A mentor for home life . . . Frontispiece. Eaton & Mains, New York, 1900. 1st ed. 400p.

2564 DE RIVAZ, EVELYN. Little French Dinners. (See Foreign sec.)

2565 FULTON, A. W. Home Pork Making. A guide for the farmer, country butcher and suburban dweller. Illus. Orange Judd: New York, 1900. 124p. & ads.

2566 MALLOCK, N. M. The Ecoomics of Modern Cookery or A Younger Son's Cookery Book. New York: Macmillan Company, 1900. vii, 378p. illus. (1st ed. 1896).

2567 THE AMERICAN COOK BOOK. By the readers of The New York Journal, Chicago American, San Francisco Examiner. 1000 recipes. Illustrated. Decorative end papers. Hearst: New York, 1901. 413p.

2568 BURRELL, CAROLINE BENEDICT. Gala-Day Luncheons. New York: Dodd, Mead & Co., 1901. 221p. illus.

2569 CURTIS, ISABEL GORDON. Left-Overs Made Palatable. Based on actual results of the best cooks, tested at the New England Cooking School. New York: Orange Judd Co. (1901). 168p. illus.

2570 PHYSICAL CULTURE COOK BOOK. Compiled by Mary Richardson and George Propheter, under direction of Bernarr MacFadden. Physical Culture Pub. Co., New York, 1901. 249p. & ads.

2571 Pierce, Ella A. The Hartley House Cook Book and Household Economist. New York: Lenthilon & Co. (c. 1901). 188p.

2572 Beard, Sidney H. A Comprehensive Guide-Book to Natural, Hygienic & Humane Diet. Unusual food reformer. Thomas Y. Crowell, New York (1902). 169p.

2573 Compton, Margaret. Grand Union Cook Book. New York: 1902. 322p. illus. with photos. (see No. 2374).

2574 Ellwanger, George H. The Pleasures of the Table. An account of gastronomy from ancient days to present times. Charming end papers; delightful illustrations. Doubleday Page and Co., New York, 1902. 1st ed. 477p.

2575 Gray, Arthur (compiler) Over the Black Coffee. Illus. by George Hood. New York: Baker & Taylor Co., 1902.

2576 Harper's Cook Book Encyclopedia. Illus. with photos. New York, Harper & Brothers, 1902. 443p. Frontis.

2577 How to Cook. New York: Frank Tousey, 1902. 80p. and book ads. Pict. cover.

2578 Howard, Arthur P. Grandmother's Cook Book. A humorous little book about indigestion. With illustrations by C. G. Moller, Jr. New Amsterdam Book Co., New York, 1902. 1st ed. 27p.

2579 Janvier, Thomas A. The Christmas Kalends of Provence. Christmas Dinner. The Great Supper. Chateau-neuf-du Pape vineyards, etc. New York, 1902. 1st ed. 261p.

2580 Martha Washington's or the Mother's Cook Book. A compendium of cookery and reliable recipes. New ed. illus. New York: Abbey Press (1902). 315p.

2581 Reynolds, Cuyler. The Banquet Book. Quotations helpful in the preparation of the toast list, afterdinner speech and address. Menus and banquet planning. Intro. by Elbert Hubbard. New York: G. P. Putnam's Sons, 1902. 475p. Frontis. by Arthur Rackham.

2582 Ronald, Mary. Luncheons: A Cook's Picture Book. A supplement to the century cook book. Illus. with over 200 photographs. The Century Co.: New York, 1902. 223p. and handwritten recipes.

2583 Seely, Mrs. L. Mrs. Seely's Cook Book. A Manual of French and American Cookery. Illus. The Macmillan Co., New York, 1902. 432p. and ads.

2584 Tasty Dishes made from tested recipes. What we can have for breakfast, dinner, tea and supper. New York: R. F. Fenno, 1902. 181p.

2585 Fletcher, Horace. The A. B. Z. of Our Own Nutrition. Illus. Frederick A. Stokes: New York (c. 1903). 1st ed. 426p.

2586 Gray, Arthur. The Little Tea Book. Illus. by George W. Hood. New York: Baker & Taylor Co. (1903). ix, 99p. Frontis. of Boswell and Johnson at the Mitre. Illus.

2587 Martyn, Charles. Martyn's Menu Dictionary. New York: The Caterer Publishing Co. (1903). 133p.

2588 Meyer, Adolphe. "Dainty Dishes," a collection of choice receipts. New York: The Caterer Publishing Co., 1903. 89p.

2589 Meyer, Adolphe. The Post-Graduate Cookery Book. A large number of special receipts, many of them original. New York; The Caterer Pub. Co., 1903. 282p. Frontis. portrait of the author.

2589a 365 Dinners suggested by M.E.N. Pict. cover. With literary quotation for each menu. New York, 1903. 186p.

2589b Cary, Elisabeth Luther; & Jones, Annie M. Books and My Food. Literary Quotations & Original Recipes for Every Day in the Year. Rohde & Haskins. New York, 1904. 1st ed. 235p.

2589c Christian, Mr. & Mrs. Eugene. Uncooked Foods & How to Use Them. Recipes, too. Frontispiece photo. Health-Culture Co., New York (1904). 246p.

2589d Foote, Dr. E. B. Health and Disease with Recipes, including Sexology. Murray Hill Pub. Co., New York, 1904. 1248p.

2589e Herrick, Christine Terhune (Ed. in Chief) Harland, Marion. Consolidated Library of Modern Cooking and Household Recipes. Vol. II. The cooking-school. Colored end papers. R. J. Bodmer: New York, 1904. 346p.

2589f Herrick, Christine Terhune (Ed. in Chief) Harland, Marion. Consolidated Library of Modern Cooking and Household Recipes. Vol. III. Many famous chefs and cooking experts included. Soups—Chowders & Fish, Meats, Poultry & Game. Colored end papers. Bodmer: New York, 1904. 346p.

2589g Herrick, Christine Terhune; & Harland, Marion. Consolidated Library of Modern Cooking & Household Recipes. Vol. IV.—Vegetables, Fruits & Cereals, Bread & Cakes, Salads & Relishes, Ices, Pastry & Other Desserts. New York: Bodmer, 1904. 346p.

2589h Herrick, Christine Terhune (Ed. in Chief) Harland, Marion. Consolidated Library of Modern Cooking and Household Recipes, Vol. V. Chafing-dish recipes, carving, beverages, mixing and serving drinks, toasts, index. Colored end papers. R. J. Bodmer: New York, 1904. 293p.

2589i Herrick, Christine Terhune. The Expert Maid-Servant. Duties and skills. Harper & Brothers, New York, 1904. 138p.

2589j Irwin, May. May Irwin's Home Cooking. Illus. Embellished with literary culinary quotes & frontis of May herself. Good cookbook & good Americana. 1904. 268p. 1st ed. New York.

2590 LINCOLN, MRS. MARY J. WHAT TO HAVE FOR LUNCHEON. Table settings and service, menus and recipes. Illustrations. Dodge: New York, 1904. 1st ed. 244p.

2591 LOW, BERTHE JULIENNE. French Home Cooking Adapted to the Use of American Households. (See Foreign sec.)

2592 MONTGOMERY, CHARLES A. The New York Cake Book; fifty recipes by a famous New York chef. (C. A. Montgomery). New York: C. A. Montgomery & Co., 1904. 60p.

2593 CORSON, JULIET. Family Living on $500 a Year. A daily reference book for young housewives. New York: Harper & Brothers, 1905. 437p.

2594 DAVIDSON, MRS. HUGH COLEMAN. Egg Dainties: How to Cook Eggs in 150 ways—English and Foreign. New York: Charles Scribner's sons, 1905. 86p. Paper.

2595 EINHORN, MAX, MD. Diet and Nutrition. Practical Problems of nutrition. William Wood, New York, 1905. 64p.

2596 FARMER, FANNY MERRITT. WHAT TO HAVE FOR DINNER. Menus with recipes necessary for their preparation. Illustrated. Dodge; New York, 1905. 1st ed. 271p.

2597 THE HOME COOK BOOK. A collection of practical receipts by expert cooks. Frontispiece in color by W. T. Smedley. Profusely illustrated. P. F. Collier & Son, New York, 1905. 1st ed. 440p.

2598 MARSHALL, NINA L. The Mushroom Book. Identification and study of fungi, with special emphasis on the edible varieties. Illus. in color and black and white, photographed by J. A. and H. C. Anderson. New York: Doubleday, Page & Co., 1905. 170p.

2599 TAYLOR, FOLWELL, BANGS. MONSIEUR D'EN BROCHETTE. A culinary picaresque. Illus. New York, 1905. 179p.

2600 THOMAS, JULIAN P. The Advantages of Raw Food. New York: the Author, 1905. 63p. Frontis. portrait of the author.

2601 "AUNT BABETTE'S" COOK BOOK. Copyrighted 1889 . . . New York City: The Bloch Publishing Co., 1906. 520p. plus 38p.

2602 GREEN, OLIVE. Everyday Luncheons. New York: G. P. Putnam's Sons (1906). 327p.

2603 GREEN, OLIVE (Myrtle Reed). What to Have for Breakfast. New York: G. P. Putnam's Sons (1906). 283p.

2604 HANKS, CHARLES STEDMAN. CAMP KITS AND CAMP LIFE. With a chapter on camp cooking. Illustrated. Charles Scribner's Sons, New York, 1906. 259p.

2605 MADDOCKS, MILDRED. Good Housekeeping Family Cook Book.

New York: The Phelps Publishing Co., 1906. 320p.

2606 MUCKENSTURM, LOUIS. Louis' Salads & Chafing Dishes. New York: Dodge Pub. Company, 1906. 113p. Wraps.

2607 THE NEW LUCILE COOK BOOK. Includes 40 recipes of the "Four Hundred." These are signed by contributors. Acker, Merrill & Condit; New York (c. 1906). 303p.

2608 ROYAL BAKER AND PASTRY COOK. A Practical Manual for Every Day Cookery. New York: Royal Baking Powder Co., 1906. 44p. and ads. Col. pict. cover.

2609 YOUMAN, A. E., MD. YOUMAN'S HOUSEHOLD GUIDE. Dictionary of Every-Day Wants. J. S. Ogilvie: New York, 1906. 539p. and ads.

2610 BERRY, RILEY M. F. Fruit Recipes, A Manual of the Food Values of Fruits and 900 Ways of Using. Photo. illus. Doubleday, Page & Co., New York, 1907. 341p.

2611 CAMPBELL, HELEN. Household Economics. Rev. ed. New York, 1907. 290p.

2612 CHITTENDEN, RUSSELL H. The Nutrition of Man. Illus. with photos. Tables. Frederick A. Stokes Co., New York (1907). 321p.

2613 DINING AND ITS AMENITIES. By a lover of good cheer. New York: Rebman, 1907. 470p.

2614 DRINKS AND DISHES—Wholesome and Delicious for the Sick and Convalescing. Also for General Family Use. New York: Borden's Condensed Milk Co., 1907. 16p. adv. booklet illus.

2615 ESCOFFIER, AUGUSTE. A Guide to Modern Cookery. (See Foreign sec.)

2616 GOODHUE, ISABEL. Meat Substitutes. New York: New York Magazine of Mysteries, 1907. 111p.

2617 GREEN, OLIVE. How to Cook Shell-Fish. New York: G. P. Putnam's Sons, 1907. 335p.

2618 GREEN, OLIVE. 1000 Simple Soups. New York: G. P. Putnam's Sons, 1907. 376p.

2619 HERRICK, CHRISTINE TERHUNE AND HARLAND, MARION. CONSOLIDATED LIBRARY OF MODERN COOKING AND HOUSEHOLD RECIPES. The contributors include many famous chefs and cooking experts. Illustrations. Vol. I. Bodmer: New York, 1907. 336p.

2620 LUST, LOUISE, MD. THE PRACTICAL NATUROPATHIC-VEGETARIAN COOK BOOK. Cooked and uncooked foods. Charts, adv. photographs. Benedict Lust: New York, 1907. 72p.

2621 SALADS—DURKEE: 1907. (See No. 2556).

2622 EMERSON, EDWARD R. BEVERAGES PAST & PRESENT. 2 Vols. A most complete and thorough treatment of all beverages, alcoholic & non—. New York, 1908. 653p. and 514p.

2623 GREEN, OLIVE. How to Cook Meat & Poultry. New York: G. P. Putnam's Sons, 1908. 504p.

2624 MONTGOMERY, CHARLES A. The New York Cake Book. 2nd ed. New York: Stoker (1908). (See No. 2592).

2625 MORSE, SIDNEY. Household Discoveries. An Encyclopedia of Practical Recipes and Processes. New York: The Success Company (1908). 536p. illus.

2626 NEWNHAM-DAVIS: LIEUT.-COL. Gourmets Guide to Europe. Imperishable record of the great day of Continental dining-out. Pict. 2nd ed. New York: Brentano's. 1908. 315p.

2627 RONALD, MARY. THE CENTURY COOK BOOK. Cooking, etiquette, serving of dinners. Frontispiece. Handwritten recipes. The Century Co., New York, 1908. 588p.

2628 TELFORD, EMMA PADDOCK. New York Evening Telegram Cook Book. Ed. by M. A. Armington. Illus. Copyright, New York Herald Co., 1908. New York City: Cupples & Leon Co., 254p. Pict. cover.

2629 VAN BUREN, SARA. GOOD-LIVING. A practical cookery-book for town and country (Revised). G. P. Putnam's Sons: New York (1908). 640p.

2630 WILLIAMS, MARY E. & FISHER, KATHARINE ROLSTON. Elements of the Theory and Practice of Cookery. A text-book of household science for use in schools. Many plates. New York, 1908. 347p.

2631 CURTIS, ISABEL GORDON. Mrs. Curtis's Cook Book. A Manual of Instruction for Everyday Cookery. New York: The Success Co., 1909. 280p. illus.

2632 CUTTER, MRS. B. B. (Sophia Genevieve Robinson). PRACTICAL RECIPES. For the whole family. Duffield: New York, 1909. 177p.

2633 DE LOUP, MAXIMILIAN. The American Salad Book. 4th ed. rev. with additional recipes. New York: Doubleday, Page & Company, 1909. 171p.

2634 FARMER, FANNIE MERRITT. CRESCA DAINTIES. A collection of practical recipes. Wraps. Reiss & Brady: New York, 1909. 32p.

2635 GANCEL'S READY REFERENCE OF MENU TERMS. A complete and concise Glossary of over 5,000 names. Small book, hard cover. John L. Schoenfeld Co., Inc.; New York (1909). 191p.

2636 JOHNSON, FLORENCE KENDRICK. Large Meals for Little Money. New York: The People's University Extension Society, 1909. 36p. Wraps.

2637 MITCHELL, MARGARET J. The Fireless Cook Book. About the construction and use of appliances for cooking by retained heat. 250 recipes. New York: Doubleday, Page & Co., 1909. 315p.

2638 MORSE, SIDNEY. Household Discoveries. An Encyclopaedia of

Practical Recipes and Processes including Mrs. Curtis's Cook Book. Success Company, New York (1909). 1024p.

2639 My Favorite Receipt. New York: Royal Baking Powder Co., 1909. 9th ed. (See No. 2456).

2640 Read, C. Stanford. Fads and Feeding. New York: E. P. Dutton and Co., 1909. 163p.

2641 Swain, Rachel. Cooking for Health. Plain Cookery with Health Hints. Health Culture Co., New York (1909). 203p.

2642 Williams, Jennie B. Us Two Cook Book. Recipes for Two Persons. A complete cook book for the young housewife. Illustrations. Barse & Hopkins: New York, 1909. 319p.

2643 Buttner, J. L. A Fleshless Diet. Vegetarianism as a Rational Dietary. New York: Frederick Stokes Co., 1910. 287p. illus.

2644 Child's Book of Recipes for Managers. New York: Child's Co. (c. 1910). 69p. Wraps.

2645 Christian, Eugene and Griswold, Mollie. 250 Meatless Menus and Recipes. To meet the requirements of people according to age, climate and work. New York: private printing, 1910. 181p.

2646 Fletcher, Horace. Menticulture, or The A-B-C- of True Living. Rev. ed. New York: 1910. 280p. (see No. 740).

2647 Foster, Olive Hyde. Cookery for Little Girls. Frontis. Partly reprints from various periodicals. New York: Duffield & Co., 1910. 157p. illus.

2648 Hiller, Elizabeth. The Practical Cookbook. To boost cooking by gas range. Pict. cover. Doherty Operating Co., New York, 1910. 153p.

2649 Kephart, Horace. Camp Cookery. By a specialist on camping. Illus. with pen drawings. Outing Publishing Co., New York. 1910. 154p. and ads.

2650 Marvin, Mrs. A. I. Mrs. Marvin's Cook Book . . New York: Cochrane Publishing Co., 1910. 80p. Wraps.

2651 Mitchell, S. Weir. A Madeira Party. Tiny book. Illus. New York, 1910. 165p.

2652 More Light. New York: Shredded Wheat Co. (c. 1910). 16p. advertising booklet, with col. pict. cover and col. pl.

2653 The Butterick Cook Book. With special chapters about Casserole and Fireless Cooking. Edited by Helena Judson. Illus. Butterick Publishing Co., New York, 1911. 359p. & vi Index.

2654 Clarke, Helen Carroll and Rulon, Phoebe Deyo. The Cook Book of Left-Overs. A handy book for the housekeeper. Harper & Brothers, New York (1911). 254p.

2655 Green, Olive. Everyday Dinners. An attractive little book of menus & recipes. G. P. Putnam's Sons, New York, 1911. 1st ed. 410p. and ads.

2656 Green, Olive. One Thousand Salads. The kinds you know about plus rabbit salad & goose salad. Wish to know what auditorium cheese is? New York: G. P. Putnam's Sons, 1911. 415p. Book ads.

2657 Hackwood, F. W. Good Cheer, The Romance of Food and Feasting. 'The Election Entertainment' by Hogarth very interesting. Black & white illus. New York: Sturgis & Walton, 1911. 416p.

2658 Harper's Camping & Scouting. Illus. New York, 1911. 398p.

2659 Helps for the Young Housekeeper. 100 tried recipes for economic catering, by an experienced housewife. New York: G. T. Long, 1911. 58p.

2660 Hexamer, F. M. Asparagus. Its Culture for Home Use & for market. Cutting, canning etc. New York, Orange Judd, 1911. 168p. Illus.

2661 Hutchison, Robert, MD. Edin., F.R.C.P. Food and the Principles of Dietetics. A textbook for medical students. With plates and diagrams. William Wood and Co., New York, 1911. 615p.

2662 Lemcke, Gesine. European and American Cuisine. New York: D. Appleton and Co., 1911. 614p. Frontis. portrait.

2663 Murray, J. Alan. The Ecoomy of Food. A popular treatise on nutrition, food, and diet. New York: D. Appleton & Co., 1911. 253p. illus.

2664 Royal ..Baker and Pastry Cook. Receipts for Home Baking and Cooking. Wraps. Royal Baking Powder Co., New York (1911). 46p.

2665 Royal Baker and Pastry Cook. Wraps. Royal Baking Powder Co., New York, 1911. 64p.

2666 Ward, Artemas (Compiled by) The Grocer's Encyclopedia. Useful information concerning foods of all kinds. Illustrations, handsome color plates. Stationers' Hall, New York, 1911. 748p.

2667 Wood, Katharine B. Quotations for Occasions. A most valuable reference for out-of-the-way quotes on horseradish, marchpane, frogs legs, whitebait, etc. New York, 1911. 200p.

2668 Cobb, Irvin S. Cobb's Bill of Fare. Illus. New York, 1912. 1st ed. 148p.

2669 Falconer, William. Mushrooms: How to Grow Them. Recipes for cooking mushrooms. Illus. New York, 1912. 169p.

2670 Gibbs, Winifred S. Economical Cooking. Planned for two or more persons. Compiled from many sources. Illustrated. New York Book Co.; New York, 1912. 157p.

2671 Hall, Mary Elizabeth. Candy-making Revolutionized. Confectionery from Vegetables. Illus. Color frontispiece. New York: Sturgis & Walton Co., 1912. 154p.

2672 Harland, Marion & Herrick, Christine Terhune: The Help-

ING HAND COOKBOOK. New York: Moffatt, Yard and Company, 1912. 340p.

2673 ISOLA, ANTONIA (Mabel Earl McGinnis). Simple Italian Cookery (See Foreign sec.)

2674 JAMES, ALICE. The Chafing Dish & Sandwiches. G. P. Putnam's Sons: New York, 1912. 1st ed. 271p.

2675 LEWIS, H. EDWIN. Diet for the Sick. From leading authorities, assisted by staff of American Medicine. New York: American Medical Publishing Co. (1912). 155p.

2676 MAUR, KATE V. SAINT. A Self-Supporting Home. Farm produce-planning. Many illus. from photographs. Macmillan, New York, 1912. 344p. and ads.

2677 POPE, AMY ELIZABETH AND CARPENTER, MARY L. ESSENTIALS OF DIETETICS IN HEALTH & DISEASE. A textbook for nurses and a guide for the household. G. P. Putnam's Sons, New York, 1912. 255p.

2678 SNOWDRIFT SECRETS. SOME CHOICE RECIPES FOR THE USE OF SNOWDRIFT. Wraps. The Southern Cotton Oil Co., New York, 1912. 48p.

2679 TELFORD, EMMA PADDOCK. Standard Paper-Bag Cookery. The author, household editor of The Delineator. New York: Cupples and Leon Co., 1912. 156p. and ads.

2680 WALLACE, LILY HAXWORTH. (Revised & edited by) THE MODERN COOK BOOK AND HOUSEHOLD RECIPES. Compiled by many of the Famous Chefs and Cooking Experts of the United States. Illustrated. Warner Library Company, New York (1912). 1127p.

2681 ALLGEMEINES REZEPT-BUCH FUER BACKER UND CONDITOREN. (See Foreign sec.)

2682 BARROLL, MARY LOUISE. AROUND THE WORLD COOK BOOK. The Culinary Gleanings of a Naval Officer's Wife. The Century Co., New York, 1913. 360p.

2683 BOOK OF VALUABLE RECIPES. For use of Arm & Hammer Soda. New York City: Church & Dwight Co., 1913. 61st ed. 34p. advertising booklet.

2684 BRYAN, GEORGE S. THE CAMPER'S OWN BOOK. For Devotees of Tent and Trail. Illus. New York, 1913. 191p.

2685 CONGREVE, A. E. The One Maid Book of Cookery. New York: E. P. Dutton & Co., 1913. 217p.

2686 FILIPPINI, ALEXANDER. THE INTERNATIONAL COOK BOOK. Over 3300 Recipes gathered from all over the World; many never published in English. Doubleday, Page & Co., New York, 1913. 1059p.

2687 FINCK, HENRY T. Food and Flavor. A gastronomic guide to Health and Good Living. Illus. by Charles S. Chapman. The Century Co., New York, 1913. 594p.

2688 HARPER'S HOUSEHOLD HANDBOOK. A Guide to Easy Ways of

Doing Woman's Work. New York, 1913. 205p.

2689 Keoleian, Ardashes H. The Oriental Cook Book. (See Foreign sec.)

2690 Lemcke, Gesine. Preserving & Pickling. A notable book by a famous food writer. New York: D. Appleton & Co., 1913. 115p.

2691 Rorer, Sarah Tyson. Recipes. Showing some uses of Wesson Oil in salads. Pamphlet, illus. New York, 1913. 48p.

2692 Williams, Mary E. and Fisher, Katharine Rolston. Elements of the Theory and Practice of Cookery. A text book of household science for schools. Illus. Macmillan Co., New York, 1913. 347p.

2693 Yates, Lucy H. The Gardener and the Cook. Choice vegetables and how to prepare them. Decorations. McBride, Nast and Co., New York, 1913. 260p.

2694 Bennett. The Vegetable Garden. With recipes. Many plates. New York, 1914. 260p.

2695 Condit, Elizabeth and Long, Jessie A. How to Cook and Why. The authors, teachers at Pratt Institute. New York: Harper & Brothers, 1914. 249p. illus.

2696 Conley, Emma. Principles of Cooking. A textbook in domestic science. Illustrated. American Book Co.: New York, 1914. 206p.

2697 Farmer, Fannie Merritt. A Book of Good Dinners. For My Friend or, What to Have for Dinner. Decorative paper. Wraps. Dodge: New York, 1914. 270p.

2698 Gillmore, Maria McIlvaine. Meatless Cookery. With special diets for heart disease, blood pressure and autointoxication. Intro. by Dr. Louis Faugeres Bishop . . . New York: E. P. Dutton & Co. (1914). 352p. and 11 not num.

2699 Goessling, Adeline O. Making the Farm Kitchen Pay. Illus. wraps. New York, 1914. 91p.

2700 Lancaster, Maud. Electric Cooking, Heating and Cleaning. Edited by E. W. Lancaster, American ed. revised by Stephen L. Coles. New York: D. Van Nostrand Co. of Brooklyn, 1914. 305p. illustrated.

2701 Larned, Linda Hull. The New Hostess of To-Day. Illus by Mary Cowles Clark. Charles Scribner's Sons, New York, 1914. 428p.

2702 Maddocks, Mildred. The Pure Food Cook Book. The Good Housekeeping recipes—how to buy—and how to cook. With intro. by Dr. Harvey W. Wiley. Over 70 illus. New York: Hearst's International Library Co., 1914. 417p. frontis. pl.

2703 Mahdah. Eat and Grow Thin. A collection of hitherto unpublished Mahdah Menus and recipes. A list of "forbidden" foods. Foreword by Vance Thompson. E. P. Dutton: New York (1914). 97p.

Col. Dinner & Diners. Where &

2704 Newnham-Davis, Lieut.-

How to Dine in London. Invaluable gastronomic material, anecdotes and all. New York, Brentano's, 1914. 376p.

2705 PEARSE, CECELIA MARIA. The Kitchen Garden and the Cook. An Alphabetical Guide to the Cultivation of Vegetables with Recipes for Cooking Them. New York: E. P. Dutton and Co., 1914. 284p.

2706 PRESCOTT, ALLEN. Wifesaver's Candy Recipes. New York (1914). 60p.

2707 ROSE, MARY SWARTZ. A LABORATORY HANDBOOK FOR DIETETICS. Text-book and reference by the professor of nutrition, Teachers College. Macmillan: New York, 1914. 127p. and ads.

2708 STORY, JOSEPHINE (Mrs. Emilie Baker Loring). For the Comfort of the Family. A vacation experiment. Illus. from photos posed by the author. New York: George H. Doran Co. (1914). 118p.

2709 WALLI, MINA. Suomalais-Amerikalainen. Keittokirja. (See Foreign sec.)

2710 WILEY, HARVEY. 1001 TESTS of Foods, Beverages and Toilet Accessories, Good and Otherwise. Hearst's International Library Co., New York, 1914. 249p.

2711 WILEY, HARVEY W., MD., MADDOCKS, MILDRED (ed.) The Pure Food Cook Book. New York: Hearst's International Library Co., 1914. 417p. Illus.

2712 WILLIAMS, ANNIE COPELAND. Never Fail Cook Book. Brooklyn: E. H. Avery, 1914. 66p. Wraps.

2713 WINTERBURN, FLORENCE HULL Novel Ways of Entertaining. Harper & Bros.: New York, 1914. 211p.

2714 BENTON, CAROLINE FRENCH. The Fun of Cooking. Illus. by Sarah K. Smith. New York: (The Century Co.), 1915. 254p.

2715 DAY, LILLIAN PASCAL. Social Entertainments. Illus. with photos. New York, 1915. 138p.

2716 GOY, SYLVAINE CLAUDIUS. LA CUISINE ANGLO-AMERICAINE, LA CUISINE DE L'AMERIQUE CENTRALE. (See Foreign sec.)

2717 LARNED, LINDA HULL. 100 Picnic Suggestions. New York: Charles Scribner's Sons, 1915. 123p.

2718 LUCK, MRS. BRIAN: The Belgian Cook-book. (See Foreign sec.)

2719 MILLER, W. H. CAMP CRAFT. Intro. Ernest Thompson Seton. Illus. "The Chef on Trail" with cook-kits and cook-fires. New York, 1915. 283p. 1st ed.

2720 PRETLOW, MARY DENSON. The Small Family Cookbook. Illus. McBride, Nast & Co., New York, 1915. 1st ed. 216p.

2721 THOMPSON, VANCE. Drink and Be Sober. New York: Moffat, Yard and Company, 1915. 213p.

2722 WARD, ARTEMAS. PROSPECTUS FOR THE ENCYCLOPEDIA OF FOODS AND BEVERAGES. The Grocer's Encyclopedia. Sample pages and beautiful plates. Appendix contains dictionary of food terms in 5 languages. Artemas Ward, New York, 1915? 110p.

2723 WERLIN, OTTO. The American Cake Baker. Port Richmond, N.Y.: The Richmond Borough Pub. & Ptg. Co.: (1915). 125p.

2724 WILLIAMS, FLORENCE. Dainties for Home Parties. A cook-book for entertainments. New York: Harper, 1915. 89p.

2725 WILLIAMS, MARY E. AND FISHER, KATHARINE ROLSTON. ELEMENTS OF THE THEORY AND PRACTICE OF COOKERY. A Text-Book of Household Science for Use in Schools. Illustrated. Macmillan: New York, 1915. 347p.

2726 BIRGE, WILLIAM S., MD., TRUE FOOD VALUES AND THEIR LOW COSTS. Sully and Kleinteich, New York, 1916. 218p.

2727 CELEBRATED ACTOR-FOLKS' COOKERIES. A Collection of Favorite Foods of Famous Players. Dedicated to the Red Cross and the Actors' Fund. Pict. cover designed by Albert Dick. Recipes autographed by actors. New York City: Mabel Rowland, Inc., 1916.

2728 CHRISTIAN, EUGENE. LITTLE LESSONS IN SCIENTIFIC EATING. 24 separate booklets, each with a lecture on food and nutrition. Collected into a titled box. Corrective Eating Society: New York, 1916. 8p. each.

2729 COCROFT, SUSANNA. WHAT TO EAT AND WHEN. Diet, infant feeding, recipes for invalids and semi-invalids. Frontispiece photograph. Illus. B. P. Putnam's Sons, New York, 1916. 366p.

2730 DAVIES, SAMUEL E. An English Butler's Canapes, Salads, Sandwiches, Drinks, etc. (See Foreign sec.)

2731 FARMER, LISSIE C. A-B-C of Home Saving. A chapter on keeping food from spoiling. Harper & Brothers, New York (1916). 114p.

2732 FURGERSON, A. N. AND JOHNSON, CONSTANCE. From House to House. A book of odd recipes from many homes. New York: E. P. Dutton & Co., 1916. 291p.

2733 GRISWOLD, FRANK GRAY. The Kittens. 1869-1916. An elite NY Dining Club listing members. Cover with portraits, menus, wine lists and history. Privately printed, Plimpton Press., N.Y., 1916. 25p.

2734 HARRISON, GRACE CLERGUE AND CLERGUE, GERTRUDE. Allied Cookery—British, French, Italian, Belgian, Russian. To aid war sufferers in the devastated areas of France. Intro. by Hon. Raoul Dandurand. Preface by Stephen Leacock and Ella Wheeler Wilcox. New York: G. P. Putnam's Sons, 1916. 108p.

2735 HERRICK, CHRISTINE TERHUNE. A-B-C of Cooking . . . New York: Harper & Brothers (1916). 110p.

2736 NEIL, MARION HARRIS (Compiled & edited by). RYZON BAKING BOOK. A practical manual for the preparation of food requiring baking powder. Illustrated. General Chemcial Company, New York, 1916. 82p.

2737 PIERCE, PAUL. NOVEL SUGGESTIONS FOR SOCIAL OCCASIONS. Party food and decor. Barse & Hopkins, New York (1916). 96p.

2738 PUTNAM, E. PUTNAM'S HOUSEHOLD HANDBOOK. Section on Cooking. New York, Croy, 1916. 327p.

2739 QUARLES. AMERICAN PHEASANT BREEDING & SHOOTING. Includes recipes for cooking. Illus. New York, 1916. 128p.

2740 SUMMERVILLE, AMELIA. Why Be Fat. Rules for weight reduction and the preservation of youth and health. New York: Frederick A. Stokes Company (1916). 89p.

2741 TABLE AND KITCHEN. Practical Cook Book; a compilation of approved cooking recipes. New York: Royal Baking Powder Co., 1916. 60p. adv. booklet.

2742 WILEY, HARVEY W., MD., 1001 Tests of Foods, Beverages and Toilet accessories, good and otherwise. Arranged by Anne Lewis Pierce. Hearst's International Library Co., New York, 1916. 344p.

2743 THE A B C OF COOKING. For men with no experience of cooking on small boats, in camps, on marches. New York: Moffat, Yard, 1917. 40p.

2744 ALSAKER, R. L., MD. How To Live on 3 Meals a Day. New York, 1917. 96p.

2745 BARROWS, ANNA AND BERTHA E. SHAPLEIGH. An Outline of the History of Cookery. Assisted by Anne D. Blitz, Technical Educ. Bulletin, No. 28. New York: Teachers College, 1917. 36p. Wraps.

2746 CHAN, SHIU WONG. The Chinese Cook Book. (See Foreign sec.)

2747 CHRISTIAN, EUGENE. Meatless & Wheatless Menus. New York, 1917. 144p.

2748 EVANS, MARY ELIZABETH. My Candy Secrets. Accurate instructions for the novice. 53 illus. from photographs to show actual processes. New York: Frederick A. Stokes Co. (1917). 146p.

2749 GREEK COOK BOOK. (See Foreign sec.)

2750 GREEN, MARY. Better Meals for Less Money. New York: Henry Holt and Co., 1917. 295p.

2751 HINTS TO HOUSEWIVES. To conserve the food supply. Booklet. Mayor Mitchel's Food Supply Committee, New York City, 1917. 112p.

2752 HOLT, EMILY. The Complete Housekeeper. Illus. New York, 1917. 402p.

2753 KITTREDGE, MABEL HYDE. The Home and Its Management. 300 inexpensive cooking receipts. New York: The Century Co., 1917. 385p. illus.

2754 LEMCKE, GESINE. CHAFING-DISH RECIPES. By the owner of the Brooklyn and New York Cooking

Colleges. D. Appleton and Co., New York, 1917. 84p.

2755 McCANN, ALFRED W. Thirty Cent Bread. How to Escape a Higher Cost of Living. New York: George H. Doran Co. (1917). 83p.

2756 MURPHY, CHARLES J. AMERICAN INDIAN CORN (Maize) A Cheap, Wholesome, and Nutritious Food; 150 Ways to Prepare and Cook It. Foreword by Jeannette Young Norton. G. P. Putnam's Sons: New York, 1917. 128p.

2757 NEIL, MARION HARRIS. Favorite Recipes Cook Book. A complete culinary guide. New York: F. M. Lupton, 1917. 504p. Wraps.

2758 NORTON, JEANNETTE YOUNG. Mrs. Norton's Cook-Book. Selecting, Cooking, and Serving for the Home Table. New York: G. P. Putnam's Sons, 1917. 634p.

2759 POPE, AMY ELIZABETH. A Dietary Computer. For Nurses. New York: G. P. Putnam's Sons, 1917. 156p.

2760 RONALD, MARY. THE CENTURY COOK BOOK. Illustrative pages from the book . . The Century Co., New York, 1917.

2761 SABIN, E. L. How Are You Feeling Now? Illus. by Tony Sarg. Pict. bds. New York, 1917. 97p.

2762 SHERMAN, HENRY C., PH.D. Food Products—By professor of Food Chemistry. Columbia University. Macmillan Co.: New York, 1917. 594p.

2763 SNYDER, MRS. SHERWOOD P. A Treatise on Food Conservation and the Art of Canning. Binghamton; Health Publishing Co., 1917. 205p. illus.

2764 WADHAMS, CAROLINE REED. Simple Directions for the Cook. Intro. by Maurice A. Bigelow, Ph. D. Dir. of the School of Practical Arts, Teachers College, Columbia Univ. New York: Longmans, Green & Co., 1917. 84p.

2765 WEAVER, LOUISE BENNETT AND LECRON, HELEN COWLES. A THOUSAND WAYS TO PLEASE A HUSBAND with Bettina's Best Recipes—the Romance of Cookery. Decorations by Elizabeth Colbourne. Burt: New York, 1917. 479p.

2766 WHAT TO EAT. How to use the science of modern dietetics for more efficient living. Illus. Auspices of the Life Extension Institute. Review of Reviews Co., New York, 1917. 48p.

2767 ANDREA, A. LOUISE. HOME CANNING, DRYING AND PRESERVING. Illus. Doubleday, Page & Co., New York, 1918. 150p.

2768 BECKWITH, MARGARET. The Family Cook Book. For Home Cooking and the Simple Life. Knickerbocker, New York, 1918. 125p.

2769 BREAZEALE, J. F. Economy in the Kitchen. New York: Frye Pub. Co., 1918. 114p. illus.

2770 CORN PRODUCTS RECIPES. Endorsed by Oscar of the Waldorf-

Astoria. Wraps. Corn Products Refining Co., New York, 1918. 64p.

2771 FOOD SAVING AND SHARING. Telling How the Older Children of America May Help Save from Famine Their Comrades Across the Sea. Illus. Prepared by The United States Food Administration. Doubleday, Page & Co., New York, 1918. 102p.

2772 FRANKS, THETTA QUAY. Daily Menus for War Service. Menus, giving calories, food substitutes. Doubleday & Co., New York, 1918. 730p. & 51p. Appendix.

2773 GILLMORE, MARIA MCILVAINE. Economy Cook Book. New York: E. P. Dutton & Co. (1918). 215p.

2774 GOUDISS, C. HOUSTON & ALBERTA M. FOODS THAT WILL WIN THE WAR AND HOW TO COOK THEM. Save wheat, meat, sugar, fat, and food. World: New York, 1918. 118p.

2775 GREENBAUM, FLORENCE KREISLER. The International Jewish Cook Book. (See Foreign Sec.)

2776 HALL, MARY ELIZABETH. War Time Recipes. Wheatless cakes, 7 meatless dishes, sugarless candies. Illus. New York, 1918. 1st ed. 163p.

2777 HAMMOND, MRS. ERICSSON. THE SWEDISH, FRENCH, AMERICAN COOKBOOK. (See Foreign sec.)

2778 HOW TO USE CORN MEAL, OAT MEAL, BARLEY, BUCKWHEAT, POTATOES, RICE, ETC. AND SAVE WHEAT FLOUR. BEST WAR TIME RECIPES. Wraps. Royal Baking Powder Co., New York, 1918. 14p.

2779 LEMCKE, GESINE. DESSERTS AND SALADS. By the owner of the Brooklyn and New York cooking colleges. D. Appleton and Co., New York, 1918. 318p.

2780 METROPOLITAN LIFE COOK BOOK. For the use of its Industrial Policy-holders. Wraps. Metropolitan Life Ins. Co. New York, 1918. 64p.

2781 MILLER, EDITH STARR. Common Sense in the Kitchen. Normal rations in normal times. New York: Brentano's, 1918. 55p.

2782 MOORE, HELEN WATKEYS. CAMOUFLAGE COOKERY. A book of Mock Dishes. Duffield & Co., New York, 1918. 106p.

2783 ORMOND, CHARLOTTE HEPBURN. The Abingdon War-Food Book. Foreword by Herbert Hoover. Recipes and menus. New York: The Abingdon Press, 1918. 58p.

2784 PARTRIDGE, PAULINE DUNWELL AND CONKLIN, HESTER MARTHA. WHEATLESS AND MEATLESS DAYS. D. Appleton and Co., New York, 1918. 225p.

2785 PURDY, MABEL DULON. Food and Freedom. A Household Book. Endorsed by the U.S. Food Administration. New York: Harper & Brothers (1918). 252p. illus.

2786 ROCKWELL, FREDERICK FRYE. SAVE IT FOR WINTER. Modern methods canning, dehydrating, preserving. Illus. Frederick A. Stokes, New York (1918). 1st ed. 206p.

2787 SHERMAN, HENRY C. PH.D. FOOD PRODUCTS. Illustrations & charts. Macmillan, New York, 1918. 594p.

2788 STOCKBRIDGE, BERTHA E. L. The Liberty Cook Book. A guide to good living combined with economy. Up to date canning and preserving. Based on U. S. Dept. of Agriculture's research. New York: D. Appleton and Company, 1918. 493p.

2789 THE TAPLEX BOOK FOR RECIPES. A receptacle for saving recipes—contains a few handwritten recipes. Designed by Lillian Alice Palmer. Taplex Corporation, New York (1918). 157p. and ads.

2790 ALSAKAR, R. L. (RASMUS LARSEN). Eating for Health and Efficiency. New York: Frank E. Morrison, 1919. 5 vols. bound in one, 498p.

2791 CARRELL, THEODORA M. A Manual of Canning and Preserving. New York: E. P. Dutton & Co., 1919. 101p.

2792 COBB, IRVIN S. Eating in Two or Three Languages. New York, 1919. 1st ed. 64p.

2793 FREDERIKSEN, JOHAN D. THE STORY OF MILK. By a graduate of the Royal Danish Agric. College. Includes some milk cookery. Illus. Macmillan: New York, 1919. 188p. and ads.

2794 HILL, JANET MCKENZIE AND ADAMS, MARGARET. CAKE AND BREAD MAGIC. Booklet, wraps. Ward Baking Co.: New York, 1919. 36p.

2795 HOPKINS, ALBERT A. HOME MADE BEVERAGES. Making alcoholic and non-alcoholic drinks in the household. Scientific American, New York, 1919. Frontis. & illus. 233p.

2796 LEMCKE, GESTINE. EUROPEAN AND AMERICAN CUISINE. By the owner of the New York Cooking School. Photograph of the author. D. Appleton & Co., New York, 1919. 618p.

2797 MOORE, CORA: 24 Little French Dinners. (See Foreign sec.)

2798 OPPENHEIMER, REBECCA W. DIABETIC COOKERY. Recipes and Menus. Introduction by Dr. A. I. Ringer. E. P. Dutton: New York (1919). 159p.

2799 PANCHARD, M. EDOUARD. Meats, Poultry and Game. How to Buy, Cook, and Carve with a Potpourri of Recipes. Preface by A. Louise Andrea. Illus. E. P. Dutton: New York (1919). 1st ed. 134p.

2800 65 DELICIOUS DISHES MADE WITH BREAD. New York: The Fleischmann Co., 1919. 32p. advertising booklet. Col. pict. cover.

2801 BAKING RAISED BREADS. Excellent recipes. Booklet; wraps. Fleischmann Co.: New York, 1920. 48p.

2803 CHRISTIAN, EUGENE AND MOLLIE GRISWOLD. ENCYCLOPEDIA OF COOKERY. 1001 Recipes and Menus,

& Rules for Cookery. Illustrations. The Corrective Eating Society, New York, 1920. 248p.

2804 DUGGAR, B. M. MUSHROOM GROWING. With Mushrooms for the Table and Recipes. Illus. New York, Orange Judd, 1920. 250p.

2805 FLEISHMANN'S RECIPES. Excellent recipes for baking raised breads. New York: Fleishmann Co., 1920. 48p. advertising booklet.

2806 HAMMOND, MRS. ERICSSON: SALAD APPETIZER COOKBOOK (See Foreign sec.)

2807 JUDSON, CLARA INGRAM. The Junior Cook Book by author of Mary Jane Series. New York: Barse & Hopkins (1920). 253p.

2808 JUDSON, CLARA INGRAM. Cooking Without Mother's Help. A story cook book for beginners . . . New York: The Nourse Co. (1920). 94p. illus. Frontis.

2809 NEW ROYAL COOK BOOK. New York: Royal Baking Powder Co., 1920. 50p. adv. booklet. Col. pict. cover.

2810 STOCKBRIDGE, BERTHA E. L. WHAT TO DRINK (THE BLUE BOOK OF BEVERAGES). Appleton, New York, 1920.

2811 VILMORIN, ANDRIEUX. The Vegetable Garden. Illus. Many cooking suggestions. English edition. New York, 1920. 803p.

2812 DONNELLY, ANTOINNETTE. How TO REDUCE. New Waistlines for Old. Diet and exercise; some recipes. Illus. D. Appleton: New York, 1921. 96p.

2813 THE EVERYDAY CAKE BOOK. A recipe for every day in the year including Feb. 29th. By G. P. New York: Moffat Yard, 1921. 98p.

2814 GOUDISS, C. HOUSTON. Give the Grape its Rightful Food Place. Wraps. Privately printed by the People's Home Journal, New York, 1921. 17p.

2815 GOUDISS, C. HOUSTON. Vegetables and Vitamines, Vol. I. A study with illustrative recipes. Privately printed by The People's Home Journal, New York (1921). 1st ed. 20p.

2816 GOUDISS, C. HOUSTON. Vegetables and Vitamines, Vol. II. Essay with illustrative recipes. Privately printed by The People's Home Journal, New York (1921). 1st ed. 23p.

2817 HAMILTON, DOROTHY M. A Primer of Cooking. New York: The Century Co., 1921. 177p.

2818 JESSUP, ELON. The Motor Camping Book. Chapters on making fires, cooking equipment & supplies, out of doors cookery. 100 illustrations; some of old cars and camp sites. G. P. Putnam's Sons: New York, 1921. 219p.

2819 ROSE, MARY SWARTZ. FEEDING THE FAMILY. Macmillan Company, New York, 1921. 449p.

2819a SALADS. Durkee, 1921. (See No. 2556).

2819b ADDAMS, JANE. Peace and Bread. New York, 1922. 1st ed. 257p.

2819c ALSAKER, R. L., MD. MAINTAINING HEALTH. A treatise about all kinds of foods; some ideas on their preparation. Success Magazine Corp., New York, 1922. 411p.

2819d BURDICK, JENNIE ELLIS. WHAT SHALL WE HAVE TO EAT? A Practical Plan for Choosing the Right Foods for Every Occasion. Wraps. The University Society: New York, 1922. 128p.

2819e GOOD HOUSEKEEPING'S BOOK OF MENUS, RECIPES AND HOUSEHOLD DISCOVERIES. Illus. Good Housekeeping, New York (1922). 253p.

2819f LANE, DOROTHY E. Nutrition and Specific Therapy. New York: The Macmillan Co., 1922. 185p. A plea for vegetarian diet.

2819g METROPOLITAN COOK BOOK. Wraps. Metropolitan Life Insurance Co., New York, 1922. 64p.

2819h MONAGHAN, ELIZABETH A. What to Eat & How to Prepare It. Preface by Sarah Gertrude Banks, M.D. George H. Doran Co., New York (1922). 185p.

2819i NEW ROYAL COOK BOOK. Wraps. Royal Baking Powder Co., New York, 1922. 50p.

2819j PUTNAM, NINA WILCOX. Tomorrow We Diet. New York: George H. Doran Co. (1922). 90p.

2820 SHERIDAN, C. MAC. The Stag Cook Book. Written for men by men. Intro. by Robert H. Davis. New York: George H. Doran Co., 1922. 197p.

2821 STOCKBRIDGE, BERTHA E. L. The Practical Cook Book . . (same as No. 2788). New York, 1922.

2822 WEAVER, LOUISE BENNETT AND LE CRON, HELEN COWLES. A Thousand Ways to Please a Family with Bettina's Best Recipes. For a family of four or more. Decorations by Elizabeth Colborne. New York: A. L. Burt Company (1922). 397p. illus.

2823 WHAT SHALL WE HAVE TO EAT? A Practical Plan for Choosing the Right Food for Every Occasion. Illus. Wraps. New York, 1922. 128p.

2824 CONRAD, JESSIE. A HANDBOOK OF COOKERY FOR A SMALL HOUSE. Preface by Joseph Conrad, the author's husband. Doubleday, Page & Co., Garden City, N.Y., 1923. 1st ed. 142p.

2825 FINCK, HENRY T.: Girth Control. A book on diet to reduce. With menus. Harper & Brothers, New York, 1923. 342p.

2826 GAGARINE, PRINCESS ALEXANDRE. (compiler and translator). The Borzoi Cook Book. (See Foreign sec.)

2827 GURNEY, LYDIA MARIA. Title: THINGS MOTHER USED TO MAKE. Published by The Macmillan Company, New York, 1923. 110p.

2828 HOUSEHOLD HELPS and GUIDE to Household Economy. Wraps. Household Publishing: New York, 1923. 70p.

2829 KEGLER, HENRI (autographed) Fancy Salads of the Big

Hotels. Including Hors d'oeuvres and cocktails (shellfish). Illus. Hotel Industry, New York, 1923. 78p.

2830 Locke, Edwin A. A.M., M.D. Food Values. Practical Tables for use in Private Practice and Public Institutions. D. Appleton & Co.: New York, 1923. 110p.

2831 Murphy, Claudia Quigley. A Collation of Cakes Yesterday and Today. History of cake making with recipes—prepared for use in teaching Culinary Arts. Printed for Claudia Quigley Murphy, New York City, 1923. 31p.

2832 Nichols, Nell B. The Farm Cook and Rule Book. Prepared especially for rural homemakers. Macmillan Co., New York, 1923. 1st ed. 295p.

2833 Rare Recipes Old and New. Contributed by relatives and friends. Compiled and edited by The Veltin School Cook Book Comm. New York City. John C. Winston Co., Philadelphia, Pa., 1923. Limited edition 911. 268p.

2834 Scotson-Clark, G. F. Eating Without Fears. A literary delight. Nicholas L. Brown, New York, 1923. 1st ed. 145p.

2835 Southworth, May E., Motorist's Luncheon Book. New York, Harper & Brothers (1923). 146p. 1st ed.

2836 Weaver, Louise Bennett and Le Cron, Helen Cowles. Bettina's Best Desserts. Illustrated by Elizabeth Colborne. A. L. Burt Co., New York (1923). 1st ed. 194p.

2837 Allen, Ida C. Bailey. Mrs. Allen on Cooking, Menus, Service. 2500 recipes. Illus. by Jack Wilbur. Garden City, N.Y.: Doubleday, Page & Co., 1924. 1001p. Ads.

2838 Allen, Ida Bailey. Home Partners; or Seeing the family through. Illus. by Jack Wilbur. New York: Priv. Print., 1924. 88p. illus.

2839 Good Housekeeping's Book of Menus, Recipes, and Household Discoveries. Illustrated. Good Housekeeping, New York, 1924. 253p.

2840 Hammond, Mrs. Ericsson. Mrs. Hammond's Salad, Appetizer Cook Book. Illus. The author: New York, 1924. 196p.

2841 Hastings, Milo. Physical Culture Food Directory. Rating of foods. MacFadden Publications, New York, 1924. Wraps. 151p.

2842 Huddleson, Mary Pascoe. Food for the Diabetic. What to eat and how to calculate it with common household measures. Introduction by Dr. Nellis Barnes Foster. Macmillan Co., New York, 1924. 75p.

2843 Jessup, Elon. Camp Grub. An out of doors cooking manual. Illustrated. Dutton: New York, 1924. 274p.

2844 Lord, Isabel Ely. Everybody's Cook Book. A Comprehensive Manual of Home Cookery. Compiled by the School of Household Science & Arts of Pratt Institute. Illustrated. End papers on 'Proportions,' Equivalents, Substitutions. Holt, New York, 1924. 1st ed. 916p.

2845 MacFadden, Bernarr. Physical Cook Book. Photograph of the author. MacFadden, New York, 1924. 1st ed. 372p.

2846 Rose, Robert Hugh. Eat Your Way to Health. A scientific system of weight control. The author, instructor Post Graduate Medical School, N.Y. New York: Funk & Wagnalls Co., 1924. 230p.

2847 Tipton, Edna S. Table Decorations. For all occasions—Illus. from photographs. Frederick A. Stokes Co.: New York, 1924. 1st ed. 128p.

2848 Weaver, Louise Bennett and LeCron, Helen Cowles. Bettina's Cakes and Cookies. Give Your Table the Bettina Touch. Illustrated by Elizabeth Colborne. Burt, New York, 1924. 1st ed. 224p.

2849 Weaver, Louise Bennett and Le Cron, Helen Cowles. When Sue Began To Cook with Bettina's Best Recipes. A beginning cook book for girls from 8 to 15. New York: A. L. Burt Company (1924). 189p. illus.

2850 Adams, Franklin Pierce; Taylor, Deems; Bechdolt, Jack. The Book of Diversion. Chapter on Food, Indoor Cooking and Campfire Cooking. Greenberg Inc., New York, 1925, 1st ed. 282p.

2851 Boulestin, X. Marcel. A Second Helping, or More Dishes for American Homes. Color frontispiece by J. E. Laboureur. F. A. Stokes Co., New York, 1925. 156p.

2852 Mrs. Caldwell's Cook Book. 500 Economical Receipts with complete Index. J. H. Sears & Co., New York (1925). 118p.

2853 Chappell, George S. The Restaurants of New York. Restaurants uptown and downtown, and around the corner, including "foreign feeding grounds." Greenberg; New York, 1925. 169p.

2854 Child, Georgie Boynton. The Efficient Kitchen. Plan, arrange, and equip a modern labor-saving kitchen. The author formerly of the Housekeeping Experiment Sta., Darien. New York: Robert M. McBride & Co., 1925. 259p.

2855 Finkel, Harry. Diet and Cook Book. For the doctor, nurse, dietitian, layman. A vegetarian cook book, including recipes and menus. Society for Public Health Education: New York (1925). 285p. and ads.

2856 Fisk, Eugene Lyman, MD. Food—Fuel for the Human Engine. What to Buy, How to Cook It, How to Eat It. The simple story of feeding the family, based on the Diet Squad Experiment in cooperation with the NYC Police Dept. and the Dept. of Nutrition, Teachers College, Columbia University. Copyright 1917 by Life Extension Institute, Inc., Copyright 1917 and 1925 by Funk &

Wagnalls Co., New York City. 68p. includes a brief bibliography of books on diet.

2857 FOODS FROM SUNNY LANDS. New York, 1925. 24p. advertising booklet. Illus. Col. plates and pict. cover.

2858 GERARD, LILLIAN WHITE. ECONOMY COOKING. How to prepare tasty dishes. Wraps. Pocket Copyright, New York, 1925. 115p.

2859 JOHNSON, CONSTANCE FULLER. When Mother Lets Us Cook. Receipts for little folk with cooking rules in rhyme. Illustrated in color. New York: Dodd, Mead and Co., 1925. 95p.

2860 LAWTON, MARY. The Queen of Cooks—and Some Kings. (The Story of Rosa Lewis, Cook to Edward VII). Many photos of prominent people. New York, 1925. 1st ed. 208p.

2861 LOCKHART, M. STANDARD COOK BOOK, for All Occasions. What to Cook, and How. New York, J. H. Sears & Co., Inc. (c. 1925). 115p.

2862 MACMILLAN, GEORGETTE. The Marvel Cook Book. New York: Street and Smith Corp. (1925). 244p.

2863 MCFEE, INEZ NELLIE. Young People's Cook Book, or How the Daytons Cook at Home and in Camp. New York: Thomas Y. Crowell Co. (c. 1925). 290p.

2864 THE METROPOLITAN COOK BOOK. Wraps. Metropolitan Life Ins. Co.: 1925, New York. 64p.

2865 RECTOR, THOMAS M. SCIENTIFIC PRESERVATION OF FOOD. Thorough study of methods of preserving foods. John Wiley & Sons, Inc., New York, 1925. 213p.

2866 SALAD DRESSINGS. New York: The Wesson Oil Snowdrift People, 1925. 27p. advertising booklet. Col. Pict. cover.

2867 SCOTSON-CLARK, G. F. HALF HOURS IN THE KITCHENETTE. A Self-Help for Small Families. D. Appleton; New York, 1925. 1st ed. 145p.

2868 SOMERS, ETHEL M. (prepared by) 100 STANDARD RECIPES. Each one tested. Wraps. Liberty, New York (1925). 64p.

2869 THE STORY OF A PANTRY SHELF. An Outline History of Grocery Specialties. Illus. with photographs of the founders of food industries. Butterick; New York (1925). 1st ed. 224p.

2870 STRATTON, FLORENCE. Favorite Recipes of Famous Women. Foreword by Florence Stratton. New York: Harper & Brothers, 1925. 99p. 1st ed.

2871 THE SUGAR PLUM. Compiled by Jeanette C. Heminway. New York: The Heminway Press, 1925. 3rd ed. rev. and enlarged. 128p.

2872 TIPTON, EDNA SIBLEY. Reducing Menus for the Hostess of Today. Jack Sprat Spreads. D. Appleton and Co.; New York, 1925. 69p.

2873 WALLACE, LILY HAXWORTH. FOODS FROM SUNNY LANDS. The

date in all its glory: figs, cocoanut. Wraps: illustrations. Dromedary Golden Dates, U.S.A. 1925. 21p.

2874 ALEXANDER, HELEN. The Helen-Alexander Cook Book. New York: Maddox & Gray, 1926. 216p.

2875 ALLEN, IDA BAILEY. THE MODERN METHOD OF PREPARING DELIGHTFUL FOODS. A little book of recipes, and anecdotes from the history of cooking. Illustrated. Corn Products Refining Co.: New York, 1926. 109p. 3p. Index.

2876 ALLEN, IDA BAILEY. 104 Prize Radio Recipes, with 24 radio homemaker's talks. Decorations by E. M. Stevenson. New York: J. H. Sears & Co., Inc., 1926. 125p. illus.

2877 BOURJAILY, BARBARA WEBB AND GORMAN, DOROTHY MAY. The Mother's Cook Book. How to prepare food for children. Intro. by Dr. Justin Garvin. New York: D. Appleton & Co., 1926. 164p.

2878 BOWLES, ELLA SHANNON. PRACTICAL PARTIES. Description and Suggestions. The Womans' Press: New York (1926). 88p.

2879 BRILLAT-SAVARIN, JEAN ANTHELME. THE PHYSIOLOGY OF TASTE. (See Foreign sec.)

2880 CHRISTIAN, EUGENE, F.S.D. EAT AND BE WELL. Eat and Get Well—menus. Alfred A. Knopf, New York, 1926. 1st ed. 133p.

2881 CRIPPEN, ALICE HOTCHKISS. FRENCH PASTRY BOOK. (See Foreign sec.)

2882 FISHER, IRVING AND FISK, EUGENE LYMAN, MD. How To Live. Rules for Healthful Living including chapter on quantity of food. Funk & Wagnalls, New York, 1926. 513p.

2883 GRACE INSTITUTE COOK BOOK. Revised. William J. Hirten Co., Inc., New York, 1926. 194p.

2884 HAMMOND, MRS. ERICSSON. Svensk-Amerikanska Kokbok. (See Foreign sec.)

2885 HARLAND, MARION. THE NEW COMMON SENSE IN THE HOUSEHOLD. Rev. by Christine Herrick—for gas and electricity. Frederick A. Stokes, New York, 1926. 499p.

2886 HEIDE, HENRY. Fancy Cake Baking. Dedicated to the Baking Industry of the U. S. Use of the products of Henry Heide. Illus. in color. Private printing, New York, 1926. 135p.

2887 LEE, JENNETTE. If You Must Ask. New York: Dodd, Mead and Company, 1926. 174p.

2888 LEONARD, IRIS F. AND WEIGERT, DORIT K. Professional Candy Making. By recognized candy lecturers, instructors and manufacturers of the incomparable Iridor Candies. New York: The Iridor School (1926). 131p. Frontis., pl.

2889 LONG, JOHN D.; LONG, J. C. Motor Camping. A chapter on Fire and Food for the camper. Illustrations and Diagrams. Dodd, Mead; New York, 1926. 380p.

2890 MACDOUGALL, ALICE FOOTE. COFFEE AND WAFFLES and teas,

sandwiches, cakes and other things. Decorative cover. Foreword by Charles Hanson Towne. Doubleday, Page: New York, 1926. 1st ed. 115p.

2891 MacFadden, Bernarr. The Miracle of Milk. How to Use the Milk Diet Scientifically at Home. Portrait of the author. Macfadden Publications, Inc., New York City, 1926. 1st ed. 204p.

2892 Macfadden, Bernarr with Milo Hastings. Physical Culture Cook Book. Macfadden Publications, New York, 1926. 372p.

2893 Moritz, Mrs. C. F. Every Woman's Cook Book. Cupples & Leon Co.; New York, 1926. 714p.

2894 Original Diets—classified and calculated, with particular reference to diets for the nephritic, the tuberculous and for children. New York: Dry Milk Co. (c. 1926). 72p. Wraps.

2895 Ramus, Carl. Outwitting Middle Age. Chapter on 'Facts About Foods.' New York, 1926. 269p.

2896 Swift, Marjorie & Herrick, Christine Terhune. Feed the Brute. Pict. cover. New York, Frederick A. Stokes Co., 1926. 174p.

2897 Van Rensselaer, Martha; Rose, Flora; Canon, Helen. A Manual of Home-Making compiled at the Department of Home Economics, New York College of Agriculture at Cornell Univ. New York: Macmillan Company, 1926. 661p. profusely illus.

2898 Wihlfahrt, Julius E. and Brooks, Robert W. A Treatise on Baking. A professional approach to baking. Standard Brands, New York, 1927. 458p.

2899 Wright, Mabel Osgood. My New York. Kitchen Days in the Sixties, Jefferson Market, Street Cries, Wedding Cake, etc. New York, 1926. 276p.

2900 Allen, Ida Bailey. The Modern Method of Preparing Delightful Foods. A small book of special recipes. Illustrations by Jack Wilbur. Corn Products Refining Co., New York, 1927. 112p.

2901 Allen, Ida Bailey. Vital Vegetables with analyses, menus and recipes. Photographs by Jack Wilbur, drawings by Edward M. Stevenson. Garden City, N.Y.: Doubleday, Page & Co., 1927. 451p.

2902 Alsaker, R. L. (Rasmus Larsen). Adventures in Cooking. New York: Grant Publications, Inc., 1927. 642p.

2903 Any One Can Bake. Compiled by the Educational Department. Illustrated. Royal Baking Powder Co., New York, 1927. 100p.

2904 Barrows, Anna. The Joys of Home Making. Tested Recipes and Hints for the Housewife. New York: Broadcasting Committee of Greater New York Gas Companies, 1927. 64p.

2905 The Butterick Book of Recipes and Household Helps. For appetizing and varied meals. Butterick Publishing Co., New York (1927). 256p.

2906 Caron, Emma C. Favorite Recipes of Famous Chefs. Many with reproduced signatures of the chefs. Robert M. McBride, New York, 1927, 1st ed. 90p.

2907 Claire, Mabel. The Busy Woman's Cook Book or Cooking by the Clock. New York: Greenberg, Publisher: 1927. 88p.

2908 Claire, Mabel. Short Cut Cookery. New York: Greenberg (1927). 120p.

2909 Fish and Sea Food Recipes covering the entire Industry. Cooking Dept. New York: U. S. Fisheries Ass'n., 1927. 97p. 4 full page pl.

2910 Fisk, Walter W. The Book of Ice-Cream Manufacturing procedures. Macmillan Co., New York, 1927. 340p.

2911 Good Housekeeping's Book of Good Meals. How to Prepare and Serve Them. A Guide to Meal Planning, Cooking and Serving. Frontispiece photograph. Good Housekeeping: New York, 1927. 256p.

2912 Hulbert, Mary Allen. Treasures of a Hundred Cooks. A Collection of Distinctive Recipes for Lovers of Good Food. New York: D. Appleton and Co., 1927. 333p.

2913 King, Mrs. John Alexander. The Gracious Art of Dining. The author, of Delineator Magazine. New York: Black Knight, 1927. 63p. Wraps.

2914 Lansdown, Lillian B. How To Prepare and Serve a Meal. New York: Social Culture Publications (1927). 62p. Wraps.

2915 McFall, Robert James. The World's Meat Production and Distribution. Charts. D. Appleton & Co., New York, 1927. 1st ed. 624p.

2916 Metropolitan Cook Book. New York: Metropolitan Life Ins. Co., New York, 1927. (See No. 2816).

2917 Rector, George. The Girl from Rector's. About the famous restaurant, its celebrated clients, and some of its dishes. Garden City, N.Y.: Doubleday, Page & Co., 1927. 226p.

2918 Reilly, Estelle M. How to Cook for Children. A Book For Mothers. Intro. by Dr. Charles Gilmore Kerley. G. P. Putnam's Sons: New York, 1927. 250p.

2919 Reynolds, Philip. The Banana. Its history, cultivation and place among staple foods. New York: Houghton Mifflin, 1927. 181p. illus.

2920 Tipton, Edna Sibley. Menus for Every Occasion. For everyday meals, for one or two people, for parties. Frederick A. Stokes: New York, 1927. 1st ed. 217p.

2921 Whitton, Mary Ormsbee. The New Servant. Electricity in the Home. When to Use Current. Illus. by Leslie Crump. Pub. for the N. Y. Edison Co. by Doubleday, Page & Co., Garden City, N. Y., 1927. 326p.

2922 ALLEN, MARGARET PRATT & HUTTON, IDA ORAM. Man-Sized Meals from the Kitchenette. The Vanguard Press: New York, 1928. 149p.

2923 ANYONE CAN BAKE. Compiled by the Educational Dept. Illustrated, color and black & white. Royal Baking Powder Co. N.Y.C., 1928. 100p.

2924 BARNES, MARY FRANCES HARTLEY. Feeding the Child from Two to Six. Intro. by Dr. Richard M. Smith. New York: The Macmillan Co., 1928. 206p.

2925 BELL, KATHARIN. Mammy's Cook Book. New York, H. Holt (1928). 295p. (see No. 154).

2926 BONNÉ, JOSEPHINE. The Continental Cook Book. 1000 and 1 Recipes of European Tradition. Translated by Edna L. Sherman. Minton, Balch, N.Y., 1928. 428p.

2927 BROWN, H. C. DELMONICO'S. A story of old New York. Valentine's Manual. Many full page plates, col. & plain. Wraps. New York, 1928. 1st ed. 64p.

2928 CLAIRE, MABEL. Plate Dinners for the Busy Woman. Greenberg; New York, 1928. 122p.

2929 DE KRUIF, PAUL. Hunger Fighters. Illus. 1st ed. New York, 1928. 376p.

2930 DICKEY, ELLEN ROSE. Economy in the Kitchen. Edward J. Clode, Inc., New York (1928). 224p. Frontis. port. of author.

2931 FOR THE HOSTESS. Handbook for entertaining by editors of Vogue, Vanity Fair, House & Garden. New York: Condé Nast Pub., 1928. 72p. Frontis. & illus.

2932 GOLD, MOLLIE AND GILBERT, ELEANOR. THE BOOK OF GREEN VEGETABLES. How to Choose and Serve Them in 200 Different Ways. D. Appleton and Co., New York, 1928. 1st ed. 190p.

2933 GOOD HOUSEKEEPING'S BOOK OF GOOD MEALS. How to Prepare and Serve Them. Good Housekeeping: New York, 1928. 256p.

2934 GRAHAM, ABBIE. Ceremonials of Common Days "of Food, of Coffee," etc. Decorative cover. New York (1928). 98p.

2935 HERRICK, W. W., B.A., M.D. (Ed-in-chief). Nelson Loose-Leaf Living Medicine, VII. Prepared under direction of International Advisory Board. Mental creation of Sir William Osler. (Food section). Thomas Nelson & Sons, New York (1928). 560p. & 23 Index.

2936 LIEB, CLARENCE W. EAT, DRINK & BE HEALTHY. An outline of rational dietetics, recipes. John Day: New York, 1928. 180p.

2937 MOFFAT, ALEX. W. The Galley Guide. Supplies, lists, recipes, menus. Yachting, Inc., New York, 1928. 157p.

2938 PARTY SANDWICHES. Pamphlet. Illus. Delineator Institute. New York, 1928. 22p.

2939 ROSE, MARY SWARTZ, PH.D. FEEDING THE FAMILY. Nutrition for each member of the family. Illustrated. Macmillan: New York, 1928. 487p.

2940 SMITH, ERNEST ELLSWORTH. Aluminum Compounds in Food. Includes report re nutrition value. New York: Paul B. Hoeber, 1928. 378p.

2941 SWANSON, C. O. Wheat Flour and Diet. The author, professor and department head of Milling Industry, Kansas State Agricultural College. New York: The Macmillan Company, 1928. 203p.

2942 THOMAS, PROFESSOR JERRY. THE BON VIVANT'S COMPANION or How to Mix Drinks as it was done at the Metropolitan Hotel & at Planters' House. Introduction by Herbert Asbury. Illus. from newspapers of 1860-1880. A handsome book. Alfred A. Knopf, New York, 1928. 169p.

2943 WOLCOTT, IMOGENE B. The Blue Gingham Cook Book. Recipes from scientific tests of famous food manufacturers. New York: W. Morrow, 1928. 481p.

2944 ADAIR, A. H. DINNERS LONG & SHORT. (See Foreign sec.)

2945 ADAM, H. PEARL. KITCHEN RANGING. Recipes from famous chefs around the world. Jonathan Cape & Harrison Smith, New York (1929). 1st ed. 400p.

2946 ALLEVI, BAPTISTIN. THE SAVARIN COOKBOOK. Scientific Cooking for Profit. Illus. Harper & Brothers, New York, 1929. 1st ed. 262p.

2947 ANY ONE CAN BAKE. Color illus. Royal Baking Powder: New York (1929). 100p.

2948 BOLITHO, HECTOR. The Glorious Oyster. His history in Rome and in Britain. How to cook him. What poets and writers have said about him. London & New York: Alfred A. Knopf. 1929. 203p.

2949 BONNEY, THÉRÈSE AND LOUISE. French Cooking for American Kitchens. (See Foreign sec.)

2950 DANE, PHOEBE. Your Home Cook Book. New York: Constructive Publishing Corp., 1929. 72p.

2951 FLEXNER, MARION W. AND MCMEEKIN, ISABELLA MCLENNAN. Food for Children and How to Cook It. Also how to get them to eat it. New York: Henry Holt & Co. (1929). 125p.

2952 FROUDE, CHARLES C. Right Food, the Right Remedy. Intro. by Royal S. Copeland, former commissioner of Public Health. New York: Brentano (1929). 306p.

2953 GALLICHAN, WALTER M. YOUTHFUL OLD AGE. How to Keep Young: chapters on food and drink and reducing. Intro. by Dr. Thurman B. Rice. Macmillan: New York, 1929. 236p.

2954 HASTINGS, MILO. PHYSICAL CULTURE FOOD DIRECTORY. A rating of foods for vitality, growth . . menus. Macfadden Publications, New York, 1929. 151p.

2955 MOORE, HELEN FRANCES. Old Family Receipts. New York: n. pub. 1929. 102p.

2956 New Delineator Recipes. From the Home Institute. Illustrated. Butterick Publishing Co.: New York (1929). 222p.

2957 Oldfield, Josiah. Eat and Be Happy. New York: D. Appleton and Co., 1929. 114p.

2958 The Royal Guide to Meal Planning. Compiled by the Educational Dept. of Standard Brands Inc. New York City: Standard Brands Inc., 1929. 100p. illus.

2959 Snyder, Madeline. My Books of Parties. Illus. New York, 1929. 191p.

2960 Three Meals a Day. Suggestions for Good Food at Low Cost. Wraps. Metropolitan Life Ins. Co.; New York, 1929. 16p.

2961 Wilder, James Austin. Jack-Knife Cookery. For a desert island—camping. Profusely illustrated with line drawings by the author. Dutton: New York, 1929. 1st ed. 186p.

2962 Charles. Cheerio. Drinks from Delmonicos. Elf: New York, 1930. 53p.

2963 Cox's Gelatine Recipes. Wraps. Cox Gelatine Co., New York, 1930. 32p.

2964 Fisher, Katharine (Director) Good Hoksekeeping's Book of Meals. Tested, Tasted and Approved. Favorite recipes. Frontispiece. Good Housekeeping, New York, 1930. 256p.

2965 Frederick, J. George. Cooking As Men Like It. Intro. by Mrs. Christine Frederick. New York; Business Bourse, 1930. 1st ed. 280p.

2966 Hauser, Gayelord. New Health Cookery. Tempo Books: New York, 1930. 132p.

2967 MacDougall, Allan Ross (autographed) The Gourmets' Almanac. Strange & exotic dishes, feast days & fast days: with proverbs, songs and a garland for gourmets. Illus. by several artists of note and talent. Covice-Friede; New York, 1930. 1st ed. 309p. & Notes.

2968 Mason, Dexter (Compiled by) The Art of Drinking or what to make with what you have. Succulent Canapes Suitable to Each Occasion. Farrar & Rinehart, New York, 1930. 76p.

2969 New Delineator Recipes. Including ten exclusive recipes by Ann Batchelder. Illustrated. Butterick Publishing Co.: New York, 1930. 222p.

2970 Snyder, Harry. Bread. A collection of popular papers on wheat, flour and bread. Biographical Sketch by Andrew L. Winton. Macmillan, New York, 1930. 1st ed. 293p.

2971 Treat, Sara. The New Thought in Cooking. Tested recipes prepared for the American Maize-Products Company. New York: Chicago: (1930). 84p. illus. Wraps.

2972 Voison, Gaston. French Cooking for All. (See Foreign sec.)

2973 Ade, George. The Old-Time Saloon, not wet—not dry—just history. New York: Ray Long & Richard R. Smith, Inc., 1931. 174p.

2974 Axtell, Luella, MD. Grow Thin on Good Food. Illus. Funk & Wagnalls Co., New York, 1931. 336p.

2975 Browne, Susanna Shanklin. The Plain Sailing Cookbook. For beginners, by a graduate of Pratt Institute Domestic Science Dept. New York, Charles Scribner's Sons, 1931. 156p.

2976 Clendening, Logan. The Care and Feeding of Adults. With Doubts about Children. A discussion of habits; no recipes. Alfred A. Knopf, New York, 1931. 1st ed. 317p., 10 Index.

2977 Dane, Phoebe. 333 New Ways to a Man's Heart. The recipes have to be good. Intro. by Professor Bristow Adams . . 3rd ed. New York: True Story Magazine, Home Maker Library (1931). 112p. illus. Wraps. Ads.

2978 Dimock, Hedley S.; Hendry, Charles E. Camping and Character. A camp experiment in character education. Foreword by William H. Kilpatrick. Illus. Association Press: New York, 1931. 364p.

2979 Dipman, Carl W. The Modern Grocery Store. Store plans & displays. Illus. The Progressive Grocer, New York (1931). 199p.

2980 Drury, John. Dining in Chicago. An intimate guide. Foreword by Carl Sandburg. Colorful end papers—gastronomical maps. John Day, New York, 1931. 1st ed. 274p.

2981 Favorite Tested Recipes. Featuring the Wonder Shredder and Grater. Wraps. Dixon Prosser, New York City, 1931. 32p.

2982 First Aid in Emergencies. What To Do Till the Doctor Comes. Brief section on special diets. Wraps. McKesson & Robbins, New York, 1931. 96p.

2983 Goldsmith, Happy. Some Biting Remarks. About you and the foods that you eat. Unusual. Flavored with the author's own illustrations. A. S. Barnes, New York (1931). 43p.

2984 Goudiss, C. Houston and Alberta M. Eating Vitamines. Illus. 3rd ed. New York, Funk & Wagnalls (1931). 129p.

2985 Haines, Edith Key. Tried Temptations. Old and New. Collected and original recipes. Farrar & Rinehart, Inc., New York (1931). 229p.

2986 Hart, Frances Noyes. Pigs in Clover. (See Foreign sec.)

2987 Littledale, Clara Savage. The Whole-Family Cook Book. Recipes nutritious for children, delicious for grown-ups. New York: The Parents' Magazine (1931). 181p.

2988 McCarthy and Rutherford. Peacock Alley, The Romance of the Waldorf-Astoria. Illus. New York, 1931. 213p.

2989 Mason, Dexter. Tipple and Snack. Good things to eat and better things to drink. Decorations. Farrar & Rinehart: New York, 1931. 83p.

2990 The Minute Chef. Adapted for restaurants, tea rooms and luncheonettes. Illustrated. Chef's Guide: Brooklyn, N. Y., 1931. 1st ed. 205p.

2991 Moody, Harriet C. Mrs. William Vaughn Moody's Cookbook. New York: C. Scribner's Sons, 1931. 475p.

2992 Neil, Marion Harris. Favorite Recipes. Cook Book. A complete culinary guide. New York: Willey Book Co., 1931. 504p.

2993 Patterson, Betty Benton. Mammy Lou's Cook Book. New York: R. M. McBride & Co., 1931. 307p.

2994 Proudfit, Fairfax. Nutrition and Diet Therapy. A Textbook of Dietetics. Macmillan Co., New York, 1931. 705p.

2995 Riesenberg, Emily. Easy Baking. Foreword by Felix Riesenberg. New York: John Day Co. (1931). 287p.

2996 Sugden, Claire. The Romantic and Practical Side of Cookery. New York, L. S. Siegfried (1931). 522p.

2997 Tummy Book. Playful little hangover from Prohibition. A prime period piece. Illus. New York, 1931. 48p.

2998 Wangner, Ellen D. The American Home Book of Outdoors. Illus. with photos. New York, 1931. 156p.

2999 The Whole-Family Cook Book. Recipes and Menus Nutritious for Children, Delicious for Grown-Ups. Parents' Magazine, New York (1931). 181p.

3000 Adams, Charlotte. The Run of the House (presentation) Housewife and hostess—not cookery, Macmillan, New York, 1932. 1st ed. 271p.

3001 Allen, Ida Bailey. Ida Bailey Allen's Modern Cook Book. 2500 delicious recipes. Garden City, N. Y.: Garden City Publishing Co., Inc. (1932). 977p. illus.

3002 Bolton, Dorothy. Kitchen Prelude. (See Foreign sec.)

3003 Brown, Bob. Let There Be Beer! History and anecdote, and recipes. Harrison Smith and Robert Haas; New York, 1932. 321p.

3004 Claire, Mabel. The Emporium's Modern Cook Book for the Busy Woman. Illus. Meier & Frank: New York, 1932. 416p.

3005 Claire, Mabel. The World's Modern Cook Book. For the busy woman. World Syndicate Pub. Co., New York (1932). 416p.

3006 Cookery for Today. Including ten exclusive recipes by Ann Batchelder. Illustrated. Delineator Institute, New York, 1932. 164p.

3007 Denison, Grace E. (Edited by) The American Home Cook Book. A volume of tested recipes.

Illus. Grosset & Dunlap, New York (1932). 1st ed. 537p.

3008 DORK, MARJORIE. REDUCE WHERE YOU NEED TO. Charts and menus. Horace Liveright, New York (1932). 63p.

3009 FITZGERALD, DOROTHY. The Quality Cook Book, Modern Cooking and Table Service. New York: Grosset & Dunlap (1932). 271p. illus.

3010 GRAVES, LULU G. FOODS IN HEALTH AND DISEASE. Macmillan, New York, 1932. 1st ed. 390p.

3011 HAUSER, BENJAMIN GAYELORD AND BERG, RAGNAR. DICTIONARY OF FOODS. With valuable notes penned in. Tempo Books, New York (1932). 1st ed. 135p. and ads.

3012 HAWLEY, EDITH. Economics of Food Consumption. Author formerly with U. S. Dept. of Agriculture. New York: McGraw-Hill Book Company, Inc., 1932. 335p.

3013 HIBBEN, SHEILA (Mrs. Paxton Hibben). THE NATIONAL COOKBOOK. A kitchen Americana. Harper & Brothers: New York, 1932. 1st ed. 452p.

3014 HUNGARIAN COOKERY. (See Foreign sec.)

3015 LOWE, BELLE. Experimental Cookery. From the Chemical & Physical Standpoint. Laboratory outline. John Wiley & Sons, New York, 1932. 498p.

3016 MACAULEY, THURSTON. The Festive Board. A literary feast. Culinary writings by great authors: Dickens, Dumas, Lamb, Hearn, Shaw, etc. New York: 1932. 144p.

3017 THE NEW YORK COOK BOOK. Institute of Nutrition. . . New York: Constructive Pub. Corp., 1932. 674p.

3018 REBOUX, PAUL (See Foreign sec.)

3019 ROYAL COOK BOOK. Wraps. Standard Brands, Inc., New York, 1932. 45p.

3020 VAN ARSDALE, MAY B., MONROE, DAY & BARBER, MARY T. Our Candy Recipes. Color illus. New York: The Macmillan Co., 1932. 202p.

3021 WEAVER, LOUISE BENNETT & LE CRON, HELEN COWLES. Bettina's Best Salads & What to Serve With Them. Illus. & color plates. A. L. Burt: New York (1932). 215p.

3022 WYNNE, SHIRLEY W., MD. Diet & Weight Control. Menus and Directions for a 30-day Diet. New York, 1932. 223p.

3023 ALL ABOUT HOME BAKING. Cakes, Cookies, Breads, Party Menus. Color photographs, illus. General Foods, New York (1933). 1st ed. 144p.

3024 BARBER, EDITH M. What Shall I Eat? By a famous nutrition authority. Illus. by Helen E. Hokinson. New York: The Macmillan Co., 1933. 107p.

3025 BEER IN THE HOME. Compliments of Jacob Ruppert, with a color photo of the Brewery, 3rd

Avenue. New York: 1933. 18p. and ads.

3026 Bond Bread Cook Book. Wraps. Bond Bread: New York, 1933. 22p.

3027 Fox, Helen Morgenthau. Gardening with Herbs for Flavor and Fragrance. Full page illus. Drawings by Louise Mansfield. New York: Macmillan Co., 1933. 334p.

3028 Good Housekeeping Cook Book. Recipes and Methods for Every Day and Every Occasion. Tested & approved by: Dorothy Marsh, Katherine Norris and Adeline Mansfield. Illus. Good Housekeeping: New York, 1933. 1st ed. 254p.

3029 Goudiss, Alberta M. Quick Meals from Market to Table for 2 or 4 or 6. Colored end papers. Photograph of the author. Forecast Publishing Co., New York, 1933. 93p.

3030 Rector, George (autographed). A la Rector. Cooking recipes. Illus. New York, 1933. Copyright by The Great Atlantic and Pacific Tea Co. 110p.

3031 Rose, Robert Hugh. How To Stay Young. New York: Funk & Wagnalls Co., 1933. 195p.

3032 Selivanova, Nina Nikolaevna. Dining and Wining in Old Russia (See Foreign sec.)

3033 Smith, Coral B. New Dishes from Left-Overs. New York: Frederick A. Stokes Co., 1933. 285p.

3034 3 Point 2 and what goes with it, the beer barrel booklet. Beach, New York, April 1933. 32p.

3035 Ullmann, Egon V., MD. Diet in Sinus Infections and Colds. Recipes and menus by Elza Mez. Macmillan: New York, 1933. 166p.

3036 Wenzel, G. L. American Menu Maker. New York: Daily News Building (1933).

3037 Whiteman, Margaret Livingston and Leighton, Isabel. Whiteman's Burden. A cheerful book of diet. Illustrations. Viking, New York, 1933. 116p.

3038 Allen, Ida Bailey. Wines and Spirits Cook Book. 456 recipes, 81 menus. Index. New York: Simon & Schuster, 1934. 366p. illus.

3039 Angostura. Famous for Foods. New York: 1934. 40p. advertising booklet. illus., with col. pict. cover.

3040 Boyer, Josephine and Cowdin, Katherine. Hay Dieting. Menus and Receipts for all Occasions (Rev. and enlarged ed). Charles Scribner's Sons, New York, 1934. 394p.

3041 Bredenbek, Magnus. What Shall We Drink? Popular Drinks, Recipes and Toasts. New York: Carlyle House, 1934. 215p.

3042 Bunyard, Edward. The Anatomy of Dessert. Wth a few notes on wine. E. P. Dutton & Co., New York, 1934. 215p.

3043 Charpentier, Henri and

SPARKES, BOYDEN. LIFE A LA HENRI. The savorous memoirs of a humorous gentleman; a chef and friend of the great of our time and of the immediate past. Photographs. Simon & Schuster, New York, 1934. 1st ed. 328p.

3044 CLAIRE, MABEL. The Modern Salad and Dessert Book. Canapes, hors d'oeuvres, sandwiches, appetizers, and party suggestions. New York: Greenberg, 1934. 304p. illus.

3045 CRADDOCK, HARRY. The Savoy Cocktail Book. A compendium of the Drinks, manners and customs of people of quality in 1930. Decorations by Gilbert Rumbold. New York: Simon and Schuster, Inc., 1934. 287p. illus. in color.

3046 DE WOLFE, ELSIE (LADY MENDL). Recipes for Successful Dining Menus and recipes. Illus. D. Appleton—Century Co., New York, 1934. 1st ed. 102p.

3047 DORRIS, NANCY. News Cook Book. More than 500 recipes from the News, N.Y.'s Picture Newspaper. Photo of author on intro. page. Pict. cover. New York: The News, 1934. 159p.

3048 ELLIOTT, VIRGINIA AND JONES, ROBERT HOWARD. Soups and Sauces. New York: Harcourt, Brace & Co., 1934. 98p.

3049 FAMILY FOOD SUPPLY. What to Buy and Why. Illus. Metropolitan Life Insurance Co., New York, 1934. 23p.

3050 GRIEVE, MRS. M. Culinary Herbs and Condiments. New York: Harcourt, Brace and Co. (1934, 2nd printing). 209p.

3051 HAMBIDGE, GOVE. Your Meals and Your Money, Budget plans and charts. Whittlesey House, New York, 1934. 190p.

3052 HIBBEN, SHEILA. THE AGA COOK BOOK. Describing the use of the Aga Stove; recipes for any kitchen. Illustrated. Amer. Gas Accumulator Co.; New York, 1934. 173p.

3053 HUDDLESON, MARY PASCOE. FOOD FOR THE DIABETIC. What to eat and how to calculate it. Intro. by William S. McCann. Macmillan: New York, 1934. 110p.

3054 JAMES, RIAN. DINING IN NEW YORK. An Intimate Guide. Repeal edition—completely revised. John Day Company, New York (1934). 271p.

3055 LUTES, DELLA THOMPSON. Table Setting and Service for Mistress and Maid. Sample menus and how to serve them. Illus. M. Barrow & Co.: New York (1934). 155p.

3056 MAIDEN, RACHEL BELL. The Canape Book. Decorations by Lucina Smith Wakefield. Pen sketches; original and selected recipes. New York: D. Appleton-Century Co., Inc., 1934. 95p.

3057 MARKS, ROBERT. Wines, How, When and What To Serve. There are pages of receipts for use of wine in cookery. New York: Schenley Import Corp., 1934. 63p.

3058 100 FAMOUS COCKTAILS in

Collaboration with Oscar of The Waldorf. The romance of wines and liquors, etiquette, recipes. Decorations by Henry Stalhut. Kenilworth, New York, 1934. 1st ed. 46p.

3059 OZIAS, BLAKE. How the Modern Hostess Serves Wine. Recipes & Menus. Illus. New York, 1934.

3060 PICTORIAL REVIEW STANDARD COOK BOOK. Methods of preparing 1000 appetizing dishes. Pictorial Review Co.: New York, 1934. 481p.

3061 ROSS, GEORGE. Tips on Tables. Being a Guide to Dining and Wining in New York at 365 Restaurants. New York: copyright by Geo. Ross, 1934. 301p.

3062 SHERMAN, HENRY C. Food and Health. Intelligent Use of Food. Illustrative Records of Meals. Macmillan Co.: New York, 1934. 296p.

3063 A TREATISE ON CAKE MAKING. To assist the baker enlarge his business. Standard Brands Inc., New York (1934). 381p.

3064 WILLIAMS, HENRY SMITH. Why Die Before Your Time. A Doctor Looks at the Food that Becomes You. Robert M. McBride; New York, 1934. 232p.

3065 WISHARD, WINIFRED (compiler). Best Recipes. New York: Elliot Publishing Co., 1934. 124p.

3066 ALLEN, IDA BAILEY. The Budget Cook Book. More than 250 recipes for popular dishes. The Best Foods, Inc., New York, 1935. 127p.

3067 ALLEN, IDA BAILEY. THE SERVICE COOK BOOK No. 2. 200 cooking tricks; 700 recipes. Spiral binding. F. W. Woolworth Co., New York, 1935. 195p.

3068 BOYER, JOSEPHINE & COWDIN, KATHERINE. Hay Dieting. Menus & receipts for all occasions. Charles Scribner's Sons, New York, 1935. 404p.

3069 FLAVOR AND COLOR in bread and sweet yeast doughs. Charts and illustrations. Corn Products Refining Co., New York, 1935. 45p.

3070 GOURMET'S BOOK OF FOOD AND DRINK. Decorations in color by Hendy. New York: Macmillan, 1935. 278p. illus.

3071 HURST, FANNIE. No Food with My Meals. New York, 1935. 1st ed. 56p.

3072 MACDOUGALL, ALICE FOOTE. Alice Foote MacDougall's Cook Book. Photos by F. S. Lincoln. New York: Lothrop, Lee and Shepherd, 1935. 292p.

3072a MAUDUIT—VICOMTE DE. The Vicomte in the Kitchenette. (see Foreign sec.)

3073 THE MYSTERY CHEF'S OWN COOK BOOK. New York: Longmans, Green, 1935. 366p.

3074 SCHLINK, F. J. EAT, DRINK AND BE WARY. All about the products sold to the public. Grosset & Dunlap, New York (1935). 322p.

3075 SIMON, ANDRÉ L. THE ART OF GOOD LIVING. Understanding Food & Drink; with a Gastronomic

Vocabulary and a Wine Dictionary. Frontispiece after Daumier. Foreword by Maurice Healy. Alfred A. Knopf, New York, 1935. 191p.

3076 SIMONSON, GERDA. "Smorgasbordet" (See Foreign sec.)

3077 AKERSTROM-SODERSTROM, JENNY. The Princesses Cook Book. (See Foreign sec.)

3078 ANDERSON, MARTHA LEE (Tested by). GOOD THINGS TO EAT. Made with Arm & Hammer or Cow Brand Baking Soda. Wraps. Small booklet. Church & Dwight Co., New York, 1936. 32p.

3079 BELL, ALBERT J., A.B., MD. FEEDING, DIET AND THE GENERAL CARE OF CHILDREN. A book for mothers and trained nurses. Illus. G. P. Putnam's Sons, New York (1936). 316p.

3080 BIDDLE, DOROTHY AND BLOM, DOROTHEA. THE BOOK OF TABLE SETTING. Variety and charm for your table. Illustrated. Doubleday, Doran & Co., New York, 1936. 1st ed. 83p.

3081 BROWN: CORA, ROSE & BOB. The European Cookbook for American Homes (From Italy, Spain, Portugal and France). Farrar & Rinehart Inc., New York (1936). 400p.

3082 BUCKSTEIN, JACOB, MD. Food, Fitness and Figure. Diet information, history of foods, and fads & fancy. Intro. by Dr. Harlow Brooks. Emerson Books, Inc., New York, 1936. 1st ed. 252p.

3083 FASCINATING CRANBERRIES AND HOW TO SERVE THEM. New York: American Cranberry Exchange, 1936. 24p. advertising booklet. Col. illus.

3084 FUNK, CASIMIR, SC.D. PH.D., & DUBIN, H.E., PH.D. VITAMIN AND MINERAL THERAPY. Practical manual. U. S. Vitamin Corp., New York, 1936. 94p.

3085 HEATON, ROSE HENNIKER. THE PERFECT HOSTESS. Unusual, 'sprightly' comments and menus. Introduction by Frank Crowninshield. Decorated by Alfred E. Taylor. E. P. Dutton: New York (1936), 160p.

3086 LORD, ISABEL ELY (Edited by) THE HOUSEHOLD COOKBOOK. A handy cookbook for homemakers. Harcourt, Brace and Co., New York, 1936. 486p.

3087 THE MYSTERY CHEF. BE AN ARTIST AT THE GAS RANGE. Successful recipes by the mystery chef. Wraps. Longmans, Green: New York, 1936. 96p.

3088 PLATT, JUNE. PARTY COOKBOOK. Carefully presented recipes. With illustrations. Houghton Mifflin; Boston, Mass., 1936. 277p.

3089 ROSE, MARY SWARTZ: PH.D. A LABORATORY HANDBOOK FOR DIETETICS. Food Values, Requirements, Problems of Dietary Calculation and Reference Tables. Macmillan, New York, 1936. 269p.

3090 TAYLOR, RUTH. The Kitchenette Cook Book. To help you save time, money and temper. New

York, Charles Scribner's Sons, 1936. 299p. Spiral Col. end papers.

3091 ABDULLAH, ACHMED. For Men Only. New York: G. P. Putnam's Sons (1937). 205p.

3092 ALL ABOUT HOME BAKING. Cakes, breads, frostings, party menus. Illustrations. General Foods Corp.; New York, 1937. 144p.

3093 AMERICA'S COOK BOOK. Col. illus. N. Y. Herald Tribune. New York, 1937. 1006p.

3094 BRADLEY, ALICE. MENU—COOK—BOOK. Menus, Marketing Lists and Recipes, January, February, March. Gay cover; spiral binding. Macmillan: New York, 1937. 241p.

3095 BRADLEY, ALICE. MENU—COOK—BOOK. Menus, Marketing Lists and Recipes. April, May, June. Gay cover: spiral binding. Macmillan: New York, 1937. 247p.

3096 BRADLEY, ALICE. MENU—COOK—BOOK. Menus, Marketing Lists and Recipes. July, August, September. Gay cover, spiral binding. Macmillan: New York, 1937. 247p.

3097 BRADLEY, ALICE. THE ALICE BRADLEY MENU—COOK—BOOK. Menus, Marketing Lists and Recipes for October, November, December. Macmillan; New York, 1937. 1st ed. 253p.

3098 BROWN: CORA, ROSE & BOB. The Country Cookbook. Cooking, canning and preserving. For home, farm, camp & trailer. The countryman Press, Weston, Vt., and Farrar & Rinehart, New York City (1937). 224p.

3099 BROWN: CORA, ROSE AND BOB. 10,000 SNACKS. A cookbook of canapes, savories, relishes. Decorations by Julian Brazelton. Farrar & Rinehart Inc., New York (1937). 1st ed. 593p.

3100 DE GOUY, LOUIS P. The Derrydale Book of Fish and Game. 2 Vols. A celebrated set of cook books. New York, 1937.

3101 EVELYN, JOHN. ACETARIA, A DISCOURSE OF SALLETS. Facs. of 1699. 1st ed. of great herbal. Brooklyn, 1937. Ltd. ed. 1,000 copies. 148p. and table.

3102 FISHER, M. F. K. Serve It Forth. History of Cooking from Hon-Zo to now. Literary and autobiographical. Illus. Colored end papers. Harper & Brothers: New York, 1937. 1st ed. 253p.

3103 FISHER, M. F. K. Serve It Forth. Biographical & Gastronomical. World Book Co.: New York (1937). 253p.

3104 FURNAS, C. C. AND S. M. MAN, BREAD AND DESTINY. The Story of Man's Food. Reynal and Hitchcock: New York (1937). 1st ed. 364p.

3105 GENERAL FOODS COOK BOOK. A key to the question of three meals a day. Illustrated. General Foods Corporation, New York, 1937. 370p.

3105a GILLETT, LUCY H. Food For

Health's Sake. New York: Funk & Wagnalls (1937). 74p. & ads.

3106 GOOD THINGS TO EAT. Breads, cakes and cookies. Pamphlet, wraps. Arm & Hammer, Church & Co., New York State, 1937. 15p.

3107 GOURLEY, JAMES E. Eating Round the World. Foreign recipe books and magazine articles in English. New York: the compiler, 1937. 51p. Wraps.

3108 HAINES, EDITH KEY. EDITH KEY HAINES' COOKBOOK. Farrar & Rinehart, New York, 1937. 1st ed. 655p.

3109 MCCANN, ALFRED W. Science of Eating. How to Insure Health in Infancy, Youth & Age. New York, 1937. 408p.

3110 MAY, EARL CHAPIN. The Canning Clan. A Pageant of Pioneering Americans. History of the canning industry. New York: Macmillan, 1937. 487p.

3111 RECTOR, GEORGE. DINE AT HOME WITH RECTOR. A book on what men like, why they like it, and how to cook it. Preface by Arthur 'Bugs' Baer. Dutton: New York, 1937. 248p. and Index.

3112 WALDORF-ASTORIA. Manual of Food, Beverages & Restaurant Service. Catering, wines & spirits, also Photos of New York. Wraps. New York: 1937.

3113 WILLSON, LOU AND HOOVER, OLIVE. MEALS ON WHEELS. A cook book for trailers and kitchenettes. Decorations by Barbara Willson. Modern Age Books: New York, 1937. 168p.

3114 BROWN, CORA, ROSE & BOB. MOST FOR YOUR MONEY COOKBOOK. Economy recipes, including chapter on mulligans, slumgullions, lobscouses and burgoos. Decorations by Julian Brazelton. Modern Age Books, New York (1938). 1st ed. 228p. and ads.

3115 BROWN, CORA, ROSE & BOB. Salads and Herbs. More than 300 recipes. J. B. Lippincott: N. Y. (1938). 274p.

3116 COOKING FOR TWO. With Menus and Recipes. Illus. Wraps. Good Housekeeping Institute, New York (1938). 34p.

3117 DE GOUY, L. P. ICE CREAM DESSERTS FOR EVERY OCCASION. 470 tested recipes. Hastings House, New York (1938). 1st ed. 281p.

3118 DIET at The Waldorf-Astoria, including special menus for children. Booklet, wraps. Waldorf-Astoria: New York, 1938. 36p.

3118a EDDY, DR. WALTER H. (Dir.) Planning Meals Rich in Vitamins. New York: Good Housekeeping Bureau, 1938. 23p. booklet.

3119 A GIFT TO THE BRIDE. A book of ready reference on a variety of subjects, including cooking. Extra large plates, colored end papers, handsome illustrations, ads. Mac Arthur Publications; New York City (1938). 1st ed. 201p. & notes & Index.

3119a LAZO, HECTOR AND BLETZ,

M.H. Who Gets Your Food Dollar? New York: Harper, 1938. 129p.

3120 LINDLAHR, VICTOR H. GUIDE TO BALANCED DIET. The right foods and how to cook them. Portrait of the author. National Nutrition Society, New York, 1938. 96p.

3121 MORPHY, COUNTESS. Recipes of All Nations. Indexed. William H. Wise & Co.; New York, 1938. 821p.

3122 MORRIS, HELEN. Portrait of a Chef. The Life of Alexis Soyer, Sometime Chef to the Reform Club. Illus. The Macmillan Co., New York and The University Press, Cambridge, England, 1938. 1st ed. 221p.

3123 ROSE, MARY SWARTZ. The Foundations of Nutrition. Illus. Col. frontis. Macmillan: New York, 1938. 625p.

3124 ROSS, ANNA; BRAND, REGINA. Modern Recipes for Radiant Health. Intro. by Max Warmbrand. Spiral. Healthful Living Publishing Co., Inc., New York, 1938. 81p.

3125 RUBINSTEIN, HELENA. FOOD FOR BEAUTY (autographed) Recipes and menus for vital loveliness. Illustrations by Robert L. Leonard. Colored end papers. Washburn, New York, 1938. 245p.

3126 SHERMAN, HENRY C. Food and Health. By a professor of chemistry, Columbia University. Macmillan Co.: New York, 1938. 296p.

3127 SPECIFICATIONS. Institute of Fine Cooking. Large notebook of Bulletins for restaurants & hotels. Bound by G. L. Wentzel (c. 1938). New York.

3128 WILLIAMS, ELLIS. IN AND OUT OF DOORS. Wild food, fruit, herbs & seasonal chart. New York, 1938.

3129 ABBOTT, MARJORIE. Half Hour Dinners. Chapters on meat, fish, hot weather dinners. Wraps. Harian Publications: New York, (1939). 1st ed. 80p.

3130 ARMITAGE, MERLE. "FIT FOR A KING" FOOD. Spice Closet by Gaige; The Art of Eating, Conroy; Food for Camping, Armitage; Table Conversation, Abbe Dimnet; and recipes of the famous. Edited by Ramiel McGehee. Drawings by Elise; decorative end papers, a handsome book. Duell, Sloan and Pearce: New York, 1939. 1st ed. 261p.

3131 ASHLEY, DIANA: WHERE TO DINE IN THIRTY-NINE. With 200 Recipes by Famous Chefs. New York, 1939. 126p.

3132 BROWN: CORA, ROSE, BOB. SOUPS, SAUCES AND GRAVIES. The Year 'Round Book for Modern Kitchens. More than 500 different recipes. J. B. Lippincott: New York (1939). 319p.

3133 BROWN: CORA, ROSE & BOB. THE SOUTH AMERICAN COOKBOOK. Including Central America, Mexico and the West Indies. Doubleday, Doran & Co., Inc., New York, 1939. 368p.

3134 BROWN, CORA, ROSE & BOB. The Wining and Dining Quiz. A

Banquet of Questions and Answers From Soup to Nuts. D. Appleton-Century Co., New York, 1939. 165p.

3135 BROWNE, CHARLES. THE GUN CLUB COOK BOOK (autographed) A Culinary Code for Appreciative Epicures. Illustrations by Leonard Holton. Scribner's, New York, 1939. 298p.

3136 DISTINGUISHED CHEESE DISHES OF SWITZERLAND. (See Foreign sec.)

3136a THE FORTIFICATION OF FOODS WITH VITAMINS AND MINERALS. Symposium at American Institute of Nutrition at Toronto. New York: Milbank Memorial Fund, 1939. 262p.

3137 GORITZINA, KYRA. Service Entrance. Memoirs of a Park Avenue Cook. New York, 1939. 315p.

3138 HARRIS, FLORENCE LA GANKE. Cooking with a Foreign Flavor. How to make exciting dishes right in your own home. New York: M. Barrows, 1939. 320p.

3139 HEWETT, MARGARET. Party Menus and Recipes. Illus. by Hiram Hurd. Henry Holt: New York, 1939. 109p.

3140 HUNT, MARY. Salad Bowl. Recipes from a famed Minneapolis Restaurant. M. Barrows: New York, 1939. 102p.

3141 LORD, ISABEL ELY. THE MODERN WOMAN'S COOK BOOK. Illustrated. Decorative end papers. Sun Dial Press, New York (1939). 479p.

3142 THE MAZOLA SALAD BOWL. Recipes reprinted from many magazines. With colorful illustrations. Corn Products Refining Co., New York, 1939. 32p.

3143 MORGAN, HELEN. YOU CAN'T EAT THAT! A manual and recipe book for those with food allergy. Foreword by Dr. Walter C. Alvarez, Mayo Clinic. Harcourt, Brace & Co., New York (1939). 1st ed. 330p.

3144 NASON, EDITH. INTRODUCTION TO EXPERIMENTAL COOKERY. New York, 1939. 317p.

3145 NORBERG, INGA. GOOD FOOD FROM SWEDEN (See Foreign sec.)

3146 RECTOR, GEORGE. DINING IN NEW YORK WITH RECTOR. A Personal Guide to Good Eating. New York 1939. 1st ed. 275p.

3147 RECTOR, GEORGE. HOME AT THE RANGE. A treatise of truly tasteful edibles. Decorative end papers, illustrations. George Rector, New York, 1939. 137p.

3148 TAYLOR, DEMETRIA AND LYNN, GERTRUDE. THE DAY BY DAY COOK BOOK. Balanced menus for every day in the year and 1047 tested recipes. Illustrations. Harper & Brothers, New York, 1939. 367p.

3149 WELLS, ENID. Living for Two. A book for the bride, with chapter on cooking. Chatty and informal. New York: David Kemp & Co., 1939. 434(1)p 1st ed.

3150 WINE WITHOUT FRILLS. Everyday Enjoyment of Imported

Wines and Spirits. Designs by Joseph Binder. Schenley Import Corp., New York, 1939. 61p.

3151 ALLEN, IDA BAILEY. MONEY-SAVING COOK BOOK. Menus with variations for a year, recipes. Decorative end papers in color. Garden City Publishing Co., New York, 1940. 481p.

3152 BARBER, EDITH M. Edith Barber's Cook Book. Putnam, N. Y. 1940. 524p.

3153 BARBER, EDITH M. SPEAKING OF SERVANTS. How to Hire, Train, and Manage Household Employees. Kitchen plans and menus. Whittlesey House: New York, 1940. 256p.

3154 BEARD, JAMES (autographed) HORS D'OEUVRES AND CANAPES. With a key to the cocktail party. Illus. M. Barrows: New York (1940). 1st ed. 189p.

3155 BORSOOK, HENRY, PH.D., MD. VITAMINS. What They are and How They Can Benefit You. By a professor of Biochemistry. A few menus. Viking Press, New York, 1940. 193p.

3156 BROWN: CORA, ROSE AND BOB. America Cooks. Practical Recipes from 48 States. Norton, New York, 1940. 1st ed. 986p.

3157 BROWN: CORA, ROSE AND BOB. THE FISH AND SEA FOOD COOK BOOK. Simple panfish to a heavenly 'bouquet de mer!' Every fish recipe including camp specialties for men. Grosset & Dunlap, New York (1940). 348p. and biographical sketch.

3158 DORRIS, NANCY. The News Offers Requested Recipes. New York: News Syndicate Co., Inc., 1940. 92p.

3159 EBERLE, IRMENGARDE. Spice on the Wind. History and Geography of "the great spices" of the world. Beautiful illustrations by Richard Jones. Decorative end papers. Holiday House: New York (1940). 1st ed. 56p.

3160 FUNK, WILFRED. If You Drink. N. Y. 1940. 1st ed.

3161 GUMPERT. (See Foreign sec.)

3162 HILLES, HELEN TRAIN. YOUNG FOOD. For children—according to age. Duell, Sloan and Pearce: New York (1940). 1st ed. 253p.

3163 OWEN, JEANNE. A WINE LOVER'S COOK BOOK. Recipes for the use of wine in cookery; liqueurs in desserts. M. Barrows, New York, 1940. 1st ed. 197p.

3164 PERRY, JOSEPHINE. COOKIE JAR. Around the World Making Cookies. M. Barrows: New York, 1940. 157p.

3165 RIPPERGER, HELMUT: Coffee Cookery. Rare recipes from chestnuts with Coffee Sauce to Coffee Chiffon Pie. George W. Stewart, 1940. 1st ed. New York. 94p.

3166 SMITH, ISABEL COTTON. The Blue Book of Cookery. Menus, economical and party recipes. Introduction by Emily Post. Illustrated. Hobart Press, New York, 1940. 1st ed. 566p.

3167 SPECIALTIES DE LA MAISON. (See Foreign sec.)

3168 THOMAS, MARIE WADE. What To Eat and How To Cook It. Recipes and Menus. G. P. Putnam's Sons, New York, 1940. 1st ed. 389p.

3169 BEARD, JAMES. Cook It Outdoors. He-man meals for outdoor fun. Back-yard cooking, too. New York: M. Barrows, 1941. 200p. illus.

3170 BRANDT, JOHANNA. THE GRAPE CURE; Pub. under the Auspices of The Order of Harmony. New York (1941). 215p.

3171 BROWN, ROSE AND BOB. LOOK BEFORE YOU COOK. A Consumers Kitchen Guide. Decorative end papers, drawings. Robert M. McBride and Co., New York (1941) 1st ed. 404p.

3172 CHANDLER, ASA C. THE EATER'S DIGEST. About foods and nutrition; no recipes. Farrar & Rinehart: New York (1941). 1st ed. 343p.

3173 COOKS' ROUND TABLE OF ENDORSED RECIPES. 12 months: 1939-1940-1941. Better Homes & Gardens; New York.

3174 CULLEN, M. O. How To Carve Meat, Game and Poultry. New York, 1941. 209p.

3175 DEL VALLE, KATHARINE. RECIPES OF A ROLLING STONE. Memories and recipes for good food. Illustrated by Prince Giorgio Abkhasi. Coward-McCann: New York, 1941. 1st ed. 217p.

3176 DE SOUNIN, LEONIE. MAGIC IN HERBS. Making everyday meals delicious. Introduction by Miriam Birdseye. M. Barrows & Co., New York, 1941. 1st ed. 208p.

3177 DRAPER, DOROTHY. ENTERTAINING IS FUN! How to be a popular hostess. Table settings, planning, and menus. With line cuts and halftone illustrations. Decorative end papers. Doubleday, Doran & Co., New York, 1941. 249p.

3177a FUNK, CASIMIR; DUBIN, HARRY AND TAUB, ABRAHAM. Ready-Reference Vitamin Manual. New York: U. S. Vitamin Corp.: (1941).

3178 HIBBEN, SHEILA. A KITCHEN MANUAL. Duell, Sloan and Pearce, New York, 1941. 1st ed. 231p.

3179 LINDLAHR, VICTOR H. THE LINDLAHR VITAMIN COOKBOOK. Charts. National Nutrition Society, New York, 1941. 319p.

3180 THE NEW HOOD COOK BOOK. 1195 Modern Recipes. Col. plates. New York, 1941. 394p.

3181 RIPPERGER, HELMUT. CHEESE COOKERY. Culinary and literary lore; recipes for cheese. George W. Stewart: New York (1941). 1st ed. 96p.

3182 RIPPERGER, HELMUT. MUSHROOM COOKERY. Recipes devoted to the mushroom in the past and the present. George W. Stewart; New York (1941). 1st ed. 96p.

3183 SMITH, ISABEL COTTON. The Blue Book of Cookery. Menus and recipes. Intro. by Emily Post. Illus. Hobart Press, New York, 1941. 566p.

3184 TRACY, MARIAN & NINO. CASSEROLE COOKERY. One dish Meals for the Lazy Gourmet. Recipes illus. Spiral. New York, 1941.

3185 WALLACE, LILY HAXWORTH. CARVING THE EASY WAY with illustrations. M. Barrows, New York, 1941. 130p.

3186 WHERE TO EAT, SLEEP AND PLAY IN THE U.S.A. Contributed by the Travelers of Today for the Travelers of Tomorrow. Listings with brief comments. The Traveler's Windfall Ass'n., New York (1941). 648p.

3187 WOOD, MARNI. PARTIES ON A SHOESTRING. Illus. New York (1941). 1st ed. 96p.

3188 ALLEN, IDA BAILEY. MONEY-SAVING COOK BOOK. Eating for Victory. Garden City Publishing Co., Inc.; New York (1942). 481p.

3189 CASE, FRANK. FEEDING THE LIONS. An Algonquin Cookbook. Food for the wise. With comments from the "lions." Drawings. Greystone: New York, 1942. 255p.

3190 ELSIE. This Is My Book of Magic Recipes . . . Made with Borden's Eagle Brand Sweetened Condensed Milk. New York: Borden Co., 1942. 23p. illus. Advertising pamphlet.

3191 FURNAS, C. C. AND S. M. Man, Bread and Destiny, 1942. (See No. 3104).

3192 HARRIS, FLORENCE LA GANKE & RIDLER, DOROTHY ABIGAIL. Food 'N' Fun for the Invalid. Decorations by Frank Lieberman. M. Barrows: New York (1942). 1st ed. 255p.

3193 HONEY, A GOOD COOK'S SECRET. About Golden Blossom Honey Recipes. Wraps. Paton: New York, 1942. 42p.

3194 KREY, OTTO. SHIP'S COOK AND BAKER. Ship's cook, chef's duty. Illus. Cornell Maritime Press, New York, 1942. 312p.

3195 MACLEVY, MONTY. Pounds Off! Illus. with photos. New York, 1942. 193p.

3196 MADDOX, GAYNOR. Eat Well for Less Money. The American Guide to Modern Nutrition. Basic Foods for Everyday Living. New York, 1942. 219p.

3197 MARTIN, GEORGE W. Come and Get It. The Complete Outdoor Chef. Illus. New York, 1942. 1st ed. 189p.

3198 MIMI TELLS YOU HOW TO PREPARE YOUR FAVORITE ITALIAN DISHES AT HOME. (See Foreign sec.)

3199 PIERCE, ANNE (Compiled and edited by) HOME CANNING FOR VICTORY. Also preserving, pickling and dehydrating. Illus. M. Barrows: New York (1942). 106p.

3200 RIPPERGER, HELMUT. SPICE COOKERY. New York (1942). 1st ed. 95p.

3201 RUSSIAN COOKBOOK FOR AMERICAN HOMES. (See Foreign sec.)

3202 SENSE, ELEANORA. AMERICA'S NUTRITION PRIMER. What to Eat and Why. Introduction by Dr. E. V. McCollum. Illus. by the Author. M. Barrows: New York (1942). 95p.

3203 SILVER, FERN. NUTRITION. An Introductory Text for use in the schools. Illustrated. D. Appleton-Century Co., New York, 1942. 168p.

3204 SMITH, HERMAN. Stina, The Story of a Cook. Illustrated by Eleanora Sense. Barrows, 1942. 1st ed. New York. 242p.

3205 TAYLOR, CLARA MAE, PH.D. FOOD VALUES IN SHARES AND WEIGHTS. By a professor of Nutrition, Columbia Univ. Color chart. Macmillan: New York, 1942. 92p.

3206 THOUGHTS FOR FOOD. A menu aid, especially for parties for brunch and bridge. Recipes for family or guests. Vanguard in co-operation with the Institute Pub. Co., New York, 1942. 323p.

3207 WALLACE, LILY HAXWORTH. The New American Cook Book. End plates & illus. in color. Thumb index. Books, Inc., New York, 1942. 930p.

3208 WING, FRED. NEW CHINESE RECIPES. (See Foreign sec.)

3209 WINN-SMITH, ALICE B. Thrifty Cooking for Wartime. General suggestions, and specific recipes. Macmillan Co., New York, 1942. 147p.

3210 WOMAN'S HOME COMPANION COOK BOOK. Foreword by Willa Roberts. Collier & Son, N.Y., 1942. Illus. 952p.

3211 ADAMS, CHARLOTTE. YOU'LL EAT IT UP. A menu for every day and every occasion. Recipes, too. M. Barrows and Co., New York, 1943. 1st ed. 308p.

3212 ALLEN, IDA BAILEY. DOUBLE QUICK COOKING FOR PART TIME HOMEMAKERS. For women who are pioneers in industry, and are part time homemakers. M. Barrows: New York, 1943. 241p.

3213 BECK, PHINEAS. CLEMENTINE IN THE KITCHEN. (See Foreign sec.)

3214 BROBECK, FLORENCE. Title: COOK IT IN A CASSEROLE. With Chafing Dish Recipes and Menus. Introduction by Hendrik Willem Van Loon. Illustrated. Published by M. Barrows & Co., Inc., New York, 1943. 1st ed. 183p.

3215 BRYAN, MARY DE GARMO. THE SCHOOL CAFETERIA. A study of management, organization, purchasing of foods and tables of food specifications. Illus. F. S. Crofts: New York, 1943. 740p.

3216 THE CANNED FOOD REFERENCE MANUAL. A publication of the Research Dept., Roger H. Lueck, Director. Illus. American Can Company, New York (1943). 552p.

3217 CLARKE. HOME CANNING IN WARTIME. Wraps. Spiral binding. New York, 1943. 123p.

3218 FISHER, M. F. K. THE GASTRONOMICAL ME. Autobiography

and food. Duell, Sloan and Pearce, New York, 1943. 1st ed. 295p.

3219 FREEMAN, MARGARET E. HERBS FOR A MEDIEVAL HOUSEHOLD. Illus. Metropolitan Museum of Art, 1943. 1st ed. 48p.

3220 THE GOOD HOUSEKEEPING COOKBOOK. Kitchen equipment, methods, selection of foods, menus and recipes. Tested. Decorative end papers. Illustrations. Farrar & Rinehart; New York, 1943. 949p.

3221 GOOD THINGS TO EAT. Gay little booklet. Arm & Hammer, Church & Co., New York City, 1943. 15p.

3222 HENDRICKSON, ROY F. Food 'Crisis.' New York, 1943. 274p.

3223 MADDOX, GAYNOR (Editor in Chief) NOBLE, RANSOM E. JR. (Managing Editor) RUSSIAN COOK BOOK. (See Foreign sec.)

3224 MARIL, LEE: Spice & Scent. Herbs in Fact & Fancy. Col. illus. New York, 1943. 63p.

3225 MEALS WITHOUT MEAT. 275 recipes. A hook-up cook book. Wraps. Dell: New York, 1943. 48p.

3226 MORE THOUGHTS FOR FOOD. A Menu Aid and recipes to match. Colored end papers. Vanguard: New York, 1943. 282p.

3227 PRIESTNALL-HOLDEN, IVIE. 750 DISHES FROM OVERSEAS. Recipes adapted to American kitchens, from all over the world. Macmillan Co., New York, 1943. 1st ed. 255p.

3228 ROBBINS, ANN ROE. Canning and Drying Vegetables and Fruit. Wraps. Thomas Y. Crowell Co., New York (1943). 1st ed. 58p.

3229 ROBBINS, ANN ROE. 100 MEAT SAVING RECIPES. Prepared during rationing. Spiral binding. Thomas Y. Crowell Co., New York (1943). 106p.

3230 ROBBINS, ANN ROE. 25 VEGETABLES ANYONE CAN GROW. With recipes. New York, 1943. 245p.

3231 ROMBAUER, IRMA S. THE JOY OF COOKING. Compilation of reliable recipes with an occasional culinary chat. Illus. by Marion Rombauer Becker. Bobbs-Merrill Co., New York (1943). 884p.

3232 SHERMAN, HENRY C. AND LANFORD, CAROLINE SHERMAN. AN INTRODUCTION TO FOODS AND NUTRITION. To make information available during period of adjustment to rationing. Macmillan Company, New York, 1943. 292p.

3233 TAYLOR, MARY L. R. Economy for Epicures. A practical menu & recipe book. Oxford University Press. N. Y., 1943. Decorated by Julian Brazelton. 511p.

3234 TAYLOR, ROSEMARY. Chicken Every Sunday—My Life with Mother's Boarders. Illus. New York, 1943. 1st ed. 307p.

3235 THOUGHTS FOR FOOD. Republished by Houghton Mifflin, New York, 1943. 372p. (See No. 3206).

3236 WASON, BETTY. COOKING WITHOUT CANS. Smith & Durrell: New York (1943). 186p.

3237 WHITE, MARION. Diet without Despair. M. S. Mill: New York, 1943. 128p.

3238 WORTH, HELEN. Down-on-the-Farm Cook Book. Tangy, sturdy recipes from many farms: Rummage pickles or Setting-Hen Farm Graham Cracker Pie. New York: Greenberg (1943). 322p.

3239 WRIGHT, RICHARDSON. The Bed-Book of Eating and Drinking. The lore of food, historical notes & anecdotes. Good things to do about cooking. Decorations by June Platt. J. B. Lippincott; New York (1943). 1st ed. 315p.

3240 WYMAN, LOLA. BETTER MEALS IN WARTIME. Tasty meals from inexpensive foods. Hundreds of new menus and recipes. New York (1943). 168p.

3241 BRADLEY, ALICE. MENU-COOK-BOOK. Menus, Marketing Lists and Recipes for a year. Gay cover; Index and Kitchen list. Macmillan: New York, 1944. 944p.

3242 BROBECK, FLORENCE. SERVE IT BUFFET. M. Barrows, New York, 1944. 1st ed. 288p.

3243 GRIFFIN, MARJORIE. How TO COOK. Describes proper methods of cooking—With pictures, Hall Publishing, U.S.A., 1944. 223p.

3244 HAUSER, GAYELORD. Diet Does It. New York, 1944. 248p.

3245 KEATING, LAWRENCE A. "IF HE COULD ONLY COOK." Men in aprons. M. S. Mill Co.: New York (1944). 186p.

3246 KREY, OTTO. Ship Steward's Handbook. Illus. New York, 1944. 170p.

3247 MABON, MARY FROST. A MEAL IN ITSELF. A Book of Soups. Duell, Sloan and Pearce, New York (1944). 1st ed. 168p.

3248 MARDIKIAN, GEORGE. DINNER AT OMAR KHAYYAM'S. (See Foreign sec.)

3249 MARIL, LEE. SAVOR & FLAVOR. Col. illus. by Author. Berries in Fact & Fancy. New York, 1944. 1st ed. 64p.

3250 PEARSON, FRANK A.; PAARLBERG, DON. Food. War and food, shortage, distribution, black market. Alfred A. Knopf, New York, 1944. 1st ed. 239p. & Index.

3251 SMITH, HERMAN. KITCHENS NEAR AND FAR. Illustrated by Eleanora Sense. Photograph of the author. M. Barrows, New York, 1944. 1st ed. 277p.

3252 SPRACKLING, HELEN. COURTESY, A BOOK OF MODERN MANNERS. For home and friends and business connections. The technique of eating. M. Barrows; New York, 1944. 306p.

3253 TAYLOR, DEMETRIA M. The Soy Cook Book. New York: 1944. 215p.

3254 WHITE, MARION. Mother Hubbard's Cookbook. Making old fashioned flavors from new fashioned products. Foreword by Oscar of the Waldorf, New York: M. S. Mill Co., Inc. (1944). 204p.

3255 WILLIAMS-HELLER, ANNIE AND MCCARTHY, JOSEPHINE. Soybeans From Soup To Nuts. General and specific directions. Foreword by Dr. Walter H. Eddy. New York: Vanguard (1944). 1st ed. 120p.

3256 ASHBROOK, FRANK G. & SATER, EDNA. COOKING WILD GAME. Meat from Forest, Field & Stream and How to Prepare It for the Table. Illus. New York, 1945. 1st ed. 358p.

3257 BAUER, W. W., MD. EAT WHAT YOU WANT! A sensible guide to good health through good eating. Introduction by Morris Fishbein, MD. Blue Ribbon Books, New York, 1945. 163p.

3258 CARHART, ARTHUR H. THE OUTDOORSMAN'S COOKBOOK. Illus. Suggestions on use of aluminum foil, dehydrated foods. Macmillan: New York, 1945. 211p.

3259 COOLEY, DONALD G. THE NEW WAY TO EAT AND GET SLIM. What you ought to weigh and how to do it. Funk: New York, 1945. 208p.

3260 GREENBERG, BETTY D. AND SILVERMAN, ALTHEA O. THE JEWISH HOME BEAUTIFUL. (See Foreign sec.)

3261 JONES, IDWAL. HIGH BONNET. Recipes interwoven in this fine story of Chefs. New York, 1945. 1st ed. 184p.

3262 KAYE-SMITH, SHEILA. KITCHEN FUGUE. The author writes about learning to cook during World War II; autobiography related to the kitchen. Harper, New York, 1945. 1st ed. 215p.

3263 PLATT, JUNE. SERVE IT AND SING—for Sell's Liver Pate. Decorations by the author. Alfred A. Knopf, New York, 1945. 1st ed. 70p.

3264 SILVER, FERN. JUNIOR FOODS AND NUTRITION. For the junior high school girl. Illus. D. Appleton-Century: New York (1945). 1st ed. 234p.

3265 WALL, ROY. FISH AND GAME COOKERY. New York, 1945.

3266 WALLACE, LILY HAXWORTH. EGG COOKERY. M. Barrows, New York, 1945. 1st ed. 169p.

3267 WHITE, MARION. SWEETS WITHOUT SUGAR. Over 200 recipes using sweetening agents other than sugar. Jacket photograph by Corn Products Refining Co. Blue Ribbon Books, New York (1945). 128p.

3268 WILLIAMS - HELLER, ANN. COOKED TO YOUR TASTE. A Vegetable Cook Book. Foreword by Walter H. Eddy, Ph.D. Essential Books; New York, 1945. 1st ed. 234p.

3269 WILLISON, GEORGE F. SAINTS AND STRANGERS. Much about good food and drink of Pilgrim fathers and their families. New York, 1945. 513p.

3270 BAKER, CHARLES H., JR. Title: THE GENTLEMAN'S COMPANION, Vol. 1: Being an Exotic Cookery Book or, Around the World with

Knife, Fork and Spoon. Published by Crown Publishers at New York, 1946. 220p.

3271 BAKER, CHARLES H., JR. Title: THE GENTLEMAN'S COMPANION, Vol. II: Being an Exotic Drinking Book or, Around the World with Jigger, Beaker and Flask. Published by Crown Publishers at New York, 1946. 217p.

3272 BEEBE, LUCIUS. The Stork Club Bar Book. New York, 1946. 136p.

3273 BEROLZHEIMER, RUTH (ed.) American Woman's Cookbook. 5000 easy-to-follow recipes. Color illus. Thumb index. Rev. ed. New York: Doubleday, 1946.

3274 BORDEN'S EAGLE BRAND MAGIC RECIPES. New York City, 1946.

3275 BRODY, ILES. THE COLONY. Portrait of a restaurant, and its famous recipes. Also about the people who ate there. Jarrolds: London, New York, 1946. 192p.

3276 EBERLE, IRMENGARDE. BASKETFUL. The Story of our Foods. Illustrated by Marion R. Kohs. Decorative end papers. Thomas Y. Crowell Co., New York (1946). 256p.

3277 ENGLE, FANNIE. FANNIE ENGLE'S COOK BOOK. Marketing economically, cooking well. Profusely illustrated. Essential Books, Duell, Sloan & Pearce, New York (1946). 186p.

3278 FITZSIMMONS, MURIEL & CORTLAND. You Can Cook If You Can Read. Viking Press: New York, 1946. 1st ed. 364p.

3279 HIBBEN, SHEILA. AMERICAN REGIONAL COOKERY. Original recipes for dishes from nearly every state. Little, Brown and Co.: Boston, 1946. 1st ed. 354p.

3280 KAISER, CLIFFORD ALLEN. GROUP FEEDING. Nutrition guide for Institutions. McGraw-Hill; New York, 1946. 1st ed. 490p.

3281 LA PRADE, MALCOLM. That Man in the Kitchen. Illus. by Robert Ferguson. Boston: Houghton Mifflin: 1946. 1st ed. 244p.

3282 LEONARD, LAURA KITTNER AND CROSBY, RUTH WALKER. THE GARLAND COOKBOOK. From the graduates of Simmons College. Illustrated. Chester R. Heck, New York, 1946. 176p.

3283 LINDLAHR, VICTOR H. Eat—And Reduce! Illus. New York, 1946. 194p.

3284 MALONE, DOROTHY. HOW MAMA COULD COOK. Biography with humor and delicious recipes. Drawings. A. A. Wyn, New York, 1946. 178p.

3285 MOFFATT, ALEX. W. THE GALLEY GUIDE. Supplies, lists, recipes, menus. Yachting, Inc., New York, 1946. 181p.

3286 SCHLINK, F. J. AND PHILIPS, M. C. MEAT THREE TIMES A DAY. Importance of meat in the diet. Facsimiles of old menus, as illustrations. Richard R. Smith, New York, 1946. Spec. ed. 194p.

3287 STANDARD, STELLA. MORE THAN COOKING. Recipes and Menus. Illus. by Fritz Kredel. Vanguard Press, Inc. New York, 1946. 1st ed. 275p.

3288 STANDEN, NIKA. REMINISCENCE AND RAVIOLI. (See Foreign sec.)

3289 TRADER VIC'S BOOK OF FOOD & DRINK. Intro. by Lucius Beebe. Col. illus. New York, 1946. 1st ed. 272p.

3290 WALLACE, LILY HAXWORTH. JUST FOR TWO. A Handbook of Cookery for the Small Household. M. Barrows: New York, 1946. 311p.

3291 WHITE, MARION. ICE CREAM DIETS. Menus and some ways to prepare low calory food. M. S. Mill: New York, 1946. 58p.

3292 WHITE, MAX. HOW I FEED MY FRIENDS. 100 Sunday Night Dishes. New York, 1946. 167p.

3293 WOODWARD, ELIZABETH. Let's Have a Party. Illus. New York, 1946. 122p.

3294 BOTSFORD, HARRY. Fish and Game Cook Book. New York, 1947. 1st ed. 290p.

3295 BROWN, BARBARA. SOUR CREAM COOKERY. M. Barrows, New York, 1947. 1st ed. 250p.

3296 CARROLL, LEONE RUTLEDGE. PRESSURE COOKERY. How to cook with any type of pressure pan. Illustrated by Jan Freeman. Spiral binding. M. Barrows: New York, 1947. 171p.

3297 COOMBS, ANNA OLSSON. Modern Swedish Cookbook. (See Foreign sec.)

3298 DE GOUY, LOUIS P. The Gold Cook Book. Intro. by Oscar of the Waldorf. New York: Greenberg (1947). 1098p. Port.

3299 DE GOUY, LOUIS P. Gourmet Cook Book of Fish and Game. Vol. I. Only fish recipes. New York, 1947. 240p.

3300 DE WOLFE, ELSIE (Lady Mendl) (autographed) Recipes for Successful Dining. Menus and Recipes. Illus. The William-Frederick Press: New York, 1947. 3rd ed. Privately Printed. 102p.

3301 GAIGE, CROSBY. MACARONI MANUAL with 200 Main Dish, Soup, Salad and Dessert Recipes, and 50 Sauces. M. Barrows: New York, 1947. 192p.

3302 HALL, WILLIAM. THE CARE AND FEEDING OF PARENTS. Illus. New York, 1947. 1st ed. 118p.

3303 KROPOTKIN, ALEXANDRA. How To Cook and Eat in Russian. (See Foreign sec.)

3304 LAVERTY, MAURA. Maura Laverty's Cook Book. (See Foreign sec.)

3305 McCUE, LILLIAN BUENO AND TRUAX, CAROL. THE 60 MINUTE CHEF. Menus, even party meals, prepared in 60 minutes or less. Macmillan Co., New York, 1947. 1st ed. 222p.

3306 MACDOUGALL, ALLEN ROSS.

AND THE GREEKS. (See Foreign sec.)

3307 OWEN, JEANNE. The Lejon Cook Book. Pict. wraps—color plates, New York, 1947. 64p.

3308 PRATT, FLETCHER AND BAILEY, ROBESON. A MAN AND HIS MEALS. A cook book without recipes. Drawings by Inga. Henry Holt: New York (1947). 1st ed. 252p.

3309 PRENTICE, E. PARMALEE. Progress: An Episode in the History of Hunger. Important culinary Americana in text & pics. Beautifully produced on coated paper. Privately printed, New York, 1947. 189p.

3310 RICHARDSON, ALICE WILSON. Just a Minute, a Book of Quick Cookery. Illus. Spiral bdg., soft cover. Procyon Press; New York (1947). 151p.

3311 RORTY, JAMES AND NORMAN, N. PHILIP, MD. TOMORROW'S FOOD. The Coming Revolution in Nutrition. Foreword by Stuart Chase. Prentice-Hall, Inc., New York, 1947. 1st ed. 258p.

3312 ALLEN, IDA BAILEY. Cook Book. Sensible economies. Permabooks, New York (1948). 274p.

3313 BRILLAT-SAVARIN, JEAN ANTHELME. THE PHYSIOLOGY OF TASTE. (See Foreign sec.)

3314 DANA, ROBERT W. WHERE TO EAT IN NEW YORK. From the Admiral to Zoe Chase. Drawings by Bill Pause. Current Books: New York, 1948. 1st ed. 240p.

3315 DE KNIGHT, FREDA (PRESENTATION COPY) A DATE WITH A DISH. American Negro Recipes—non-regional. Foreword by Gertrude Blair. Drawings by S. Lodico. Hermitage Press, New York, 1948, 1st ed. 426p.

3316 THE ECONOMY COOK BOOK. Compiled by the Staff of the Research Kitchen. The Journal of Living, New York, 1948. 128p.

3317 ELISOFON, ELIOT. Food is a Four Letter Word. Intr. by Gypsy Rose Lee. New York, 1948. 175p.

3318 FENWICK, MILLICENT. VOGUE'S BOOK OF ETIQUETTE. A complete guide to traditional forms and modern usage: manners, ceremonies, weddings, entertaining, clothes. Simon & Schuster, New York, 1948. 658p.

3319 FOOD GUIDE TO BETTER HEALTH. Compiled by the Staff of the Journal of Living. The Journal of Living, New York, 1948. 122p.

3320 LO PINTO, MARIA & MILORADOVICH, MILO. The Art of Italian Cooking. (See Foreign sec.)

3321 MACKALL, LAWTON. KNIFE AND FORK IN NEW YORK. Where To Eat—What To Order. McBride; New York, 1948. 1st ed. 249p.

3322 MARIL, LEE. CRACK AND CRUNCH. Nuts in Fact and Fancy. New York, 1948. 1st ed. 64p.

3323 PELLEGRINI, ANGELO M. THE UNPREJUDICED PALATE. Cooking, philosophy and literature. New

York, 1948. 1st ed. 235p. Macmillan Co.

3324 SIMON, ANDRÉ. FRENCH COOK BOOK. (See Foreign sec.)

3325 SIMPSON, JEAN I. PH.D., AND TAYLOR, DEMETRIA M., A.M. with the technical cooperation of The Frozen Food Foundation . . . The Frozen Food Cook Book. A complete guide to the preparation, cooking & preservation of frozen foods. Recipes, charts, lists & menus New York: Simon & Schuster (1948). 1st ed. 493p.

3326 WELCH, MARY SCOTT. Your First Hundred Meals. A how-to book for new home-makers. Unusual. Every meal complete on one page. New York. Scribner's, 1948. 200p. spiral bdg.

3327 ARFMANN, FLORENCE (Compiled by) THE TIME READER'S BOOK OF RECIPES. Illustrations by Erdoes. Dutton, New York, 1949. 1st ed. 252p.

3328 BATCHELDER, ANN. Ann Batchelder's Cookbook. 500 recipes from her Ladies' Home Journal pages. New York: M. Barrows, 1949. 312p.

3329 BEARD, JAMES A. THE FIRESIDE COOK BOOK. For Beginner and Expert; 1217 recipes and 400 color pictures. Illustrations by Alice & Martin Provensen. Decorative end papers. Simon & Schuster, New York, 1949. 1st ed. 322p.

3330 THE BROWN DERBY COOKBOOK. The story of the Brown Derby, its specialties and recipes. Foreword by Robert H. Cobb. Introduction by Marjorie Child Husted. Doubleday; New York, 1949. 1st ed. 272p.

3331 CAMPBELL, JEAN HAMILTON; KAMERAN, GLORIA. SIMPLE COOKING FOR THE EPICURE. Special recipes simplified to a reasonable point. Viking: New York, 1949. 1st ed. 204p.

3332 CHAO, BUWEI YANG. How To Cook and Eat In Chinese. New York, 1949. (see Foreign sec.)

3333 CONASON, EMIL G., MD. AND METZ, ELLA. THE SALT-FREE DIET COOK BOOK. Lear; New York, 1949. 144p.

3334 COOMBS, ANNA OLSSON. THE SMORGASBORD COOKBOOK. (See Foreign sec.)

3335 DE GOUY, LOUIS P. THE PIE BOOK. Technical data, pastry and pie recipes, chiffon pies and topping and glazing. By a Master Chef. Greenberg; New York, 1949. 1st ed. 380p.

3336 DE GOUY, LOUIS P. THE SOUP BOOK. General information, hot and cold soups and consommes, clear and cream soups. Their garnishes. By a Master Chef. Greenberg; New York, 1949. 1st ed. 414p.

3337 ESQUIRE'S HANDBOOK FOR HOSTS. Cooking with a flair. Illustrated by L. J. Allen plus some Esquire drawings and girls. Colored end papers. Grosset & Dunlap, New York, 1949. 288p.

3338 GAIGE, CROSBY. DINING WITH MY FRIENDS. Adventures with Epicures. Menus and recipes, and the people who contribute them. Crown: New York (1949). 1st ed. 292p.

3339 HILL, AMELIA LEAVITT. The Complete Book of Table Setting, Service, Etiquette, Flower Arrangement, Recipes. Handsome illustrations. Greystone: New York (1949). 288p.

3340 JONES, RUSSELL K.; NORTON, C. MCKIM. The Cruising Cookbook. Easy-to-cook meals on a two-burner stove. W. W. Norton: New York, 1949. 302p.

3341 KIRKLAND, ALEXANDER—ASSISTED BY SHAFFER, MURIEL. Title: RECTOR'S NAUGHTY '90s COOKBOOK. More than 400 tantalizing recipes; Embellished with Anecdote and Gossip. Decorations by Bob Cato. Gay end papers. Photographs of personalities of the period. Doubleday & Co., Inc., Garden City, N. Y., 1949. 1st ed. 247p.

3342 THE MYSTERY CHEF (John MacPherson) Never Fail Cook Book. The Mystery Chef: New York, 1949. 190p.

3343 NEWELL, TAYLOR. The New Century Cook Book. Illus. New York, 1949. 1st ed. 595p.

3344 OPERATION VITTLES. From Aviation Operations Magazine. Photos by courtesy of U. S. Armed Forces. Conover-Mast Publications: New York, 1949. 110p.

3345 PADDLEFORD, CLEMENTINE. HOW AMERICA EATS. Best recipes of 1949. Selected and tested by the author. Wraps. United Newspapers Magazine Corp. New York, 1949. 21p.

3346 PARKER, ELINOR. COOKING FOR ONE. A godsend for those who live alone and like to cook. Thomas Y. Crowell, New York, 1949. 122p.

3347 POPE, ANTOINETTE & FRANCOIS. Antoinette Pope School Candy Book. Photos. New York, 1949. 1st ed. 112p.

3348 SIMON, ANDRÉ L. A Dictionary of Gastronomy. Compiled by the President of the Wine and Food Society of London. Farrar, Straus & Co.: New York, 1949. 264p.

3349 THE TIME READERS BOOK OF RECIPES. Illus. New York, 1949. 1st ed. 252p.

3350 TRACY, MARIAN. Cooking Under Pressure. Decorations by Julian Brazelton. Varied recipes & new uses for the pressure cooker. Boards. Viking Press, New York, 1949. 160p.

3351 TURGEON, CHARLOTTE (translated & adapted by). TANTE MARIE'S FRENCH KITCHEN. (See Foreign sec.)

3352 WEST, BETTY M. Diabetic Menus, Meals and Recipes. Intro. by Russel F. Rypins, MD. Chief, Diabetic Clinic, Mt. Zion Hospital, San Francisco. Doubleday & Co., Garden City, N.Y., 1949. 254p.

3353 WONG, RICHARD. Enjoy Chinese Cooking at Home. (See Foreign sec.)

3354 ADAMS, CHARLOTTE. HOME ENTERTAINING. A Complete guide to party-giving; including dinner parties, outdoor fireplace parties; for people of all ages; what to eat and what to wear. Decorations by Margaret Jervis. Crown, New York, 1950. 1st ed. 443p.

3355 BEROLZHEIMER, RUTH (editor). American Woman's Cook Book. Contains 5000 easy-to-follow recipes. Thumb-indexed. 230 half-tones, many in color. New York: Garden City Books, Doubleday & Co., 1950. New and rev. ed. 856p.

3356 BONI, ADA. THE TALISMAN ITALIAN COOK BOOK. (See Foreign sec.)

3357 BOTHWELL, JEAN. Onions Without Tears. A collection of Intriguing Recipes. From the Egyptians to now. Illustrations by Mararet Ayer; decorative end papers with "measures." Hastings House: New York (1950). 1st ed. 166p.

3358 BROBECK, FLORENCE. Chafing Dish Cookery. 200 recipes to cook at the table. Menus. 7th printing. New York: M. Barrows, 1950. 222p.

3359 EARLY, ELEANOR (autographed) NEW YORK HOLIDAY. All about New York, including things to eat. Rinehart & Co.: New York (1950). 1st ed. 376p.

3360 FOLSOM, ANNE. THE CARE AND TRAINING OF HUSBANDS. Food and drink among many household illus. Pict. bds. New York (1950).

3361 THE FORD TREASURY OF FAVORITE RECIPES FROM FAMOUS EATING PLACES. Through the Pennsylvania Dutch country, to antebellum mansions in the old South, through the Ozarks, across Texas to the Pacific shores. Compiled by Nancy Kennedy. Art Dir. Arthur Lougee. Simon & Schuster, New York, 1950. 252p.

3362 GOURMET COOK BOOK. Recipes from all parts of the world, 2300 of them. Pen and ink vignettes by Henry Stalhut. New York: Gourmet, 1950. Beautiful col. illus.

3363 GROSS, LOUISE HABERBUSH. MEATS, POULTRY AND GAME. Funk & Wagnalls, New York, 1950. 1st ed. 299p.

3364 THE HOLIDAY COOK BOOK. Charming holiday drawings by Vee Guthrie—in color. Peter Pauper Press, New York, 1950. 61p.

3365 KNOPF, MILDRED O. THE PERFECT HOSTESS COOK BOOK. With an introduction by June Platt. Design and Decorations by Warren Chappell and Fritz Kredel. Knopf, New York, 1950. 1st ed. 498p. xxii Index.

3366 MACAULEY, CAMILLE. Eating Together. A cookbook for diabetics and their families. Foreword by Solomon Strouse, M.D. Farrar, Straus; New York (1950). 1st ed. 419p.

3367 MILORADOVICH, MILO. The Art of Cooking with Herbs and Spices: A Handbook of Cooking with Herbs and Spices. New York: Doubleday & Co., 1950. 304p.

3368 MULVEY, RUTH WATT AND ALVAREZ, LUISA MARIA. GOOD FOOD FROM MEXICO. (See Foreign sec.)

3369 MUNRO, D. C., MD. You Can Live Longer Than You Think. In favor of meat eating for a long life. New York, 1950. 211p.

3370 NEARING, HELEN & SCOTT. The Maple Sugar Book. Account of the Art of Sugaring. New York, 1950. 271p.

3370a PILLSBURY, ANN. Baking Book. New York: Pocket Books, 1950. 372p. and ads.

3371 POLLIO, ALBERT. RICOTTA AND MOZZARELLA RECIPE BOOK. (See Foreign sec.)

3372 SARA, DOROTHY. A Primer for Hostesses. A shortcut to effective entertaining for the newlywed or busy career woman. New York: M. Barrows, 1950. 128p.

3373 SERANNE, ANN. The Complete Book of Home Baking. Encyclopedic coverage. New York: Doubleday & Co., 1950. 386p. illus.

3374 TEAGUE, RUTH MILLS. COOKING FOR COMPANY. Colored illustrations. Published by Random House, New York, 1950; 1st printing. 309p.

3375 TURGEON, CHARLOTTE. COOKING FOR CHRISTMAS. Menus and recipes for every course, including the cup that cheers. Decorations by the Strimbans. Oxford University Press: New York, 1950. 1st ed. 116p.

3376 WHEELER, ELMER. FAT BOY'S BOOK. How Elmer lost 40 lbs. in 80 days. Illustrations by Carl Rose. Wraps. Avon Publishing Co., New York, 1950. 127p.

3377 WRIGHTNOUR, ELEANOR. Basic Guide to Good Cooking. A Practical Handbook. Illus. Grosset & Dunlap; New York (1950). 96p.

3378 BARBER, EDITH M. The Party Sampler. With actual samples of cake ornaments inside front cover. Sterling Pub.: New York, 1951. 63p.

3379 BROWN: CORA, ROSE AND BOB. THE EUROPEAN COOKBOOK. The Four-in-One Book of Continental Cookery: Italy, Spain, Portugal, France. Prentice-Hall, Inc., New York (1951). 418p.

3380 BURTON, KATHERINE AND RIPPERGER, HELMUT. FEAST DAY COOKBOOK. Describing the traditional feast day dishes of many lands. David McKay Co.: New York, 1951. 194p.

3381 DAVIS, ADELLE. Let's Cook It Right. Good health comes from good cooking. More than 350 basic recipes, and delicious variations. New York: Harcourt, Brace, 1951. 626p.

3382 DE BOTH, JESSIE. It's Easy To Be A Good Cook. General help with ideas to make simple dishes unusually delicious. Recipes. Garden City Books: Garden City, New York (1951). 1st ed. 254p.

3383 DE GOUY, LOUIS P. The Oyster Book. Illus. New York, 1951. 1st ed. 175p.

3384 Essipoff, Marie Armstrong. Making the Most of Your Food Freezer. New ideas, new techniques, new recipes. Illustrations. Rinehart & Co.: New York, 1951. 1st ed. 310p.

3385 Firuski, Elvia and Maurice (Edited by) The Best of Boulestin. (See Foreign sec.)

3386 Flexner, Marion. Quick Cooking from the Top of the Stove. Over 1000 time saving recipes. Wraps. Illus. New York, 1951. 144p.

3387 Fredericks, Carlton. Eat, Live and Be Merry Nutrition. A fortnight of meals with recipes. Drawings. Wraps. Paxton-Slade; New York (1951). 112p.

3388 Gofman, Helen F. and Others. The Low Fat, Low Cholesterol Diet: What To Eat and How To Prepare It. Doubleday & Co., New York, 1951. 371p.

3389 Hauser, Gayelord. Look Younger, Live Longer. Practical advice about a way of life—diet suggestions. Farrar, Straus & Young: New York (1951). 335p.

3390 Hibben, Sheila and Jordan, Sara M. Good Food For Bad Stomachs: 500 Delicious and Nutritious Recipes for Sufferers from Ulcer and other Digestive Disturbances. Introduction by Harold W. Ross. New York: Doubleday & Co., 1951. 255p.

3391 Holberg, Ruth Langland. The Buffet Cookbook. Crowell: New York (1951). 214p.

3392 James, Rian. Dining in New York. Suggestions & cautions & recipes. John Day: New York (1951). 266p.

3393 Koten, Bernard. The Low Calory Cookbook. Non-fattening recipes for people who love good food. Foreword by Dr. Donald B. Armstrong. Random House, New York (1951). 1st ed. 253p.

3394 Lincoln, Miriam, MD. Danger! Curves Ahead! How To Prevent and Correct Overweight. Many photos. New York, 1951. 138p.

3395 Lynes, Russell. Guests, or How To Survive Hospitality. Illus. New York, 1951. 80p.

3396 Post, Edwin M. Director, The Emily Post Institute. The Emily Post Cookbook. A handsomely printed and presented book of recipes from a famous hostess. For cook-less epicures. Colored end papers. Designed and illustrated by Marshall Lee. Funk & Wagnalls, New York, 1951. 1st ed. 384p.

3397 Rhode, Irma. Cookbook for Fridays and Lent. Eggs, vegetables, fish. Introduction by Robert I. Gannon, S.J. McKay; New York, 1951. 1st ed. 187p.

3398 Robbins, Ann Roe. 100 Meat-Saving Recipes. Most take only a short time to prepare. Economical meals. Thomas Y. Crowell: New York (1951). 116p.

3399 Sachs, Hilda. So Your Child Won't Eat! Diet, How To Prepare and Serve Food to Children. General Hints. With a special section on Psychological Problems by Dr. Samuel Karelitz. Illus. with drawings. Sterling Publishing Co.: New York (1951). 61p.

3400 SCHOONMAKER, FRANK. Dictionary of Wines. Edited by Tom Marvel. Illus. by Oscar Fabrès. Hastings House, New York (1951). 1st ed. 120p.

3401 SCHWARTZ, ESTHER K. WITH RUTH KOOPERMAN. THE HAMBURGER COOK BOOK. 200 distinctive ways of using ground beef to achieve greater variety in the daily menu. Abelard: New York, 1951. 213p.

3402 STANDARD, STELLA. Whole Grain Cookery. Nearly 500 recipes, all tasty and nutritious, made from varied grains, some enhanced by herbs. Sesame candy. New York: The John Day Co., 1951.

3403 TRACY, MARIAN. MORE CASSEROLE COOKERY. "150 Brand-New Recipes" demonstrating the growing versatility of the casserole. Spiral binding—Decorations by Marguerite Burgess. Viking: New York, 1951. 160p.

3404 201 TASTY DISHES FOR REDUCERS. Including the famous Victor H. Lindlahr 7-day reducing diet. The Journal of Living, New York, 1951. 128p.

3405 VESTER, KELLY G. HOSPITALITY: A TWENTIETH-CENTURY FRONTIER. A Manual for Restaurant Owners. Illus. Exposition Press: New York (1951). 112p.

3406 WENKER, MARY ALBERT. The Art of Serving Food Attractively. Suitable garnishes for every type of food. New York: Doubleday & Co., 1951. 190p. illus.

3407 THE WORLD'S FAVORITE RECIPES. From the United Nations. Bds. with flags in colors. New York, 1951. 1st ed. 59p.

3408 ALLEN, IDA BAILEY. SOLVING THE HIGH COST OF EATING. A cookbook to live by. Farrar, Straus & Young, Inc.: New York, 1952. 545p.

3409 ALLEN, IDA BAILEY. STEP-BY-STEP PICTURE COOK BOOK. New York: Grosset & Dunlap (1952). 247p. Illus.

3410 BEAN, RUTH. All-in-one Oven Meals. Time-saving, work-saving menus, with over 350 recipes. New York: M. Barrows, 1952. 224p.

3411 BERTHOLLE, LOUISETTE; BECK, SIMONE; RIPPERGER, HELMUT. WHAT'S COOKING IN FRANCE. (See Foreign sec.)

3412 BONOMO, JOE. CALORIE COUNTER AND CONTROL GUIDE. A program for reducing including 21 days of balanced eating. Wraps. Bonomo Culture Institute, New York, 1952. 64p.

3413 BOUTELL, ZELLA. The Home Freezer Book for Better Living. All the ways to make your freezer help you. Viking Press: New York, 1952. 448p.

3414 BROBECK, FLORENCE. Cooking with Curry. (See Foreign sec.)

3415 BROBECK, FLORENCE. The Good Salad Book. 347 salads, with a special health and reducing section. Dressings, too. New York: M. Barrows, 1952. 192p.

3416 CHAN, SOU. The House Of Chan Cookbook. (See Foreign sec.)

3417 DANIELS, BEBE; ALLGOOD, JILL. THE COMPLETE BOOK OF SALADS. 282 recipes, including favorites of famous people. Prentice-Hall, Inc., New York, 1952.

3418 DE FLOREZ, CARLOS. Candlelight and Cookery—Remembrances and Recipes. Bond Wheelwright: New York (1952). 177p.

3419 DENIS, PAUL. CELEBRITY COOKBOOK. Favorite recipes of famous people. With photographs. Rockport Press, Inc.: New York, 1952. 94p.

3420 DISHES MEN LIKE. Pamphlet. Illus. Pub. by Lea & Perrins: New York, 1952. 64p.

3421 "ELSIE" (with the aid of Harry Botsford) Elsie's Cook Book. Tested Recipes of Every Variety by Elsie the Cow. Bond Wheelwright Co., N. Y., 1952. Wraps. 374p.

3422 FISH COOK BOOK. From the Institute. Wraps. Color illustrations. GOOD HOUSEKEEPING INSTITUTE, New York, 1952. 40p.

3423 HEARTMAN, CHARLES F. (Compiled by) CUISINE D'AMOUR, A COOK BOOK FOR LOVERS. In part the Squire of Baudricourt's cuisine; and a modern adaptation of nearly 200 historical recipes from many countries. Limited edition reprint, 1952. Boar's Head Books, New York. 184p. and Bibliography.

3424 HOLIDAY BOOK OF FOOD AND DRINK. Illus. Originally the chapters in this book were food features in Holiday Magazine. New York, 1952. 341p.

3425 HONG, WALLACE YU. The Chinese Cook Book. (See Foreign sec.)

3426 IRWIN, WILLIAM WALLACE. The Garrulous Gourmet. (See Foreign sec.)

3427 JOLLIFFE, NORMAN, MD. Reduce & Stay Reduced. Illus. Simon & Schuster: New York, 1952. 1st ed. 235p.

3428 JONES, IDWAL. CHEF'S HOLIDAY. A mixture of food and adventure and humor. Illustrated by Roger Duvoisin. Longmans, Green: New York, 1952. 210p.

3429 LOEB, ROBERT H. JR. SHE COOKS TO CONQUER. Chatty writing of recipes. Illustrated by Laura Jean Allen. Wilfred Funk, Inc., New York (1952). 121p.

3430 LO PINTO, MARIA. The Art of Making Italian Desserts. (See Foreign sec.)

3431 MACLAREN, HALE AND AXE, EMERSON WIRT. BE YOUR OWN GUEST. Once a Week Cooking; a section on Wines. Houghton Mifflin Co., Boston, 1952. 1st ed. 178p.

3432 METZELTHIN. THE AVON IMPROVED COOK BOOK & PRACTICAL

GUIDE TO PRESSURE COOKING. Wraps. New York, 1952. 255p.

3433 MILORADOVICH, MILO. Home Garden Book of Herbs and Spices. Growing, preparing and preserving all culinary herbs and spices in your garden or kitchen. Endpapers. New York: Doubleday & Co., 1952.

3434 MITCHELL, LEONARD JAN. Luchow's German Cookbook. (See Foreign sec.)

3435 MITCHELL, MARGOT FINLETTER. THE BUSY GIRLS' COOKBOOK. For girls who like to be hospitable. Easy recipes. Pictures by Alanson. Decorative cover and end papers. Coward-McCann, New York, 1952. 84p.

3436 1000 RECIPE COOK BOOK. Illus. Wraps. New York, 1952. 98p.

3437 OWEN, JEANNE. Book of Sauces. Tantalizing tricks to make a specialty of the simplest dish. New York: M. Barrows, 1952. 4th printing. 160p.

3438 PARKER, ELINOR. Entertaining Single handed, a Book of Easy Dinners. New York, 1952. 120p.

3439 PEPPER, BEVERLY. The Glamour Magazine After Five Cookbook. Over 300 menus, 1000 different dishes to be prepared—easily and quickly. New York: Doubleday & Co., 1952. 258p. illus.

3440 PILLSBURY, ANN. 300 PILLSBURY PRIZE RECIPES. Every recipe from a contest winner. Paperback book. Dell: New York, 1952. 383p.

3441 POPE, A. & F. A COOK'S QUIZ. New York, 1952.

3442 SHOUER, LOUELLA G. QUICK AND EASY MEALS FOR TWO. Index. Illus. Henry Holt: New York, 1952. 288p.

3443 SIDON, ALICE. CONTINENTAL DESSERT DELICACIES. 200 desserts, European heirlooms. M. Barrows: New York (1952). 186p.

3444 STEGNER, MABEL. Electric Blender Recipes. Save time, and produce easier meals. 3rd printing. New York: M. Barrows, 1952. 224p.

3445 TRACY, MARIAN. The East-West Book of Rice Cookery. 150 international recipes for using rice in varied dishes. Viking Press: New York, 1952. 160p.

3446 TRACY, MARIAN (Selected by) FAVORITE REGIONAL RECIPES OF AMERICA. Coast to Coast cookery. Collected by America's Food Editors. Grosset & Dunlap: New York, 1952. 318p.

3447 WOODY, ELIZABETH. Cook Book. From McCall's Magazine Staff. Wraps. Pocket Books, New York (1952). 376p.

3448 ADAMS, CHARLOTTE. HOUSEKEEPING AFTER OFFICE HOURS. Includes marketing, food planning & preparation. Harper: New York (1953). 1st ed. 210p.

3449 ANDERS, NEDDA CASSON. Complete Cookbook for Infrared Broiler and Rotisserie. Mouth watering recipes, and instructions for care and use of appliance. Illus. 5th printing. New York: M. Barrows, 1953. 224p.

3450 BEROLZHEIMER, RUTH (edited by) BOND BREAD COOK BOOK. Pamphlet. Illus. New York, 1953. 22p.

3451 BEST RECIPES OF 1953. Illus. New York, 1953. 124p.

3452 BOURGAIZE. One Pot Cookery. Spiral bdg. New York, 1953. 126p.

3453 BOUTELL, ZELLA. The Christmas Cook Book. Over 500 recipes to help make your Christmas meals, as well as everyday ones, festive. Viking Press: New York, 1953.

3454 CANNON, POPPY. The Can-Opener Cookbook. Tells all about the very best ways to use cans and openers. New York: Crowell (1953). 281p.

3455 COOKIE COOK BOOK. From 'Today's Woman.' Wraps. Many pl., one in color. New York, 1953. 144p.

3456 DAVENPORT, JONATHAN. WEIGHT REDUCING HANDBOOK. A common-sense program for losing weight easily and safely. Wraps. Illus. Fenwick Publishing Co., New York, 1953. 94p.

3457 GARRISON, LOUIS. DELICIOUS SEAFOOD RECIPES. Crowell, New York, 1953. 1st ed. 204p.

3458 GIVEN, META. The Modern Family Cookbook. Easy recipes, menus, shopping advice, money-saving tips. New York: Garden City Books, Doubleday, 1953. 640p. illus.

3459 HILL; RADCLIFFE. FOOD TO MAKE YOU FAMOUS. A Book of Elegant Cookery. New York 1953, 1st ed. 310p.

3460 HOGNER, D. C. Herbs From The Garden To The Table. Illus. by Nils Hogner. Modern gardening and cooking with overtones of romance and tradition. New York: Oxford University Press, 1953. 236p.

3461 LAPOLLA, GARIBALDI M. Italian Cooking for the American Kitchen. (See Foreign sec.)

3462 LAPOLLA, GARIBALDI M. The Mushroom Cook Book. (See Foreign sec.)

3463 101 CAKES. Recipes compiled from The American Home Magazine. Spiral bdg. Charts of preparation time, vitamin and calory content. New York: Doubleday & Co., 1953. Illus. Index.

3464 101 CASSEROLES. Recipes from The American Home Magazine. Spiral bdg. Charts: preparation time, vitamin and calory content. New York: Doubleday & Co., 1953. Illus. Index.

3465 101 MEATS. Recipes from The American Home Magazine. Spiral bdg. Charts of preparation time, vitamin and calorie content. New York: Doubleday & Co., 1953. Illus. Index.

3466 101 PIES. Recipes from The American Home Magazine. Spiral bdg. Charts of preparation time, vitamin and calorie content. New York: Doubleday & Co., 1953. Illus. Index.

3467 101 QUICKIES. Recipes from The American Home Magazine.

Spiral bdg. Charts of preparation time, vitamin and calory content. New York: Doubleday & Co., 1953. Illus. Index.

3468 101 SALADS. Recipes from The American Home Magazine. Spiral bdg. Charts of preparation time, vitamin and calorie content. New York: Doubleday & Co., 1953. Illus. Index.

3469 PIERCY, CAROLINE B. THE SHAKER COOK BOOK. Not by Bread Alone. Collected time-tested Shaker recipes; plus the heart-warming "old fashioned" ideas about food. Gen'l ed., Charlotte Adams. Illustrated by Virginia Filson Walsh. Eastern States map as end papers. Crown Publishers: New York, 1953. 1st ed. 283p.

3470 PLATT, JUNE AND KERR, SOPHIE. THE BEST I EVER ATE. Recipes by June Platt and Reading by Sophie Kerr. Rinehart, New York, 1953. 234p.

3471 POLLIO, ALBERT. RICOTTA AND MOZZARELLA RECIPE BOOK. (See Foreign sec.)

3472 SARDI, VINCENT, SR.; GEHMAN, RICHARD. Sardi's (signed presentation). The story of a famous restaurant. Henry Holt, New York (1953). 1st ed. 244p.

3473 SERANNE, ANN. Your Home Freezer. Definitive book. New York: Doubleday & Co., 1953. 222p. illus.

3474 SIMON, ANDRÉ: FOOD. In "Pleasures of Life Series," New York, 1953. Col. plates. 272p.

3475 SMALL, MARVIN. REDUCE WITH THE LOW CALORIE DIET. A new kind of cook book and instant calorie counter. Wraps. Pocket Books, New York, 1953. 221p.

3476 WECHSBERG, JOSEPH. Blue Trout & Black Truffles. The Peregrinations of An Epicure. An armchair guide to good eating. Illus. Knopf, New York, 1953. 304p.

3477 WHEELER, ELMER. THE FAT BOY'S CALORIE GUIDE. Reduce while you eat. Wraps. Avon Periodicals, New York, 1953. 64p.

3478 ADAMS, CHARLOTTE. Easter Idea Book. Ideas, recipes, menus, gifts. Color frontis., photos, drawings. New York: M. Barrows, 1954. 192p.

3479 ANCESTRAL RECIPES OF SHEN MEI LON. (See Foreign sec.)

3480 BEARD, JIM. Jim Beard's Complete book of barbecue & rotisserie cooking. Magazine format. Illus. and decorations. New York: Maco Magazine Corp., 1954. 144p.

3481 BEARD, JIM. THE COMPLETE COOKBOOK FOR ENTERTAINING. Menus for everything, and recipes. Drawings by H. Rosenbaum. Bobbs-Merrill: New York, 1954. 144p.

3482 BEARD, JAMES A. AND AARON, SAM. HOW TO EAT BETTER FOR LESS MONEY. Dine, wine and entertain like a gourmet, on a budget. Appleton-Century-Crofts, New York, 1954. 317p.

3483 BENNETT, PAUL POGANY AND CLARK, VELMA R. The Art of

Hungarian Cooking. Mrs. Bennett, a native Hungarian, offers 222 tested recipes. 16 drawings by Willy Pogany. New York: Doubleday & Co., 1954. 223p.

3484 CANNON, POPPY. THE BRIDE'S COOKBOOK. Recipes arranged with serving ideas. Dedicated to her husband, Walter White. Illustrations by Byron Goto. Henry Holt: New York (1954). 1st ed. 400p.

3485 CARTER, GERMAINE. The Home Book of French Cookery. (See Foreign sec.)

3486 DE GOUY, LOUIS P. The Master Chef's Best. Appetizers, Snacks, Punches and Cocktails. For parties. Wraps. Harian Publications, Greenlawn, N.Y. (1954). 173p.

3487 ESCOFFIER, A. The Escoffier Cook Book. (See Foreign sec.)

3488 KIENE, JULIA. Electric Fryer-Cooker Recipes. Recipes and menus for the new appliance that does most any kind of cooking at the flick of a switch. New York: M. Barrows, 1954. 256p.

3489 KOTKIN, LEONID, MD. Eat, Think and Be Slender. Figuring things right. Wraps. Imperial Books, New York, 1954. 188p.

3490 LEONARD, LEAH W. JEWISH COOKERY. (See Foreign sec.)

3491 MCCARROLL, MARION CLYDE. SUMMER COOKBOOK. Hot and cold dishes, food for picnics, barbecues, week end guests. Barrows, New York (1954). 1st ed. 188p.

3492 MCCARTHY, MARGUERITE GILBERT. THE QUEEN IS IN THE KITCHEN. 500 new recipes. Scribner's: New York, 1954. 232p.

3493 MANN, GERTRUDE. Apple Cooking. New York: Coward-McCann Inc.: 1954. 92p.

3494 THE SECOND FORD TREASURY OF FAVORITE RECIPES FROM FAMOUS EATING PLACES. Recipes tested by the Women's City Club of Detroit. Collected from Maine to California. Compiled by Nancy Kennedy. Art Director, Arthur Lougee. Simon & Schuster, New York, 1954. 253p.

3495 TURGEON, CHARLOTTE (trans.) Tante Marie's French Pastry. (See Foreign sec.)

3496 WALDO, MYRA. THE COMPLETE ROUND-THE-WORLD COOKBOOK. Recipes gathered by Pan American World Airways from the 84 countries they serve. Illustrations. Doubleday & Co.: New York, 1954. 480p.

3497 WALLACE, LILY HAXWORTH. THE AMERICAN FAMILY COOK BOOK. Everything for the kitchen stove. Decorative end papers. Books: New York, 1954. 831p.

3498 WASON, BETTY. DINNERS THAT WAIT. Leisurely service when you have guests. Exotic foods. Line Drawings by Margot Tomes. Colored end papers. Doubleday: New York, 1954. 1st ed. 216p.

3499 WEISER, FRANCIS X. THE EASTER BOOK. Customs and food. Illus. by Robert Frankenberg. Harcourt, Brace: New York (1954). 1st ed. 224p.

3500 ABBOTT, ANITA. Magic Half Hour Dinners. Menus, shopping lists, recipes. Wraps. Harian Publications, Greenlawn, New York. (1955). 128p.

3501 ANDORS, LISA; ABBOTT, ANITA. SIMPLE MASTERPIECES OF FRENCH COOKING. (See Foreign sec.)

3502 BAKER, IVAN. COMPLETE VEGETARIAN RECIPE BOOK. Plants in all their glory. Citadel Press: New York, 1955. 1st ed. 168p.

3503 BEARD, JIM. THE COMPLETE CASSEROLE COOKBOOK. Illus. with step-by-step photographs and amplified by herb & spice list and wine chart. Bobbs-Merrill, New York, 1955.

3504 BETTER HOMES & GARDENS JUNIOR COOK BOOK. 6 sections of recipes with illus. drawings. For children old enough to read. Meredith: New York, 1955.

3505 BLANCH, LESLIE. Around the World in Eighty Dishes. For Children 10 and up. From 30 different countries. Harper: New York, 1955.

3506 BROWN, BOB. THE COMPLETE BOOK OF CHEESE. Descriptions and history, anecdotes and recipes. Introduction by Clifton Fadiman. Illus. by Eric Blegvad. Random House, New York (1955). 1st ed. 316p.

3507 BROWN, HELEN EVANS AND BEARD, JAMES A. The Complete Book of Outdoor Cookery. If it can be cooked over charcoal, indoors or out, this book tells how. New York: Doubleday & Co., 1955. 255p. illus. Index.

3508 BRUNNER, LOUSENE ROUSSEAU. Magic With Leftovers. From canapes to desserts. 300 recipes. Harper: New York, 1955.

3508a CATANZARO, ANGELA. Mama Mia Italian Cookbook. (See Foreign sec.)

3509 CONRAD, MARIAN L. Allergy Cooking. Over 600 recipes and menus for all types of allergies. Crowell: New York, 1955.

3510 DINGLE, JOHN. International Chef. An autobiography. New York, 1955. 1st ed. 253p.

3511 ELKON, JULIETTE. The Honey Cookbook. More than 250 recipes, some from early Egypt. Alfred A. Knopf, New York, 1955. 1st ed. 159p. & xii Index.

3512 FLEXNER, MARION W. Cocktail-Supper Cookbook. For the new American meal, the keynote is informality. The menus and recipes will delight any gourmet. New York: M. Barrows, 1955. 256p.

3513 GIVEN, META. Meta Given's Modern Encyclopedia of Cooking. This revised edition has thousands of recipes, time and money-saving ideas, plus 365 daily menus. Two vol. New York: Garden City Books, Doubleday & Co., 1955. 1502p. illus.

3514 GRIFFITH, CORINNE. Eggs I

Have Known. A movie star's collection of recipes of famous people. New York, 1955. 230p.

3515 HOLBERG, RUTH LANGLAND. THE BUFFET COOKBOOK, enlarged edition. Thomas Y. Crowell, New York, 1955. 276p.

3516 KAUFMAN, WILLIAM I., Editor. COOKING WITH THE EXPERTS. Published by Random House, New York, 1955. 1st ed. 248p. plus Brief Biographies of TV's Best Cooks.

3517 KEYES, FRANCES PARKINSON. THE FRANCES PARKINSON KEYES COOKBOOK. From New England, through Washington, to the South and the World. Illustrations, photographs. Decorative end papers—drawings. Doubleday: New York, 1955. 1st ed. 322p.

3518 LAKLAN, CARLI AND FREDERICK, THOMAS. Gifts From Your Kitchen. Wonderful recipes, each with its own clever packaging idea. Photos and sketches. New York: M. Barrows, 1955. 256p.

3519 LEDERMAN. The Slim Gourmet. New York, 1955. 240p.

3520 LEONARD, LEAH W. The Jewish Holiday Cook Book. (See Foreign sec.)

3522 MURPHY, AGNES. THE AMERICAN EVERYDAY COOKBOOK. Menus, charts, and time tested recipes. Colored end papers with charts. Random House: New York (1955). 1898 recipes. 20p. charts and Index.

3523 PEPPER, BEVERLY. POTLUCK COOKERY. Illustrated by the author. Doubleday, New York, 1955. 1st ed. 284p.

3524 PREZZOLINI: Spaghetti Dinner. (See Foreign sec.)

3525 PROFITABLE FOOD AND BEVERAGE OPERATION. Edited by Joseph Brodner, CPA; Howard M. Carlson, CPA; Henry T. Maschal, CPA. Management guide. With charts and illustrations. Ahrens: New York, 1955. 424p.

3526 RUDOMIN, ESTHER. Let's Cook Without Cooking. For children 6-10 yrs. Recipes in clear, big print. No cooking. Crowell: New York, 1955.

3527 SCHULER, ELIZBETH. German Cookery (Mein Kochbuch). (See Foreign sec.)

3528 SERANNE, ANN. The Complete Book of Home Preserving. Over 100 ways of canning, jelly making, pickling, brining, smoking, freezing, etc. New York: Doubleday & Co., 1955. 384p. illus.

3529 SPECIALTY OF THE HOUSE. 100 favorite recipes from 100 famous cooks. Decorative end papers—with signatures of cooks. Florence Crittenton League: New York, 1955. Col. pictorial boards. 116p.

3530 TAGLIENTE, MARIA LUISA. ITALIAN COOKBOOK. (See Foreign sec.)

3531 TAYLOR, MARIAN YOUNG (MARTHA DEANE) COOKING FOR COMPLIMENTS. 600 fascinating recipes—with the gourmet touch. Drawings by Mary Anna Winkler. M. Barrows, New York, 1955. 312p.

3532 TRACY, MARIAN. THE PEASANT COOKBOOK. Dishes from 39 foreign countries adapted to American tastes. Illustrations by Marguerite Burgess. Hanover House, New York, 1955. 1st ed. 224p.

3533 TROUP, LORIS. THE TASTING SPOON. A seasoning guide for spices, herbs, condiments etc. Citadel Press: New York, 1955.

3534 ADAMS, CHARLOTTE. EAT-WELL DIET BOOK. Diets for every weight. Over 200 tempting recipes. Cover Ektachromes by Joe Long. Inside drawings by Ralph Stein. Random House, New York (1956). 128p.

3535 AVENELL, VICTOR M. DE SABROSO. (See Foreign sec.)

3536 BARR, STRINGFELLOW; STANDARD, STELLA. The Kitchen Garden Book: Vegetables from Seed to Table. How to raise 32 vegetables, and surprising, delicious ways to serve them. Viking Press: New York, 1956. 384p. and Index.

3537 BEARD, JAMES. The Summer Food and Drink Portfolio. Reprint from Gentry magazine. New York: Sherry Wine & Spirits Co., Inc., 1956. G pages.

3538 CHAMBERLAIN, NARCISSA. The Omelette Book. All you would want to know about the omelette —with over 300 recipes. New York: Alfred A. Knopf, 1956. 192p.

3539 CULINARY ARTS INSTITUTE (compilers). The American Peoples Cookbook. America's best cooks and their prize-winning recipes. 1000 photographs, drawings and color plates. New York: Hanover House, 1956. 600p.

3540 DE PRATZ, CLAIRE. FRENCH HOME COOKING. (See Foreign sec.)

3541 FAVORITE RECIPES FROM THE UNITED NATIONS. 170 Dishes. Illus. Plastic, col. pict. bds. New York, 1956. 96p.

3542 GANCEL'S CULINARY ENCYCLOPEDIA OF MODERN COOKING. Concise glossary. Over 8000 recipes and 300 articles. Small book, hard cover. Radio City Bookstore: New York, 1956. 507p.

3543 GRAY, PETER. The Mistress Cook. Cooking in the grand manner; to stimulate the imagination and the palate. Recipes from 12 countries and 6 centuries. New York: Oxford University Press, 1956. 352p. and decorations by Vito Giallo.

3544 KASDEN, SARA. Love and Knishes: (See Foreign sec.)

3545 KIRK, DOROTHY (editor). The Woman's Home Companion Cook Book. A reprint with new chapters on freezers, pressure cookers, child feeding, weight control, and recipes revised for modern cooking. 66 photos and drawings. New York: Garden City Books, Doubleday & Co., 1956. 951p.

3546 MUNDT, ERNEST. Birth of a

Cook, A Gastronomical Autobiography. He learned to appreciate good food the hard way—by preparing it for himself and his friends. New York: Alfred A. Knopf, 1956. 256p.

3547 Smallzried, Kathleen Ann. The Everlasting Pleasure. The enthralling history of American cooking from 1565 to 2000. Appleton—Century—Crofts, Inc., New York (1956). 1st ed. 344p.

3548 Tracy, Marian. Casserole Cookery Complete. Combined ed. of 'Casserole Cookery' and 'More Casserole Cookery' with new recipes added. Viking Press, New York, 1956. 192p. & Index.

3549 Tselementes, Nicholas. Greek Cookery. (See Foreign sec.)

3550 Waldo, Myra. The Round-The-World Cook Book. 300 unusual, easy-to-follow recipes from 84 foreign countries. Wraps. Bantam Books, New York, 1956. 230p.

3551 Allen, Ida Bailey. 159 exciting easy-do-meals with sausage. Illus. Spiral binding. Union Carbide Corp., New York, 1957. 48p.

3552 Erlanger, Baba and Pierce, Daren. The Complete Martini Cook Book. What to cook after each martini; not to be taken too seriously. It brings joy even to a bibliographer. Illustrated by Elizabeth Fraser. Spiral binding. Random Thoughts Publishing Co., New York, 1957. 32p.

3553 Gourmet's Guide to Good Eating. By the editors of Gourmet Magazine. Where to eat in the U.S.A. Simon and Schuster, New York, 1957. Wraps. 232p.

3554 Harvey, Peggy. Season to Taste. A first-rate gourmet book for the harried and hurried hostess. New York: Alfred A. Knopf, 1957. 288p.

3555 McBride, Mary Margaret. Harvest of American Cooking, a thousand selected recipes from all over the country. G. P. Putnam's Sons, New York, 1957.

3556 Pereyra De Aznar, Marina and Froud, Nina. (See Foreign sec.)

3557 Rowland, Joan. Good Food From the Near East. (See Foreign sec.)

3558 Turkish Recipes. (See Foreign sec.)

3559 Valldejuli, Carmen Aboy. The Art of Caribbean Cookery. (See Foreign sec.)

3560 Williams, Margaret. The Well-Fed Bridegroom. Recipes and ideas for the new homemaker. New York: Doubleday & Co., 1957. 192p. illus.

3561 Allen, Ida Bailey. Gastronomique. 1000-plus gourmet recipes. Line drawings. New York: Doubleday & Co., 1958. 384p.

3562 A Breakfast 'Manifesto.' The Gourmet Society. New York: Business Bourse, 1958. 28p. Plastic binding.

3563 Chamberlain, Samuel. Italian Bouquet. (See Foreign sec.)

3564 DAVID, ELIZABETH. Italian Food. (See Foreign sec.)

3565 DONOVAN, MARIA KOZSLIK. The Far Eastern Epicure. (See Foreign sec.)

3566 FLEXNER, MARION. Cooking the Smart Way. Nearly 400 delectable recipes from the author's files and world travels. New York: M. Barrows, 1958. 220p.

3567 KAIN, IDA JEAN AND GIBSON, MILDRED B. Stay Slim For Life. How to diet painlessly. New York: Doubleday & Co., 1958. 206p. illus.

3568 LASASSO, WILMA REIVA. The All-Italian Cookbook. (See Foreign sec.)

3569 OCHOROWICZ - MONATOWA, MARJO. Polish Cookery. (See Foreign sec.)

3570 PADDLEFORD, CLEMENTINE. A Flower for My Mother. A famous food editor writes about her mother and a good way of life. Food, too. New York: Henry Holt (1958). 1st ed. 64p.

3571 PHILOMÈNE. French Family Cooking in Plain English. (See Foreign sec.)

3572 PLATT, JUNE. The June Platt Cook Book. A class cook book for gourmets. New York: Alfred A. Knopf, 1958. 512p.

3573 ROOT, WAVERLEY. The Food of France. (See Foreign sec.)

3574 SIMMONS, AMELIA; AN AMERICAN ORPHAN. American Cookery. A Facsimile of the First Edition, 1796 (three known copies extant). Essay by Mary Tolford Wilson. Ltd. ed. 800. Oxford University Press, New York, 1958. 82p. Boxed.

3575 THOUGHTS FOR BUFFETS. Compiled by a group of Chicago hostesses, arranged by menu. New York: Houghton Mifflin, 1958. 424p.

3576 TOKLAS, ALICE B. Aromas and Flavors of Past and Present. With introduction and comments by Poppy Cannon. New York: Harper & Bros. (1958). 1st ed. 164p.

3577 WALDO, MYRA. BEER AND GOOD FOOD. Brighten your menus and recipes with beer & ale. End paper photographs in color. Line drawings. Doubleday & Co., New York, 1958. 1st ed. 264p.

3578 WATT, ALEXANDER. Paris Bistro Cookery. (See Foreign sec.)

3579 ADAMS, JOAN. FOODARAMA PARTY BOOK: Lavishly illus. in full color. Recipes, table settings, decorations and games. E. P. Dutton: New York, 1959. 128p.

3580 BAKER, CHARLES H., JR. The Esquire Culinary Companion. Exotic Cookery Book and exotic drinking book. A two-in-one volume. New York, Crown Publishers, 1959. 328p.

3581 BELLIN, MILDRED GROSBERG. The Jewish Cook Book. (See Foreign sec.)

3582 BEST OF THE BAKE-OFF COLLECTION. Pillsbury's Best 1000 Recipes. Cherished family favorites from all over America. New York: Grosset & Dunlap, Inc., 1959. 608p. illus. (many in col.)

3583 BROWN, HELEN EVANS AND PHILIP. The Boys' Cookbook. Sure-fire recipes. Linecuts. New York: Doubleday Junior Books, 1959. 285p.

3584 CRANWELL, JOHN PHILIPS. Fast and Fancy Cookery. Delectable dishes in a minimum of time. Linecuts. New York: Doubleday & Co., 1959. 239p.

3585 DIRECTOR, ANNE. Standard Wine Cook Book. How to Use Wine. New York: Doubleday & Co., 1959 reissue.

3586 DONON, JOSEPH. The Classic French Cuisine. (See Foreign sec.)

3587 ENCYCLOPEDIC COOKBOOK. Prepared in the Culinary Arts Institute. New, rev. ed. Photos (many in col.), thumb-index. Diagrams. New York: Grosset & Dunlap, Inc., 1959. 1100p. illus.

3588 THE FARM JOURNAL'S COUNTRY COOK BOOK. By the Editors. Delicious recipes from country kitchens. Illus. in full color. Thumb-indexed. New York: Doubleday & Co., 1959. 420p.

3589 GOLDBERG, MOLLY AND WALDO, MYRA. The Molly Goldberg Jewish Cookbook. (See Foreign sec.)

3590 KEYS, ANCEL AND MARGARET. Eat Well and Stay Well. Comprehensive study of relationship between diet, cholesterol and good health, with menus and recipes. Foreword by Dr. Paul Dudley White. New York: Doubleday and Co., 1959. 359p.

3591 KNOPF, MILDRED O. Cook, My Darling Daughter. A cook book brimful of completely new recipes and invaluable cookery secrets. New York: Alfred A. Knopf, 1959. 672p.

3592 MACKARNESS, DR. RICHARD B. Eat Fat and Grow Slim. How to lose weight on an unusual high-fat, high-protein, low carbohydrate diet. Diagrams. New York: Doubleday & Co., 1959. 165p.

3593 MATSON, RUTH A. Cooking by the Garden Calendar. How to prepare the produce of orchard and garden. New York: Doubleday & Co., 1959. 258p. Linecuts.

3594 MATSON, RUTH A. Gardening for Gourmets. How to grow and prepare fresh garden produce. Linecuts. New York: Doubleday & Co., 1959. 262p.

3595 MILORADOVICH, MILO. The Art of Fish Cookery. Over 500 taste-pleasing fish recipes. New York: Doubleday & Co., 1959 reissue.

3596 PINKERTON, KATHRENE. Cooking Afloat. The complete cruising cook book's 350 recipes that have been approved by sea appetites. Illus. by Ginnie Hofmann. New York: M. Barrows, 1959. 288p.

3597 ROOSEVELT, NICHOLAS. Good Cooking. Stresses the true essentials of good food and how to prepare it. With a credit to Bob Brown's European Cookbook. New York: Harper & Brothers (1959). 1st ed. vi, 340p.

3598 ROSEN, RUTH CHIER (edited by) RESTAURANT-TOUR. A guide to the best dining in the U. S. with a favorite recipe from each restaurant. Plastic index cards, spiral binding. Richard Rosen Associates: New York, 1959. 176p. and ads.

3599 SERANNE, ANN. The Art of Egg Cookery. The most complete collection of egg recipes. New York: Doubleday & Co., 1959. Reissue. 192p.

3600 STANDEN, NIKA. The Art of Cheese Cookery. Recipes and menus. New York: Doubleday & Co., 1959. 192p.

3601 STREET, JULIAN. Table Topics. A collection of pieces about food and wine by the noted gourmet. New York: Alfred A. Knopf, 1959. 328p.

3602 WHITE, LORETTA. The Good Egg. Over 175 recipes for leftover egg whites/or yolks. On white or yellow paper according to kind. Spiral bdg., board covers. Line decorations. New York: Rand McNally & Co., 1959. 192p.

3603 ADAMS, CHARLOTTE. The SAS World-Wide Restaurant Cookbook. Random House, N. Y., 1960. 398p.

3604 BOTAFOGO, DOLORES. The Art of Brazilian Cookery. (See Foreign sec.)

3605 BRACKEN, PEG. I Hate To Cook Book. Light-hearted, surefire recipes and menus. Delightful illustrations by Hiliary Knight. New York: Harcourt, Brace, 1960. 192p.

3606 BROWN: CORA, ROSE & BOB. The Wine Cook Book. Culinary elegance; wine in food; wine with meals. Wraps. Roving Eye Press for Bob Brown Books, New York, 1960. 462p. Paper.

3607 CAMPBELL, THORA HEGSTAD. Potluck Party Recipes. Tasty recipes by housewife, who is a home economics authority. New York: Rand McNally & Co. (Oct. 1960). 192p. and illus. by Kay Lovelace Smith.

3608 CATANZARO, ANGELA. Italian Desserts and Antipasto. (See Foreign sec.)

3609 CHAMBERLAIN, NARCISSE. The Flavor of France. (See Foreign sec.)

3610 CHANG, ISABELLE. What's Cooking at Changs'. (See Foreign sec.)

3611 CLAIBORNE, CRAIG (editor). The New York Times Cook Book. A collection of over a thousand recipes. Sections on foreign recipes; material on herbs and spices, sources for foreign ingredients; essay on wine. New York: Harper & Bros. (Nov. 1960). 736p. illus. (many in full col.)

3612 CONIL, JEAN. GASTRONOMIC TOUR DE FRANCE. (See Foreign sec.)

3613 JONES, RUSSELL K.; NORTON, C. MCKIM. The New Cruising Cookbook. A new ed. Over 350 recipes for Easy-to-Cook meals on a two-burner stove. W. W. Norton. New York, 1960.

3614 MCCUAIG, ELIZABETH BONNELL. THE HOSPITALITY COOKBOOK: Favorite Recipes from Ministers' Wives. From U. S. and Canada. Selected for usefulness in entertaining at moderate cost. E. P. Dutton: New York, 1960. 256p.

3615 THE MASTER CHEF'S OUTDOOR GRILL COOKBOOK. By the Staff of Culinary Arts Institute. More than 300 recipes; a special Hospitality Section. Grosset & Dunlap, Inc., New York, 1960. Wraps. 64p. liberally illus. in col. and in black & white.

3616 NICKERSON, DOYNE. 365 Ways To Cook Hamburger. New York: Doubleday & Co. (Oct. 1960). 144p. illus.

3616a PADDLEFORD, CLEMENTINE. How America Eats. A famous columnist visits homes and restaurants over America, and brings you the best recipes of all. New York; Scribner's, 1960. 512p. illus.

3617 TRUAX, CAROL (editor). Ladies' Home Journal Cookbook. Over 2000 superb recipes from quick and easy to adventurous and exotic, with 2 big bonus features: (1) many color illustrations, each next to the recipe it illustrates; and (2) complete chapters on Preserving & Freezing, Your Kitchen, Diet, and Menus & Manners. New York: Doubleday & Co. (Sept. 1960). 608p.

3618 VAN DER TUUK, MARIANNE GRONWALL. Swedish Cooking at Its Best. (See Foreign sec.)

3619 WALDO, MYRA. Cooking For The Freezer. Over 150 recipes that yield dinner for tonight and partly prepared dishes for future meals which need only last minute touches when taken from the freezer and reheated. New York: Doubleday & Co. (Nov. 1960). 240p.

3620 WILDMAN, FREDERICK, JR. The Spice Wheel. Choose your seasonings with the expert aid of the wheel. Just dial. New York: M. Barrows, 1960. 1st ed.

3621 WILDMAN, FREDERICK, JR. The Wine Wheel. Dial for the right wines to go with your menu. New York: M. Barrows, 1960. New edition.

3622 Woman's Day COLLECTOR'S COOKBOOK. Gourmet cooking made easy. Recipes selected from Woman's Day. With Intro. by James Beard; illus. by Joseph Low. E. P. Dutton: New York, 1960. 320p.

3623 THE EAGLE COOK BOOK and household manual of domestic and foreign recipes. Brooklyn, N.Y.: Eagle Library Pub. (19-?). 95p. and ads. Illus. Wraps.

3624 AUNT PRISCILLA. ONE HUNDRED RECEIPTS. New and original. Wraps. Rand Sea Moss Farine Co., New York City, n.d. 16p.

3625 BIG BOY BARBECUE BOOK. Shows how easy it is to cook on

spit or grill. Full col. photos, drawings and diagrams. Tantalizing recipes. Spiral. New York: Grosset & Dunlap, Inc., n.d.

3626 BURRILL, KATHARINE AND BOOTH, ANNIE M. The Amateur Cook. Illus. by Mabell Arwell. New York: Frederick A. Stokes, n.d. 296p.

3627 CHAO, BUWEI-YANG. FOOD FOR PHILOSOPHY. (See Foreign sec.)

3628 THE CONFECTIONER'S HANDBOOK. New York: Dick & Fitzgerald, n.d. 79p. Wraps.

3629 CRANBERRIES. And how to cook them—varied recipes. Booklet, wraps, colorful illustrations. Eatmore Cranberries; New York, n.d. 38p.

3630 FARMER, FANNY MERRITT. The Fanny Merritt Farmer Calendar. For every day of the year. Wraps with silk tie cord. New York: Dodge Pub. Co., n.d. Unnumbered p.

3631 GREENWICH VILLAGE GOURMET. Studio Cookery. Favorite Recipes of 100 Villagers prominent in all of the Arts. Ring binder. New York City. 127p.

3632 THE HERITAGE OF SPICES. A History. Interesting illustrations. American Spice Trade Ass'n., New York, n.d. 16p.

3633 HEWITT, EMMA CHURCHMAN. CORN PRODUCTS COOK BOOK. Wraps. Corn Products Refining Co., New York, no date. 48p.

3634 HOW TO BE A CORDIAL HOST. More drinks than food recipes. Small booklet, wraps. Canada Dry Distillers, New York, n.d. 16p.

3635 IN WELCHER STADT WOHNEN SIE? (See Foreign sec.)

3636 LEMCKE, GESINE. THE PURE COOK BOOK. Compiled by the Principal of greater New York Cooking School & pub. by Pure Baking Powder Co. Booklet. 124p.

3637 MARTYN, CHARLES. Foods and Culinary Utensils of the Ancients. Compiled from standard historical works. New York: The Caterer Publishing Co., n.d. 72p. illus.

3638 MILLER, WARREN H. THE OUTDOORSMAN'S HANDBOOK. Camp Cooking & Grub Lists. New York, nd.

3639 NEILL, E. The Everyday Cook and Receipt Book. New York: The Great American Tea Co. n.d. 315p.

3640 OVERWEIGHT AND UNDERWEIGHT. Food values—and exercise. Wraps. Metropolitan Life Insurance Co., New York, n.d. 32p.

3641 THE PRACTICAL COOK BOOK. (See Foreign sec.)

3642 QUICK TRICK COOKERY. Minute Meals and Recipes. Full page illus. in color; other illus. Wraps. American Can Co., New York, n.d. 47p.

3643 RECIPES. Booklet, Wraps. Borden's Condensed Milk Co., N.Y.C. 32p.

3644 RORER, MRS S. T. DAINTY

DESSERTS. Using Dunham's Cocoanut. Small booklet, wraps. Dunham: N.Y.C. 32p.

3645 SHERSON, ERROLL. Two Hundred Ways of Cooking Fish. A special section on the making of Fifty Succulent Sauces to serve with fish. New York: Frederick A. Stokes Co., n.d. 154p. Frontis. and illus.

3646 SNYDER, RICHARD. 27 SPECIAL CREATIONS FOR CAKE DECORATORS. Illus. New York, n.d. 32p.

3647 SOME GOOD THINGS TO BAKE. Presto Cake Flour (Self-Rising) to help you bake good cakes. New York: n.d. 40p. advertising booklet. Col. illus.

3648 SO YOU'RE GOING TO COOK. Wraps. The Home News: New York, n.d. 48p.

3649 WAFFLES. How to make them, and what to do with left-over batter. Small booklet, wraps. Illus. Brooklyn Edison Co., New York, n.d. 27p.

North Carolina

3650 MCKINNEY, EMMA AND WILLIAM. NORTH CAROLINA'S DIXIE-LAND RECIPES. A Rare Collection of Choice Southern Dishes. Pict. cover. Chicago (1922). 147p.

3651 KLAPP, RUSSELL. Guilford Wedding Bells—and homes, prepared in the interest of new homes and homemakers in Guilford County. Greensboro: R. Klapp (c. 1927). 127p. and ads.

3652 BELL, HELEN PECK & CAMPBELL. THE LIFE ABUNDANT, Containing a few suggestions for the preparation of Natural Foods. Wilmington, 1935. 142p.

3653 THE CHAPEL HILL COOK BOOK. Autographed recipes. Wraps. Compiled by The Woman's Auxiliary of the Presbyterian Church, Chapel Hill, 1935. 88p.

3654 THE SOUTHERN COOK BOOK. Fine old recipes compiled & edited by Lustig, Sondheim & Rensel. Decorations by H. Charles Kellum. Covers of wood; ring binding. The Three Mountaineers, Asheville, 1938. 48p.

3655 BROWN, MARION. Title: THE SOUTHERN COOK BOOK. 1st edition. Published by the University of North Carolina Press, Chapel Hill, 1951. 371p.

3656 ULMER, MARY (autographed) BECK, SAMUEL E. TO MAKE MY BREAD. Preparing Cherokee Foods. Illustrated with drawings by Goingback Chiltoskey. Photos of Aggie Lossiah by Juanita Wilson. Museum of the Cherokee Indian, Cherokee, 1951. 71p.

3657 MT. PLEASANT'S TREASURE OF PERSONAL RECIPES. 1st Baptist Church. Plastic bdg. Mt. Pleasant. 1952. 56p.

3658 THE PARISH PANTRY. St. Philip's Episcopal Church, Quaint illus. Spiral bdg. Durham, 1954. 280p.

3659 FAVORITE RECIPES OF THE LOWER CAPE FEAR. Ministering Circle, Wilmington, 1956. 193p. illus.

3660 PORTER, KATE HUTCHER. A LOOK INTO NEW LIFE. Cloth. Wraps. North Carolina, 1956. 70p.

3661 THE CHRIST CHURCH COOK BOOK. Autographed recipes. Illus. Pictorial wraps. Publ. by the Woman's Auxiliary of Christ Church, Raleigh, n.d. 112p.

3662 COOKING ROUND THE WORLD AND AT HOME. Autographed recipes. Pictorial wraps. Plastic spiral binding. St. Paul's Auxiliary, Monroe, n.d. 64p.

North Dakota

3663 PIKE, GRANVILLE ROSS AND CLARA J. Dining Room and Kitchen. The No. 1 Aard Cook Book. Fargo: E. A. Webb, 1889. 64p. and ads.

3664 NASH, MRS. F. B. Lessons on the Gentle Art of Cookery. Fargo: Commonwealth Publishing Co., 1892. 79p.

3665 KOOK KEYS; Containing choice recipes and menu suggestions. (Fargo:) Beta Chapter, Phi Upsilon Omicron, North Dakota Agricultural College, 1930. 71p.

3666 JUBILEE COOK BOOK. 1st Methodist Church. Plastic. Fargo, 1949. 156p.

Ohio

3667 THE HOUSEHOLD COMPANION FOR 1871. To All Housekeepers This Little Volume, Consisting of One Hundred Good Recipes, is Cordially Dedicated. Wraps. Cincinnati, 1871. 27p.

3668 PRESBYTERIAN COOK BOOK. Compiled by the ladies of the First Presbyterian Church, Dayton: Crooke & Co., 1873. 183p. Paper.

3669 FOLLETT, ELIZA G. The Young Housekeeper's Assistant. Sandusky: Register Steam Printing Establishment. 1874. 141p.

3670 PORTSMOUTH MONUMENTAL COOK BOOK. Compiled by the ladies of the Soldiers' Aid Society. Portsmouth: J. W. Newman, 1874. Signed recipes. 185p.

3671 PRACTICAL RECEIPTS OF EXPERIENCED HOUSEKEEPERS. Compiled by the ladies of the Seventh Presbyterian Church of Cincinnati. Cincinnati: no pub., 1874. 191, 6p. Paper.

3672 HAWHE, MRS. H. J. "The Eclipse," for hotel and home cooking suitable for rich and poor. Columbus: Glenn, printer, 1875. 53p.

3673 BUCKINGHAM, JANE W. THE HOUSEKEEPER'S FRIEND: A practical cook-book, compiled by a lady of Zanesville, and sold for the benefit of the Home of the Friendless. Zanesville: Sullivan & Parsons, 1876. Some recipes signed. 117p.

3674 CENTENNIAL BUCKEYE COOK BOOK. Signed recipes. Compiled by The Women of the First Congregational Church, Marysville. Shearer: Marysville, 1876. 1st ed. 384p.

3675 JERMAIN, FRANCES D. Tried and True Recipes. The home cook book, compiled from recipes contributed by ladies of Toledo and other cities: published for the joint benefit of the Home for Friendless Women and the Orphans' Home . . Toledo: T. J. Brown, Eager & Co., 1876. 304p. Autographed recipes.

3676 PRESBYTERIAN COOK BOOK. Compiled by the Ladies of the 1st Presbyterian Church. John H. Thomas, Dayton, 1876. 178p.

3677 WILCOX, ESTELLE WOODS (Anon.) Centennial Buckeye Cook Book. Compiled by the women of the First Congregational Church, Marysville, Ohio. Marysville: J. H. Shearer & Son, 1876. 384p.

3678 TRIED AND APPROVED. Buckeye Cookery and Practical Housekeeping. Compiled from original recipes. 2nd ed. Marysville, Buckeye Pub., 1877. 464p.

3679 WILCOX, ESTELLE WOODS. Buckeye Cookery and Practical Housekeeping. 2nd ed. Marysville: Buckeye Pub. Co., 1877. 464p.

3680 BROWN, FRANK M. Brown's Excelsior Recipe Book. Over 500 excellent recipes and other valuable information. Macedonia: Brown Brothers, 1878. 170p.

3681 QUINN, C. L. The Practical Recipe Book for families, confectioners and bakers. Cincinnati: Central Book Concern, 1879. 87p. Wraps.

3682 KIRKPATRICK, MRS. THOMAS JEFFERSON. Farm and Fireside Practical Cook Book. About 1000 recipes selected from 20,000. Springfield: Farm and Fireside Co., 1881. 64p. Wraps.

3683 OUR COOK IN COUNCIL. A manual of practical and economical recipes for the household. Jefferson: The Ladies of the Congregational Church, 1881. Some autographed recipes. 161p.

3684 PRESBYTERIAN COOK BOOK. Dayton: 1883. 178p.

3685 THE HUNTER SIFTER COOK BOOK. Valuable receipts and information for every housekeeper. Cincinnati: The Hunter Sifter M'f'g. Co., 1884. Wraps.

3686 PRESBYTERIAN COOK BOOK. Compiled by the Ladies of the First Presbyterian Church. 10th ed. Historical Publishing Co., Dayton, 1886. 178p.

3687 BUELL, MARIA NYE (compiler). Centennial Cookery Book. Sold for the benefit of the Woman's Centennial Association of Marietta, Ohio . . . Marietta: Times Print, 1887. 145, 16p.

3688 THE KENTON COOK-BOOK. Prepared by the Kenton Cook-Book Co. . . Kenton: W. M. Beckman (1888). 141p.

3689 PULTE, MRS. J. H. Domestic Cook Book. A practical guide in the preparation of food; useful hints for the household. Cincinnati: Geo. W. Smith, 1888. xvi, 370p.

3690 SEASON, MRS. EVA A. (compiler). The Ohio Farmer's Home Guide Book. Cleveland: The Ohio Farmer, 1888. 128p. illus.

3691 THE TRIED AND TRUE COOK BOOK. Standard Receipts compiled by The Ladies of the Miles Avenue Church of Christ. Contemporary advertisements. Cleveland, 1888. 156p.

3692 The Weekly Bee Cook Book. The largest collection of . . receipts ever embodied in one volume. Information for every housekeeper, upon every subject. Toledo: Toledo Bee Co., 1888. 277p. illus.

3693 Presbyterian Cook Book. Compiled by the Ladies of the 1st Presbyterian Church, Dayton, Ohio. F. H. Crago, Wheeling, West Va., 1889.

3694 Kirkpatrick, Mrs. T. J. (Compiled by) The Modern Cook Book. More than 1000 Recipes and Practical Suggestions to Housekeepers. Fully illus. Springfield: Mast, Crowell & Kirkpatrick (1890). 320p.

3695 The Adelaide Cook Book. By a leader of society and a most noted entertainer. Cincinnati, L. Wise & Co., 1893. 479p.

3696 Crowell, John S. (Anon.) The Standard Cook Book for practical housewives . . . Springfield: Mast, Crowell & Kirkpatrick (1894). 320p.

3697 Dayton Evening Herald Cook Book . . . Dayton: The Herald Pub. Co., 1894. 320p. illus.

3698 Recipes Tried and True. Compiled by the Ladies' Aid Society of the 1st Presbyterian Church of Marion. One contributor Mrs. Mary Dickerson (Dickerson was maiden name Pres. Harding's mother). Press of Kelley Mount, Marion, 1894. 1st ed. 181p. and ads.

3699 Kitchen Echoes. A careful compilation of tried and approved recipes. 2nd ed. Ladies of Raper M. E. Church, Dayton, 1895. 80p. and ads.

3700 The Massillon Cook Book compiled by the Ladies of St. Timothy's Parish. (Massilon: Lookout Pub., 1895). Oblong, 156p.

3701 The Canton Favorite Cook Book . . . Ladies of the First Baptist Church. Canton: Roller Print. Co. (1896). 192p.

3702 The Domestic Echoes. A Careful Collection of Tried and Approved Recipes by the Members and Friends of the Ladies' Auxiliary and King's Daughters of the W.F.M.S. of Third St. M. E. Church. Columbus, 1897. 99p. Interesting ads.

3703 The Dorcas Cookery. Local and contemporary ads. Compiled by The Ladies of Cleveland Dorcas Society. Plain Dealer Job Rooms; Cleveland, 1897. 135p.

3704 The New American Cook Book. "The Recipes in this Cook Book were contributed by more than 200 practical . . . housekeepers, Celebrated Chefs and Prominent Women." Interesting illus. Springfield (1897). 383p.

3705 Trinity Guild Cook Book. By the Ladies Guild of Trinity Church, Fostoria, Ohio. Laning Printing Co., Norwalk, 1897. 176p. and ads.

3706 Culinary Arts for All Housekeepers. Published by the ladies' Bible class (Lucius Boughton, teacher), Bowling Green, Ohio. Toledo: B. F. Wade, 1898. 136p. and ads.

3707 Neff, Isabel Howard. A Text Book of Cookery for the Use of Schools. Cincinnati: no pub., 1899. 57p.

3708 St. Paul's M. E. Church Directory 1899 and Cook Book. Many interesting ads. Includes 18p. directory of church membership. Toledo, 1899. 182p.

3709 Sargeant, Kate. 100 Receipts. — About Mushrooms. Charles Orr: Cleveland, 1899. 52p.

3710 A Cookbook from Fostoria, Ohio. Illustration of the First Presbyterian Church. Wraps . . 1904. 198p.

3711 Presbyterian Cook Book. Picture of First Presbyterian Church of Fostoria, Ohio. Ads, including one of a carriage. Review Printing Co., Fostoria, 1904. 198p.

3712 Wilson, James S. Modern Candy Making. Everything about making choice candies. Akron: Saalfield Pub., 1904. 83p. Wraps.

3713 The Association Cook Book. Compiled by the Women's Association. First Congregational Church, Cleveland, 1905. 122p. and ads.

3714 North, Abbie A. and Espey, Mary H. Harris Cook Book. Cincinnati: Press of Jennings and Graham (c. 1905). 247p.

3715 The Presidential Cook Book. Adapted from The White House Cook Book. Frontispiece: Mrs. Edith Carew Roosevelt. Illustrated. Saalfield: Akron, 1905. 440p.

3716 Youngstown Cook Book. Compiled by the Ladies of the First Presbyterian Church. The Vindicator Printing Co., Youngstown, 1905. 210p.

3717 The Best Yet Cook Book. An every day guide for the millions. Tested by Kentucky Women. Try Jeff Davis Pudding. Marietta: S. A. Mullikin (1907). Unnumbered pages. Wraps.

3718 Popular Dainties. (Findlay, 1907). Wraps. 48p.

3719 Tried and Approved Recipes. By the Epworth League of the First M.E. Church of Barnesville, Ohio. Montfort & Co., Cincinnati, 1907. 103p. and ads.

3720 Weeter, Elizabeth M. The Lutheran Cook Book. A compilation of carefully selected and tried recipes for three times every day eating. 4th ed. Newark: 1907. 110p. and ads.

3721 Cook Book Dedicated to the Public. By the Ladies of the First Presbyterian Church of East Liverpool. Jos. Betz Printing Co., East Liverpool, 1908. 156p. and ads.

3722 The Art of Home Candy Making. Illus. Wraps. Pub. by The Home Candy Makers, Canton (1909). 2nd ed. 109p.

3723 Brighton's Best Cook Book. Wraps. Ads. The M.E. Aid Society. December 1910. Brighton. 153p.

3724 DEAVER, MARGUERITE. The Christ Hospital Cook Book. A collection of tried and approved recipes. Cincinnati, Press of Jennings and Graham, 1910. 273p.

3725 LLOYD, ELLA BENTLEY. Grandma's Cook Book. A collection of tried recipes., from Portsmouth, O. Cincinnati: the author, 1910. 228p.

3726 MARTIN, MARIA EWING. Recipes from the Old Country and the New, collected and published for the benefit of the New Straitsville social and athletic club. Columbus: The F. J. Heer Printing Co., 1910. 340p. and ads.

3727 THE PEOPLE'S HOME LIBRARY. 3 practical books: home medical book by T. J. Ritter, MD.; home recipe book by Mrs. Alice G. Kirk; home stock book by W. C. Fair. Cleveland: R. C. Barnum Co., 1910. Frontis. plates, portraits. Wraps.

3728 ZELL, MARTHA PEARL. Practical Cookery . . Xenia (1910). 77p.

3729 CRAIG, SARAH E. WOODWORTH. Scientific Cooking with Scientific Methods. Cincinnati: Standard Publishing Co., 1911. 404p.

3730 THE COOK BOOK DE LUXE. Simple and elaborate recipes; party menus. Huebner-Toledo Breweries Co., Toledo (1912). 224p.

3731 THE BUCKEYE WAY COOK BOOK; a cook book with an ideal . . . Cincinnati: Powell & White (1913). 108p. illus.

3732 CAMPBELL, MATILDA G. A Textbook of Domestic Science for High Schools. The author an instructor in Home Ec., Toledo, Ohio. New York: The Macmillan Co., 1913. 219p. illus.

3733 COOK BOOK. Recipes Furnished by the Ladies of the First Congregational Church, Akron, Ohio. Oilcloth cover. Ads. Published by the 1913 December Band., Akron, 1913. 108p.

3734 LEONARD, CECILIA. The American Ladies Cook Book. Cleveland: R. Cony & Company, 1913. 496p. illus.

3735 SNYDER, SHERWOOD. A TREATISE ON FOODS. Complete List of Recipes for the Hygienic Preparation of Food Products. Menus. Health Publishing Co., Dayton, 1913. 281p.

3736 BRIGHTON'S BEST COOK BOOK. Rev. January, 1914. (See No. 3723).

3737 THE COMMUNITY COOK BOOK. Representative of the best cookery —for the average American woman. Cincinnati: Powell & White, 1914. 116p. Wraps.

3738 COOK BOOK OF TESTED RECIPES. Compiled Under Direction of The Ladies' Aid Society. Oilcloth cover. Lakewood M. E. Church, Lakewood (c. 1914). 200p.

3739 COOK BOOK OF THE WOMAN'S EDUCATIONAL CLUB. Signed recipes, local ads. Toledo, 1914. 247p.

3740 HAMILTON COOK BOOK, compiled by the women of the First Methodist Episcopal Church. Hamilton: Brown & Whitaker (1914). 343 (1)p.

3741 OUR OWN COOK BOOK. Edited by the Young Women's Guild of Pilgrim Congregational Church. Title on cover THE PILGRIM COOK BOOK. Oilcloth cover. Cleveland, 1914. 128p. and ads.

3742 SIMMS, VIRGINIA SHRIVER. Favorite Recipes of the members of the National Editorial Association. East Liverpool: J. H. Simms, 1914.

3743 VAUGHN, KATE BREW. Culinary Echoes from Dixie. McDonald Press: Cincinnati (1914). 270p.

3744 GOOD THINGS TO EAT . . . Ladies' Aid Society of the High Street United Brethren Church . . . Dayton: The Otterbein Press (1915). 79p. Cover-title: The Housekeeper's Companion. Ads.

3745 KNORR, ELIZABETH H. (Jessie Melch). Every Day Cook Book. Cincinnati: F. Shipman (1915). 100p.

3746 BONNÉ, JOSEPHINE. AUSTRIAN-HUNGARIAN COOKBOOK. (See Foreign sec.)

3747 THE CLEVELAND SOROSIS COOK BOOK. Autographed recipes. Oilcloth cover. Printed by W. Kneale, Cleveland, 1916. 144p. and ads.

3748 THE OTTERBEIN COOK BOOK . . . Ladies' Aid Society, Cowden Memorial United Brethren Church. Dayton: The Otterbein Press (1916). 100p. and ads.

3749 TESTED RECEIPTS. By the Women of the Seventh Presbyterian Church. Original, literary, unusual. Revised 1916. Cincinnati. 194p. and ads.

3750 GROSSMAN, MARY ELIZABETH. Mary Elizabeth's Cook Book. Columbus: The Champlin Press (1917). 120p.

3751 LIBERTY COOK BOOK. Practical contribution in the present emergency. Recipes for War Cake, Hoover Cookies, etc. Wraps. Published under the auspices of The Woman's City Club, Cincinnati, 1917-1918. 32p.

3752 PARLOA, MARIA. Canned Fruit, Preserves and Jellies. Household Methods of Preparation. Saalfield, Akron (1917). 101p.

3753 UTILIZATION OF FOOD. Recipes prepared by the Home Economics Dept., Ohio State University. Issued by Agricultural Division, Ohio Branch, Council of National Defense, Columbus: 1917. 44p. Wraps.

3754 DELICIOUS FIRELESS COOKED DISHES. Color plates. Wraps. The Toledo Cooker Co., Toledo (1918). 12p.

3755 DODDRIDGE, AMELIA. Liberty Recipes. Indianapolis Instructor of Cooking. Cincinnati: Stewart & Kidd Co., 1918. 106p.

3756 LIPPMAN, BETTY F. (Anon.) Aunt Betty's Cook Book. Cincinnati: The Bacharach Press (c. 1918). 97p.

3757 Royal Canners' Guide. A complete book of instructions on canning. Cincinnati: Royal Supply Co., 1918. 38p.

3758 The Cleveland Sorosis Cook Book. A new edition of the 1916 book by the same title. Oilcloth cover. Cleveland, 1919. Printed in Chicago: T. Rozck & Co.

3759 Gilbert, George F. The Doughboy Cook Book. 232 of the most valuable recipes, endorsed by leading chefs and medical authorities . . . Mansfield, O.: Doughboy Publishing Co. (1919). 31p.

3760 Hill, Janet McKenzie. Recipes for Everyday. Colored end papers, and illustrations. Booklet, wraps. Procter & Gamble: Cincinnati, 1919. 96p.

3761 Recipes. Dainties, salads and clever hints. Lorain: Lorain Printing (1919). 48p.

3762 Children's Mission Cook Book. (Canton:) Pub. by the Children's Mission (1920). 179p.

3763 Allen, Mrs. Ida Bailey. Golden Rule Cook Book. Menus for every day; 200 tested recipes. Illustrated. Ads. Handwritten recipes. Wraps. Citizens' Wholesale Supply Co., Columbus, 1921. 144p.

3764 Harding, Adelaide May. The Borrowings . . . Lorain: 1921. 112p. and ads. Wraps.

3765 Hill, Janet. The Whys of Cooking. Illus. Wraps. Procter & Gamble: Cincinnati, 1921. 106p.

3766 Tasty Dishes. Ads indicate date as follows: Doughboy Flour, back cover; 1st National Bank, front cover. Wraps. Ladies' Aid Society, First Methodist Episcopal Church, Findlay (c. 1921). 64p.

3767 A Feast of Good Things. Prepared by the Members of the Glad Hand and Friendship Classes of the Church School. Wraps. Goss Memorial Reformed Church, Kenmore, 1922. 286p. and ads.

3768 Fordyce, Claude. Trail Craft. Illus. Cincinnati, 1922. 202p.

3769 Hill, Janet McKenzie. Balanced Daily Diet. Wraps. Col. Illus. Procter & Gamble, Cincinnati (1922). 100p.

3770 Mother's Club Cook Book. Barnesville, 1922. 208p.

3771 Neil, Marion Harris. A Calendar of Dinners with 615 Recipes. A story of Crisco and methods of cooking. Procter & Gamble; Cincinnati, 1922. 231p.

3772 A Cook Book of Recipes. Compiled Under Direction of the Woman's Association of Plymouth Church. Local ads. Shaker Heights, circa 1923-1924. 156p.

3773 Cook Book of Tested Recipes. Oilcloth cover. Compiled by the Women of the Cleveland Heights Presbyterian Church, Cleveland, 1923. 254p.

3774 A Feast of Good Things. The Third Edition First Presbyterian Cook Book, prepared by the ladies of the Church. Wraps. Tiffin, 1923. 214p.

3775 NEIL, MARION HARRIS. MRS. NEIL'S COOKING SECRETS. Illus. Pictorial wraps. Procter & Gamble Co., Cincinnati, 1923. 128p.

3776 THE NEW PERFECTION COOK BOOK. How to operate oil cook stoves & ranges. Illustrated-wraps. Cleveland Metal Products: Cleveland, 1923. 64p.

3777 COOK BOOK OF THE TOLEDO FEDERATION OF WOMEN'S CLUBS. Ads. Wraps. Toledo, 1924. 214p.

3778 A FEW COOKING SUGGESTIONS. Illus. leaflet. Procter & Gamble, Cincinnati, 1924. 16p.

3779 COOK BOOK OF TESTED RECEIPTS. Compiled Under Direction of the Ladies' Aid Society. 10 pages of recipes which "appeared in the first Cook Book published by our Society" and headed "In Memoriam." Oilcloth cover. Lakewood M. E. Church, Lakewood (c. 1925). 255p.

3780 TESTED AND SIGNED COOKING RECIPES. Oilcloth wraps. Title on cover: Olena Parent-Teacher Cook Book. Ads. Ladies of the Olena Parent-Teacher Ass'n., Olena, 1925. 184p.

3781 SPLINT, SARAH FIELD. Smoothtop Cookery with gas the modern fuel. The author, of McCall Magazine, in collaboration with C. E. Fitchen, Home Economics Dir. Cleveland, Standard Gas Equipment Corp. (1926). 63p. and ads. Wraps.

3782 WILLIAMS, HELEN W. Cook Book, published by the Cincinnati Business Women's Club—tested and recommended recipes. Cincinnati (1926). 96p. and ads.

3783 THE BOOK OF 1000 RECIPES. Compiled by the Parish Guild of St. Paul's Episcopal Church. Oilcloth cover. Norwalk, 1927. 312p. and ads.

3784 BRADLEY, ALICE. ELECTRIC REFRIGERATOR MENUS AND RECIPES. Prepared especially for the General Electric Refrigerator by the Principal of Miss Farmer's School of Cookery. Illustrated—color prints. General Electric; Cleveland, 1927. 144p.

3785 BRIGODE, LOUISA. French Recipes . . . (See Foreign sec.)

3786 DEBOTH, JESSIE M. FROZEN DESSERTS AND SALADS MADE IN FRIGIDAIRE. Wraps. Color illus. Frigidaire Corp., Dayton, 1927. 48p.

3787 DEFENSIVE-DIET LEAGUE OF AMERICA (International) Bulletins Nos. 1 to 60. The Spitzer, Toledo. Nov. 1924 to Oct. 1928. 480p. and 12 Index.

3788 FRIGIDAIRE RECIPES. Prepared especially for automatic refrigerators with 'cold control.' Illustrated. Frigidaire Corp. Dayton, 1928. 78p.

3789 HARTER, SUNOLIA VAUGHN. 80/20 COOK BOOK AND FOOD MANUAL. Day by day . . Meal by meal. With recipes, formulas and order of work. Charts and vitamin tables. Defensive-Diet League of America: Toledo, 1928. 211p.

3790 MELVILLE, MARTHA. Something Different To Serve. Cleveland: the author, 1928. 44p. Wraps.

3791 SPLINT, SARAH FIELD. THE ART OF COOKING AND SERVING. 549 tested recipes. Illustrated. Procter & Gamble: Cincinnati, 1928. 252p.

3792 TEMPTING KOSHER DISHES. 112 Choice Recipes. Printed in English and Jewish. Enlarged 2nd ed. Illus. Pictorial wraps. Manischewitz Co., Fine Matzo Bakers, Cincinnati, 1928. 80p.

3793 YOUNGSTOWN COOK BOOK. Akron: The Superior Print. & Lithograph Co., 1928. 269p. incl. pl. (See No. 3716).

3794 COOK BOOK. Compiled by the Junior Board. Recipes autographed. Oilcloth cover. Woman's Hospital Association, Cleveland, 1929-1930. 172p. and ads.

3795 FRIGIDAIRE RECIPES. Illustrated. Frigidaire Corp., Dayton, 1929. 92p.

3796 GOOD THINGS TO EAT. Parent-Teacher Association of Highland Avenue School. Columbus: The Association, 1929. 72p. and ads.

3797 THE LUTHERAN COOKBOOK . . compiled by the Spindler-Burnett Bible Class, First Lutheran Church, Dayton, Ohio . . . Dayton, 1929. 127p. 2nd ed., rev. and enl.

3798 TOMB, EVVA SKELTON (compiler). The Bowling Green Cook Book . . . (Bowling Green:) Printed by Wood County Democrat, 1929. 143p. and ads.

3799 DOMESTIC REVIEW. Recipes, Menus, Household Hints, Poisons and their Antidotes. Wraps. Ladies Aid Society, Howard M. E. Church. Findlay (1930 calendar). 24p. and ads.

3800 NEW DELIGHTS FROM THE KITCHEN. Prepared and tested by the Kelvinator home economics department, Detroit, Mich. Dayton: Reynolds & Reynolds (c. 1930). 64p. illus. in color. Wraps.

3801 QUINLAN, MARY ELLEN. Universal Cook Book. Rev. with Advice to the Housewife. World Syndicate Publishing Co., Cleveland, 1930. 752p. illus.

3802 THE SILENT HOSTESS TREASURE BOOK. Wraps. General Electric, Cleveland, 1930. 103p.

3803 SPLINT, SARAH FIELD. THE ART OF COOKING AND SERVING. Illustrated; color photographs. Procter & Gamble, Cincinnati, 1930. 252p.

3804 TEMPTING KOSHER DISHES. (See Foreign sec.)

3805 COOK BOOK of The Junior Board of the Woman's Hospital Association. Cleveland, 1931-1932. 173p. and ads.

3806 FRIGIDAIRE RECIPES. Wraps. Illustrated. Frigidaire Corp., Dayton, 1931. 48p.

3807 BELL, LOUISE PRICE. KITCHEN FUN. Teaches children to cook successfully. Illus. Harter Publishing: Cleveland, 1932. 1st ed. 27p.

3808 CARTER, WINIFRED S. GOOD THINGS TO EAT FROM OUT OF THE

Air. 136 tested radio recipes. Booklet: wraps. Procter & Gamble: Cincinnati, 1932. 71p.

3809 Claire, Mabel. The World's Modern Cook Book. For the Busy Woman; including a Complete Guide to Kitchen Management. Cleveland, Ohio, 1932. 416p. Illus.

3810 The Silent Hostess Treasure Book. Refrigerator foods. Illustrated. Wraps. General Electric: Cleveland, 1932. 103p.

3811 The New Art of Buying, Preserving and Preparing Foods. Cleveland: General Electric Kitchen Institute, 1933. 112p. illus. Wraps.

3812 Powell, Maude. A Cook Book for Hard Times. Columbus: the author, 1933. 44p. Mimeo.

3813 The Art of Cooking and Serving. Cincinnati: Procter & Gamble (1937). 252p.

3814 Carter, Winifred S. Cooking Hints and Tested Recipes. Illustrated leaflet. Wraps. Procter & Gamble Co., Cincinnati, 1937. 32p.

3815 The Children's Mission Cook Book. The Children's Mission, Inc., Canton (1937). 288p. and ads.

3816 The Everyday Cook Book. World Syndicate: Cleveland, 1937. 157p.

3817 The New Art of Modern Cooking. A Complete Book of Favorite Recipes and Suggested Menus. Color illus. Spiral binding. General Electric Co., Cleveland, 1937. 112p.

3818 The New Handy Cook Book. Wraps. The Women's Association of the 1st Congregational Church, Akron, 1938. 64p.

3819 Snow, Glenna. Glenna Snow's Cook Book. Home Tested Recipes by Beacon Journal Readers. Thumb index. Akron Beacon Journal Co., Akron, 1938. 396p.

3820 Cook Book. Compiled by the Housewives of Garfield-Trinity Baptist Church. Spiral binding. Cleveland (c. 1940). 123p.

3821 Fairmont Fare. Wartime in thrift time. Amusing illus. Ads. Spiral binding. Picture of Church on cover. Fairmont Church, Shaker Square (c. 1941). 336p.

3822 Gamble, Margaret Turner and Porter, Margaret Chandler. Your Food Dollar. How to Spend it Wisely. World Publishing Co., Cleveland, 1942. 279p.

3823 Wolberg, L. R., M.D. Weight Control Through Proper Diet. Cleveland, 1942. 321p.

3824 Kreps, E. Camp & Trail Methods. Outdoor Bake Oven, Camp Cooking on cover, utensils, provisions, preserving. Ill. Columbus (1944). 273p.

3825 The Art and Secrets of Chinese Cookery. (See Foreign sec.)

3826 London & Bishov. (Edited by) Complete American-Jewish Cookbook. (See Foreign sec.)

3827 London, Robert and Anne. Cocktails and Snacks. A bartender's guide and cookbook for people who entertain. World: Cleveland, 1953. 1st ed. 236p.

3828 Miladys Own Book. By the Pansy Chapter, No. 34 of the Order of the Eastern Star. Oberlin (19-?) 54p. and ads.

3829 Unity Church Choice Recipes. Cleveland (19-?).

3830 Alter, Jeannette C. Our Woman's Exchange. Xenia: The Xenia Republican Press, n.d. 156p.

3831 Cook Book. Tried Recipes, Kings Daughters, Grace Church, Ravenna. n.d. 2nd ed. 225p.

3832 Dayton Woman's Club Cook Book. Compiled by the Tea Room Committee. Wraps. Dayton Woman's Club, Dayton, n.d. 111p.

3833 Golden Rule Foods. The Golden Rule Way. Wraps. Color illus. The Citizens' Wholesale Supply Co., Columbus, n.d. 122p.

3834 The Ohio Apple Cook Book. Revised edition. Leaflet. The Ohio Apple Institute, Inc., n.d. Painesville, 8p.

3835 Presbyterian Cook Book. Compiled by the Earnest Workers Missionary Society. Number Two. Boards. Cadiz, n.d. 129p.

3836 Westinghouse Kitchen-Proved Electric Range. Recipes to help you serve better meals. Charts and illus. Mansfield, O.: Westinghouse Electric & Manufacturing Co. n.d. 140p. Spiral. Wraps.

Oklahoma

3837 Blake, Cora Bonnell (Beardslee), "Mrs. E. N. Blake." (editor) . . . Practical and Dainty Recipes; Luncheons and Dinner Giving in Woodward, Oklahoma . . . (Woodward: Press of the W. A. Pyne Prtg. Co., 1907). 106p.

3838 Horton, Mabel Marie. Home-Makers Cook Book. The author an instructor of home economics, dietitian of the U.S. Army, A.E.F. Oklahoma City, Harlow Printing Co., 1920. 196p.

3839 The Way to a Man's Heart. Tulsa Business and Professional Women's Club, Inc. (Tulsa, Okla.:) The Tulsa Business Women's Club, Inc. (1924). 273p.

3840 The Way to a Man's Heart, "Good Cooking." The Tulsa Business Women's Club, Inc. (Tulsa, Okla.:) Tulsa Business and Professional Women's Club, Inc. (1929). 403p.

3841 The Indian Cook Book. By the Indian Women's Club. Tulsa, Indian Women's Club, 1933. 18p.

3842 Smith, Dorothy W. (compiler). Kiowa Recipes, Kiowa Agency, Anadarko, 12p. mimeographed. 1934.

3843 Canning. Kerr home canning book. Kerr Glass Manufacturing Corp., San Springs, 1939. Informative, well illus. 56p. and ads. Wraps.

3844 Glasstone. The Food You Eat. A practical guide to home

nutrition. Univ. of Okla. Press, Norman, 1943. 1st ed. 277p.

3845 Favorite Recipes. Tested and approved by Readers of The Cherokee Messenger, Cherokee, n. d. 80p.

Oregon

3846 The Web-Foot Cook Book . . . San Grael Society of the First Presbyterian Church. Portland: W. B. Ayer & Co., 1885. (i) x-xv, 218p.

3847 Cook Book, A.N.W. Autographed recipes. The Artistic Needleworkers Cook Book. Wraps. Marshfield, 1905. 105p.

3848 Falls City Cook Book. 1st Presbyterian Church. Oregon City, 1907. 77p.

3849 Rose City Cook Book. Autographed recipes. Published by the Ladies' Aid Society, Sellwood Presbyterian Church. Press of Schwab Printing Co., Portland, 1908. 69p.

3850 Evening Star Grange Cook Book. Autographed recipes. Ads. Wraps. Published by Evening Star Grange; printed by Hyatt; Portland (c. 1910). 79p.

3851 The Neighborhood Cook Book. Compiled under the auspices of the Portland Section, Council of Jewish Women. Ads. Photo of The Neighborhood House. Oilcloth covers. Press of Bushong & Co., Portland (before 1913). 334p.

3852 The Portland Woman's Exchange Cook Book. Portland, 1913. 279p.

3853 The Neighborhood Cook Book . . . National Council of Jewish Women. Portland: (Press of Bushong & Co.), 1914. 329p., 1 illus. 2nd ed. Ads.

3854 Rose City Park Cook Book. Autographed recipes. Wraps. Ads. Compiled and published by Domestic Science Circle of Rose City Park Club. Portland, 1915. 58p.

3855 Chapel, Inie Gage (Aunt Prudence). An All-Western Conservation Cook Book. Items from the kitchen department of the Evening Telegram. Portland: Modern Printing & Pub. Co., 1917. 288p.

3856 Recipes—Our Friends' and Our Own. Autographed recipes, collected and compiled by the Ladies' Aid Society. Photo of the Church on title. Wraps. Wichita Evangelical Church, Milwaukie, 1924. 112p.

3857 Cook Book. Front and back pages missing, including the title page. Signed recipes. The Woman's Auxiliary to B.P.O.E. Portland (c. 1925). 254p.

3858 Cupid's Book of Good Counsel. Presented free to the Bride and Groom. Compiled and published by E. F. Kiessling & Son. Ads. Pictorial boards. Portland (c. 1925). 91p.

3859 The Mutual Improvement Club Cook Book. Signed recipes. The Ladies of Rock Creek and Muddy Creek (Oregon) 1925. 160p.

3860 Gamma Phi Beta Cook

Book. Edited by the Mother's Club of Gamma Phi Beta of Portland. Art work by Florence Hartman of Nu Chapter. Autographed recipes, giving Chapter of each contributor. Ads. Wraps. Ratelle Printing Co., Oregon (c. 1926). 200p.

3861 Thousand Tested Treats. Cook Book . . Silverton, no pub., 1929. 221p.

3862 Collins, Dean. The Cheddar Box, Vol. I. Learning about Tillamook cheese. The diary of a cheese investigator. Recipes for cheese. Colored end papers. Portland, 1933. 1st ed. 293p.

3863 The Courier Cook Book. Grants Pass: The Grants Pass Daily Courier, 1933. 168p.

3864 Longston, Jessica and Brownlow, L. Bernice. Favorite Recipes of foods we like to cook. Rev. and enl. with additions from Jeannette Cramer . . decorations by Quincy Scott. St. Helens: Mist Pub. Co., 1933. 41p. col. pl.

3865 Bernards, Celia and Hadwen, Sibylla. Good Foods for Better Health. Budgets, kitchen equipment, recipes. Bernards and Hadwen, Portland, 1934. 209p.

3866 Cook Book compiled by Home Economics Committee, Beaverton Grange. Autographed recipes. Ads. Wraps. Advertising sold and book printed by Beaverton Enterprise. Oregon, 1934. 80p.

3867 Cook Book. Compiled by Members of the Mothers' Club of Mr. Scott Assembly No. 15, Order of the Rainbow and Their Friends. Autographed recipes. Ads. Wraps. Portland, 1935. 92p.

3868 Cook Book. Autographed recipes, giving Chapter of each contributor. Ads. Pictorial wraps. Spiral plastic binding. Pub. by University of Oregon Mothers. Portland, 1938. 152p.

3869 Teachers Can Cook. Grant High School Cook Book. Sponsored and Edited by the Grant High School Faculty. Autographed recipes. Pictorial wraps. Spiral plastic binding. Portland, 1944. 97p.

3870 Cooking 'round the World and at Home. Compiled by American Legion Auxiliary, Springfield Unit No. 40 of Springfield, Oregon. Autographed recipes. Ads. Pictorial wraps. Spiral plastic binding. Springfield (1948). 63p.

3871 Trinity Cook Book. Sponsored by the Council of Women, Trinity Episcopal Church. Autographed recipes. Wraps. Spiral binding. Portland (c. 1949). 160p.

3872 Recipes from the Nile. Nydia's Autographed Book of Favorite Recipes. Spiral binding. Pictorial wraps. Ads. Illustrated. Private printing: Portland, c. 1951. 318p.

3873 Speidel, William C. Jr. You Can't Eat Mount Rainier! Illus. by Bob Cram. Binfords & Mort: Portland, 1955. 134p.

3874 Grace Church Cook Book. Autographed recipes. Portland, 268p.

3875 WOMEN OF ROTARY. Autographed recipes. Wraps. Portland. n.d. 46p. (unnumbered).

Pennsylvania

3876 MACKENZIE, COLIN. Mackenzie's Ten Thousand Receipts. New edition, carefully revised and rewritten, and containing the Improvements and Discoveries up to Date of Publication, January, 1868. By a Corps of Experts. 496p. (Pittsburgh ? Pa.)

3877 STERRITT, LAURA C. The Erie Cook Book. A large collection of recipes for domestic cookery, care of the sick, house plants, and party menus. Erie: W. P. Atkinson's Steam Printing House, 1881. 272p.

3878 PITTSBURGH TESTED RECIPES . . . Trinity Methodist Episcopal Church. Pittsburgh: Press of Stevenson & Foster, 1885. 178p. and ads.

3879 GEMS FOR THE KITCHEN . . . Young Ladies Society of Christ Church, Towanda, Pa. Towanda: Reporter-Journal Print Co., 1886. 62p.

3880 BOSSON, M. B. (Compiled by) AUNT MENA'S RECIPE BOOK. Sold for the benefit of the Baptist Orphanage, Angora. Portrait of the author—frontispiece. The National Baptist, Philadelphia, 1888. 1st ed. 209p.

3881 ELLSWORTH, MILON W. AND TINNIE. Our Society Cook Book. About 1200 tried, reliable and economical recipes . . . Harrisburg, Pennsylvanis Publishing Co., 1888. 363p. illus.

3882 THE WARREN COOK BOOK . . . Second Auxiliary Missionary Society of the Presbyterian Church. Warren: The Ledger Print, 1888. 190p.

3883 ARNOLD, MRS. M. S. (Compiled by) NINTH REG'T FAIR COOK BOOK. Autographed recipes. Wraps. Wilkes-Barre, 1889. 80p. and ads.

3884 STERLING, MARY D. The Alumnae Cookbook. Well-tested recipes for table dainties, contributed by graduates of the Girls' High and Normal School. Philadelphia: Burk & McFetridge, 1891. 83p. Wraps.

3885 THE SCOTIA. Autographed recipes by the Ladies of the Scotia Circle. Charming illustrations. First Presbyterian Church, New Castle (1895). 158p. and ads.

3886 WILLIAMSPORT COOK BOOK . . . Woman's Auxiliary of the Young Men's Christian Association. Williamsport: Scholl Bros., printers and binders, 1895. 336p.

3887 THE COOK AND THE CUPBOARD. A choice collection of recipes issued by the Ladies Auxiliary of the Oak Lane Presbyterian Church. Philadelphia: (c. 1896). 166p.

3888 SCHRAMM, HANNAH (Anon.) Deutsch-Amerikanisches Kochbuchlein. (See Foreign sec.)

3889 THE CARBONDALE COOK BOOK of tried and tested recipes prepared by the young lady workers of the Methodist Episcopal Church. Carbondale: C. R. Munn, 1898. 131p. and ads.

3890 NEGLEY, KATE EDNA. The Negley Cook Book. The author, a teacher in the McKinley School kitchen. Pittsburgh: The Index Press, 1898. 184p.

3891 SPLER, LOUISE. Valuable and Tried Receipts. Pittsburgh, Stevenson & Foster Co., 1898. 208p.

3892 KELLER, SARAH (KULP), "Mrs. J. A. Keller." The Pennsylvania German Cook Book . . . containing 560 excellent recipes . . . Alliance: (R. M. Scranton Prtg. Co., 1902). 71p. 2nd ed.

3893 THE WARREN COOK BOOK. 2nd ed. Warren: Mirror Print., 1903. 272p. (see No. 3882).

3894 TRINITY REFORMED COOK BOOK. Autographed recipes. Wraps. Wilkinsburg, 1905. 79p.

3895 COOK BOOK. Autographed recipes. Mrs. Wm. Strohecker's Class. Wraps. Lewisburg, 1906. 104p.

3896 THE JAMESTOWN COOK BOOK. Practical recipes for practical cooks. Autographed and some handwritten. Wraps. The Ladies Aid Society of the First Methodist Episcopal Church, Jamestown, 1906. 138p.

3897 THE GERMANTOWN D.A.R. COOK BOOK. The Germantown Chapter of the Daughters of the American Revolution of Pennsylvania. Germantown, 1907. 48p.

3898 GIGER, MRS. FREDERICK SIDNEY. COLONIAL RECEIPT BOOK. Celebrated Old Receipts used a century ago by Mrs. Goodfellow's Cooking School. Also Creole and Moravian receipts. Good photographs of the hospital. For Hospital of the University of Pa. Frontispiece of the Students' Ward. John C. Winston: Philadelphia, 1907. 275p.

3899 600 OPEN SECRETS IN COOKERY. Signed recipes. Ladies of St. Katharine's Guild of the Church of the Good Shepherd. Scranton, 1907. 173p.

3900 THE WARREN COOK BOOK. 3rd ed. Warren: Mirror Print, 1908. 267p. (see No. 3882).

3901 KAUFMAN, NETTIE M. (Anon.) OUR SISTERS' RECIPES. Compiled in Pittsburgh, Penna. Contributed by many kind hearts and in a worthy cause. Pittsburgh: J. A. Perley (1909). 224p.

3902 DEY, HARYOT HOLT. THE STORY OF WASHDAY. With some of Mrs. S. T. Rorer's copyrighted recipes for preserving fruits, jellies, etc. Wraps. Standard Oil Co., Pa. (c. 1910). 37p.

3903 THE '98 COOKBOOK OF TRIED AND APPROVED RECIPES (revised) Compiled by the Young Ladies' Society of the First Presbyterian Church—signed recipes. Decorative end papers. Scranton, 1910. 158p. 24p. ads.

3904 THE HOME ADVISER. Ladies' Aid Society of the Olivet Methodist Episcopal Church. New edition . . . Coatesville: The Society, 1911. 132p., front. 2nd ed.

3905 PRESBYTERIAN COOK BOOK. Thoroughly tested; some autographed. The Golden Workers' Society of the First Presbyterian Church, Sharon (1911). 220p. and ads.

3906 ROHN, JOSEPHINE TROUT (HALL), "Mrs. M. O. Rohn." Lancaster County Tested Cook Book . . . (Lititz: The Express Print. Co.), 1912. 268p.

3907 THE WARREN COOK BOOK. 4th ed. Warren: Warren Mirror Print, 1912. 262p. (see No. 3882).

3908 BOOK OF RECIPES for the Domestic Science Department of the Altoona High School. Altoona, n. pub. (1913). 85p.

3909 WALLACE, HELEN BRUCE. Historic Paxton, her days and her ways, 1722-1913. Family recipes contributed by the Woman's Aid Society of Paxton Church. Edited with historical sketches. Privately printed. Harrisburg: The Publishing House of the United Evangelical Church, 1913. 235p. Frontis, plates, plan, facsimiles.

3910 CANDY MAKING. Illus. Woman's Institute Library of Cookery, Scranton (1914).

3911 THE CHILDREN'S INDUSTRIAL HOME BENEFIT COOK BOOK. Of Priceless "Tried and Tested" Dauphin County Recipes. Illustrations of children in the Home. Local and contemporary advertising. Children's Industrial Home, Harrisburg, circa 1914. 158p.

3912 ARCHER, MARY. Belgian Relief Cook Book. Reading: Reading Eagle Co., 1915. 299p.

3913 KLEBER, MRS. L. O. (Compiled by) THE SUFFRAGE COOKBOOK. Contributors and portraits of pro-suffrage personalities. The Equal Franchise Federation of Western Pennsylvania. 1915. 244p.

3914 NICHOLS, MRS. H. S. PRENTISS (compiler & editor). The Philadelphia New Century Club Book of Recipes, contributed by members of the club. Philadelphia: The J. C. Winston Co., 1915. 255p.

3915 PRACTICAL RECIPES COOK BOOK. Compiled by the Ladies' Aid Society of St. John's Evangelical Lutheran Church, of Ogontz, Pa. Ads. Jenkintown, 1915. 124p.

3916 TESTED RECIPES . . . Ladies' Auxiliary of the Maple Avenue Hospital. (Du Bois: Printed by C. J. Bangert & Son, 1917). 213p. incl. plates. Ads.

3917 WITT, CLARA. The Rose Cross Aid Cook Book. Taught at "Beverly Hall." Authorized by R. Swinburne Clymer. Quakertown: for Kansas City Chapt. of Rose Cross Aid, 1917. 192p.

3918 TWENTIETH CENTURY CLUB WAR TIME COOK BOOK. Pittsburgh: Pierpont, Siviter, 1918. 167p. Signed recipes.

3919 WOMAN'S INSTITUTE LIBRARY OF COOKERY—No. 1. Essentials: cereals, bread, hot breads. Illustrated. Woman's Institute of Domestic Arts & Sciences: Scranton (1918). 227p. xiii index.

3920 WOMAN'S INSTITUTE LIBRARY OF COOKERY—No. 4. Salads, sandwiches, cold and frozen desserts, cakes, cookies, and puddings, pastries and pies. Illustrated. Woman's Institute of Domestic Arts and Sciences, Scranton (1918-1919). p. 245, 20 and 10 Index.

3921 WHAT WILL WE HAVE TO EAT? Reconstruction recipes. Spence Bible Class of the First Presbyterian Church. Uniontown: The Spence Bible Class (1919). 64p.

3922 CANNING, PRESERVING & JELLY MAKING. Made easy by using a canner. Small booklet, wraps. Wear-Ever Co.; Pa. (c. 1920). 23p.

3923 TESTED RECIPES. Autographed. Wraps. Guild Society of Christ's Lutheran Church of Milton, 1920. 168p.

3924 THE WARREN COOK BOOK. 5th ed. Warren: Newell Press, 1920. 299p. illus. (see No. 3882).

3925 ESSIG, MERCY RICHARDS. The Modern Club Book of Recipes, contributed by members and their interested friends . . . Philadelphia: The John C. Winston Co., 1921. 348p.

3926 HANOVER COOK BOOK. Favorite recipes compiled and published by committee of ladies from the Library Association. Hanover (1922). 283p. plates. 3rd ed. rev. and enl.

3927 FAVORITE RECIPES. (Augmented Edition) Signed recipes. The Woman's Club of York, 1923. 192p. and Ads. Wraps.

3928 THE HOUSEWIFE'S GUIDE. The Ladies of Guys Mills, Congregational Ladies Aid, Guys Mills, 1923. 98p.

3929 MOTHER'S FAVORITE COOK BOOK. Autographed recipes. Directory . . ads. Calvary Methodist Episcopal Church, Williamsport (c. 1923). 48p.

3930 ROHN, MRS. MAHLON O. MRS. ROHN'S LANCASTER COUNTY TESTED COOK BOOK. Choicest recipes from the garden spot of Pa. Wraps. Colored end papers. Private printing: Cleveland, Ohio, 1923. 286p.

3931 MARTHA WASHINGTON LOG CABIN COOK BOOK. By the Martha Washington Guild, Valley Forge, Pa. Valley Forge: The Martha Washington Guild (1924). 132p.

3932 THE OAK LANE COOK BOOK . . . All Work Together Society of the Oak Lane Baptist Church of Philadelphia, Pa. . . . (Philadelphia: Printed by Public Ledger Co., 1924). 160p. incl. front. illus.; ads.

3933 THE PUNXSUTAWNEY COOK BOOK. Tested Recipes. 4th ed. Punxsutawney, 1924. 191p.

3934 VILLAGE FAIR COOK BOOK. By the Comm. Downingtown, 1924. 107p.

3935 HUDSON, ETHEL FELDKIRCHNER. Recipes from McCann's

Cooking School. Pittsburgh: McCann & Co., Inc. (1925). 40p.

3936 WOMAN'S INSTITUTE LIBRARY OF COOKERY—No. 1. Essentials: cereals, bread, hot breads. Illus. Woman's Institute of Domestic Arts & Sciences: Scranton, 1925. 226p. and indices.

3937 WOMAN'S INSTITUTE LIBRARY OF COOKERY—No. 2. Milk, Butter, and Cheese, Eggs, Vegetables. Woman's Institute of Domestic Arts and Sciences, Scranton, 1925. 211p.

3938 WOMAN'S INSTITUTE LIBRARY OF COOKERY—No. 3. Soup, meat, poultry and game, fish and shell fish. Illustrated. Woman's Institute of Domestic Arts and Sciences, Inc., Scranton, 1925. 244p.

3939 WOMAN'S INSTITUTE LIBRARY OF COOKERY—No. 5. Fruit: desserts, canning and drying; jelly making, preserving and pickling, confections, beverages, the planning of meals. Illustrated. Woman's Institute of Domestic Arts & Sciences, Scranton, 1925. 299p.

3940 PENNSYLVANIA STATE GRANGE COOK BOOK. Autographed recipes. Penna. State Grange: Harrisburg, 1926. 168p.

3941 EVERYDAY COOK BOOK OF TESTED RECIPES. Autographed recipes. Wraps. End pages in color. Ads. Prepared by the Ladies of St. Peter's Episcopal Church, Waterford, 1927. 136p.

3942 FERNS, CATHARINE V. THE KITCHEN GUIDE. Rules and recipes. Wraps. Chester Times, Chester, 1927. 128p.

3943 WOMAN'S INSTITUTE LIBRARY OF COOKERY—No. 2. Milk, butter and cheese, eggs, vegetables. Illustrated. Woman's Institute of Domestic Arts & Sciences, Scranton, 1927. 211p.

3944 DELICIOUS PECANO RECIPES. Pulverized pecan recipes. Wraps. The Pecano Manufacturing Co., Manheim, 1928. 27p.

3945 HOME ECONOMIST. Recipes, menus, household hints. Names and addresses of committee. Wraps. First Presbyterian Church, Carbondale, 1928. 38p.

3945a HOSTESS REFERENCE BOOK. Recipes, invitations, introductions, serving. Autographs and initials of contributors. Wraps. Ladies' Aid Society, Methodist Episcopal Church. Carbondale (c. 1928). 36p. and ads.

3946 THOMAS, MRS. EDITH MAY (BERTELS). Mary at the Farm, and Book of Recipes Compiled During her Visit among the "Pennsylvania Germans" . . . 2nd ed. Harrisburg: Evangelical Press, 1928. 423p. illus. plates, ports.

3947 THE NEW CENTURY CLUB COOK BOOK. Pub. by the New Century Club, West Chester, Pa. (West Chester, 192-?). 153p. and ads.

3948 ARCADIAN COOK BOOK. Signed recipes. Compiled by the Arcadians. First Methodist Episcopal Church, Crafton (c. 1930). 71p. and ads.

3949 SILVERMAN, HARRY G. Congratulations . . Compiled, edited and copyright by the author. Altoona: (1930). 320p. and ads.

3950 Heinz Book of Meat Cookery. Wraps. Pittsburgh, 1932. 56p.

3951 Smith, Esther L. Susie's Cook Book. 1st ed. Stroudsburg: Monroe Publishing Co. (1932). 284p.

3952 Hille, Elsie Audrey. Love, Health, and the Cook Pot. 1st ed. Pittsburgh, Hille Publishing Co. (1933). 305p. illus. Col. plates, portrait.

3953 The Globe-Times Cook Book of Old-Fashioned Recipes . . . Bethlehem: Globe-Times, 1934. 104p.

3954 Old Family Recipes. From St. Martin's Parish. Autographed recipes. Woman's Auxiliary of St. Martin's Church: Radnor (1934). 71p.

3955 Things We Grow in Our Kitchens. Planned menus and recipes signed by members. Decorative end papers, drawn & designed by Dorothy Ellen and Esther Somers. Spiral binding. Fox Chapel Garden Club, Sharpsburg, 1934. 268p.

3956 Dorman, William K., and Davidow, L. S. (compilers). Pennsylvania Dutch Cook Book of Fine Old Recipes . . . Reading (1935). 48p.

3957 Au, M. Sing. The Chinese Cook Book. (See Foreign sec.)

3958 Morrow, Kay. 'Round the World Cookery. Compiled and edited by Kay Morrow, Hazel Hemminger, Pauline Dubin, S. Claire Sondheim. Decorations by H. Charles Kellum. Reading: Culinary Arts Press, 1936. 64p. illus. Wraps.

3959 Pennsylvania Dutch Cook Book. Fine old recipes made famous by the early settlers in Penna. Booklet. wraps. Illus. Culinary Arts Press. Reading, 1936. 48p.

3960 Watts, Nellie (compiler). The Cookie Book. The author, of the Extension Service, Ohio State Univ. and U. S. Dept. of Agric. Reading: Culinary Arts Press, 1936. 48p. illus. Wraps.

3961 Aurand, Ammon M. Jr. Little Known Facts About the Amish & Mennonites. Booklet, illus. Privately printed, Harrisburg, 1938. 4p. recipes.

3962 Reed, Anna Wetherill. The Philadelphia Cook Book of Town & Country. Decorations by Filby Edmunds. Barrows: N. Y. 1940. 346p. Illus.

3963 Smedley, Emma. Institution Recipes. For use in Cafeterias, Schools, Hospitals. 6th ed. rev. Private printing: Media, 1940. 360p.

3964 Smith, Esther L. The Official Menu Book of the Hay System. Introduction by William Howard Hay, M.D. Decorations, Hay System Publications, Mount Pocono (1940). 1st ed. 421p.

3965 Soya Enters the Kitchen. Soy bean recipes. Wraps. Penna. Soya Products Co., Williamsport, (1940). 32p.

3966 AGRICULTURAL ALMANAC. Wraps. John Baer's Sons, Inc., Lancaster, 1942. 32p.

3967 RODALE, ED. J.I. NATURAL BREAD. Wraps. By the Editor of 'Organic Gardening.' Emmaus, 1944. 48p.

3968 HALL, JEANNE M. AND EBNER, BELLE ANDERSON. 500 Recipes by Request. American recipes with the accent on Pennsylvania Dutch. New York: M. Barrows, 1948. 320p.

3969 HUTCHISON, RUTH. The Pennsylvania Dutch Cook Book. Harper, N.Y., 1948. 1st ed. 213p. Decorative end papers.

3970 RECIPES FROM SUSQUEHANNA VALLEY. Reproduced handwritten and autographed recipes. Compiled by St. Martha's Guild. Spiral binding. Muncy Evangelical Lutheran Church, 1948. 425p.

3971 RETTEN & THOMPSON. MANUAL OF MUSHROOM CULTURE. With recipes. Wraps. Many plates. Toughkenamon, 1948. 272p.

3972 D.A.R. COOK BOOK. Reproduced handwritten, autographed recipes. Spiral binding. The Valley Forge Committee, Valley Forge (1949). 267p. xi index.

3973 HARK, ANN. Pennsylvania German Cookery. Assisted by Preston A. Barba. Drawings by Eleanor Barba and Edward Smith. Allentown: Schlecter (1950). 258p. illus.

3974 SHOWALTER, MARY EMMA. MENNONITE COMMUNITY COOKBOOK. Favorite Family Recipes. Drawings by Naomi Nissley. Colored photographs by M. T. Brackbill. Authorized by The Mennonite Community Association, Scottdale. Published by the John C. Winston Company, Philadelphia, 1950. 1st ed. 496p.

3975 STOKES, ETHEL W. AND HUBER, MARY H. THE MAIN LINE COOK BOOK. The World's finest recipes in the Philadelphia Main Line tradition. Foreword by Joseph Hergesheimer. Colored end papers. Abelard: New York, 1950. 1st ed. 227p.

3976 THE ANNIVERSARY COOK BOOK OF THE COSMOPOLITAN CLUB OF PHILADELPHIA. Illustrations by Louise B. Gay. Spiral binding. Privately Printed, Philadelphia, 1952. 64p.

3977 MITCHELL, MARGARET. Cutco cook book. Meat & Poultry Cookery Vol. 1. Line illus. by Frank Marcello. Col. end papers. New Kensington; Cutco Div., Aluminum Cooking Utensil Co., Inc., 1956. 128p.

3978 HUTCHISON, RUTH. The New Pennsylvania Dutch Cook Book. Illus. by Tim Palmer. Some recipes from the time George Washington learned to like them at Valley Forge. End papers map. New York: Harper & Brothers (1958). 2nd ed. rev. 240p.

3979 THE BEST-EVER COOK BOOK. Autographed recipes. Compiled by the Ladies' Aid Society of the M. E. Church, Ralston. n.d. 164p. Ads.

3980 SCIENCE LEAFLETS (on cover) COOKING CLASS LEAFLETS, School district of Philadelphia. 28 leaflets —Collected and newly bound. Colored illustrations.

3981 RUSSELL, I. K. Romance of the Holes in Bread. "An introduction to the life of Louis Pasteur." Foreword by David Starr Jordan. Chemical Publishing Co., Easton, 156p.

3982 ST. JOSEPH'S HOSPITAL BENEFIT COOK BOOK. Ladies' Auxiliary, St. Joseph's Hospital. Lancaster (19-?). 184p. and ads.

Philadelphia, Penna.

3983 THE AMERICAN PRACTICAL COOKERY-BOOK. Housekeeping made easy and economical. By "a practical housekeeper." Illustrated with 50 engravings. J. W. Bradley, Philadelphia, 1861. 319p.

3984 LANDIS, CLARA S. The Improved Hygienic Cook-Book and Domestic Economizer. Philadelphia: C. S. Landis, 1864. 61p.

3985 MOSS, MARIA J. A Poetical Cook Book. Recipes preceded by verses, some quoted, others "evidently original." Philadelphia: C. Sherman, Son & Co., 1864. 144p.

3986 PETERSON'S NEW COOK BOOK; or, Useful and practical receipts for the housewife, and the uninitiated. 858 new and original receipts. Philadelphia: T. B. Peterson (c. 1864). 533p.

3987 GOODFELLOW, MRS. Mrs. Goodfellow's Cookery As It Should Be. A new manual: original receipts, domestic beverages, salting and curing meats. Wines: yeasts, bills of fare. Philadelphia; T. B. Peterson & Brothers (1865). 362p. illus.

3988 THE NATIONAL COOK BOOK. By a lady of Philadelphia. A practical housewife. Philadelphia: T. B. Peterson (1866). 301p. Paper.

3989 ALEXANDER, CHARLES W. Alexander's Family Friend. A collection of the most valuable information and recipes on every subject of everyday life. Philadelphia, C. W. Alexander (1867). 79p.

3990 PETERSON, MRS. M. E. Peterson's Preserving, Pickling & Canning Fruit Manual. Many of the recipes original from housewives of experience. Philadelphia: G. Peterson & Co., 1869. 72p.

3991 THE HOUSEHOLD TREASURE, or, The Young Housewife's Companion. Complete instructions and receipts for breakfast dishes, bread, biscuits, etc. Illus. col. engravings. Philadelphia: J. T. Huey, 1871. 158p. and ads.

3992 LEVY, ESTHER. A Cookery Book. (See Foreign sec.)

3993 MASON, MARY. The Young Housewife's Counsellor and Friend: containing directions in every department of housekeeping. Including the duties of wife and mother . . . Philadelphia: J. B. Lippincott & Co., 1871. 380p.

3994 FROST, S. ANNIE. What I Know About Cooking. A book

for families in town or in country; from the experience of old housekeepers. Carefully indexed. Philadelphia: William B. Evans & Co. (1872). 454p.

3995 LEWIS, DIO. Our Digestion: or, My Jolly Friend's Secret. Philadelphia: Geo. Maclean, 1872. 407p.

3996 LESLIE, ELIZA. Miss Leslie's New Cook Book. A complete manual of domestic cookery in all its branches. Philadelphia, T. B. Peterson & Brothers, c. 1873. 662p. illus.

3997 PAUL, SARA T. Cookery from Experience. A practical guide for housekeepers in the preparation of every day meals. More than 1000 domestic receipts. Philadelphia: Porter and Coates (1875). 338p.

3998 CHEVALIER DE RIVAZ, VICTOR. ROUND THE TABLE. Lippincott & Co., Phila., 1876. Illus. 303p.

3999 MYERS, MRS. ELLA E. THE CENTENNIAL COOK BOOK AND GENERAL GUIDE. Practical receipts: cookery, remedies, farm hints, events of last century. Illustrated. Rebound. J. B. Myers, Philadelphia, 1876. 403p.

4000 THE NATIONAL COOKERY BOOK, compiled from original receipts, for the women's centennial committees of the International Exhibition of 1876. Philadelphia: Women's Centennial Executive Committee, 1876. 357p. (copyright by Mrs. E. D. Gillespie).

4001 WESTMINSTER COOK-BOOK. Every recipe tried and proved. Philadelphia; Hollowbush & Carey, 1876. 64p.

4002 LEES-DODS, MATILDA. The Culinary Art: or, Science in the Kitchen. The author of the Kensington School of Cookery, London. Philadelphia: Enterprise Publishing Co., 1879. 64p.

4003 HOWSON, MRS. H. Home Cookery. 250 Tested Receipts. Philadelphia: Jackson Brothers, printers, 1880. 100, 3p.

4004 MYERS, ELLA E. The Home Cook and Receipt Book, and General Guide. In 3 parts: Cookery, family medicines, farming hints. Philadelphia: Burlock & Co. (1880). 320p. illus.

4005 HOWSON, MRS., H. Home Cookery. Philadelphia, 1881. (See No. 4003).

4006 WRIGHT, MRS. JULIA MCNAIR. THE COMPLETE HOME. An Encyclopaedia of Domestic Life & Affairs. The Household; some recipes, too. A volume of practical experiences popularly illustrated: engravings, and colored lithographs. J. C. McCurdy: Philadelphia, 1882. 583p.

4007 FROST, ANNIE. OUR NEW COOK BOOK AND HOUSEHOLD RECEIPTS. Carefully selected and indexed. Philadelphia: American Publishing Co., 1883. 454p.

4008 PELTZ, GEORGE A. The Latest and Best Cook Book . . Over 800 valuable recipes. Edited by a skilled corps of practical experts.

Philadelphia: The Cottage Library Publishing House, 1884. 369p. illus.

4009 RORER, MRS. SARAH TYSON (HESTON). The Queen of the Kitchen. A collection of southern cooking receipts. Peterson & Bros.: Philadelphia (1886). 412p.

4010 RORER, MRS. S. T. MRS. RORER'S PHILADELPHIA COOK BOOK. A manual of Home Economies. Principal of Philadelphia Cooking School. Frontispiece photograph of the author. Arnold: Philadelphia, 1886. 1st ed. 581p.

4011 TILTON, MRS. E. STEVENS (compiler & illustrator). Home Dissertations—Skill in Cookery & Nicety in the Appointments at Home. Good 'Gay Nineties' Americana. Quaint illus. Pict. cover. Woodman & Co., Philadelphia, 1886. 175p.

4012 WARD, ARTEMAS (Compiled by) THE GROCERS' HAND-BOOK AND DIRECTORY. Food descriptions —for the grocers shelf. Illustrated —color plates. Philadelphia Grocer Publishing Co.: Philadelphia, 1886. 305p.

4013 RORER, MRS. S. T. Canning & Preserving. Philadelphia. Arnold & Company, 1887. 69p.

4014 RORER, MRS. S. T. Hot Weather Dishes. Philadelphia, 1888. 104p.

4015 VOLLMER, WILLIAM. THE UNITED STATES COOK BOOK. (See Foreign sec.)

4016 HARLAND, MARION. House and Home. A complete cook book and housewife's guide. Philadelphia: P. W. Ziegler & Co., 1889. 516p. Frontis. portrait.

4017 CLARKE, ANNE. THE IDEAL COOKERY BOOK. Edgewood Pub. Co., Phila., 1891. 319p.

4018 PETERSON'S NATIONAL COOK BOOK. Philadelphia: T. B. Peterson (c. 1891). 301p. Paper.

4019 PORTER, MRS. M. E. The New World's Fair Cook Book and Housekeeper's Companion. Contains carefully prepared and practically tested recipes . . with things every housekeeper should know . . Philadelphia: J. E. Potter & Co. (c. 1891). 485p. illus.

4020 FULLERTON, MARY. Table, Home, and Health. The American authority upon all household and culinary topics. Health and medical department. Philadelphia: J. H. Moore & Co., 1892. 798p. Frontis. plates.

4021 ANDREWS, LUCY C. Choice Receipts. Arranged for the Gas Stove. Philadelphia: The United Gas Improvement Co., 1893. 110p.

4022 RORER, MRS. S. T. QUICK SOUPS. A little book. Arnold & Company, Philadelphia (1894). 71p.

4023 RORER, MRS. S. T. Sandwiches. A little book, well planned. Philadelphia: Arnold & Co. (1894). 72p.

4024 WRIGHT, JULIA MACNAIR. (Compiler). Ladies' Home Cook Book—with Bills of Fare by Marion Harland. Philadelphia: Manufacturers' Book Co. (1896). 532p.

4025 BROOKS, EDWARD. Course in Cooking for the Public Schools of Philadelphia. By the Supt. of Schools. Philadelphia: Buck & McFetridge Co., 1897. 111p. Wraps.

4026 COOKE, MAUDE C. Breakfast, Dinner and Supper; or, What to eat and how to prepare it . . . Philadelphia; National Publishing Co. (1897). 608p. illus. Col. frontispiece.

4027 TABLE TALK'S COOK BOOK. Practical Recipes by Leading American Authorities. Table Talk Pub. Co.: Philadelphia, 1897. 503p.

4028 JOHNSON, HELEN LOUISE. THE ENTERPRISING HOUSEKEEPER. Suggestions for breakfast, luncheon and supper. Booklet: wraps. Illustrations of appliances. Enterprise Manufacturing Co.: Philadelphia, 1898. 80p.

4029 RORER, MRS. S. T. Good Cooking. The author, of the Philadelphia Cooking School, and Culinary Editor of the Ladies' Home Journal. Philadelphia: Curtis Publishing Co.: (1898). 245p. Frontis. port. of author.

4030 RORER, MRS. S. T. MADE OVER DISHES. Preparation of palatable dishes. Arnold and Co.: Philadelphia, 1898. 78p. and ads.

4031 RORER, MRS. S. T. Bread and Breadmaking. Philadelphia (1899). 82p. & ads.

4032 JOHNSON, HELEN LOUISE. THE ENTERPRISING HOUSEKEEPER. Suggestions for breakfast, luncheon & supper. Booklet. Wraps. Enterprise Manufacturing Co., Philadelphia, 1900. 80p.

4033 REES, JENNIE DAY. The Complete Cook Book. Philadelphia: David McKay, 1900. 320, xix p.

4034 BREADS AND BISCUITS. For every day in the year. Selected from the experts. Philadelphia: George W. Jacobs, 1901. 169p. illus.

4035 HALL, H. FRANKLYN. 300 Ways To Cook and Serve Shell Fish, Terrapin, Green Turtle, etc. By Chef of Boothby Hotel Co. Philadelphia: Christian Banner Print (1901). 102p. and ads.

4036 THE PRACTICAL HOUSEKEEPER AND CYCLOPEDIA OF DOMESTIC ECONOMY . . . AND 5000 PRACTICAL RECIPES AND MAXIMS. Keeler-Raleigh, Philadelphia, 1901.

4037 365 BREAKFAST DISHES. For each and every day in the year. Selected from the experts in cooking schools and magazines. Philadelphia: George W. Jacobs, 1901. 169p. illus.

4038 RORER, SARAH TYSON. MRS. RORER'S NEW COOK BOOK. By the author of valuable works on cookery. Illustrated. Arnold and Co., Philadelphia (1902). 1st ed. 731p. and ads.

4039 365 LUNCHEON DISHES. One for every day in the year. Illus. Jacobs: Philadelphia (1902). 151p.

4040 RORER, MRS. S. T. New Ways for Oysters. A little book of specialties. Philadelphia: Arnold & Co., 1903. 57p.

4041 365 DINNER DISHES. Selected from the experts. For every day. Philadelphia: George W. Jacobs, 1903. 177p. illus.

4042 RORER, MRS. S. T. Dainties, appetizers, cocktails, cakes, desserts. Philadelphia: Arnold & Co., 1904. 90p. and cook book ads.

4043 RORER, MRS. S. T. World's Fair Souvenir Cook Book. Louisiana Purchase Exposition, St. Louis. Philadelphia: Arnold and Co. (1904). 202p.

4044 SACHSE, HELENA V. How To Cook for the Sick & Convalescent. J. B. Lippincott Co., Philadelphia, 1904. 297p.

4045 SMEDLEY, EMMA. Institution Recipes in use at The Johns Hopkins Hospital & Drexel Institute Lunch Room. Privately printed; Philadelphia, 1904. 121p.

4046 RORER, MRS. S. T. Cakes, Icings and Fillings. Arnold & Co.: Philadelphia, 1905. 98p.

4047 RORER, SARAH TYSON. MRS. RORER'S EVERY DAY MENU BOOK. Illustrations of decorated tables. Arnold and Co., Philadelphia, 1905. 1st ed. 300p.

4048 COLLING, EMILY MARIAN. POPULAR DISHES. A collection of recipes from lectures. Private printing, Penna. 1906. 175p.

4049 FRIEDENWALD, JULIUS; RUHRAH, JOHN. DIETETICS FOR NURSES. A text book for training schools. W. B. Saunders: Philadelphia, 1906. 363p. and ads.

4050 JOHNSON, HELEN LOUISE. THE ENTERPRISING HOUSEKEEPER. Suggestions for breakfast, luncheon and supper. Wraps. Enterprise Manufacturing Co., Philadelphia, 1906. 96p.

4051 SMITH, MRS. JACQUELINE HARRISON. Famous Old Receipts Used a Hundred Years and More in the Kitchens of the North and the South . . . J. C. Winston Co., Philadelphia, 1906. 331p.

4052 TABLE TALK'S ILLUSTRATED COOK BOOK. Table Talk Pub. Co.: Philadelphia, 1906. 144p.

4053 365 TASTY DISHES. A Tasty Dish for Every Day in the Year. Decorations. George W. Jacobs & Co., Philadelphia (1906). 1st ed. 213p.

4054 HARLAND, MARION. MARION HARLAND'S COOK BOOK. Home made yeast, bread sponge and breakfast breads, meats, vegetables, soups, etc. Wraps. Crawford, Philadelphia, 1907. 157p.

4055 RORER, MRS. S. T. My Best 250 Recipes. Philadelphia: Arnold and Company (1907). 162p.

4056 WILEY, HARVEY, M.D., PH. D. FOODS AND THEIR ADULTERATION. Origin, manufacture and composition of food products. Food Standards, Food Laws. Colored plates and illustrations. P. Blakiston's Son & Co., Philadelphia, 1907. 625p. and ad.

4057 RORER, MRS. S. T. Dainty Dishes For all the Year Round. Wraps—charming cover drawing.

North Brothers Mfg. Co., Philadelphia, 1908. 64p.

4058 365 Foreign Dishes. Selected, for every day in the year. Philadelphia: George Jacobs, 1908. 154p.

4059 Hogan, Louise E. How To Feed Children. A manual for mothers, nurses and physicians. 9th ed. rev. Philadelphia: J. B. Lippincott Co., 1909. 249p. illus.

4060 Spring, Helen M. and Coolidge, Catherine J. Individual Recipes in Use at Drexel Institute. Philadelphia: The Avil Printing Co., 1909. 64p.

4061 365 Orange Recipes. An Orange Recipe for Every Day in the Year. Illustrations. Decorative end papers. Jacobs: Philadelphia, 1909. 158p.

4062 365 Vegetable Dishes. A vegetable dish for every day in the year. Decorative end papers. Drawings. Jacobs: Philadelphia, 1910. 205p.

4063 Farmer, Fannie Merritt. Catering for Special Occasions with Menus & Recipes. Recipes for all the holidays. Illustrated with Half Tone Engravings of Set Tables. Decorations by Albert D. Blashfield. McKay, Philadelphia, 1911. 1st ed. 240p.

4064 O'Donnell, T. C. The Family Food. Penn. Publishing Co., Philadelphia, 1911. 261p.

4065 Fryer, J. E. The Mary Frances Cook Book or adventures among the kitchen people. Winston, Philadelphia (c. 1912).

4066 Neil, Marion Harris, M.C.A. How to Cook in Casserole Dishes. Delicious food, well served. Illustrated. McKay; Philadelphia, 1912. 1st ed. 252p.

4067 Rorer, Mrs. S. T. Many Ways for Cooking Eggs. Rev. and enl. edition. Philadelphia: Arnold & Company (1912). 101p.

4068 Smith, George Carroll. What To Eat and Why. Philadelphia: W. B. Saunders Co., 1912. 310p.

4069 Child's Recipes for Cooking and Preparing; Serving and Portion List. Philadelphia: G. F. Lasher (c. 1913). 2p. and 90 leaves. Wraps.

4070 Cramp, Helen. The Institute Cook Book. Planned for a family of four. Economical recipes. Illustrated. Some handwritten recipes. International Institute, Philadelphia (1913). 1st ed. 507p.

4071 Ferns, Catharine V. The Kitchen Guide. Philadelphia: D. De Benedictis, 1913. 191p.

4072 Lorand, Arnold. Health and Longevity through Rational Diet. Practical hints. About food substances, vegetarianism, "table d'hote" diet. Philadelphia: F. A. Davis Co., 1913. 416p.

4073 Follett, Mrs. John Dawson. Table Decorations and Delicacies; a complete hand-book for the hostess. Philadelphia: The John C. Winston Co. (1914). 121p. illus.

4074 Harbison, Edith Gwendolyn (Compiled by) Low Cost Re-

CIPES. By the Associate Editor of 'TABLE TALK MAGAZINE' Philadelphia; Jacobs, 1914. 208p.

4075 NEIL, MARION HARRIS, M.C. A. CANNING, PRESERVING AND PICKLING. By the cookery editor of the Ladies' Home Journal. Illustrations. McKay; Philadelphia, 1914. 1st ed. 284p.

4076 RORER, MRS. S. T. MRS. RORER'S PHILADELPHIA COOK BOOK. A manual of Home Economies. Arnold & Co., Philadelphia (1914). 581p. & ads.

4077 NEIL, MARION HARRIS. The Something-Different Dish. Illustrations and half the recipes appeared earlier in The Ladies' Home Journal. David McKay, Philadelphia (1915). 1st ed. 128p.

4078 FISH, ADA Z. American Red Cross Text-Book on Home Dietetics. Illus. Philadelphia: P. Blakiston's Son & Co. (1917). 118p.

4079 LOW-COST MEALS FOR HIGH-COST TIMES. Philadelphia: The New Housekeeping Dept., The Ladies' Home Journal, 1917. 32p. Wraps.

4080 LYMAN, BENJAMIN SMITH. VEGETARIAN DIET AND DISHES. Portrait of author. Philadelphia, 1917. 1st ed. 416p.

4081 POWELL, OLA. Successful Canning and Preserving. Practical handbook for schools, clubs and home use. Philadelphia: J. B. Lippincott Co., 1917. 371p. illus.

4082 RORER, S. T. Mrs. Rorer's Key to Simple Cookery. Philadelphia: Arnold and Co. (1917). 208p.

4083 STROUSE, SOLOMON AND PERRY, MAUDE A. Food for the Sick. A manual for physician and patient. The author, physician at Michael Reese Hosp., Chicago; and associate, the dietitian. Philadelphia, W. B. Saunders Company, 1917. 270p.

4084 WRIGHT, MARY M. Preserving and Pickling. 200 recipes for these and other good things. Philadelphia: Penn Pub., 1917. 168p.

4085 HITCHCOCK, NEVADA DAVIS. The Record War-time Cook Book, arranged by Mrs. Hitchcock, domestic science expert of the Philadelphia Record. Philadelphia; The Philadelphia Record (1918). 239p. illus.

4086 LIMERICK, MARGARET CLERK. Recipes and Combinations. . . . Philadelphia, The John C. Winston Co., 1918. 31p.

4087 NEIL, MARION HARRIS. The Thrift Cook Book. The author, former cookery editor "The Ladies' Home Journal." Illus. from photos. Philadelphia: David McKay (c. 1919). 373p.

4088 WILSON, MRS. MARY A. MRS. WILSON'S COOK BOOK. New recipes based on present economic conditions. Formerly Queen Victoria's cuisiniere. Frontispiece. J. B. Lippincott: Philadelphia & London (1920). 502p.

4089 RASKIN, XAVIER. French Cook Book for American Families. (See Foreign sec.)

4090 WRIGHT, MARY M. Hospitality. Recipes and Entertainment Hints for All Occasions. Philadelphia: Penn Pub., 1922. 223p.

4091 WELLMAN, MABEL THACHER. Food Planning and Preparation. A junior course in food study with a recipe book for use at home and at school. Philadelphia: J. B. Lippincott Company (1923). 334p. illus.

4092 FRIEDENWALD, JULIUS, M.D.; RUHRAH, JOHN, M.D. DIETETICS FOR NURSES. Training school handbook for nurses. Illus. W. B. Saunders: Philadelphia, 1924. 474p.

4093 WRIGHT, MARY M. Salads and Sandwiches. "Tempting dishes . . which are deliciously eatable." Philadelphia, Penn Pub., 1924. 197p.

4094 FRYER, JANE EAYRE. The Winston Cook Book. Guaranteed recipes for a family of four. Economical. Special chapters on home economics, entertaining, diet. Philadelphia: John C. Winston Co. (1926). 533p. Frontis., illus. plates.

4095 WHEELER, RUTH AND HELEN. TALKS TO NURSES ON DIETETICS AND DIETOTHERAPY. A text-book and reference. W. B. Saunders: Philadelphia, 1926. 184p.

4096 LUDY, ROBERT B. AND FUNK, JOHN CLARENCE. How To Live Longer. Illus. by Walt Huber. Verses by J. C. Funk. Philadelphia: David McKay Co. (1927). 149p.

4097 WHEELER, RUTH AND HELEN. Food and Nutrition. American Red Cross Text-Book. Frontispiece photograph. P. Blakeston's Son & Co., Philadelphia (1927). 123p.

4098 WELLS, HELEN M. FOOD AND HOW TO COOK IT. Illus. Philadelphia, National Publishing Co. (1928). 496p.

4099 CAREY, NANCY. SOUP TO NUTS. A Selection of Choice Recipes. Wraps. Illus. by C. H. Sykes. Macrea Smith Co., Philadelphia (1929). 186p.

4100 O'LEARY, IRIS PROUTY (Caroline). The Art of Cooking for Two: or Feeding Peter. Philadelphia: J. B. Lippincott Co. (1931). 206p.

4101 WOOD, BERTHA M.; WEEKS, ANNIE L. FUNDAMENTALS OF DIETETICS. A text-book for nurses and dietitians. Illus. W. B. Saunders: Philadelphia, 1932. 254p.

4102 THE COOK BOOK OF THE COSMOPOLITAN CLUB OF PHILADELPHIA (presentation by Directress). Illustrations by Louise B. Gay. Spiral binding. Privately printed: Philadelphia, 1936. 65p.

4103 RITZ, MARIE LOUISE. CESAR, HOST TO THE WORLD. Illus. Philadelphia, 1936.

4104 BARBORKA, CLIFFORD J. TREATMENT BY DIET. For physicians—method of prescribing diets. Illus. J. B. Lippincott: Philadelphia (1937). 642p.

4105 COPELAND, F. S. Mrs. Copeland's Guest Book. A book about entertaining in Washington. Philadelphia, 1937. 127p.

4106 Brown: Cora, Rose & Bob. Fish & Sea Food Cook Book. J. B. Lippincott Co., Philadelphia & N. Y. (1940). 1st ed. 349p.

4107 Diat, Louis (presentation copy) Cooking A La Ritz. Subtle and artful cooking, by a famous chef. Frontispiece photograph of the author. Lippincott, Philadelphia, 1941. 524p.

4108 Bridges, Milton Arlanden; Mattice, Marjorie R. Food and Beverage Analyses. Practical dietetics for the student doctor and nurse by the late director of medicine, Dept. Hosp., N.Y.C. Lea & Febiger, Philadelphia (1942). 344p.

4109 Robertson, Helen; MacLeod, Sarah; & Preston, Frances. What Do We Eat Now? A guide to wartime housekeeping. J. B. Lippincott: Philadelphia (1942). 370p.

4110 Diat, Louis. Home Cookbook. (See Foreign sec.)

4111 Cooper, Lenna F.; Barber, Edith M.; Mitchell, Helen S. Nutrition in Health and Disease. The work of three nutrition specialists. 128 illustrations and 4 colored plates. Lippincott: Philadelphia, 1947. 10th ed. 729p.

4112 Potter, Margaret Yardley. At Home on the Range or How to Make Friends with Your Stove. Decorative end papers. Lippincott: Philadelphia, 1947. 1st ed. 214p.

4113 Young, Chic. Soups, Salads & Sandwiches Cookbook. Recipes selected, and book illus. by the author. 277 ways to prepare attractive meals quickly. Philadelphia: McKay (1947). 1st ed. 141p.

4114 Widdifield, Hannah. Widdifield's New Cook Book. Popular and approved methods for cooking and preparing all kinds of food. T. B. Peterson and Brothers, Philadelphia (1956). 410p. and ads.

4114a Spicer, Dorothy Gladys. Feast Day Cakes from Many Lands. Folklore, recipes and song. Illus. in two col. Philadelphia: John C. Winston, 1960. 176p.

4115 Carton, Paul. Simple Vegetarian Cookery. McKay: Philadelphia, n.d.

4116 Douglas, Elizabeth. The Cake and Biscuit Book. Philadelphia: David McKay, n.d. 130p.

4117 Douglas, Elizabeth. The Pudding and Pastry Book. Philadelphia; David McKay, n.d. 170p.

4118 King, C. H. Cake Decorations and Desserts. Philadelphia, Arnold & Co., n.d. 153p.

4119 Robinson, W. Mushroom Culture. Modes of Cooking, and Edible Fungi. Illus. Philadelphia, n.d. 172p.

4120 Ukranian Cook Book. (See Foreign sec.)

4121 Yeo, Burney, M.D. Food in Health and Disease. Philadelphia, n.d. 583p.

Rhode Island

4122 Wallace, Lily Haxworth. The Rumford Complete Cook

Book. Rumford Chemical Works, Providence, 1908. 1st ed. 236p.

4123 Goold, Mary. The New England Cook Book. Newport: The Milne Printery, 1909. 180p.

4124 Recipes. Women's League 1st Baptist Church, Providence (c. 1910). 44p. and ads. Wraps.

4125 Farmer, Fannie Merritt. The Rumford Cook Book. Wraps. Rumford Chemical Works, Providence, no date (c. 1911). 48p.

4126 Wallace, Lily Haxworth. The Rumford Complete Cook Book (see No. 4122). Providence, 1926.

4127 Cakes to Cheer About. 25 recipes. Booklet, wraps. Rumford Chemical Works, R.I., 1941. 16p.

4128 Wallace, Lily Haxworth. The Rumford Complete Cook Book (See No. 4122). Providence, 1944. 36 ed.

4129 Little Compton Garden Club Cook Book. 2nd ed. Revised and enlarged. Plastic binding. R. I. 1947. 218p.

4130 Charting Your Courses. Recipes from Famous Rhode Island Eating Places. Illustrated by William Cotton Schoentzler, Edith Ballinger Price, Ruth Lepper Gardner. Published by the 20-30 group of St. George's Church, Newport. 1st ed. 1948. Spiral binding. 399p.

4131 Recipes from Padanaram Kitchens by Members of The Red Circle. Mimeo, wraps. n.p., n.d. R.I. 81p.

4132 Rhode Island's Hostess Cook Book. Both American and foreign dishes. Rhode Island Ass'n. for the Blind: Providence. Spiral binding. 160p. and ads.

4133 Second Presbyterian Church Sponsor. Favorite Recipes of 2nd Pres. Providence 9. 86p. & ads. Autographed Recipes. Wraps.

4134 Wells, Eleanor. Nationality Recipes. YWCA, Providence. 44p.

4135 Wilson, Mary A. Recipes pub. by Rumford. Booklet. Providence. 65p.

South

4136 Porter, Mrs. M. E. Mrs. Porter's New Southern Cookery Book. Carefully prepared and practically tested recipes for all kinds of plain and fancy cooking. Prince George Court-House. Porter: Philadelphia, 1871. 1st ed. 416p.

4137 Hill, Mrs. A. P., "Mrs. E. Y. Hill" . . . Mrs. Hill's New Cook Book. A system for private families in town and country especially adapted to the southern states. New and enl. ed. G. W. Dillingham Co.: New York, 1898. Illus. 416p.

4138 Knowles, Laura Thornton. Southern Recipes. Tested by the author. G. H. Doran, New York (1913). 61p.

4139 Mcculloch-Williams, Martha. Dishes and Beverages of the Old South. Principally family recipes. Decorations by Russel Crofoot. McBride Nast & Co.: New York, 1913. 1st ed. 318p.

4140 VAUGHN, KATE BREW. CULINARY ECHOES FROM DIXIE. McDonald Press, Cincinnati (1914). 1st ed. 270p. and ads.

4141 MCKINNEY, EMMA AND WILLIAM. Aunt Caroline's Dixieland Recipes. A rare collection of choice southern dishes. Gold Seal Corp.: Chicago (1922). 147p.

4142 PRETLOW, MARY DENSON (compiled by). Old Southern Receipts. R. M. McBride: New York, 1930. 228p.

4143 PATTERSON, MRS. BETTY BENTON. Mammy Lou's Cook Book. R. M. McBride: New York, 1931. 307p.

4144 LUSTIG, LILLIE S.; SONDHEIM, S. CLAIRE; RENSEL, SARAH. (Compiled and Edited by) THE SOUTHERN COOK BOOK OF FINE OLD RECIPES. Includes some of the carefully guarded secrets of southern cookery. Decorations by H. Charles Kellum. Culinary Arts: Reading, 1935. 48p.

4145 OLD DIXIE RECIPES. Southern Cook book. 322 Recipes. Booklet. Pict. cover. Reading, 1939. 48p.

4146 FLEXNER, MARION W. DIXIE DISHES. A cross section of foods from the South; good things about cooking with a charcoal brazier, and corn breads and cakes. Illustrated by C. Robert Perrin. Hale, Cushman & Flint: Boston (1941). 1st ed. 161p.

4147 SOME FAVORITE SOUTHERN RECIPES OF THE DUCHESS OF WINDSOR. With a Foreword by The Duchess of Windsor and Introduction by Mrs. Franklin Delano Roosevelt. Frontispiece, Color Photograph of the Duchess of Windsor. Scribner's; New York, 1942. 1st ed. 180p.

4148 BURDETTE, KAY (Translated from Southern Lore) COOKERY OF THE OLD SOUTH. A book on brown paper . . authentic and in keeping with early hand printed guides. Kitchen adventures in ante-bellum days. Wraps: brown paper and leather lace. No place, no date. 152p.

4149 STRATFORD HALL COOK BOOK. Recipes of the Directors and Friends of Robert E. Lee Memorial Foundation. Signed recipes of Mrs. Roosevelt, Mrs. du Pont etc. Spiral pict. bdg. n.p. n.d.

South Carolina

4150 PINCKNEY, ELIZA LUCAS. Recipe Book of 1756. A handwritten book of recipes: some printed and some reproduced. Medical and food recipes. South Carolina Society of the Colonial Dames of America, S.C. 29p.

4151 STONEY, LOUISA CHEVES SMYTHE, "Mrs. Samuel Gaillard Stoney." Carolina Rice Cook Book. Charleston: Carolina Rice Kitchen Association (1902). 91p. and ads.

4152 MILADY'S OWN BOOK. Fort Sumter Chapter of the South Carolina Division of the Children of the Confederacy. Charleston (1905?). 53p. and ads.

4153 GRAVES, CLARA N. Cookery Text Book by the director of domestic science in the YWCA of Monaghan Mills. Greenville, Peace Printing Co., 1910. 56p. Wraps.

4154 AMONG THE POTS AND PANS. Autographed recipes. Pictorial wraps, tied with cord. Pee Dee Chapter, D.A.R., Bennettsville, 1911. 64p. and ads.

4155 THE CHESTER COOK BOOK. Edited by the Ladies Aid. Wraps, tied by cord. Baptist Church, Chester (c. 1912). 112p. and ads.

4156 EUSTIS, CELESTINE. Fifty Valuable and Delicious Recipes Made with Corn Meal. Cover-title. Aiken Standard Press: Aiken, 1917. 18p.

4157 RHETT, BLANCHE S. (Compiled by) GAY, LETTIE (Edited by) 200 YEARS OF CHARLESTON COOKING. Like nothing else in the world. Introduction and explanatory matter by Helen Woodward. Illustrations. Cape & Smith: New York (1930). 1st ed. 289p.

4158 RANDLE, HELEN GERTRUDE. Feeding the Family. Health cook book. The author, assisted by J. H. Tilden, Lilian Gunter Davis, Greenville: Helen Randle Health Publications (1934). 118p.

4159 RHETT, BLANCHE S. (Compiler) and GAY, LETTIE (Editor). 200 Years of Charleston Cooking. Harrison, Smith & Robert Haas: New York, 1934. 305p. (See No. 4157).

4160 CHARLESTON RECIPES. Edited by the Junior League of Charleston. Cover by Margaret Walker. Autographed recipes. Plastic spiral binding. Pictorial wraps. Charleston (1947). 196p.

4161 CHARLESTON RECEIPTS. Collected by the Junior League of Charleston. Autographed recipes. Plastic spiral binding. Pictorial wraps with map of Charleston environs. Charleston, 1950. 308p.

4162 SOUTH CAROLINA COOK BOOK. A collection of recipes by the S. C. Council of Farm Women. Illustrated. Univ. of South Carolina: Columbia, 1954. 426p.

4163 COASTAL CAROLINA COOKING. Compiled by the Women's Auxiliary to the Ocean View Memorial Hospital, Myrtle Beach, S.C. Illustrated by Russell Henderson. Spiral binding. Walker, Evans & Cogswell, Charleston, 1958. 1st ed. 327p. ads, index.

South Dakota

4164 HISTORY AND COOK BOOK. Lady Helpers of the First Congregational Church. Gann Valley, 1924. 88, 140p. and ads.

4165 WILDER, SUSAN Z. New Meat Dishes. Extension Circular No. 268. South Dakota State College of Agric. and Mech. Arts. Brookings, 1927. 8p.

Tennessee

4166 THE HOUSEKEEPER'S FRIEND . . . The Guild of the Holy Name of Grace Church. Memphis: Degaris Prtg. Co., 1897. 145p.

4167 HUGGINS, MOLLIE. Tennessee Model Household Guide. Nashville: Publishing House, Methodist

Episcopal Church, South, 1897. 300p.

4168 The Central Baptist Cook Book . . . Dorcas Society of the Central Baptist Church, Chattanooga. n.p. (1900?). 148p. and ads.

4169 Columbia Cook Book. Issued by the Ladies Aid Society of the First Baptist Church of Columbia, Tenn. Louisville, Ky.: Press of the Bradley & Gilbert Co. (1902). 155p. 2nd ed.

4170 Lillard, Mrs. Reese. Tennessee Cook Book . . . Nashville: McQuiddy Printing Co , 1904. 294p.

4171 How We Cook in Tennessee. Compiled by the Silver Thimble Society of the First Baptist Church. Jackson, 1906. 316p.

4172 Knoxville Cook Book. A Collection of Practical Tested Recipes . . . for the Benefit of the Girls' Department of the Knox County Industrial School. Revised edition. Cloth. Woman's Building Board, Knoxville, 1907. 325p. Ads.

4173 Reese, Mrs. Jennie Day. The Kitchen Manual. Many recipes "entirely new, originated by the author." Thumb index. Privately printed, Memphis, 1907. 372p.

4174 Wilson, Mary Elizabeth Lyles and Huggins, Mollie. Good Things To Eat. Everybody's favorite. Nashville: Pub. House of the M. E. Church, South, 1909. 383p.

4175 Wilson, Mary Elizabeth Lyles and Huggins, Mollie. Mrs. Wilson's Cook Book. A complete collection of recipes and useful household information. Nashville: Foster & Parkes, 1914. 160p.

4176 For the Bride. Memphis: American Advertising Ass'n. (1915?). 137p. and ads.

4177 Rudd, Fay Mooring and Kayser, Francesca E. Cooking and Sewing Outline. Tennessee Coal, Iron and Railroad Co., Tenn. (1917?).

4178 Wilson, Mary A. Modern Cooking. (She was Queen Victoria's Cuisiniere, and instructor of cooking for the U. S. Navy). Memphis: Students Educational Pub. (1920). 410p.

4179 Wilson, Betty Lyles. Betty Lyles Wilson's New Cook Book. Rev. and illus. A Complete Collection of Original Recipes and Useful Household Information. Frontispiece portrait of author. 5th ed. Marshall & Bruce Co., Nashville, 1924. 166p.

4180 Calvary Church Circle Cook Book. Autographed recipes. Ads. Cloth. Memphis, 1925. 202p.

4181 Washington, Mrs. George Augustine. The Sewanee Cook Book. A collection of autographed recipes from southern homes and plantations. Baird-Ward: Nashville, 1926. 207p.

4182 Wilson, Owen H., MD. The Care and Feeding of Southern Babies. A guide for mothers, nurses and baby welfare workers in the South. Illustrated. Cokesbury; Nashville, 1926. 131p.

4183 THE EVERY DAY COOK BOOK. Compiled by The Woman's Auxiliary of the First Presbyterian Church of Chattanooga, Tenn. For the benefit of the Bachman Orphanage. Privately printed, Tenn. 1931. 100p.

4184 WEBBER, MARTIN I. 13 PARTY PLANS FOR ADULTS. Nashville (1931). 165p.

4185 STANFIELD, ELIZABETH W. White Lily Flour Cook Book. Knoxville: J. A. Smith & Co. (1932). 98p. and ads.

4186 TURNER, H. A. The Cook's Handy Andy . . Bristol: H. A. Turner (1932). 206p.

4187 THE CHAPEL OF THE GOOD SHEPHERD COOK BOOK. Autographed Recipes, all tried and some of them cherished. Lookout Mountain. Compiled and edited by Chapter VII of the Woman's Auxiliary of Saint Paul's Church, Chattanooga, 1933. 156p. and ads.

4188 ROBERTS, MRS. FLORENCE (MCMAHON). Dixie Meals. Printed for the author, Nashville: Parthenon Press (1934). 310p. illus.

4189 DENISON, GRACE E. MODERN HOME COOK BOOK. Valuable information and kitchen tested recipes. Southern Publishers, Inc., Kingsport, 1938. 534p. and some written recipes.

4190 HOUGEN, RICHARD TORGOR. Look No Further. Illus. by Robert D. Bigelow. Nashville: McQuiddy Press (1951). 240p.

4191 RYWELL, MARTIN. Mexican Cook Book. (See Foreign sec.)

4192 RYWELL, MARTIN (Compiled by). TENNESSEE COOKBOOK. More than 300 Tasty Tennessee Recipes. Illus. Wraps. Pioneer Press, Harriman, 1952. 61p.

4193 RYWELL, MARTIN (Compiled by). WILD GAME COOK BOOK. For the hunter, housewife, epicure. More than 350 recipes. Wraps. Pioneer Press, Harriman, 1958. 72p.

4194 COLUMBIA COOK BOOK, 675 Tested Recipes. Ladies' Auxiliary of the First Baptist Church, Columbia, Tenn. 3rd ed. Nashville: Marshall & Bruce Co., n.d. 171p. Ads.

Texas

4195 K.K.K. COOK BOOK . . . Compiled by the Kute Kooking Klub of Honey Grove, Tex. Cincinnati: Press of the Robert Clarke Co., 1894. 111p.

4196 THE EL PASO COOK BOOK. Compiled by the Ladies' Auxiliary of the Y.M.C.A. El Paso, Herald News Co., 1898. 166p. and ads.

4197 THOMPSON, LILIE C. The "Epicurean" or, connoisseur manual, embracing a choice selection of original receipts . . . Waco. n. pub., 1898. 91p. Frontis. portrait.

4198 THE JUNIOR LEAGUE OF DALLAS COOK BOOK. 2nd ed. revised and enlarged. 45 menus, 250 additional recipes. Dallas (n.d. c. 1900). 264p.

4199 THE GUILD COOK BOOK OF TESTED RECIPES. Many autographed recipes. Compiled by St. Paul's Guild of St. Paul's Episcopal Church, 1888. Waco, 1901. 2nd ed. 287p. and many interesting ads.

4200 RICE COOK BOOK. 200 Receipts for Preparing Rice. Compiled and Issued by the Passenger Dept. of the Southern Pacific. Interesting photos of scenes along Southern Pacific route. Copyright by S. F. B. Morse, Houston (1901). Wraps. 66p.

4201 HOUSTON CIVIC CLUB COOK BOOK. Arranged by Mrs. C. M. Crawford and the ladies of the . . . Club. (Houston, 1906). 128p.

4202 MEXICAN COOKING. (See Foreign sec.)

4203 THE FREDERICKSBURG HOME KITCHEN COOK BOOK. Ladies Auxiliary. Fredericksburg: The Ladies Auxiliary, 1916. 141p. front., plates.

4204 LAWRENCE, MARY MINERVA. . . . Six Texas Food Products; Recipes and Food Values. Austin: The University of Texas (1918). 22 (2) p. (Texas. University. Bulletin no. 1823. April 20, 1918).

4205 THE FREDERICKSBURG HOME KITCHEN COOK BOOK. 2nd ed. (Fredericksburg): The Public School Auxiliary, 1921. 165p. (See No. 4203).

4206 CHITWOOD, IDA M. Mrs. Ida M. Chitwood's Choice Recipes, Food Charts and Reducing Method. Fort Worth, The Bunker Printing Products Corp. (1927). 5, 112p.

4207 THE FREDERICKSBURG HOME KITCHEN COOK BOOK. 3rd ed. (Fredericksburg): Public School Auxiliary (1927). 170p. (See No. 4203).

4208 BONNER, MARY DAVENPORT. The Club Woman's Cook Book. Tyler: The author, 1928. 208p.

4209 TURNER, MRS. E. V. (Compiled by) HOLLAND'S COOK BOOK. A collection principally from Holland's Magazine. The Texas Farm & Ranch Pub. Co., Dallas, 1928. 1st ed. 334p.

4210 OLIVER, SADIE C. Aunt Sara's Culinary Hand-Book. By a professor of home economics, San Antonio P.S. San Antonio: Globe Printing Co. (1931). 120p. Wraps.

4211 COX, MAGGIE (PARKER). The Parker Cook Book: published for the benefit of the First Presbyterian Church . . . Abilene: Abilene Printing and Stationery Co. (1932). 416p. illus. Frontis. Ads.

4212 COMET UNCOATED WHITE RICE RECIPES. Col. pictorial wraps. Illus. San Antonio (1934). 22p.

4213 NELSON, GEORGE LUTHER (editor). Home Cooking; kitchen tested recipes. San Antonio: Neolon Sales Service (1934). 190p. illus. 1st ed.

4214 THE JUNIOR GUILD COOK BOOK. St. Luke's Episcopal Church. Wraps. Mineral Wells, Texas, 1935. 120p.

4215 MEXICAN COOKERY FOR AMERICAN HOMES. (See Foreign sec.)

4216 COOPER, VIRGINIA M. THE CREOLE KITCHEN COOK BOOK. Famous New Orleans Recipes. Illustrations of New Orleans. Naylor: San Antonio, 1946.

4217 GORDON, BRICK. THE GROOM BOILS AND STEWS. A man's cook book for men. On the Southern side. Want to make a corndodger? Illustrations by Frank Anthony Stanush. Naylor: San Antonio (1947). 1st ed. 178p.

4218 CROSBY, THEORA W. AND STINNETT, IRBY. SEAFOOD AND WILD GAME COOK BOOK. Preponderance from Gulf Coast cooks. Reliable and indispensable recipes. Naylor Co.; San Antonio (1948). 1st ed. 177p.

4219 COLEMAN, ARTHUR & BOBBIE. The Texas Cook Book. Culinary & Campfire Lore from the Lone Star State. Tall eating . . . & tall tales. New York: A. A. Wyn, 1949. 256p.

4220 TRAHEY, JANE (Editor) A TASTE OF TEXAS. 300 tested, mouth-watering recipes. Compiled for Neiman-Marcus by Marihelen McDuff. Random House: New York, 1949. 1st ed. 303p.

4221 WHAT'S COOKING IN SOUTH TEXAS. Autographed recipes. Ads. Wraps. The Chancel Woman's Club of Kingsville and Bishop, 1950. 96p.

4222 COOPER, JOE E. WITH OR WITHOUT BEANS. A compendium to perpetuate the internationally-famous bowl of chili (Texas Style). Gay end papers. Illustrations. Henson, Dallas, 1952. 1st ed. 247p.

4223 COUCH, MATTIE TERRELL. Party Cook Book. Barbecues and Baking—larruping old Southern recipes, interspersed with grandmother's comments. San Antonio: Naylor Co. (1953). 1st ed. 73p. Charming drawings.

4224 STRACHAN, CLARICE B. The Diabetic's Cookbook. Medical Arts Publishing Foundation. Houston, 1955.

4225 SHELTON, HERBERT M. The Hygienic System. Orthotrophy—Vol. II. Dr. Shelton's Health School, San Antonio, 1956. 591p.

4226 STOKER, CATHARINE ULMER. CONCHA'S MEXICAN KITCHEN COOK BOOK. (See Foreign sec.)

4227 YOUNG, ALICE ERIE. Discovering Mexican Cooking. (See Foreign sec.)

4228 WHITE HOUSE CEREALS. Natural Brown Rice, White Rice, Ricena, Rice Flakes, Corn Flakes. Booklet shaped like a package of cereal. Pictorial wraps. Standard Rice Company, Inc., Houston, n. d. 47p.

Utah

4229 THE COSMOPOLITAN COOK AND RECIPE BOOK. American, French, German, English, Irish and other National Dishes, both costly and economical. Household & medical remedies and miscellany. Ogden: Eugene Friederich, 1890. 398p. and ads.

4230 MILLER, ELIZABETH M. (Mrs. Glen) Sarah Daft Home Cook

Book. A collection of choice and tested recipes contributed by the members of the board and their friends. 3rd ed. rev. Kaysville: Inland Printing (1923). 242p. Illus. by M. R. Trenam. Many local ads.

4231 MEDLOCK, ADDISON. EAT, DRINK, TO BE HEALTHY and Tomorrow You Live. The author a "Dietotherapist," Priv. Printed, wraps. Salt Lake City, 1933. 98p.

4232 STROWIG, NELL AND REES, RUTH. Recipe Book for Home Economics Classes. Salt Lake City, 1933. 176p. Cover design by Cornelius Salisbury.

Vermont

4233 HAYES, EMILY. DINING ROOM NOTES: A Practical Hand-Book for Housekeepers. Carefully prepared recipes, using products of the Health Food Co. Crowell: Brattleboro, 1885. 208p.

4234 THE LADIES' HANDBOOK & HOUSEHOLD ASSISTANT. A Manual of Religious & Table Etiquette: A Selection of Choice Recipes for Plain & Fancy Cooking & a Compend. of Rules, Tables & Suggestions of Infinite Variety in Every Household. Pub. in Behalf of the Universalist Church. Springfield, 1886. 79p. & ads.

4235 YOUNG MOTHER HUBBARD'S CUPBOARD. Autographed recipes. Wraps. Pub. by the Young Ladies of the 1st Baptist Society, Brattleboro, 1889. 50p. & ads.

4236 EXCELSIOR COOK BOOK . . . Congregational Church. Rutland, 1891. 135p.

4237 COMPOSITIONS OF MANY COOKS, by West Rutland ladies. Rutland, 1892. 32p.

4238 THE KING'S DAUGHTERS' COOK BOOK. Containing Choice Gleanings From Many Households. Autographed recipes. Cloth. Pub. by The Golden Rule Circle of King's Daughters, Springfield, 1897. 119p. & ads.

4239 THE DEWEY COOK BOOK. Autographed recipes. Frontispiece photo of Admiral Dewey's birthplace. Compiled by the Women of the Auxiliary to the Young Men's Christian Ass'n., Montpelier, 1899. 131p.

4240 BERNE, CARL. BERNE'S HOME ASSISTANT. Bennington, 189? 315p.

4241 CRYSTAL LAKE COOK BOOK. Autographed recipes. Women's Literary Club of Barton, Vermont, for the Benefit of the Library and Reading Room. St. Johnsbury, 1902. 96p. and ads.

4242 THE LAMOILLE VALLEY COOK BOOK, published by the ladies of the Congregational Church of Johnson, Vermont . . . (Johnson), 1904. 149 (1) p.

4243 LADIES AID SOCIETY OF THE METHODIST EPISCOPAL CHURCH of Springfield, Vt., choice selection of tested recipes. Wraps. Wm. H. Nichols Cookbook Pub. Co., Morrisville, 1907. 105p. and ads.

4244 THE MOUNT MANSFIELD COOK

BOOK. Choice Selection of Tested Recipes from Many Households. Over 400 recipes. Wraps. Ladies' Aid Society of the Methodist Episcopal Church, Stowe, 1907. 105p. and ads.

4245 THE NEW MEMPHREMAGOG COOK BOOK. Ladies of the Congregational Church, Newport, Vt. . . . Newport: Press of Express and Standard, 1907. 152p. illus. and ads.

4246 THE AMSDEN COOK BOOK. Published by the Union Ladies' Aid Society, Amsden, Vermont. 3rd ed. Ludlow, R. S. Warner, 1909. 128p. Wraps.

4247 BOOK OF TESTED RECIPES AND HELPFUL HOUSEHOLD IDEAS. Trinity Episcopal Church, Rutland, 1911. 143p. illus.

4248 THE LABAREE COOK BOOK. Autographed recipes. Illus. Wraps. Vermont (c. 1912). 39p. and ads.

4249 WHAT TO COOK AND HOW TO COOK IT. Pictorial wraps. White River Junction (1912). 66p.

4250 THE GREEN MOUNTAIN COOK BOOK. Autographed recipes. Oilcloth wraps. Ladies of the Jeffersonville Cemetery Ass'n. 2nd ed. Essex Junction, 1913. 114p.

4251 MY LADYE'S COKE BOOKE. Autographed recipes. Wraps. Brattleboro Woman's Club. 3rd ed. Brattleboro, 1916. 211p.

4252 ECONOMY COOK BOOK. Ladies' Industrial Society of the First Baptist Church. Rutland: (Tuttle Co.), 1917. 40p. and ads.

4253 THE MONTPELIER WOMAN'S CLUB COOK BOOK. Many interesting ads. Autographed recipes. Boards. Montpelier (1921). 151p.

4254 VERMONT COOK BOOK. Each recipe bears the name of the town or village from which it comes. Wraps. Methodist Ladies Aid Society, Burlington, 1927. 80p.

4255 THE VERMONT COOK BOOK. Barton: Gilpin, Hunt & Co., Inc., 1929. 256p.

4256 VERMONT MAPLE SUGAR AND SYRUP. Bulletin of the Vermont Department of Agriculture, No. 38. Pamphlet, illus., wraps. Montpelier, Vermont, Feb. 1, 1930. 45p.

4257 TYLER, HELEN ELIZABETH. The Green Mountain Cook Book, by Aristene Pixley (pseud.). Brattleboro: Stephen Daye Press, 1934. 96p.

4258 BROWN: CORA, ROSE & BOB. The Country Cookbook. The Countryman Press, Vermont, 1937. 1st ed. 224p.

4259 PITKIN, ROYCE S. MAPLE SUGAR TIME. For boys who want to eat 'Sugar" on snow. Illustrated with drawings by Clifford A. Bayard and with photographs. Daye: Vermont, 1937. 64p.

4260 BROWN, BOB. Homemade Hilarity. Country Drinks, Both Hard & Soft. Wraps. The Countryman Press, Weston, 1938. 1st ed. 16p.

4261 OUT OF VERMONT KITCHENS. Repro. Handwritten recipes with autographs. Spiral binding. Compiled by Trinity Mission of Trinity Church, Rutland and Women's Service League of St. Paul's Church, Burlington, 1939. 1st ed. 400p.

4262 HILDEBRAND: LOUISE & JOEL. CAMP CATERING or How to Rustle Grub for Hikers, Campers, Mountaineers, Packers, Canoeists, Hunters, Skiers & Fishermen. Illus. Daye Press: Brattleboro, 1941. 102p.

4263 THE NEW HOOD COOK BOOK. 1195 Modern Recipes. Illustrated; clear print, good paper with large margins for notes on each recipe. H. P. Hood & Sons, Vermont (1941). 394p.

4264 PIXLEY, ARISTENE. THE GREEN MOUNTAIN COOK BOOK. A brief history of the Spirit in as well as recipes of Vermont food. Daye: New York, 1941. 1st ed. 90p.

4265 OUR FAVORITE RECIPES. Autographed recipes. Wraps. Londonderry School Club. Londonderry, 1945. 74p.

4266 OUT OF VERMONT KITCHENS. Vermont, 1945. (See No. 4261).

4267 OUT OF VERMONT KITCHENS. Vermont, 1949. (See No. 4261).

4268 PEARL, MARY. VERMONT MAPLE RECIPES. Recipes collected and tested through the years. Illustrations by Edward Sanborn. Decorative end papers. Spiral binding. Mary Pearl: Vermont, 1952. 87p.

4269 CHOW, DOLLY (MRS. C. T. WANG) CHOW! (See Foreign sec.)

4270 GORTON, AUDREY ALLEY. The Venison Book. How to Dress, Cut Up and Cook your Deer. Illus. by George Daly. Wraps. The Stephen Greene Press, Brattleboro, 1957. 78p.

4271 GORDON, JEAN. ROSE RECIPES. Customs, facts, fancies. Rose lore from 14 centuries. Illustrations. Red Rose Publications, Woodstock, 1958. 100p.

4272 ONE HUNDRED CHOICE RECEIPTS FOR THE BENEFIT OF TRINITY CHURCH MISSION. Rutland, n.d. 80p. illus.

Virginia

4273 CONFEDERATE RECEIPT BOOK. A compilation of over 100 receipts, adapted to the times. Richmond: West & Johnston, 1863. 29p. Wraps.

4274 HOUNIHAN, JOHN D. Bakers' and Confectioners' Guide and Treasure. A practical guide to bread, cracker, cake and pastry baking. How to make all kinds of candy, ice creams, custards, jams, etc. Over 850 recipes. Staunton: John D. Hounihan (1877). 363p. illus. 20 full p. monochrome pl.

4275 TYREE, MARION CABELL (editor). Housekeeping in Old Virginia. Contributions from 250 ladies in Virginia and her sister states distinguished for their skill in the culinary art. Autographed recipes, including some by Mrs. Robert E. Lee. New York: G. W. Carleton & Co., 1877. 528p.

4276 YEAGER, JOHN G. Recipes for the World; for the useful and ornamental arts of cooking and baking. Staunton: Staunton Spectator Job Office, 1877. 43p. Wraps.

4277 SMITH, MARY STUART (HARRISON). Virginia Cookery-Book. Contains many famous Southern recipes. New York: Harper & Bros., 1885. 352p.

4278 TODD, MARGARET M. (anon.) The Noble Cook. The real need of every household . . Alexandria: Gazette Book and Job Office, 1887. 2, 18, 1p. Wraps.

4279 ARMSTRONG, MARY FRANCES. ON HABITS AND MANNERS. Normal School Press, Hampton, 1888. 204p.

4280 DONNAN, MRS. WILLIAM S. A Collection of Virginia Recipes. Richmond: Whittet & Shepperson, 1890. 87p.

4281 FAUNTLEROY, MRS. A. M. Tried Receipts. The "Housekeeper," of Staunton, Virginia. Staunton: Mrs. A. M. Fauntleroy, 1891. 99p. Wraps. Menus.

4282 MCPHAIL, MRS. CLEMENT CARRINGTON. F.F.V. Receipt Book. West, Johnston & Co.: Richmond, 1894. 287p.

4283 CRINGEN, MRS. JOHN W. INSTRUCTION IN COOKING. Hill Pr. Co., Richmond, 1895. 327p.

4284 ROSSER, ELIZABETH (WINSTON), "Mrs. T. L. Rosser." Housekeepers' and Mothers' Manual. E. Waddey Co.: Richmond, 1895. 604p.

4285 GLOVER, E. T. The Warm Springs Receipt-Book. Compiled between 1881 and 1894. Richmond: B. R. Johnson Publishing Co., 1897. 395p.

4286 MOORE, CARRIE PICKETT. The Way to the Heart, Hints to the Inexperienced; a collection of tested Virginia recipes . . . Richmond: Whittet & Shepperson, 1905. 155p.

4287 FITCHETT, L. S. Beverages & Sauces of Colonial Virginia. 1607-1907. Regional sources of unusual drinks such as White Apron Sauce with Sherry. New York: Neale Pub., 1907. (1st ed.)

4288 BOMBERGER, MAUDE ADA. Colonial Recipes from Old Virginia and Maryland Manors. Neale Pub. Co.: New York & Washington, 1907. 107p.

4289 THE ROANOKE COOK BOOK. Favorite recipes by some of Roanoke's good housekeepers. Woman's Civic Betterment Club. Roanoke: Stone Printing & Manufacturing Co., 1907. 162p.

4290 POINDEXTER, CHARLOTTE MASON (Compiled by) JANE HAMILTON'S RECIPES. Delicacies from the Old Dominion — Fredericksburg, Va. A. C. McClurg & Co., Chicago, 1909. 1st ed. 191p.

4291 OLD VIRGINIA COOKING. Retail Grocers' Association of Richmond, Inc., Richmond, Va., editor. (Richmond:) Richmond Press, Inc., printers, 1910. 159p. and ads.

4292 BIVINS, S. THOMAS. The Southern Cook Book. A manual of cooking and list of menus, including recipes by noted cooks and caterers. Press of the Hampton Institute: Hampton, 1912. 239p.

4293 McCulloch-Williams, Martha. Dishes and Beverages of the Old South. Decorations by Russel Crofoot. Exceptional dishes. New York: McBride, Nast & Co., 1913. 318p.

4294 Church, Edith and Leete, Bertina A. Practical Patriotic Recipes. Hampton: The Hampton Normal and Agricultural Institute, 1918. 16p. Wraps.

4295 A Few Recipes from Virginia . . . Hampton Chapter of the Daughters of the American Revolution, Hampton Chapter (191?). 60p. and ads.

4296 Lyford, Carrie Alberta. A Book of Recipes for the Cooking School, by the director of home economics at Hampton Normal and Agric. Institute. Hampton: Hampton Normal and Agricultural Institute (1921). 299p.

4297 Virginia Cookery Book. Traditional recipes. Virginia League of Women Voters, Richmond, 1921. 192p.

4298 Moeschler, Velma. Virginia Cookery. Roanoke: Roanoke Prtg. Co. (1930). 115p. frontis.

4299 The Monticello Cook Book. Recipes, cooking hints, household hints. The Univ. of Virginia Hospital League, sponsor. Wraps. Charlottesville, 1931. 1st ed. 93 (1)p.

4300 Goldenberg, Henrietta P. Tried and True Recipes. Lynchburg, Mutual Press (1932). 116p. Frontis. portrait.

4301 Moncure, Blanche Elbert (Collected by) Emma Jane's Souvenir Cook Book and Some Old Virginia Recipes. Wraps. Williamsburg, 1937. 87p.

4302 The Monticello Cook Book. Recipes, cooking hints, household hints. The Univ. of Virginia Hospital League, sponsor. Wraps. Jarman's: Charlottesville, 1937. 140p. & ads.

4303 Bullock, Helen. The Williamsburg Art of Cookery. Reproduction of an old Virginia cookbook of 1742 as one of the craft projects of the Colonial town. Leather bound—handmade paper, ink. Colonial Williamsburg Inc., 1939. 276p.

4304 Kimball, Marie. The Martha Washington Cook Book. Profusely illustrated. End papers of The Kitchen Garden of Mount Vernon. Coward-McCann, New York, 1940. 1st ed. 212p.

4305 The Garden Club of Virginia, Favorite Recipes, 3 from each club member, in autograph. Lynchburg, 1942.

4306 Recipes from Old Virginia. Compiled by The Virginia Federation of Home Demonstration Clubs. Illustrated by Mrs. N. R. Perkins. Spiral binding. Dietz, Richmond, 1946. 287p.

4307 Nos Meilleurs Recettes. (See Foreign sec.)

4308 De Virginia Hambook. By De Ol' Virginia Hamcook. Booklet. Virginia, 1948. 63p.

4309 WYMAN, ETHEL M. (Compiled and edited by) AN UNITED NATIONS COOK BOOK. Autographed recipes from all over the World. Sponsored & Revised by Circle Four of Old St. Paul's Church, Norfolk, Va. and Circle Six of St. John's Church, Hampton, Va. Washington, D.C., 1948. 44p. Wraps.

4310 THE MONTICELLO COOK BOOK. Dishes from Ancient & Modern Times by the Ladies of Charlottesville and the County of Albemarle. Compiled for the University of Virginia Hospital Circle. Spiral Binding; Interesting sketches. Dietz Press: Richmond (1950). 157p.

4311 DAVIS, NORMA A. TRADE WINDS COOKERY. Tropical Recipes for All America. Spiral binding Dietz Press, Inc., Richmond, (1956). 1st ed. 215p.

4312 VIRGINIA COOKERY—PAST AND PRESENT. Including a Manuscript Cook Book of the Lee and Washington Families. Signed recipes. Spiral Binding . . Cover by Marguerite Burgess. The Woman's Auxiliary of Olivet Episcopal Church, Franconia, 1957. 449p.

4313 SAUER'S CHOICE RECIPES. For cakes and pies and drinks. Small booklet, wraps. Sauer: Richmond. n.d. 24p.

4314 THE SECOND BAPTIST CHURCH COOK BOOK. A useful collection of practical tested and approved recipes. Woman's Auxiliary of the Second Baptist Church, Richmond. 223p.

4315 SOUTH BOSTON COOK BOOK. Signed recipes. Benefit of The Helping Hand Society of South Boston Baptist Church. Private printing, Richmond. n.d. Autographed recipes. Ads. 144p.

Washington

4316 CLEVER COOKING . . . Women's Guild of St. Mark's Church. Seattle: Metropolitan Print. & Binding Co., 1896. 319p. and ads.

4317 PHELAN, CHARLES. Dried Fruit. Its care, protection from worms, packing, storing. Seattle: Phelan & Co., 1902. 44p. Wraps. Illus.

4318 EDWARDS, PERMELIA. The Table and Its Service. An encyclopedia of "how-to's" including cooking. Spokane: n. pub. (1905). 488p.

4319 PUGET SOUND COOK BOOK. Published by L. St. M. P., Seattle: 1906. 128p. and much adv. Recipes signed.

4320 ARONSON, MRS. SIGISMUND (compiler). One Thousand Recipes, under auspices of the Ladies' Auxiliary to Temple de Hirsch . . . Seattle: Merchants Print. Co., 1908. 194p. 1st ed.

4321 JENNINGS, LINDA DEZIAH (compiler). Washington Women's Cook Book. Autographed recipes published by The Washington Equal Suffrage Association. Seattle: Trade Register Print, 1909. 256p. Pictorial cloth covers. "Votes for Women," "Good Things to Eat."

4322 HAZZARD, DR. LINDA BURFIELD, M.D. Fasting for the Cure of Disease. Wraps. Hazzard Pub. Co., Seattle, 1910. 161p.

4323 THE SEATTLE BRIDE'S COOK BOOK. Seattle: Union Advertising Co. (c. 1911). 104p. Ads. Pictorial boards.

4324 HAINES, MARY LEWIS. Helpful Hints for Housewives. Olympia: The Recorder Press (1913). 216, xii p. Wraps.

4325 DE LONG, WILLARD W. AND BELLE D. Seattle Home Builder and Home Keeper. Seattle: Commercial Publishing Co., 1915. 160p. illus. and ads.

4326 SWEZY, ISABELLE CLARK. Can't Fail Cook Book. Seattle: John Vitucci Company (1915). 64p. and promotion for Vitucci olive oil.

4326a ECONOMY COOK BOOK. Every Receipt Tested. Published in the interest of the equipment fund. Tacoma, Wash.: Womna's Club House, 1917. Unnumbered p. Ads.

4327 ST. MARGARET'S GUILD COOK BOOK. Autographed recipes. Ring book, heavy paper. For St. Luke's Church, Vancouver. 86p. & ads. (c. 1920).

4328 GARDINER, H. W. (compiler). Recipes and Menus of Noted Pacific Coast Chefs . . . Seattle Culinary Association, Inc. Seattle, 1923. 127p. illus. Contains ads.

4329 KAHN, LEAH BARASH. Kiddy Kookery. Menus and recipes for feeding children from 6 mo. to 6 yrs. Aided by Miss Martha Koehne, ass't. Prof. Home Econ., & Dr. H. L. Moon, child specialist. Illus. by Ruth Kreps. Seattle: Kiddy Kookery Publishing Co., 1923. 92p.

4330 CHOICE RECIPES by Seattle Women. Compiled for the benefit of the Seattle Fruit & Flower Mission. Seattle: Lowman & Hanford, 1924. 393p. and ads. Signed recipes.

4331 THE HIGHLAND CIRCLE COOK BOOK. Very best recipes from the ladies of Longview. Longview: authors, 1925. 111p. and ads. Paper.

4332 DONNELLY, ACHSA P. AND TOURTELLOTTE, JANET P. Cooking for Connoisseurs as Theresa Capell Does It. Seattle: The Seattlite, Inc. (1930). 40p.

4333 WHAT THE COOK SAID. Landscape Association of the Cathedral of St. John the Evangelist. Spokane: Printed by Wakefield-Park Co. (1931). 192p. Frontis.

4334 WONDER SHREDDER RECIPES. Favorite Tested Recipes featuring the Wonder Shredder. Seattle: Dixon Prosser, Inc. (1931). 32p. Wraps.

4334a KITCHEN BOUQUET. Compiled for Seattle Children's Orthopedic Hospital by Maude G. Palmer. About herbs and things to put them in. Seattle, Wash.: Covered in brown building paper, tied with red twine. 16p. mimeo. Spring, 1935.

4334b GIRL SCOUT ..COOK BOOK. Signed recipes published by the Tacoma Girl Scout Council. Tacoma, Wash.: (193?). 50p. mimeo. with oilcloth cover.

4335 COOK BOOK. Autographed recipes, compiled by Members of San Juan Rebekah Lodge, Orcas Island Rebekah Lodge. Wash.: 1941. 107p. Ads. Wraps.

4336 FROM DANISH KITCHENS. (See Foreign sec.)

4337 JUNIOR AID COOK BOOK. Henri, Sponsor of Yakima Day Nursery. Autographed recipes reproduced in the handwriting of the contributor. Yakima: Yakima Bindery and Prtg. Co., 1944. 397p. illus. Spiral, pictorial wraps.

4338 AURORA COOK BOOK. Swedish Tabernacle, Spokane: n.d. 46p. Ads. Wraps.

4339 COOK BOOK compiled by the Altrusa Club of Seattle. Dedicated to the memory of Ruth E. Forsberg. Autographed recipes. Seattle: n.d. 64 mimeo. p. Spiral. Pict. wraps.

4340 DESSERTS BY JUNIOR AID, compiled by the Junior Aid Members, Sponsors of the Yakima Day Nursery. Autographed recipes. Yakima: n.d. 79p. illus. Pictorial colored wraps.

4341 DORCAS DAINTIES, Bethany Presbyterian Church. Seattle. 48p. n.d. Autographed recipes.

4342 TESTED RECIPES. By the Ladies of the First Lutheran Church. Autographed recipes. Tacoma: n.d. 136p. illus. Picture of Church on cover. Ring binding.

West

4344 WESTERN COOKERY. Compiled by Kay Morrow & Hazel Hemminger. Decorations by Warren Troutman. Wraps. Culinary Arts Press; Reading, Pa., 1936. 48p. Wraps.

4345 CALLAHAN, GENEVIEVE A. SUNSET ALL-WESTERN FOODS COOK BOOK. TYPICAL WESTERN FOODS: How to pick the best of the offerings; how to cook and serve them attractively. Decorative end papers. Profusely illus. Lane Publishing Co., San Francisco (1949). 284p.

4346 BROWN, HELEN. WEST COAST COOK BOOK. Recipes from Washington, Oregon and California. Historical notes and comments. Little, Brown & Co., Boston, Mass., 1952. 1st ed. 443p.

4347 GARY, LAMORA SAUVINET. The Pacific Hostess Cookbook. Glamorous food: some from Hawaii. Colored end papers with herb lists. Coward-McCann, New York (1956). 1st ed. 256p.

West Virginia

4348 PRESBYTERIAN COOK BOOK. Compiled by the Ladies of the First Presbyterian Church of Dayton, Ohio. Cragg: Wheeling, 1889. 178p.

4349 THE TWIG COOK BOOK. Autographed recipes, compiled by The Twigs, a group of organizations working for the benefit of the Ohio Valley General Hospital. Thumb Index. Ads. Oilcloth cover. Illus. Wheeling. (c. 1920's). 196p.

4350 CLUB HOUSE COOK BOOK. Autographed recipes, compiled by Young Women's Department, Conservation Department, American Home Department, of the Charleston Woman's Club. Oilcloth covers. Rose City Press: Charleston, 1929. 475p.

4351 GEORGE WASHINGTON BICENTENNIAL COOK BOOK, compiled by the Woman's Club of Charles Town, 1932. 20p.

4352 FLETCHER, L. E. (Compiled by) BRIDE'S COOK BOOK. "Through the courtesy of Mr. J. M. Slack, our County Clerk, this book is handed to you on your wedding day." Ads. Oilcloth covers. Photo of Club House. Pub. by Rose City Press: Charleston, 1934. 183p.

Wisconsin

4353 ADAMS, ABBY MERRILL. SENSE IN THE KITCHEN. A Manual of the Art and Science of Cooking. "We are under special obligations to Mrs. Leonard of La-Crosse, Wis." Contains 689 recipes. Syracuse, N.Y. and LaCrosse, 1879. 338p.

4354 DIE HAUSFRAU, GATTIN UND MUTTER. (See Foreign sec.)

4355 THE GOOD CHEER COOK BOOK. Ladies Aid Society of the Episcopal Church. Chippewa Falls: Herald Print, 1889. 320p.

4356 CLARKE, MARY LAMSON. THE STAR CRYSTAL COOK BOOK. Flint: Milwaukee, 1890. 136p. Wraps.

4357 FINNEY, JESSIE AND EATON, ALICE. The King's Daughters Cook Book. Reliable recipes from experienced housekeepers. Pub. by the ladies of the Charity Circle. Signed recipes. Oshkosh: Wis.: W. M. Castle, 1891. 304p. and ads.

4358 BISCUITS AND DRIED BEEF. A Panacea. By L. H. M. Milwaukee: Young Churchman Co., 1894. 76p.

4359 MAGIE, MRS. J. (Compiled by) THE MILWAUKEE COOK BOOK. Respectfully dedicated to the Wisconsin Training School for Nurses. Ads. Milwaukee, 1894. 380p.

4360 CAMPBELL, HELEN. Household Economics. Lectures given in the Univ. of Wisc. Bibliography. G. P. Putnam's Sons: New York (1896). 290p. & ads.

4361 DAVIDIS, HENRIETTE. Praktisches Kochbuch für die Deutschen in Amerika. (See Foreign sec.)

4362 JAMISON, MRS. JENNIE A. (editor). The Wisconsin Cook Book for 1897-'98. Neenah: W. C. Jacobs & Son, 1897. 28p.

4363 CHOICE RECIPES. Compiled under the auspices of the Ladies of the 1st M.E. Church of Menasha, Wisconsin. Oshkosh, 1899. 82p.

4364 THE CHARITY CIRCLE COOK BOOK. Pub. by The Charity Circle of King's Daughters of Oshkosh. Ads. Castle-Pierce Co., Oshkosh, 1902. 424p.

4365 The Oakland Cook Book. Compiled by the Members of the Ladies' Society of the Free Baptist Church. Ads. Oakland Centre, 1902. 187p.

4366 The West Bend Cook Book . . . Milwaukee: Press of Gillet & Co. (1902). 294p.

4367 The Federation Cook Book. Compiled by members of the Women's Clubs of Whitewater. Ads. Oilcloth cover. Whitewater Gazette Print: Whitewater, 1903. 176p.

4368 Capital City Cook Book. Compiled by the Woman's Guild of Grace Church. Merchants' advertising helped print it. Madison, 1906. 156p.

4369 Thomson, Helen Mar. Monarch Cook Book. Kitchen-tested recipes for every-day use. Beaver Dam: Malleable Iron Range Co. (1906). 143p. and 32p. ads.

4370 The Milwaukee Cook Book. Edited and pub. by the Ladies of Kingsley Methodist Church. Illus. by Milwaukee scenes. Ads. Houtkamp Printing Co., Milwaukee. 1907. 302p.

4371 The West Bend Cook Book: compiled from recipes contributed by ladies of West Bend; originally published for the benefit of St. James' Society, West Bend. Lake Mills: H. E. Crump (1907). 416p.

4372 Cook Book. A Collection of Favorite Recipes contributed by the Ladies of the Presbyterian Church of Neenah, George Banta Pub. Co., Menasga. Oct. 1908. 68p.

4373 Meir, Mrs. Lina (Wachtelborn). Aechte deutsche Kochkunst: the art of German cooking and baking: verfasst und hrsg. von Frau Lina Meier, geb. Lina W. Meier (German cooking teacher). 1909. 484p. port. (English and German texts in parallel columns). Milwaukee.

4374 Waupun Cook Book. 2nd Ed. Dedicated to the Ladies of Waupun and vicinity by Mrs. H. D. Bell and Mrs. C. A. Rank. Compiled by Ladies of Waupun. Schaar Bros., Fond du Lac, 1909. 263p. and ads.

4375 Caloric Book of Recipes. A Compilation; more than 300 superior recipes of all kinds. Adapted to the Caloric Cookstove. Illustrated. Caloric Co.: Janesville, 1910. 152p.

4376 Cook Book. Compiled by St. Agnes' Guild, All Saints' Church. Ads. Appleton. (c. 1910). 256p.

4376a "Caloric" Book of Recipes. A compilation especially adapted to the improved caloric bookstove, whose immediate ancestor was the "hay-box." Janesville, Wisc.: The Caloric Company, 1911. 152p. Index and Special Recipe p.

4377 A Cook Book of 450 Original Receipts. Tested and Recommended by 150 Lake Geneva Housewives. Pub. by the Ladies of the Congregational Church of Lake Geneva, 1911. 181p. and ads.

4378 The Door County Cook Book. Compiled by the Ladies' Aid

Society of Hope Congregational Church. Ads. "From the Famous Land of Cherries." Door County Democrat Print, Sturgeon Bay, 1911. 188p.

4379 BUZZACOTT'S MASTERPIECE. The complete hunters', trappers' and campers' library of valuable information. Recipes, too. Illustrated. McMains & Meyer, Milwaukee, 1913. 1st ed. 544p.

4380 KANDER, MRS. SIMON (Lizzie Black). The "Settlement" Cook Book. Compiled by Mrs. Kander, assisted by Mrs. Henry Schoenfeld, Mrs. Isaac D. Adler. Recipes used in the Settlement cooking classes, the Milwaukee P.S. and gathered from other reliable sources. For benefit of the Settlement . . 7th ed. Milwaukee Press of J. H. Yewdale & Sons Co. (1915). 488p. illus.

4381 PARSONS, FLORENCE CROSBY (Compiled by) EVERY WOMAN'S HOME COOK BOOK. An economical, Practical Guide for the 20th Century Housekeeper. Hamming-Whitman Co.: Racine, 1915. 224p.

4382 WAUWATOSA COOK BOOK. Pub. by the Woman's Club of Wauwatosa. (c. 1915). 192p. Ads.

4383 CUNIBERTI, JULIA LOVEJOY (Anon.) Practical Italian Recipes for American Kitchens. (See Foreign sec.)

4384 THE EAST MILWAUKEE COOK BOOK . . . Ladies' Aid Society of the Luther Chapel. (Milwaukee: Printed by Germania Pub. Co.), 1917. 126p., 1 illus. ads.

4385 THE EPHRAIM COOK BOOK. Compiled by the Ladies' Aid Society of the Moravian Church. Door County Advocate Print. Ephraim, 1921. 153p. and ads.

4386 KANDER, MRS. SIMON (Compiled by) The Settlement Cook Book. Tested Recipes from the Settlement Cooking Classes, the Milwaukee Public School Kitchens, the School of Trades for Girls, and Experienced Housewives. 11th Ed. Enlarged and Revised. The Settlement Cook Book Co., Milwaukee (1921).

4387 HOW TO MAKE AND KEEP FRIENDS. Dedicated to our Alma Mater and all those who assisted in making this book a success. Illus. with photos of College. Ads. Wraps. Pub. by, Twin City Chapter of St. Mary's Alumnae of Prairie du Chine. Wisc. (c. 1922). 172p.

4388 MEIER, MRS. LINA. THE ART OF GERMAN COOKING AND BAKING. (See Foreign sec.)

4389 THE SHOREWOOD COOK BOOK . . . (Albany), 1922. 160p., 1 illus. (Wis.)

4390 THE LA CROSSE COOK BOOK. Pub. under Auspices of Ladies' Aid Society of the 1st Presbyterian Church. 2nd Ed. Inland Printing Co., La Crosse, 1923. 321p. and ads.

4391 THE WOMAN'S ALLIANCE COOK BOOK . . . 4th ed. . . Stevens Point: Worzalla Pub. Co., 1924. 236p.

4392 THE BRIDE'S COOK BOOK . . . Stout Institute. Menomonie: The Home-maker Pub. Co. (1925). 163p. plates. (Printed on one side of page only).

4393 EVERY WOMAN'S HOME COOK BOOK. As above. Revised and Reprinted. Whitman Pub. Co., Racine, 1925. 212p.

4394 FIRST CONGREGATIONAL CHURCH COOK BOOK. Wraps. Castle-Pierce Co.: Oshkosh, 1925. 126p.

4395 THE EPHRAIM COOK BOOK. Wisconsin Rapids: Tribune Ptg. Wks., 1926. 160p.

4396 KANDER, MRS. SIMON (Compiled by) THE SETTLEMENT COOK BOOK. Tested recipes from the Settlement cooking classes, and the public school kitchens. Thumb index. Settlement Cook Book Co.: Milwaukee, 1926. 15th ed. 624p.

4397 THE CLUB WOMAN'S COOK BOOK. Menomonee Falls: The Woman's Club, 1928. 162p. and ads.

4398 THE HOSTESS BOOK, by the editor of the woman's page of the Milwaukee Journal, decorations by Bettie Lenz . . . Milwaukee: The Journal Co., 1928. 60p. illus.

4399 ODELL, EMERY A. A HISTORY OF GREEN COUNTY'S CHEESE INDUSTRY. A history of Limburger in Wisconsin. Booklet. Monroe, 1928. 17p.

4400 CLARK, E. C. (Compiled by) A Book of Famous Recipes by Famous Cooks from Thousands of American Homes. Section on Vitamins. Ads. Wraps. Milwaukee (1930). 1st ed. 64p.

4401 KITCHEN TREASURES; A recipe book of prize winners in the kitchen treasure hunt . . . (Milwaukee:) The Milwaukee Journal, Public Service Bureau (1930). 156p. illus. ("1st ed.")

4402 THE WEST BEND COOK BOOK. Compiled from Recipes contributed by Ladies of West Bend. Pub. by St. James Episcopal Church, and by St. Elizabeth's Guild: West Bend (1930). 416p.

4403 CONNELL, STELLA M. The Rainbow Cook Book. More menus and recipes than the colors in the rainbow. Menominee Falls: 1931. 183, 11p.

4404 A BOOK OF PRACTICAL RECIPES FOR THE HOUSEWIFE. "Grateful acknowledgment made to more than 13,000 housewives willing to contribute favorite recipes." Wisconsin News; Milwaukee (1932). 244p.

4405 SCHULMAN, B. DONALD. Favorite Recipes of the famous movie stars . . Milwaukee, Editor, 1934. 80p. Wraps. Illus. Ads.

4406 HONEY: FOLDERS: 1) Honey & some of its Uses—U.S. Dept of Agriculture (1936). 2) Prost & Colahan Adv. List of Foreign & Domestic Honeys. 3) American Honey Institute—A few recipes. Wisc. 8p. +1+1.

4407 TWENTIETH CENTURY CLUB. Spiral binding. Wraps. Castle-Pierce: Oshkosh, 1896-1936. 145p.

4408 New Milwaukee Cook Book. With list of 30 artists who illustrated the autographed recipes. Visiting Nurse Ass'n. Milwaukee, 1938. 318p.

4409 Allen, Ida Bailey. The Common Sense Cook Book. 200 Recipes and 100 Puzzling Food Questions and their answers. Pictorial board covers. Whitman Pub. Co.: Racine, 1939. 122p.

4410 Kenwood Methodist Cook Book. Ads. Spiral binding. Wisc. 1939. 202p.

4411 George, Iola F.; Goold, Alice G. Foods for Home and Trade. Assistance of Girls' Trades and Technical High School acknowledged. Spiral binding. Wraps. City of Milwaukee, 1942. 310p.

4412 Old Favorite Honey Recipes. Wraps. American Honey Institute, 1945. 52p.

4413 Hamilton Beach Food Mixer. Instructions and Tested Recipes. Wraps. Col. illus. Hamilton Beach Co., Division of Scovill Mfg. Co., Racine, 1947. 50p.

4414 New Favorite Honey Recipes. Foreword by Dr. Morris Fishbein on Honey. Decorations. Spiral. American Honey Institute, 1947. 56p.

4415 National Presto Cooker. Instructions, Recipes, Time Tables. Illus. Wraps. National Pressure Cooker Co., Eau Claire, 1948. 127p.

4416 Recipes and Instructions for Waterless Cooking. Illus. Wraps. Flavo-Seal de Luxe Aluminum Ware. West Bend, 1948. 22p.

4417 Wisconsin's Folkways in Foods. Each recipe a family favorite & gift of the people who made Wis. great in the first 100 years of Statehood. Nationality Foods, Wisconsin Home Economics Ass'n. 1948. 40p. booklet.

4418 Our Pet Recipes. The Baileys Harbor Woman's Club. Spiral binding. 1950. 90p. and ads.

4419 Look 'n Cook by Junior Auxiliary, Evangelical Deaconess Hospital. Each section printed on different color paper. Spiral binding. Milwaukee, 1951.

4420 Balke, May. A Few of My Favorite Recipes. Advertising booklet, Carnation Milk Products Co., Oconomowoc. n.d. 16p.

4421 Columbus Cook Book. Educational Association of Columbus. n.d. 181p. and ads.

4422 How to Prepare Fish the Sportsman's Way and Seafood Cookery. Booklet. Milwaukee. 94p.

4423 Kitchen Guide. Quality recipes, carefully selected. Valuable household suggestions. Aluminum Goods Manufacturing Co.; Manitowoc, n.d. 252p.

4424 Recipes from the French. Presented by the French Club of Central High School. Courtesy of Mrs. Earl Foizie. Illus. Wraps. Superior, n.d. 20p.

4425 TASTY CHEESE RECIPES. Mimeo. booklet. Wisc. State Dept. Agric. 62p.

4426 VIKO COOK BOOK. Recipes from the Viko Aluminum Test Kitchen. Manitowoc. 252p.

Wyoming

4427 WOMAN'S CLUB HIGH ALTITUDE COOK BOOK. The Laramie Prtg. Co., Laramie, 1922. 96p.

4428 HOT LUNCHES for Wyoming rural schools. (Laramie), 1923. 11p. (Wyoming University. Agricultural College. Extension Division, Circular no. 5).

4429 SHERMAN, LUELLA. Wyoming honey for Wyoming people. (Laramie), 1925. 4 l. (Wyoming. University. Agricultural College. Extension. Circular no. 17).

4430 HIGH ALTITUDE COOK BOOK. A compilation of tested and tried recipes. Phi Upsilon Omicron, Delta Chapter, Wyoming University. Laramie, 1930. 164p.

4431 THIESSEN, EMMA J. Vegetable Cookery at High Altitudes. Bulletin No. 180, of Agric. Experiment Station. Wyoming University, Laramie, 1931. Illus. 32p.

4432 JENNINGS, EVANGELINE. Handbook for first year Wyoming 4-H food club work. Laramie, 1932. 47p. (Wyoming University, Agricultural College. Extension Division. Circular no. 42).

You Solve It

4433 DANVILLE COOK BOOK. Danville, Fred E. Warner, 1890. 163p.

4434 LOURT, H. S. 50 CHOICE RECIPES, of Mexican & Spanish Dishes. (See Foreign sec.)

4435 CROSSWAY RECIPES. 'Compliments of the author, Edith A. Hartwell' inscribed on inner cover. 1 Kitchen illus. n.p., 1917-1918. Wraps. 87p.

4436 AUNT JENNY'S FAVORITE RECIPES. Delicious, Economical and Easy to Make with the 'purer' all-vegetable shortening Spry. Advertising booklet. Pictorial wraps in color. 50p. illus. n.p., n.d. (1920's).

4437 FAVORITE RECIPES. A little ring-binder book by the Grace Presbyterian Church from Heaven-Knows-Where. Circle A, 1940. A poem, too! We pay you 25¢ for taking this. Postpaid. First come, first served.

4438 PRESCRIPTIONS FROM THE DOCTOR'S WIFE. Autographed recipes. Compiled by The Women's Auxiliary to the Alumni Association of C.M.E. Plastic Cover, spiral. 70p. & ads. n.p. (1941).

4439 SACRED HEART ACADEMY GUILD COOK BOOK. Autographed recipes, from the members of the Guild. Unnumbered pages, plastic spiral binding. n.p., n.d. (c. 1940's).

4440 BWA COOKIE JAR. Autographed recipes. Mimeo. Wraps handmade. Unnumbered pages, n. p., n.d.

4441 COOK BOOK. Compliments of John S. Ogden. Candidate for

County Treasurer. Wraps. Photo of author. n.p., n.d., no pub. 16p.

4442 COOK BOOK. What the Westminster Men Eat and How Their Wives Prepare It. Signed recipes. Spiral binding. Where and when pub'd.? You solve it. 100p.

4443 COOK-OUT RECIPES. For outdoors parties. All the makings from your co-op market. Small leaflet—wraps. No date, place, or publisher. 17p.

4444 FOOD FARE. Autographed recipes compiled by The Friendship House Board of Delta Sigma Epsilon. Spiral. n.p., n.d. 56p.

4445 A FRIEND IN NEED. Grove Hall Universalist Church Parish. n.d. n.p. Wraps.

4446 KOHLER VILLAGE GARDEN CLUB COOK BOOK. Autographed recipes. From soups to desserts. Wraps—Small booklet. no place, n.d. 119p.

4447 OUR GENTLEMEN'S FAVORITE RECIPES. Signed recipes. The Irving Park Woman's Club, 1927. 89p.

Foreign Section

Canal Zone

4448 CRISTOBAL COOK BOOK. Panama, 1921. 121p. Ads. Wraps.

4449 TROPICAL COOK BOOK. Panama, n.d., n. pub., 172p.

Central Europe

3483 BENNETT, PAULA POGANY AND CLARK, BELMA R. The Art of Hungarian Cooking. Mrs. Bennett, a native Hungarian, offers 222 tested recipes. 16 drawings by Willy Pogany. New York: Doubleday & Co., 1954. 223p.

3746 BONNÉ, JOSEPHINE. Austrian-Hungarian Cookbook. Tausend Und Ein Rezept. Akron, Ohio: 1916. 540p.

1671 FEICHELT, MELANIE. 200 Famous Viennese Recipes selected by the compiler. Foreword by Miss Marjorie Mills. Boston: no pub., 1931. 134p. Frontis. port. of the author.

3014 HUNGARIAN COOKERY; recipes new and old. New York: St. Marks Printing & Pub. (1932). 271p. Wraps.

978 MATA SKRZYNKA SKARBOW. Chicago, Ill.: Dr. Peter Fahrney & Sons, 38p. Wraps.

3569 OCHOROWICZ - MONATOWA, MARJO. Polish Cookery—the Universal Cook Book by Poland's most famous cookery expert. Trans. by Jean Karsavine. The kind of cookery little known here. New York: Crown Pub., 1958. 320p.

2005 ROSICKY, MARY. Bohemian-American Cook Book. Tested and practical recipes for American and Bohemian dishes. An English trans. of the Bohemian language book. Omaha, Nebr.: National Printing Co., 1915. 305p. Frontis. port. of the author.

844 ROZNER, JAN F. Dyeta Domowa; Kuchnia Ekonomiczna. Polish Cookery. Chicago, Ill.: 1919. 76p. and ads.

Far Eastern

3479 ANCESTRIAL RECIPES OF SHEN MEI LON. New York: 1954. Thumb index, spiral, boxed.

3825 THE ART AND SECRETS OF CHINESE COOKERY. Recipes. Archbold, Ohio: La Choy Food Products, 1949. 27p. illus. in color. Wraps.

3957 AU, M. SING. The Chinese Cook Book. Both cookery and the order of serving. Decor. by Warren G. Troutman. Reading, Pa.: Culinary Arts Press (c. 1936). 47p. Wraps.

809 BOSSE, SARA AND WATANNA, ONOTO. Chinese-Japanese Cook Book. Chicago: Rand McNally, 1914. 120p. plus 4p. for memo.

3414 BROBECK, FLORENCE. Cooking With Curry. Fabulous Indian, Malayan and Hawaiian recipes. New York: M. Barrows, 1952. 192p.

2746 CHAN, SHIU WONG. The Chinese Cook Book. More than 100 recipes for everyday food, unique dishes too. New York: Frederick A. Stokes, 1917. 201p.

3416 CHAN, SOU. The House of Chan Cookbook. A famous New York restaurateur combines his knowledge of exotic cookery with the ingredients obtainable at any neighborhood grocery. 10 linecuts by Siu Lan Loh. New York: Doubleday, 1952. 190p.

3610 CHANG, ISABELLE. What's Cooking at Changs'. The Key to cooking Chinese. Nearly 400 tested recipes. New York: Liveright, 1960. 282p.

3332 CHAO, BUWEI YANG. How to Cook and Eat in Chinese. Rev. enl. ed. A comprehensive introduction to cookery and customs. Preface by Pearl Buck. Jacket design from T'ang Dynasty. Illus. with sketches, New York: John Day, 1949. 282p.

3627 CHAO, BUWEI-YANG. Food for Philosophy. Brief extracts from "How to Cook and Eat in Chinese." Booklet with colored end papers. Published in cooperation with the East and West Ass'n. 1250 copies for private distribution. New York: John Day, n.d. 15p.

106 CHINESE AND ENGLISH COOK BOOK. San Francisco, Cal.: Chang Jan, 1913. 287, 50, B p.

4269 CHOW, DOLLY (Mrs. C. T. Wang). Chow! Secrets of Chinese cooking with selected recipes. Illus. by Henry Liu. Vermont; Tuttle, 1954. 174p.

2115 DE WILDT, MRS. Selected Indonesian Recipes. Booklet Javanese Rice table, etc. Paterson, N.J.: n.d. 12p.

3565 DONOVAN, MARIA KOZSLIK. The Far Eastern Epicure. Menus and recipes. Linecuts; index. New York: Doubleday, 1958.

94 GILBRETH AND BOSSUE. Chinese and English Cook Book. Frontis. at back. Last 34p. conversational phrases in Chinese and English. San Francisco, Cal.: Fat Ming Co. (Japanese & American Press). 1910. 344, 34p.

3425 HONG, WALLACE YU. The Chinese Cook Book. 500 of the best Chinese recipes, many little known in the United States of America. New York: Crown, 1952. 288p.

2689 KEOLEIAN, ARDASHES H. The Oriental Cook Book. Wholesome, Dainty and Economical Dishes of the Orient, adapted to American Tastes and methods of preparation. Portr. frontis. New York: Sully & Kleinteich, 1913. 349p.

178 KWONG, GEORGE I. AND MAGPIONG, PACIFICO. Oriental Culinary Art. An authentic book of recipes from China, Korea, Japan and the Philippines. Los Angeles, Cal.: the author (1933). 115p. (Title page at back, pages numbered from back to front of book).

3826 LONDON & BISHOV. (Edited by) COMPLETE AMERICAN-JEWISH COOKBOOK.

893 MANDARIN CHOP SUEY COOK BOOK. Authentic translations of the best recipes of leading Chinese chefs; directions for preparation of Chinese dishes. Chicago: Pacific Trading Co., 1928. 96p. Wraps.

90 MIYAGAWA, Y. Entree and Salad Cookery. The book was printed in Japanese characters in Japan, with the exception of the preface by M. H. Simmons, Med. Dir., U.S.N., dated 1907. San Francisco, Cal.: Aoki Taiseido, 1909. 235, 22p.

2282 MOORE, ALICE. Chinese Recipes. Letters from Alice Moore to Ethel Moore Rook. Cover design by Royal Rook. Garden City, N. Y.: Doubleday, Page, 1923. 113p. Frontis. of small Chinese holding a steaming dish.

1751 NOLTON, JESSIE LOUISE. Chinese Cookery in the Home Kitchen. Editor of the Chicago Inter-Ocean. Detroit, Mich.: Chino-American Pub. (1911). 62 unnumbered p.

104 OHATA, SUSUMU ICHITARO. Cook's Cook Book. In Japanese, with names of recipes in English. San Francisco, Cal.: Hinomoto Book Co., 1912.

3208 WING, FRED. New Chinese Recipes. Spiral. Illus. New York: 1942. 44p.

3353 WONG, RICHARD. Enjoy Chinese Cooking at Home. Cook delicious Chinese food with whatever cooking materials you have at home. By the proprietor of Dragon Inn. New York: New Moon Pub., 1949. 1st ed. 89p. Wraps.

French

2944 ADAIR, A. H. Dinners Long and Short. Rational French recipes, menus and good service. Preface by Sheila Kaye-Smith; intro. by X. Marcel Boulestin; illus. by J. E. Laboureur. New York: Alfred A. Knopf, 1929. 1st ed. 217p. & xv Index.

3501 ANDORS, LISE AND ABBOTT, ANITA. Simple Masterpieces of French Cooking. Recipes and menus. Spiral, stiff paper covers. New York: Harian Publications, 1955.

2515 BABET. 99 Practical Methods of Utilizing Boiled Beef and the CLARK, VELMA R. The Art of Hun-Original Recipe for Stewed Chicken. Translated from French by A. R. New York: John Ireland, 1893. 123p. illus.

3213 BECK, PHINEAS. Clementine in in the Kitchen. About a French cook in a Massachusetts town. Illus. by Samuel Chamberlain; vignettes by Henry Stahlhut. Pub'd. in cooperation with Gourmet Magazine. New York: Hastings House, 1943. 1st ed. 228p.

3411 BERTHOLLE, LOUISETTE; BECK, SIMONE; RIPPERGER, HELMUT. What's Cooking in France. Learn to cook the French way. Drawings by Otto Fried. Spiral. New York: Washburn, 1952. 60p.

3002 BOLTON, DOROTHY. Kitchen Prelude. Mes Metiers. Trans. from the French. New York: E. P. Dutton (1932). 309p.

2949 BONNEY, THÉRÈSE AND LOUISE. French Cooking for American Kitchens. New York: R. M. McBride, 1929. 295p.

3785 BRIGODE, LOUISA. French Recipes . . . Mt. Vernon, O.: Manufacturing Printers Co., 1927. 210p.

2879 BRILLAT-SAVARIN, JEAN ANTHELME. The Physiology of Taste. Meditations on Transcendental Gastronomy. A complete translation from the French. Foreword by Frank Crowninshield. New York: Boni & Liveright, 1926. 1st ed. 359p.

3313 BRILLAT-SAVARIN, JEAN ANTHELME. The Physiology of Taste. Meditations on Transcendental Gastronomy. A complete translation from the French with preface by Charles Monselet. De Luxe Black and Gold Ed. New York: Liveright (1948). 361p.

402 BROWN, MARGARET. Margaret Brown's French Cookery Book. From the Plainest Cookery to the Most Elaborate French Dish. Washington, D.C.: Rufus H. Darby, 1886. 120p.

2558 CARON, PIERRE. French Dishes for American Tables. Author formerly chef at Delmonico's. Trans. and ed. by Mrs. Frederic Sherman. New York: D. Appleton, 1899. 231p.

3485 CARTER, GERMAINE. The Home Book of French Cookery. Simple and traditional dishes, designed for Americans. Index. New York: Doubleday & Co., 1954. 278p.

3609 CHAMBERLAIN, NARCISSE. The Flavor of France: In Recipes and Pictures. By 3 authors: Samuel (artist, photographer). his wife Narcissa (expert cook) and their daughter who planned the book. Nostalgic views of France and its food. Hastings House, New York, 1960.

3612 Conil, Jean. Gastronomic Tour de France. Desc. of each province, list of culinary specialties and complete recipes for some of the dishes mentioned. Illus. with photos and maps. New York: E. P. Dutton, 1960. 384p.

1803 Corbett, Lucy and Sidney. French Cooking in Old Detroit Since 1701. Hors d'Oeuvres in a log cabin. Recipes from pre-Revolution days. Detroit, Mich.: Wayne Univ., 1951. Spiral. 178p.

2881 Crippen, Alice Hotchkiss. French Pastry Book. Gives complete instructions for making French Pastry. New York: Brentano's, 1926. 1st ed. 103p. illus.

2439 Déliée, Felix J. The Franco-American Cookery Book. 2000 recipes of the caterer and chef of New York, Union and Manhattan Clubs. Menu for dinner for 8 for every day of the year, and recipes to match. New York: G. P. Putnam's Sons, 1884. 626p.

3540 De Pratz, Claire. French Home Cooking. Edited by Georgia Lingafelt. A chapter on wine by Jeanne Owen. Completely rev. ed. of a book published over 30 years ago. Over 500 recipes. Combined French & English index. New York: E. P. Dutton, 1956. 320p.

2564 De Rivaz, Evelyn. Little French Dinners. Edited by a famous Chef. New York: New Amsterdam Book Co., 1900. 110p.

4110 Diat, Louis. Home Cookbook. French Cooking for Americans with recipes, customs and savory foods. Foreword by Monty Woolley. Philadelphia, Pa.: J. B. Lippincott (1946). 1st ed. 309p.

3586 Donon, Joseph. The Classic French Cuisine. A complete cook book distilling a master French chef's lifetime experience. New York: Alfred A. Knopf, 1959. 368p.

2615 Escoffier, A. A Guide to Modern Cookery. New York: McClure, Phillips, 1907. 691p.

3487 Escoffier, A. The Escoffier Cook Book. A guide to the fine art of cookery. 2973 recipes. New York: Crown, 1954. 923p.

3385 Firuski, Elvia and Maurice (editors). The Best of Boulestin. Recipes and writings of the man who was not a professional chef but a gentleman amateur whose restaurant remains one of the fine eating places of the world. New York: Greenberg, 1951. 1st ed. 332p.

2716 Goy, Sylvaine Claudius. La Cuisine Anglo-Americaine, La Cuisine de l'Amerique Centrale by the Chef to Astor, Vanderbilt, Mackay & Goelet families. Privately printed in French, 1915. 489p.

2986 Hart, Frances Noyes. Pigs in Clover. Eating one's way through France. Menus in French.

No recipes. New York: Doubleday, Doran. 1931. 297p.

3426 Irwin, William Wallace. The Garrulous Gourmet. French home cooking. Foreword by Fred Allen. New York: McBride (1952). 1st ed. 208p.

1646 Jacques, Marie. Colette's Best Recipes. A book of French cookery. Boston: Little, Brown, 1925. 1st ed. 229p.

2591 Low, Berthe Julienne. French Home Cooking Adapted to the Use of American Households. New York: McClure, Phillips & Co., 1904. 332p. illus.

1702 Lucas, Dione. The Cordon Bleu Cook Book. Drawings by Phoebe Nicol. Boston: Little, Brown, 1947. 1st ed. 322p.

2797 Moore, Cora. 24 Little French Dinners. How to cook and serve them. New York: E. P. Dutton, 1919. 124p.

699 Morenci, L. R. The French Cook. Over 500 genuine French recipes, with special instructions incidental to the art of pure and wholesome cooking. Chicago: The Illustrated Pub. Co. (1886). 160p.

4307 Nos Meilleurs Recettes. By the Club Feminin de Liaison Franco-Americaine. Manassas, Va.: (1947). 1st ed. 58p. and ads. Ring binding.

3571 Philomène. French Family Cooking in Plain English. New York: Doubleday & Co., 1958. 258p.

2526 Ranhofer, Charles. The Epicurean—Analytical & Practical Study of the Culinary Art. A Franco-American Encyclopedia. 800 illus. New York: the author, 1894. 1183p.

860 Raskin, Xavier. The French Chef in Private American Families. A book of recipes. Chicago, Ill.: Rand McNally, 1922. 1st ed. 700p.

4089 Raskin, Xavier. French Cook Book for American Families. 2200 recipes, including 800 French recipes and hundreds of new American ones. Philadelphia: David McKay (1922). 713p.

3018 Reboux, Paul. Diet for Epicures. 1st ed. of a translation from the French by Iris Barry. New York: 1932. 297p.

3573 Root, Waverley. The Food of France. A book for gourmets to read and savor. Maps. New York: Alfred A. Knopf, 1958.

3324 Simon, André. French Cook Book. New edition revised by Crosby Gaige. French recipes for Americans. New York: Grosset & Dunlap (1948). 342p.

3167 Specialites De La Maison. French recipes in English from notable list of contributors incl. Vincent Astor, Pearl Buck, Dukes & Duponts, Rockefellers & Vanderbilts. Preface by Louis Bromfield, decorations by Alajalov, jacket by Clement Hurd. New York: American Friends of France, 1940. 1st ed. 108p. and ads.

966 STEARNS, OSBOURNE PUTNAM. PARIS IS A NICE DISH. Its Recipes and Restaurants. Chicago, H. Regnery Co., 1952. 169p. illus.

1904 TANTY, FRANCOIS. French Cookery for Every Home by the late "Chef de Cuisine of the Emperor Napoleon II." 438 recipes. Illus. 70 full page ads of the finest food and drink in America 60 years ago. St. Louis, Mo.: Peter Nicholson, 1893. 157p.

1994 TAYLOR, CAROLINE N. French Sauces and Entrees. Park Plaza Hotel. St. Louis, Mo.: Clarke-Sprague Co., n.d. 96p. Wraps.

3351 TURGEON, CHARLOTTE (translator). Tante Marie's French Kitchen. Recipes used for generations by French families. Decorated by Julian Brazelton. New York: Oxford Univ. Press, 1949. 323p. French & English Index.

3495 TURGEON, CHARLOTTE (translator). Tante Marie's French Pastry. Tante Marie shows you there is nothing mysterious, complicated or even extravagant about making pastries. New York: Oxford Univ. Press, 1954. 160p.

2972 VOISIN, GASTON. French Cooking for All. New York: Frederick A. Stokes, 1930. 187p.

3578 WATT, ALEXANDER. Paris Bistro Cookery. A guide to 50 Paris bistros and their specialties. Recipes, menus and food lore. Endpaper maps. New York: Knopf, 1958. 196p.

German

2681 ALLGEMEINES REZEPT-BUCH FUER BACKER UND CONDITOREN. Erster band. Herausgegeben vom Verleger. Druck und Verlag von Louis A. Roswaag, New York (c. 1913). 128p.

4361 DAVIDS, HENRIETTE. Praktisches Kochbuch für die Deutschen in Amerika. In German. Portrait of the author as frontis. Milwaukee, Wis.: G. Brumder, 1897. 2nd Amer. ed. 646p.

4354 DIE HAUSFRAU, GATTIN UND MUTTER. Praktische Anleitung für deutsch-amerikanische Hausfrauen. Milwaukee, Wis.: W. W. Coleman (1880). 456p. Paper.

817 FRIES, ALFRED. Amerikanische Gerichte. Illustriert. By the Chef, Pompeian Grillroom, Congress Hotel. Chicago, Ill.: (1915). 191p. Frontis. portr. of author.

2559 GILLETTE, MRS. F. L. AND ZIEMANN, HUGO. Das "Weisse Haus" Kochbuch. An encyclopedia of cookery . . in German. Frontis. portr. of Ida Saxton McKinley. New York: Das Morgen-Journal (1899). 651p.

3161 GUMPERT. Health Under Hitler. Heil Hunger! Trans. from German. Chapter on food. New York: 1940. 128p.

2499 HELLSTERN, CHARLES. Deutsch-Amerikanisches Illustriertes Kochbuch. New York: G. Heerbrandt, 1891. iv, 504, 17, xxiv, xiv p. Ads.

2468 HELLSTERN, CHARLES. Kochbuch. Both German and English index. New York: G. Heerbrandt, 1888. 594p. illus. plus 17p. plus Index.

2463 HARLAND, MARION. Gesunde Vernunft im Haushalte. Ein Handbuch praktischer Hausfrauenschaft. Ubersetzt von Marie Pabke. New York: C. Scribner's Sons, 1887. 577p.

3635 IN WELCHER STADT WOHNEN SIE? In German. New York: Grand Union Tea Co., n.d. 286p.

2248 MALZBENDER'S PRACTICAL RECIPES BOOK FOR BAKERS AND PASTRY COOKS. In English and German. Buffalo, N.Y.: 1912. 162p. Pict. cover.

4373 MEIER, MRS. LINA (WACHTELBORN). Aechte deutsche Kochkunst: the art of German cooking and baking: verfasst und hrsg. von Frau Lina Meier, geb. Lina W. Meier (German cooking teacher). English and German texts in parallel columns. Milwaukee, Wis.: 1909. 1st ed. 484p. & frontis. portr.

4388 MEIER, MRS. LINA. The Art of German Cooking and Baking. Milwaukee, Wis.: the author, 1922. 414p. and frontis. portr. 2nd ed.

3434 MITCHELL, LEONARD JAN. Luchow's German Cookbook. Story and favorite recipes of America's most famous German restaurant. Introduction and illustrations by Ludwig Bemelmans. New York: Doubleday & Co., 1952. 224p.

2002 PFUHL, ALEXIS CONSTANTIN CARL. Science of Health. German Cook Book. Omaha, Nebr.: Douglas Printing Co., 1912. 31p.

2134 SCHLICKEYSEN, GUSTAV. Fruit and Bread. A Scientific Diet. Trans. from the German by M. L. Holbrook, M.D. Appendix. Illus. Danville, N.Y.: Austin Jackson & Co., 1877. 227p.

3888 SCHRAMM, HANNAH (Anon.) Deutsch-Amerikanisches Kochbuchlein. Von Dorle. Pittsburgh, Pa.: Printing Co. (1896). 48p. Wraps.

3527 SCHULER, ELIZABETH. German Cookery (Mein Kochbuch). The famous best-selling modern German cookbook, translated and adapted to American use. 500 extra good recipes. New York: Crown, 1955. 224p.

2494 SCHULTZ, PAULINE (Anon.) Grand Union Kochbuch, eine leicht verstandliche und praktische Anweisung. New York: Grand Union Tea Co. (1890). 286p.

723 STIEFEL, IFA (editor). St. Paul's Bazaar Kochbuch und Geschaeftsfuerhrer . . . Chicago: Druck von F. Kressmann & Bro., 1892. 138p.

2502 THEISE, WILLIAM (Anon.) Haushaltungs-Kochbuch, ein vollstandiges Handbuch praktischer. New York: M. J. Ivers & Co., 1891. 102p. Wraps.

4015 VOLLMER, WILLIAM. The United States Cook Book. A Complete Manual for Ladies, Housekeepers and Cooks. With particular reference to the climate and production of the U.S. 165p. in German facing 165 translated into English. Philadelphia, Pa.: 1888.

2496 WEHMAN'S DEUTSCH-AMERIKANISCHES KOCHBUCH . . in German. New York: n.d. 126p. (c. 1890).

Italian

3356 BONI, ADA. The Talisman Italian Cook Book. Correct recipes for the best of every style of Italian Cooking. In English. New York: Crown, 1950. 292p.

3608 CATANZARO, ANGELA. Italian Desserts and Antipasto. ala Mama Mia. Inspired recipes and glossary. New York: Liveright, 1960. 314p.

3508a CATANZARO, ANGELA. Mama Mia Italian Cookbook. The home book of Italian cooking. New York: Liveright, 1955. 286p.

3563 CHAMBERLAIN, SAMUEL. Italian Bouquet. By an artist and photographer. Beautifully illus. Trans. from the Italian by Narcissa Chamberlain. Very selective and subtle recipes. New York: Gourmet (1958). 593p.

4383 CUNIBERTI, JULIA LOVEJOY (anon.) Practical Italian Recipes for American Kitchens . . . Janesville, Wis.: Gazette Printing Co. (1917). 32p.

129 CUSIMANO, JACK. Economical Italian Cook Book. Many new and delicious receipts designed especially to meet the high cost of living. Los Angeles, Cal.: the author, 1917. 53p. and frontis. portrait.

3564 DAVID, ELIZABETH. Italian Food. New York: Alfred A. Knopf, 1958. 362p.

2673 ISOLA, ANTONIA (Mabel Earl McGinnis). Simple Italian Cookery. New York: Harper & Brothers, 1912. 68p.

3461 LAPOLLA, GARIBALDI M. Italian Cooking for the American Kitchen. Illus. by the author. New York: Wilfred Funk, 1953. 274p.

3462 LAPOLLA, GARIBALDI M. The Mushroom Cook Book. An entertaining and nourishing way to become acquainted with the mushroom: fresh, canned or dried. Decorated by the author. New York: Wilfred Funk, 1953. 128p.

3568 LASASSO, WILMA REIVA. The All-Italian Cookbook. Cherished recipes, many written down for the first time, and each distinctive to its own Italian town and time. New York: Macmillan, 1958. 268p. illus. frontis. and drawings.

3430 LO PINTO, MARIA. The Art of Making Italian Desserts. Over 250 recipes for desserts, candies, confections, preserves, liqueurs and punches. New York: Doubleday, 1952. 223p.

3320 LO PINTO, MARIA & MILORADOVICH, MILO. The Art of Italian Cooking. 200 recipes, history and definitions of ingredients, menus for every occasion. Glossary. New York: Doubleday, 1948. 202p. illus.

3198 MIMI TELLS YOU HOW TO PREPARE YOUR FAVORITE ITALIAN DISHES AT HOME. New York: Friebele Press, 1942. 24p. booklet.

3371 POLLIO, ALBERT. Ricotta and Mozzarella Recipe Book. New York: (1950). Advertising booklet. 32p. illus.

3471 POLLIO, ALBERT. Ricotta and Mozzarella Recipe Book. New York: Aiello Dairy Maid, 1953. 20p. illus.

3524 PREZZOLINI. Spaghetti Dinner. A history of Spaghetti eating and cooking. New York: 1955.

362 RIELLO, MARY CARMEN. ITALIAN COOK BOOK, Written in English. New Haven, Conn. 1948. 62p.

3288 STANDEN, NIKA. Reminiscence and Ravioli. Classic Italian recipes and family life. New York: William Morrow, 1946. 1st ed. 148p.

3530 TAGLIENTE, MARIA LUISA. Italian Cookbook. In English. Illus. by Reisie Lonette. New York: Kingsport Press, 1955. 320p.

Jewish

3581 BELLIN, MILDRED GROSBERG. The Jewish Cook Book. This is the successor of the famous Aunt Babette Cook Book, the first Jewish cookbook in English. New York: Doubleday, 1959. 444p.

1411 THE CENTER TABLE. Compiled under the Auspices of the Sisterhood and Mother's Club of Temple Nishkan Tefila for the benefit of the New Jewish Center. Boston, Mass.: 1922. 213p. Ads. Autographed recipes.

656 THE CHICAGO JEWISH YEAR BOOK, 1930. A cook book of tested recipes for refined tastes. Chicago: The South Shore Temple, 1930. 159p.

3589 GOLDBERG, MOLLY AND WALDO, MYRA. The Molly Goldberg Jewish Cookbook. Read first, then enjoy a delightful collection of mouthwatering recipes from many lands. Each section introduced by Molly's inimitable comments. New York: Doubleday, 1959. 320p. illus.

2775 GREENBAUM, FLORENCE KREISLER. The International Jewish Cook Book. 1600 recipes according to Jewish dietary laws. Recipes of America, Austria, Germany, Russia, France, Poland etc. New York: Bloch Pub., 1918. 419p.

3260 GREENBERG, BETTY D. AND SILVERMAN, ALTHEA O. The Jewish Home Beautiful. Festival days; history and customs, menus and recipes. New York: The Women's League of the United Synagogue of America, 1945. 136p. illus.

3544 KASDEN, SARA. Love and Knishes: An Irrepressible Guide to Jewish Cooking. Illus. by Louis Slobodkin. Chapters on Cholent, Tzimmes, Yom Kippur Cookery, Cocktails. New York: Vanguard Press, 1956. 192p.

2245 LEITER, MRS. HENRY AND VAN BERGH, MISS SARA (Compilers). The Flower City Cook Book. The Sisterhood, affiliated with Congregation Berith Kodesh, Rochester, N.Y.: 1911. 1st ed. 188p.

3490 LEONARD, LEAH W. Jewish Cookery. In accordance with the Jewish Dietary Laws. New York: Crown, 1954. 497p.

3520 LEONARD, LEAH W. The Jewish Holiday Cook Book. Special holiday foods and food customs, in accordance with dietary laws. New York: Crown, 1955. 192p.

3992 LEVY, ESTHER. A Cookery—in accordance with the rules of the Jewish religion. Adapted for Jewish housekeepers; with medicinal recipes and other valuable information. Philadelphia: W. S. Turner, 1871. 200p.

3826 LONDON, ANNE & BISHOV, BERTHA K. (Editors). Complete American-Jewish Cookbook. Contains glossary of special Yiddish terms. Cleveland & New York: (1952). 623p. illus. with photos.

3641 THE PRACTICAL COOK BOOK. Compiled by The Sisterhood of the West End Synagogue. New York: n.d. 121p.

2258 RECIPES TRIED AND TRUE. Sisterhood of Temple Emanuel (Yonkers, N.Y.:) Truan Press, 1913. 122p.

3792 TEMPTING KOSHER DISHES. 112 choice recipes. Printed in English and Jewish. 2nd ed. enl. Cincinnati, O.: Manischewitz Co., Fine Matzo Bakers, 1928. 80p. illus Pict. wraps.

3804 TEMPTING KOSHER DISHES. Prepared from Matzo Products. Cincinnati, O.: B. Manischewitz Co., 1930. 79p. English, 79p. Hebrew. Illus. in color. Decorative end papers.

Latin American

3604 BOTAFOGO, DOLORES. The Art of Brazilian Cookery. Over 300 authentic Brazilian recipes, adapted to American entertaining by Brazil's foremost cooking teacher. New York: Doubleday & Co., 1960. 240p. illus.

4448 CRISTOBAL COOK BOOK. Panama, Canal Zone: 1921. 112p. and ads. Wraps.

4449 TROPICAL COOK BOOK. College club cook book; recipes from the men-folks, and 'special native recipes.' Ring binder. Panama, Canal Zone: n.d. n. pub., 172p.

3559 VALLDEJULI, CARMEN ABOY. The Art of Caribbean Cookery. West Indian dishes ready to prepare in American kitchens, with both Caribbean and English names. New York: Doubleday & Co., 1957. 254p. illus.

Mexican—Spanish

15 ARIZONA MEXICAN COOK BOOK. Tucson, Ariz.: n.d. 72p. illus. Pict. wraps.

3535 AVENELL, VICTOR M. DE SABROSO! An introduction to Spanish cookery. New York: Las Americas Pub. (1956). 62p.

1686 EL COCINERO ESPANOL. Tested Recipes of Famous Spanish

Dishes. Sold for the benefit of Milk Fund for Spanish Babies. 87 recipes. Boston, Mass.: Medical Bureau to Aid Spanish Democracy (June 1938). Spiral bdg., pict. wraps. 45p. (In English).

2125 FERGUSSON, ERNA. Mexican Cookbook. An unusually attractive book of Mexican recipes. Illus. by Vidaurreta. Santa Fe, N.M.: Rydal, 1934. 1st ed. 119p.

220 HAFFNER-GINGER, BERTHA. California Mexican-Spanish Cook Book. Selected recipes. n.d., n. pub. 111p. illus.

4434 LOURT, H. S. 50 Choice Recipes, of Mexican and Spanish Dishes. Privately published, n.p., n.d. (1905?). 32p.

4215 MEXICAN COOKERY FOR AMERICAN HOMES. Paperback pamphlet published by Gebhardt's. San Antonio, Tex.: 1936. 62p. illus. in color.

4202 MEXICAN COOKING. The Flavor of the 20th century—that real Mexican tang. San Antonio, Tex.: Gebhardt Chili Powder Co. (before 1910). 44p. illus. Wraps.

89 MIDDLETON, MAY. Recipes from Old Mexico. Compiled and translated (each page has one recipe in both English and Spanish). San Jose, Cal.: Melvin & Murgotten, 1909. 36p. Wraps.

3368 MULVEY, RUTH WATT AND ALVAREZ, LUISA MARIA. Good Food From Mexico. A book to read or to cook by. New York: M. Barrows (1950). 1st ed. 290p.

3556 PEREYRA DE AZNAR, MARINA AND FROUD, NINA. The Home Book of Spanish Cookery. Real Spanish dishes from various regions of Spain, with a special section on fish. New York: M. Barrows, 1957. 256p.

1987 PET MILK CO'S. Guia Para El Cuidado Prenatal. Illus. Wraps. Pet Milk Co., St. Louis, Mo., 1955. 50p.

1972 RICHARDSON, MYRTLE. Genuine Mexican and Spanish Cookery Recipes for American Homes. Kansas City, Mo.: 1934. 32p. booklet. Pict. cover.

4191 RYWELL, MARTIN (Compiled by) MEXICAN COOK BOOK. More than 300 tasty recipes. Wraps. Pioneer, Harriman, Tenn. 1952. 70p.

4226 STOKER, CATHARINE ULMER. Concha's Mexican Kitchen Cook Book. Recipes from Aztec and Mexican kitchens, handed down for generations. Stories of customs in the land of Montezuma. San Antonio, Tex.: Naylor (1958). 5th ed. 244p.

4227 YOUNG, ALICE ERIE. Discovering Mexican Cooking. Patricia Peters Stephenson assisted and did the illustrations too. Theodosia Moreno Samano helped with information on Mexican food and customs. A gay little book with delicious recipes. San Antonio, Tex.: Naylor Co. (1958). 61p.

2112 ZELAYETA, ELENA. Elena's Secrets of Mexican Cooking. More than 500 recipes from South-of-the-Border. You can add tang to regular meals. Englewood Cliffs, N.J.: Prentice-Hall, 1958. 224p.

Near Eastern

2749 GREEK COOK BOOK. In Greek; recipe titles in English. New York: Atlantis (1917). 283p.

3306 MACDOUGALL, ALLEN ROSS. And the Greeks. A book of Hellenic Recipes. New York: Near East Foundation (c. 1942). 109p. Pict. cover.

3248 MARDIKIAN, GEORGE. Dinner at Omar Khayyam's. War conservation printing. Foreword by William Saroyan; intro. by Joseph Henry Jackson. New York: Viking, 1944. 150p.

3557 ROWLAND, JOAN. Good Food From The Near East. Favorite Recipes from 12 Countries—a new culinary world. M. Barrows; New York (1957). 274p.

3549 TSELEMENTES, NICHOLAS. Greek Cookery. By an international authority on European and Oriental cooking. Decorations. New York: D.C. Divry, 1956. 239p. and ad.

3558 TURKISH RECIPES. Illus. booklet. Recipes "borrowed" from book of the Turkish-American Women's Cultural Society, pub. in Ankara. This one pub'd. by Turkish Information Office, New York, 1957. 36p.

Russian

2826 GAGARINE, PRINCESS ALEXANDRE (compiler and translator). The Borzoi Cook Book. New York: Alfred A. Knopf, 1923. 247p.

3303 KROPOTKIN, ALEXANDRA. How to Cook and Eat in Russian. The most popular national dishes. (In English). New York: G. P. Putnam's Sons (1947). 1st ed. 270p.

3223 MADDOX, GAYNOR (Editor in Chief) AND NOBLE, RANSOM E. JR. (Managing Editor). Russian Cook Book. A War-Time edition for American Homes. New York: Russian War Relief, 1943. 95p. Spiral binding.

3201 RUSSIAN COOKBOOK FOR AMERICAN HOMES. By a distinguished editorial board including Charlotte Adams, Ripperger, and Clementine Paddleford. Pict. bds. Ring binder. New York: 1942. 94p.

3032 SELIVANOVA, NINA NIKOLAEVNA. Dining and Wining in Old Russia. New York: E. P. Dutton, 1933. 1st ed. 154p.

4120 UKRANIAN COOK BOOK. 76 traditional recipes. Philadelphia, Pa.: n.d. 82p.

Scandinavian

3077 AKERSTROM — Söderström, Jenny. The Princesses Cook Book. Trans. from the Swedish by Carlson. Photos of 3 Swedish princesses on cover. New York: 1936. 315p.

3297 COOMBS, ANNA OLSSON. Modern Swedish Cookbook. Over 250 recipes from smorgasbord to desserts and party food. Decorations by Irene Aronson. New York: A. A. Wyn (1947). 196p.

3334 COOMBS, ANNA OLSSON. The Smorgasbord Cookbook. Over 200 new recipes, nearly all to be prepared the day before a party. New York: A. A. Wyn (1949). 240p.

4336 FROM DANISH KITCHENS. Compiled by the Annex Club of St. John's Lutheran Church, to preserve favorite Danish recipes. Seattle, Wash.: 1941. 5th ed. Spiral bdg. 144p.

2806 HAMMOND, MRS. ERICSSON. Salad Appetizer Cookbook. 1st supplement to the "Swedish French American Cookbook." New York: Privately printed (c. 1920). 1st ed.

2884 HAMMOND, MRS. ERICSSON. Svensk-Amerikanska Kokbok. In Swedish. New York: the author (1926). 390p. illus.

2777 HAMMOND, MRS. ERICSSON. The Swedish, French, American Cookbook. New York: the author, 1918. 480p. illus.

744 HEMMETS DROTTNING KOKBOK. Iva Tusen Vardefulla Recepter (many with facsimile autographs of donors). Chicago: Fort Dearborn Pub. (1899). 604p. illus. (A Swedish translation of the "Home Queen Cook Book.")

805 HEMMETS KOKBOK. Chicago: 1913. 248p.

2332a LANDSTAD-JENSEN, MAGNY. Norwegian Recipes. Brooklyn, N. Y.: 1947. 175p. Pict. cover on plastic bds.

3145 NORBERG, INGA. Good Food From Sweden. Includes the Smorgasbord. New York: M. Barrows, 1939. 186p.

758 NY NORSK-DANSK OG AMERICANSK KOGEBOG. Recipes in double columns: Danish and English. Chicago, Ill.: John Anderson Pub., 1905. 418p. illus.

1066 "QVINNAN OCH HEMMETS" NYA KOKBOK. Swedish cook book. Pictorial cloth covers. Cedar Rapids, Iowa. 1922. 302p.

3076 SIMONSON, GERDA. "Smorgasbordet" Swedish Hors d'Oeuvres. 300 Recipes. New York: Albert Bonnier, 1935. 104p. illus. Spiral bdg.

1261 SMORGASBORD COOK BOOK. Featuring Smorgasbord. Autographed recipes. Pictorial wraps. Spiral. Illus. Bethesda Ladies' Aid, Maryland. n.d. 69p.

741 SVENSK-AMERIKANSK KOKBOK. Swedish-English Cookbook with recipes in both languages. Chicago, Ill.: Engberg-Holmberg Pub., 1897. 378p. illus. Pict. cover. Book ads.

735 SWEDISH-ENGLISH COOK BOOK. English text opposite the Swedish. Illus. Pictorial boards. Chicago, Ill.: Engberg-Holmberg Pub., 1895. 378p.

352 SWEDISH SMORGASBORD AND 500 OTHER FAMOUS RECIPES—SWEDISH AMERICAN COOK BOOK. Edited by West Hartford Ladies Aid Society. Autographed recipes. Spiral bdg. Pictorial wraps. Emanuel

Evangelical Lutheran Church, Hartford, Conn., 1941. 159p. ads.

1824 VALLENTIN, C. A. Praktisk Illustrierad Kok-Bok for Svenskarne/Amerika. Minneapolis, Minn.: Svenska Bok-och Musikhandelus Forlag, 1889. 410p. illus.

3618 VAN DER TUUK, MARIANNE GRONWALL. Swedish Cooking At Its Best. Genuine Smorgasbord; most popular traditional dishes. New York: Rand McNally & Co., 1960. Col. photos and black and whites.

867 WALLI, MINA. Keittokirja, Kolmas, Korjattu ja Laajennettu Painos Cook Book. 3rd ed. revised and enl. Chicago: A.S.S.K. Kustantama (1923). 390p. (Finnish and English).

2709 WALLI, MINA. Suomalais-Amerikalainen. Keittokirja. New York: 1914. 350p. (Text in double columns; Finnish in one, English in the other.)

Western European

2730 DAVIES, SAMUEL E. An English Butler's Canapes, Salads, Sandwiches, Drinks, etc. New York: Hirschler Books (1916). 109p.

3136 DISTINGUISHED CHEESE DISHES OF SWITZERLAND. Authentic recipes. New York: Switzerland Cheese Assoc., 1939. 15p. illus. Wraps.

2063 LAFAYETTE REFORMED CHURCH. Old Dutch Receipts. From the homes of Communipaw and Lafayette. Issued by the Ladies of the church. Newark, N.J.: Holbrook, 1885. 43p. and ads.

3304 LAVERTY, MAURA. Maura Laverty's Cookbook. With a section on diet by Sybil Le Brocquy and decorations by Louis Le Brocquy.* New York: Longmans, Green, 1947. 149p. *A literary cook book —wisdom and humor—recipes with an Irish accent.

2718 LUCK, MRS. BRIAN. The Belgian Cook-book. The pick of a great national cuisine that should be better known and more used. New York: E. P. Dutton, 1915. 151p.

3072a MAUDUIT, VICOMTE DE. The Vicomte in the Kitchenette. Illus. by Mary Shepard. Covici, Friede: New York, 1935. 146p.

Index of Authors

Index of Titles

Frontispiece from "The Century Cook Book" Chicago 1894

Index of Place of Publication

Index of Book Prices

Where two prices are given for the same title, the difference is based on the edition.

No.	*Price*	*No.*	*Price*	*No.*	*Price*	*No.*	*Price*
4	$5.50	198	$2.25	282	$ .75	342	$2.50
8	7.50	199	3.50	293	5.25	343	2.50
11	1.50	200	3.75	294	4.50	344	2.50
12	10.25	201	3.50	295	3.75	345	5.00
19	12.50	202	1.25	296	5.50	348	2.75
19a	2.50	204	6.50	297	.75	350	4.75
20	9.25	205	1.50	298	5.50	353	3.50
41	5.50	206	4.50	299	4.95	354	1.00
47	6.50	207	4.75	300	5.00	355	5.00
53	5.00	208	1.75	301	.75	356	3.25
61	3.25	209	2.50	302	10.00	357	3.50
62	8.75	210	1.75	303	.75	359	2.50
70	2.25	211	.50	304	.75	361	4.50
76	3.25	212	.75	305	4.75	364	.25
82	5.50	216a	.50	306	5.00	366	2.75
88	3.75	223	6.50	307	.75	369	1.75
95	5.50	233	5.75	309	.75	370	1.50
108	5.75	241	6.50	310	.75	373	2.50
112	4.50	244	8.50	311	5.75	375	2.75
134	2.25	250	1.75	313	5.00	376	1.00
135	7.50	253	11.50	314	8.50	377	3.75
	3.50	254	18.50	317	4.50	378	4.50
142	6.00	256	10.00	318	4.50	380	4.50
144	3.50	262	6.50	319	.75	381	3.50
	5.50	264	6.75	320	4.50	388	4.50
147	5.50	265	9.75	322	3.75	391	4.75
148	2.50	266	14.50	323	2.75	392	1.75
153	5.50	270	4.50	324	3.75	393	8.75
160	12.50	272	2.00	326	4.75	395a	2.25
169	5.00		7.50	327	3.50	400	4.75
	7.50	273	8.00	329	.75	407	4.50
172	3.00	274	6.50	330	1.00	420	1.25
188	2.75	276	12.50	331	3.75	422	1.35
189	2.75	282	6.50	332	4.25	423	7.50
190	4.50	285	9.50	333	.75	426	2.75
192	1.25	286	8.50	334	3.75	430	1.75
195	2.50	288	3.75	335	5.50	431	4.75
197	2.25	290	.75	340	.75	432	5.00

433	$8.50	532	$4.75	715	$5.00	847	$1.25
435	1.25	533	3.25	717	4.95	850	7.50
436	3.50	534	1.75	722	5.50	854	4.50
438	1.25	536	2.00	728	5.00	856	3.75
439	1.75	543	2.75	731	8.50	857	3.75
440	3.50	547	14.50	732	4.75	858	3.95
441	1.00	549	14.00	733	5.25	860	6.50
443	3.50	550	14.50	737	5.25	864	3.50
445	4.50	552	9.75		3.75	869	7.50
446	.75	562	2.75	738	5.25	875	1.00
452	1.75	570	17.50	742	4.25	879	1.50
454	4.50	573	12.50	747a	5.00	883	1.75
455	1.75	580	6.50	748	.75	884	1.75
456	1.00	582	4.75	754	4.50	885	3.50
458	5.00	584	9.75	757	2.75	885a	.75
461	4.50	603	4.25	769	6.50	886	2.50
467	5.00	609	4.50		7.50	886a	.75
468	4.50	610	5.00	770	4.25	888a	.75
469	3.50	618	2.95	772	5.75	891	1.75
470	4.50	624	2.75	774	9.50	894	5.50
471	1.00	628	3.50	775a	4.00	895	2.75
472	1.00	635	4.75	776	4.75	898	5.50
473	1.25	636	4.50		3.75	899	2.75
474	1.00	640	1.75	778	6.50	902	2.25
477	1.00	649	3.50	781	10.50	903	1.75
481	1.50	653a	5.00	786	4.50	906	6.00
482	2.75	658	3.75	791	4.75	909	2.75
484	2.25	660	3.75	793	6.50	911	2.50
487	6.50	664	4.75	803	4.75	915	1.75
493	2.75	665	3.25	806	4.50	916	2.75
494	3.50	667	4.50	810	9.50	918	2.75
495	6.75	673	4.25	813	4.50	921	1.25
498	4.50	673a	2.95	816	1.00	922	4.75
498a	2.50	676	5.00	820	3.50	927	2.25
506	14.50	678	4.25	820a	.75	931	3.50
513	4.75	679	3.50	821	1.25	934	2.50
518	4.25	687	6.50	826	1.25	936	1.25
519	5.50	703	6.50	829	1.50	937	3.75
521	4.75	707	4.50	831	1.25	940	4.50
522	5.50	708	2.75	832	3.25	941	5.50
523	4.95	709	8.50	837	3.75	945	4.75
524	35.00	713	4.75	839	8.50	947	2.75
530	3.50	714	4.75	842	3.95	947a	.75

947b	$ .75	1036	$3.75	1259	$3.75	1499	$5.50
947c	.75	1037	1.75	1272	4.50	1500	7.50
947d	.75	1040	6.00	1279	3.75	1505	9.75
947e	.75	1041	4.75	1290	1.75	1517	9.50
947f	.75	1056	6.50	1295	1.00	1519	12.50
947g	.75	1072	2.50	1296	1.00	1532	4.00
947h	.75	1082	3.95	1301	5.00	1533	6.25
947i	.75	1096	4.75	1302	4.75	1538	6.50
948	1.75	1099	1.50	1304	1.50	1539	12.25
	3.75	1103	4.75	1306	4.50	1542	1.75
948a	.75	1105	4.75	1330	6.50	1546	14.50
948b	.75	1136	2.75	1331	1.50	1548	6.50
948c	.75	1137	3.75	1333	1.00	1553	6.00
948d	.75	1138	1.95	1336	2.75	1557a	4.50
948e	.75	1140	4.95	1346	5.75	1559	4.25
948f	.75	1142	4.95		4.75	1563	3.50
948g	.75	1143	4.95	1352	7.50	1564	3.50
949	1.50	1147	75.00	1360	2.75	1566	3.25
950	2.75	1165	2.75	1363	19.50	1570	6.50
	3.75	1174	5.50	1364	4.50	1571	4.75
952	3.25	1177	4.75	1368	6.50	1572	2.75
953	1.75	1178	2.75	1379	1.75	1573	2.75
954	2.75	1179	3.50	1395	5.50	1575	2.50
955	3.50	1180	3.25	1414	4.00	1576	2.50
956	3.75		4.25	1415	3.50	1580	5.00
958	5.25	1183	1.50	1425	4.50	1583	2.75
960	5.75	1184	4.50		6.50	1584	2.75
963	1.00	1185	3.50	1428	1.25		2.50
964	3.75	1186	3.00	1435	3.95	1587	3.75
965	3.50	1199	2.75	1441	3.75	1589	3.50
967	1.00	1209	5.50	1448	4.75	1590	2.00
968	1.00	1211	5.25	1457	5.50	1597	5.50
969	1.00	1221	8.50	1466	5.00	1599	2.25
971	3.75	1227	5.50	1468	5.00	1600	5.75
972	4.95	1230	7.75	1481	4.50	1601a	4.75
973	.50	1237	2.00	1483	2.75	1602	1.75
977	.75	1248	3.50	1484	5.25	1604	1.75
978	.75	1250	6.50	1485	1.00	1605	2.75
1011	3.75	1252	4.75	1489	3.75	1608	1.50
1012	3.50	1253	3.50	1491	6.50	1614	2.50
1027	5.75	1253a	5.00	1493	10.00	1616	1.25
1030	2.75	1257	6.50	1495	15.00	1617	3.75
1032	5.75	1258	2.00	1498	9.50	1618	1.25

1620	$4.50		$6.50	1841	$5.75	1974	$2.25
1623	2.50	1702	5.00	1842	3.50	1975	2.25
1624	2.50	1703	3.75	1843	7.50	1980	5.50
1628	2.50	1704	3.75	1845	9.50	1982	9.50
1631	1.50	1705	5.50	1851	4.50	1983	4.50
1633	1.50	1706	4.95	1852	4.75	1984	7.50
1635	1.00	1710	3.75	1853	8.50		5.25
1636	2.25	1711	5.50	1854	3.50	1985	1.25
1638	3.75	1718	17.50	1859	4.75	1986	5.50
1639	2.75	1726	14.50	1864	4.75	1989	4.75
1641	3.50	1729	3.75	1866	4.50	1990	3.95
1642	1.50	1734	17.50	1867	3.25	2012	6.50
1643	4.50	1740	12.50	1868	5.50	2013	4.75
1646	4.25	1741	4.75	1870	2.50	2020	5.50
1648	3.50	1744	6.50	1872	1.75	2021	4.50
	4.25	1748	7.50	1873	2.50	2025	2.50
1649	3.25	1753	3.50	1875	3.25	2028	3.75
1651	2.75	1754	2.50	1877	4.25	2030	6.50
1652	3.50	1759	1.25	1878	3.50	2031	4.75
1654	4.75	1762	4.75	1880	1.75	2032	9.50
1655	3.50	1769	5.50	1881	5.00		4.95
1656	3.00	1771	6.50	1883	3.95	2033	4.75
1658	1.25	1773	5.75	1884	2.50	2034	4.75
1659	3.50	1779	4.75	1885	4.50	2035	4.75
1665	3.75	1783	4.75	1886	1.25	2036	4.95
1668	4.50	1794	4.25	1887	2.25	2043a	6.50
1670	4.50	1798	7.50	1888	4.50	2054	.50
1672	3.50	1802	5.50	1889	2.75	2059	3.75
1675	3.25	1803	6.25	1890	3.50	2076	4.75
1676	1.75	1806	4.25	1894	4.50	2080	3.25
1680	4.25	1813	5.00	1914	6.50	2095	6.75
1682	8.50	1814	5.50	1916	3.00	2099a	3.50
1684	6.00		4.25	1929	5.75	2100	7.50
1687	1.75	1815	4.75	1937	4.50	2101	1.75
1688	4.75	1816	50.00	1939	4.50	2101a	6.50
1690	4.75	1817	8.50	1942	5.00	2107	6.25
1691	2.25	1821	4.75	1949	2.75	2108	3.50
1692	3.50	1822	10.00	1951	4.75	2109	15.50
1693	4.50	1830	8.50	1955	1.75	2110	3.50
1696	3.75	1831	6.75	1960	8.75	2111	3.95
1697	4.75	1837	5.00	1961	1.75	2112	3.95
1699	3.50	1839	8.10	1964	1.25	2113	3.50
1700	3.75	1840	2.75	1968	6.50	2114	6.40

2125	$7.50	2262	$1.00	2334	$4.75	2440	$1.75
2126	7.50	2265	5.00	2336	4.50	2448	2.75
2130	2.75	2267	4.75	2337	.50	2452	3.00
2131	19.75	2270	6.50	2338	5.50	2472	6.00
2139	2.00	2274	6.75	2339	4.25	2475	2.75
2140	2.00	2277	2.50	2340	5.50	2479	7.50
2143	12.50	2278	.50	2341	2.50	2480	6.50
2144a	7.75	2283	3.75	2342	5.50	2481	6.50
2147	2.00	2284	1.25	2344	.95	2484	5.50
2150	1.50	2285	1.75	2345	3.95	2491	6.50
2153	2.00	2288	5.00	2346	4.00	2493	4.25
2155	2.00	2291	6.50	2347	2.95	2499	8.50
2159	2.00	2292	4.75	2349	1.50	2500	4.75
2162	6.50	2294	4.75	2350	.50	2504	2.75
2164	14.50	2296	1.50	2352	1.00	2506	5.75
2165	2.00	2298	4.75	2352a	3.25	2516	4.50
2166	4.50	2299	3.25	2353a	19.50	2517	1.50
2168	9.50	2300	1.00	2359	4.50	2523	12.50
2171	14.00	2301	7.50	2363	8.75	2527	1.75
2172	3.25	2302	.50	2369	8.50	2529	5.00
2173	5.50	2303	4.75	2369b	2.00	2530	3.50
2179	2.00	2305	2.25	2369d	4.75	2532	2.50
2184	2.00	2306	3.25	2369e	9.75	2536	7.50
2188	2.00	2312	7.50	2369g	7.50	2539	3.75
2192	2.00	2314	.50	2373	2.00	2540	5.75
2197	2.00	2315	6.50	2376	4.50	2547	2.50
2199	8.50	2316	3.75	2379	2.00	2548	2.75
2201	2.00	2317	4.25	2380	5.75	2551	3.95
2205	14.00	2320	5.50	2382	2.50	2552	1.75
2206	5.00	2321	8.00	2384	2.00	2554	4.75
2207	5.00	2322	3.50	2388	2.00	2556	4.75
2212	2.00	2323	4.50	2392	8.75	2557	10.00
2214	6.50	2325	4.95	2397	2.00	2559	5.50
2217	8.50	2326	1.00	2401	6.50	2563	2.75
2218	6.50	2327	3.25	2403	19.50	2565	3.50
2223	4.00	2328	3.25	2404	4.50	2567	2.75
2230	2.50	2329	2.75	2406	3.50	2570	4.75
2232	6.50		1.50	2407	2.00	2572	4.75
2234	6.50	2330	1.75	2409	8.25	2574	14.00
2238	6.25	2330a	1.00	2411	2.00	2578	4.75
2239	4.75	2330b	1.00	2416	6.25	2582	3.50
2245	8.50	2331	4.75	2426	5.25	2589b	6.75
2249	5.25	2332	3.50	2427	1.25	2589c	3.50

2589d	$3.75	2696	$4.25	2804	$4.50	2872	$2.75
2589e	2.50	2697	4.75	2812	1.95		.95
2589f	2.50	2701	4.75	2815	4.75	2873	1.00
2589h	2.50	2703	1.75	2816	4.75	2875	1.25
2589i	1.75	2707	2.75	2817	2.50	2878	1.75
2590	4.25	2710	3.75	2818	2.50	2879	5.50
2595	3.75	2722	4.50	2819	1.50	2880	4.75
2596	7.50	2725	2.50	2819a	1.00	2881	2.75
	4.50	2726	2.50	2819c	2.50	2882	4.50
2597	4.75	2728	18.50	2819d	2.25	2883	3.50
	3.75	2729	3.50	2819e	1.95	2884	2.75
2604	4.75	2731	.95		1.25	2885	3.50
2609	5.50	2736	3.75	2819g	.50	2886	9.50
2619	2.50	2737	5.50	2819h	2.75	2889	4.25
2620	4.75	2742	2.75	2819i	1.00	2890	3.75
2621	1.75	2749	9.50	2824	6.50	2891	3.75
2626	4.75	2751	2.75		4.75	2892	2.50
2627	3.50	2754	4.75	2827	2.00	2894	2.25
2629	5.75	2756	2.50	2828	1.50	2898	5.50
2632	5.25	2762	2.75	2829	4.25	2900	1.25
2634	2.25	2765	4.25		3.25	2903	2.50
2635	4.75	2766	3.25	2830	1.75	2905	1.75
2638	3.75	2767	2.75	2831	9.75	2906	4.00
2641	4.75	2768	2.75	2832	4.75	2909	3.50
2642	3.75	2770	2.75	2833	4.75	2910	3.75
2649	1.75	2771	1.95	2836	4.75	2911	3.75
2653	2.50	2774	1.25	2839	2.75		1.75
	5.50	2778	.85	2841	2.75	2915	3.75
2654	4.25	2779	4.75	2842	1.25	2916	.50
2655	2.50	2780	.75	2843	4.75	2918	2.00
2656	7.95	2782	4.75	2844	5.00		1.75
2661	6.75	2784	2.75	2845	2.50	2920	3.50
2664	1.00	2786	1.75	2847	2.50		5.50
2665	2.75	2787	2.75	2848	4.50	2921	2.50
2666	35.00	2789	2.25	2852	1.75	2923	2.75
2670	2.25	2793	3.50	2853	4.75	2926	6.25
2676	2.50	2794	1.00	2855	4.75	2931	1.25
2678	1.75	2796	6.50	2858	.75	2932	4.75
2680	3.75	2797	4.50	2864	.50	2933	3.25
	5.50	2798	2.25	2865	3.50	2935	1.25
2686	5.25	2799	4.75	2867	1.75	2936	3.75
2692	2.25	2801	1.25	2868	1.00	2937	5.50
2693	6.50	2803	2.50	2869	5.50	2939	1.50

2940	$2.50	3021	$2.75	3089	$2.75	3138	$2.75
2942	8.50	3023	1.75	3090	4.00	3140	2.50
2944	6.50	3026	1.50	3092	3.50	3141	2.75
	4.50	3028	2.75	3094	2.00	3142	2.50
2945	3.75	3029	2.50	3095	2.00	3143	2.75
2946	3.75	3030	5.50	3096	2.00	3145	3.25
2953	3.50	3034	6.50	3097	3.00	3147	4.50
2954	2.75	3035	1.75	3098	6.50	3148	3.50
2956	2.25	3037	3.75		6.00	3149	2.75
2960	1.00	3040	3.50	3099	9.00	3150	2.25
2961	4.75	3042	5.50		9.75	3151	3.75
2962	3.75	3043	5.50	3102	8.50	3152	3.50
2963	1.00	3046	6.50	3103	5.50	3153	1.75
2964	1.50	3049	1.25	3104	3.50	3154	3.75
	1.00	3051	1.75	3105	2.75		4.50
2967	25.00	3052	6.50	3105a	2.25	3155	5.50
2968	2.75	3053	3.00	3106	.50	3156	11.50
2969	3.50	3054	6.00	3108	2.50	3157	3.00
2970	4.75		2.75	3111	5.50	3159	4.95
2976	3.75	3055	2.25	3112	4.75	3160	4.50
2978	2.25	3058	6.95	3113	3.75	3162	3.75
2979	1.75	3059	3.50	3114	4.50	3163	4.50
2980	5.50	3060	3.25	3115	8.50	3164	3.00
2981	2.25		2.50	3116	.75	3166	4.50
2982	.50	3062	2.50	3117	7.75	3167	5.00
2983	2.50	3063	5.50	3118	1.00	3168	2.75
2985	4.75	3064	1.25	3118a	1.00	3169	2.75
2986	4.75	3066	1.25	3119	2.75	3171	5.50
2989	2.75	3067	1.95	3119a	1.75	3172	4.75
2990	6.50	3068	2.75	3120	2.75	3173	1.35
2994	2.50	3069	2.75	3122	4.75	3175	4.75
2999	2.50	3074	2.25	3124	3.75	3176	5.00
3000	6.00	3075	6.50	3125	7.50	3176	3.50
3003	5.50	3078	1.00	3126	3.75	3177	3.75
3005	4.50	3079	2.75		2.50	3177a	.75
3006	1.95	3080	1.75	3127	1.00	3178	4.00
3007	2.75	3081	8.50	3129	5.50	3179	1.75
3008	1.00	3082	3.50	3130	9.75	3181	4.25
3010	2.50	3084	2.50	3132	5.50	3182	3.25
3013	8.50	3085	6.50	3134	3.25	3183	4.75
	5.00	3086	2.50	3135	4.00	3185	2.35
	7.50	3087	1.00	3136	1.00	3186	3.75
3015	2.75	3088	10.00	3136a	1.50	3188	1.75

3189	$12.50	3254	$3.95	3315	$8.50	3364	$2.50
3192	2.75	3255	3.75	3316	2.50	3365	5.00
3193	1.25	3256	5.00	3318	8.50	3366	2.50
3194	4.50	3257	2.75	3319	4.00	3367	3.50
3199	1.50	3259	3.75	3320	2.95	3368	3.75
3202	2.50	3260	4.00	3321	4.75	3370a	1.75
3203	2.50	3262	4.25	3323	5.50	3372	2.50
3204	4.00	3263	5.95	3324	3.50	3373	3.95
3205	4.50	3264	2.00	3325	5.50	3374	5.00
3206	3.75	3266	2.25	3326	2.75	3375	3.75
3207	3.75	3267	2.50	3327	3.75		2.75
3209	1.75	3268	4.75	3328	2.75	3376	.95
3210	4.75	3270	5.00	3329	6.00	3377	1.75
3211	4.75	3271	5.00	3330	7.50	3379	7.50
3212	1.75	3273	3.95	3331	4.25	3380	5.00
3213	4.75	3274	.50	3332	3.75	3381	3.50
	5.25	3275	2.75	3333	5.00	3382	2.50
3214	4.75	3276	4.95	3334	4.50	3384	4.50
3215	4.75	3277	4.50	3335	6.75	3385	5.00
3216	4.75	3279	5.75	3336	4.50	3387	.95
3218	6.50	3280	6.00	3337	4.50	3388	3.95
3220	5.00	3282	2.75	3338	6.50	3389	2.75
3221	1.00	3284	3.50	3339	4.50	3390	3.75
3223	4.00	3286	3.50	3341	4.75	3392	2.75
3225	1.00		4.75	3344	3.75	3393	3.25
3226	3.75	3288	3.75	3345	.75	3396	6.50
3227	3.75	3290	3.50	3346	2.75	3397	4.25
3228	1.25	3291	2.75	3347	2.50	3398	2.75
3229	2.75	3294	3.00	3348	5.50	3399	1.25
3231	3.50	3295	4.50	3350	2.00	3400	6.50
3232	2.75		3.00	3351	5.50	3401	4.00
3233	7.50	3296	2.25		4.75	3402	3.95
3238	4.75	3297	4.75	3352	1.75	3403	3.50
	5.00	3300	8.50	3354	5.50	3404	2.50
3239	7.50	3301	3.25	3355	3.95	3405	4.75
3241	4.75	3303	8.50	3356	4.50	3406	2.95
3242	3.50	3305	2.75		3.00	3408	4.75
3243	4.50	3307	2.75	3357	4.75	3410	3.50
3247	3.50	3308	3.50	3358	3.00	3411	3.75
3248	4.75	3311	2.75	3359	5.50		2.25
3250	3.50	3312	.95	3361	1.95	3412	.25
3251	3.25	3313	4.50	3362	10.00	3413	4.95
3252	3.75	3314	4.75	3363	4.25	3414	2.95

3415	$2.95	3472	$4.75	3525	$7.50	3576	$3.50
3416	3.50	3473	3.95	3527	3.00	3577	4.95
3419	5.00	3475	.95	3528	5.00	3578	3.00
3421	3.25	3476	4.50	3529	5.25	3580	5.00
3422	2.50	3477	.50	3531	3.75	3581	3.50
3423	5.50	3478	3.50		2.95	3582	4.95
3425	3.00	3480	1.50	3532	5.50	3583	2.95
3426	4.75	3481	2.75	3534	2.75	3584	3.75
3428	4.75	3482	4.50	3536	4.95	3585	1.95
3429	4.50	3483	3.50	3537	1.25	3586	5.00
3430	2.95	3484	5.00	3538	3.50	3587	5.95
3431	4.75	3485	2.95	3539	4.95	3588	4.95
3433	3.50	3486	2.00	3540	3.50		5.95
3434	3.50	3487	7.50	3542	7.50	3589	2.95
3435	3.75		3.95	3543	7.00	3590	3.95
3437	2.75	3488	3.00	3544	3.50	3591	4.95
3439	2.95	3490	3.75	3545	4.95	3592	2.95
3440	1.00	3491	4.50	3546	4.00	3593	3.95
3443	4.75		3.00	3547	6.00	3594	3.95
	2.75	3492	4.00	3548	2.95	3595	2.95
3444	3.00	3494	1.95	3549	6.50	3596	3.50
3445	2.95	3495	4.50	3550	1.00	3597	4.50
3446	5.50	3496	4.95	3551	1.50	3598	4.75
3447	.95	3497	3.75	3552	2.50	3599	1.95
3448	3.50	3498	3.75	3553	3.75	3600	1.95
3449	3.00	3499	3.75	3554	3.95	3601	4.50
3453	3.95	3502	4.50	3556	3.75	3602	2.95
3454	4.25	3506	10.00	3557	3.50	3603	4.95
3456	.50		5.00	3559	3.95	3604	3.95
3457	4.00	3507	3.95	3560	3.00	3605	3.75
3458	4.95	3508a	3.00	3561	4.95	3606	2.50
3460	5.00	3511	3.75	3563	12.50	3607	2.95
3461	3.00	3512	3.95	3564	5.00	3608	3.50
3462	2.95	3513	7.95	3565	3.95	3609	5.95
3463	1.00	3515	4.25	3566	3.95	3610	3.50
3464	1.00	3516	4.75	3567	3.95	3611	7.50
3465	1.00	3517	4.50	3568	4.50		9.00
3466	1.00	3518	3.95	3569	3.00	3612	7.95
3467	1.00	3520	2.50	3570	2.50	3613	4.50
3468	1.00	3522	4.25	3571	2.95	3614	3.95
3469	4.50		3.25	3572	5.00	3615	2.00
	5.25	3523	4.50	3573	10.00	3616	2.95
3470	10.00		4.00	3574	15.00	3616a	10.00

3617	$5.95	3784	$1.00	3915	$5.00	4006	$15.00
3618	3.95	3787	4.75	3919	2.75	4010	8.50
3619	3.95	3788	3.50	3920	2.75		4.25
3620	1.50	3789	4.50	3922	1.75	4012	5.75
3621	1.50	3791	2.25	3923	5.50	4022	1.75
3622	3.95	3795	1.00	3927	4.75	4023	1.75
3624	2.75	3799	2.75	3929	3.75	4028	5.00
3625	1.00	3801	3.75		3.50	4030	1.75
3627	3.50	3802	4.75	3930	4.50	4032	2.75
3629	1.00	3803	1.75	3936	2.25	4038	4.50
3630	5.50	3804	4.50	3937	2.75	4040	1.75
3632	2.50	3805	5.50	3937a	5.75	4042	1.75
3633	2.25		4.50	3938	2.75	4047	5.75
3634	.25	3806	1.00	3939	3.50	4048	6.50
3640	.75	3807	4.75	3940	3.75	4049	1.25
3641	4.25	3808	1.00	3941	4.50	4050	2.50
3642	1.25	3810	1.00	3942	3.75	4053	2.50
3643	1.50	3816	1.75	3943	2.75	4054	.75
3644	2.75	3822	2.50	3944	2.50	4056	7.50
3648	1.75	3825	1.00	3945	2.75	4057	3.75
3649	1.25	3826	4.95	3945a	3.25	4061	2.50
3653	3.75	3827	4.00	3948	4.75	4062	2.50
3654	2.75	3836	1.95	3954	4.50	4063	7.50
3656	1.75	3857	4.75	3955	5.50		2.75
3674	19.75	3859	5.75	3959	2.75	4066	2.75
3691	9.75	3860	5.50	3962	5.95	4070	3.75
3694	7.50	3862	9.75	3963	2.75	4074	.95
3703	6.75	3865	3.50	3964	2.75	4075	5.25
3710	7.50	3872	6.50	3965	1.25		3.75
3715	4.50		5.50	3966	1.50		1.50
3717	4.25	3880	14.25	3968	3.50	4076	5.00
3730	4.75	3883	5.50	3969	5.25	4077	6.75
3735	4.75	3885	13.75	3970	6.50	4088	3.75
3739	5.50	3894	8.50	3972	5.50	4092	3.25
3747	4.50	3895	6.50	3974	7.75	4095	2.75
3752	2.50	3896	7.50	3975	6.50	4097	.95
3760	2.25	3898	14.50	3976	3.50	4099	3.25
3763	3.75	3899	4.75	3977	2.95	4101	2.50
3769	1.50	3902	2.50	3978	3.95	4102	3.50
3771	1.00	3903	3.75	3979	12.50	4104	4.00
	1.25	3905	4.75	3980	7.50	4106	4.50
3772	5.50	3911	8.75	3983	14.25		3.50
3776	1.00	3913	9.50	3999	34.00	4107	5.00

4108	$6.75	4163	$5.50	4267	$4.50	4345	$4.75
4110	6.75	4180	6.50	4268	3.75	4346	5.25
	4.95	4182	3.75	4269	3.25		4.95
4111	5.00	4183	4.75	4270	1.95	4347	4.75
4112	3.50	4189	2.75	4271	5.00	4348	14.50
4113	2.50	4191	2.50	4290	6.75	4360	2.75
4114	14.50	4193	3.50	4297	3.00	4361	9.75
4122	5.50	4215	2.75	4301	8.50	4368	5.75
4125	2.75	4216	3.75	4302	4.25	4375	4.50
4126	2.75	4217	4.75	4303	6.50	4376a	4.25
4127	.50	4218	4.75		6.00	4379	7.50
4128	1.25	4219	4.75		5.00	4381	5.75
4130	5.50	4220	4.75	4304	5.00		5.50
4132	5.95	4222	3.75	4306	3.75	4386	4.50
4133	2.95	4223	2.25	4309	4.50	4388	4.50
4136	13.75	4225	3.50	4310	6.50	4396	3.75
4139	9.75	4226	3.75	4311	4.00	4412	1.25
	7.25	4227	1.95		2.50	4414	1.25
4140	8.75	4230	8.50	4312	4.50	4423	1.75
4144	1.25	4233	9.75	4313	1.00	4435	4.50
4146	8.50	4243	4.75	4315	3.75	4438	4.50
	5.25	4258	5.00	4326a	3.75	4440	6.50
4147	3.75	4259	2.75	4327	7.50	4441	5.00
4148	5.00	4260	1.50	4334a	2.25	4442	4.50
4150	6.50	4261	5.50	4334b	2.25	4443	.50
4157	8.50	4263	6.50	4336	3.00	4444	2.75
4161	2.75	4264	4.75	4339	3.60	4446	3.75
4162	4.50	4266	4.75	4344	2.50	4447	4.75

Frontispiece from "The American Cookery Book" Philadelphia, 1861. A kitchen in Civil War days.